THE THEORY OF BUYER BEHAVIOR

The Wiley Marketing Series

The Theory of
BUYER
BEHAVIOR

JOHN A. HOWARD

AND

JAGDISH N. SHETH

Columbia University

John Wiley & Sons, Inc.

NEW YORK · LONDON · SYDNEY · TORONTO

Library of Congress Catalogue Card Number: 78-82975

SBN 471 41657 6

Printed in the United States of America

To LYNN, JEFFREY, AND PETER
and
To MADHU

Preface

The purpose of this book is to provide a theoretical structure that, in addition to serving the usual functions of a theory, focuses the findings in behavioral science on issues of public and private practice, thus building "pathways" along which the buyer behavior specialist can "find his way" to the body of knowledge of basic science and the basic scientist can approach the problems of buyer behavior. Our objective in developing such a structure thus was not only to further basic research in buyer behavior and so create a firm body of knowledge, but in the meantime, to make the available knowledge more accessible to public and private practice.

The need for a structure to guide basic research is obvious. Probably few fields of human activity have available so many facts as do companies on the buying behavior of their customers. Unfortunately, each of these bits and pieces of data stands alone, isolated and of limited usefulness, instead of being integrated into a whole, which would endow each part with the meaning that emerges from the whole. At the same time there are available many tested propositions from behavioral science, especially psychology, each of which could bring a few of the bits and pieces of data together to yield a pattern of meaning. However, each proposition, alone provides so little leverage in obtaining meaning that to the practitioner it seems trivial. Hence the available propositions also need to be brought together and be converted into a comprehensive structure. This structure would guide the researcher in fitting the data together in such a way that some of their now hidden meaning would be laid bare. Once the meaning became apparent, it would motivate refinements in definition, in the data collected to conform to the definition, and in the precision with which the relationship is estimated. This effort could endow buying behavior with sufficient meaning to make possible substantial predictions about it.

The needs of practice, both public and private, for such predictions are urgent. Companies are devoting great resources to "influencing" the buyer—the consumer, the institutional buyer, and the industrial buyer— but there is little systematic knowledge about how to proceed. In public practice, which has recently developed equally insistent demands, decisions are currently being taken with even less systematic knowledge than is employed in business. This public need is obviously not new. Such matters as antitrust and truthfulness of advertising have been significant for many years, but, because of a number of social and technological factors, their nature and importance have changed.

These objectives dictate certain directions in creating theoretical structure. They dictate a focus on the buyer's capacity to process information. They lead to an emphasis on the mostly goal-directed aspects of human behavior instead of the less functional features. Also, they cause attention to the characteristics of behavior that are common to most people instead of an emphasis on individual differences. They urge that more effort be directed to field studies than to the laboratory because policy decisions, public and private, must be based on buying behavior as it occurs in the complex field setting. This, in turn, causes us to emphasize certain aspects of behavior such as perception. They highlight the need for dealing with overt behavior as well as with constructs short of behavior. Finally, they encourage the search for the kind of variables that can economically incorporate individual differences that significantly exist under field conditions.

This attempt to build a structure may seem presumptuous to the reader. One of the authors, Howard, was commissioned by the Ford Foundation in 1960 to do a somewhat similar task, which resulted in *Marketing: Executive and Buyer Behavior* (Columbia University Press, 1963). Out of that effort grew the first attempt at systematic theory building (see Chapters 3 and 4, *Marketing Management*, 2nd ed., R. D. Irwin, 1963). Our intent is to modify and extend the earlier work in a more systematic, comprehensive, and rigorous way.

The book represents a truly joint piece of work, so that it is difficult to say which one of us was responsible for what. The endless discussions required in this type of effort obscure the source of most of the ideas. We can say, however, that J. N. Sheth took primary responsibility for Chapters 2, 6, 7, and 9 and J. A. Howard for Chapters 3, 4, 5, and 8.

John A. Howard
Jagdish N. Sheth

New York
June 1969

Acknowledgments

For initial financial support of this five-year project we are indebted to the Chauncy Williams Fund for Research on Industrial Buying. The late Chauncy Williams, former editor of Sweet's catalog, a long-standing, standard source of industrial buying information, exhibited remarkable imagination and vision in making available funds for research in industrial buying, a field that is just now beginning to be subjected to systematic research.

This book represents an attempt to bring industrial buying and consumer buying together under one umbrella. Since the buyer is the ultimate focus of all marketing effort, industrial marketing research can benefit in two ways from being integrated into buyer behavior research. First, such integration can stimulate the teaching of industrial marketing in business schools, both in the United States and abroad, where industrial marketing has taken second place to consumer marketing, even to the point of being entirely omitted. In our opinion, it is not appropriate to have two separate arrays of courses, one in industrial marketing and the other in consumer marketing. Basic knowledge does not conveniently "slice" in that manner. Instead, study of both consumer markets and industrial markets should be included in all marketing courses. Second, transfer of knowledge between the two areas will be facilitated. Currently, we see growing evidence, in marketing journals and on the part of academic researchers, of an effort to modify consumer marketing techniques so as to make them appropriate for industrial markets. We surmise that, as a consequence, we can also expect a reverse flow of ideas —from industrial to consumer marketing. For these two reasons we believe that this book will help to achieve Chauncy William's vision of providing an intellectual foundation for industrial marketing.

The General Electric Foundation supported the project for three years, and Joseph Bertotti, the director, was helpful in a number of ways.

William F. Ogden was a constant source of stimulation, and teaching at General Electric's Crotonville center was one of the sources of the conviction that marketing management seriously needs a systematic theory.

The Chemstrand Corporation, now the Textile Division of Monsanto Company supported our study for one year.

Finally, the Buyer Behavior Project, a large research program devoted to testing the theory provided considerable intellectual support. This project was financed by the Ford Foundation through the University of Chicago, and in that connection we are grateful to Dr. Marshall A. Robinson whose imaginative but demanding criticism was very helpful. Also, we are indebted to the General Foods Corporation for its financial support of the project and for providing a market laboratory. Equally important, however, were the human resources of the corporation. James L. Beuide displayed the imagination and encouragement that caused us to attempt to test out the theory. A. Ossip, currently Marketing Research Manager, Post Division, was in many ways of immense help to us, particularly in his insistence on questioning the relevance of the findings, which helped to create a demanding but intellectually healthy environment for the study. B. R. Panettiere, Director of Marketing Research Services, gave freely his time, his valuable ideas, and the help of his staff. Also, we express appreciation to C. W. Cook, Chairman of the Corporation, who opened up a number of splendid opportunities for us, making it possible to work with such an effective marketing organization.

The Buyer Behavior Project was also supported by Parker-Kalon Company and by the Market Research Corporation of America. Samuel G. Barton, Chairman of the Board of Market Research Corporation of America, showed a remarkable interest in and an understanding of the process of creating new knowledge. Dr. Jack Abrams, Vice President of the Market Research Corporation of America, was a helpful and imaginative critic.

Finally, in connection with the Buyer Behavior Project, we owe Paul F. Lazarsfeld, Quetelet Professor of Social Science at Columbia University, a great debt. Aided by Professor Allen Barton, Professor Lazarsfeld brought to the project not only the splendid tradition of the Bureau of Applied Social Research, but also an unusual depth of substantive understanding, of methodological expertise, and of warm, kindly personal advice. To have worked with him is a cherished experience.

The project would not have been possible without Professor Abraham Shuchman, a colleague and friend. We sometimes felt that Professor Shuchman's criticism of some of our pet ideas was a bit abrasive, but we learned that he was one of the finest intellectual taskmasters with whom we have had the pleasure of working. Professor Johan Arndt was especially helpful as a critic on Chapter 8.

Many others were helpful in developing the theory. Professor William J. McGuire, Jr., now of the University of California at San Diego, played a far more important role than he is aware of. In addition to his criticism of parts of some early drafts, his knowledge and deep interest in applied psychology have had a profound effect on our thinking. His own work, with its breadth, incisiveness, and balance, was an inspiration for us. Professor Daniel Katz, University of Michigan, carefully went over two late drafts of the manuscript, and his criticisms, both specific and general, were of immense benefit. His straightforward, candid evaluation was in the highest tradition of American scholarship. We are most grateful to him. Professor John J. Sherwood, Purdue University, was also a helpful critic.

We are indebted to a number of marketing educators and researchers as well. These include Joel Cohen, University of Illinois, Paul Green, University of Pennsylvania, Philip Kotler, Northwestern University, John G. Myers, University of California at Berkeley, William Lazer, Michigan State University, J. A. Lunn, Research Bureau Ltd., London, John O'Shaughnessy, Columbia University, and Alvin Silk, Massachusetts Institute of Technology. We are particularly grateful to John G. Myers and John O'Shaughnessy for making exceedingly valuable and extensive suggestions on the manuscript.

We also thank Brian M. Campbell, George S. Day, Shlomo Lampert, Claude R. Martin, Terrence V. O'Brien, Robert Parket, Paul A. Pellemans, Michael Perry and S. Prakash Sethi for their involvement in testing parts of the theory as doctoral candidates at Columbia Business School.

For direct encouragement and favorable intellectual and physical environment we are indebted to Dean Courtney C. Brown. Dean Brown, in addition to having many other splendid qualities, is a perceptive man of marked idealism, an idealism that has sometimes been contravened by the myths about research that pervade institutions of higher learning. Once he is fully persuaded of the integrity of the intention to contribute to the body of knowledge that is useful to practicing management, his support is enthusiastic. We think of him not only as the man who must allocate resources within the school, but also as a good friend.

Dean G. C. Owens in his imaginative and sympathetic understanding of our purposes has wherever possible in terms of the broad needs of the school contributed in many, many ways to our effort. He is one of those rare associate deans who in a quiet, unassuming way are able to make a profound difference in the effectiveness of an academic institution.

We are deeply grateful to Richard A. Harriman, Research Assistant, who performed many tasks always with great skill, an amazing alacrity, and unfailing good humor.

Finally, Judith R. Clarke, with her competence, boundless energy, charm, and splendid sense of humor made the completion of the manuscript much easier.

J. A. H.
J. N. S.

Contents

THE THEORY OF BUYER BEHAVIOR

The Nature of the Theory, and a Summary

Theory: Function, Need, and Structure

The purpose of this book is to describe, apply, and assess those elements of the theory of human behavior that we believe to be essential for understanding the range of activities that we call "buying." Specifically, the book focuses on brand choice, but because related activities are included, we call it a theory of buyer behavior rather than merely brand choice. Also, we speak of buyer behavior instead of consumer behavior because our research has suggested that at a general level the industrial buyer and the consumer buyer are quite similar.

Chapter 1 is intended to provide perspective for this specific theory by considering standard concepts and terminology from philosophy of science and in this way we hope to better understand its nature and role. The nontechnical, marketing-sophisticated reader may, therefore, prefer to skip this chapter and move on to Chapter 2 for a summary of the theory, but others will benefit from such an understanding. People working in the field of buyer behavior, hence making contributions to it, come from a great variety of backgrounds. Learning theorists, social psychologists, personality theorists, economists, sociologists, operations researchers, communication researchers, and so forth, all tend to approach theory with subtly different points of view, depending on the particular way in which the respective body of knowledge has developed historically. Each sees theory as serving some functions and not others;

for example, operations researchers are inclined to regard theory as almost solely a predictive device. The more philosophical setting in this chapter can provide a common umbrella for these disparate views and set forth a better rationale for developing the theory.

Philosophy of science holds that we identify a theory by its structure—its parts and the relationships among the parts—and that there are certain dimensions by which a structure can be described. Furthermore, there are certain functions that theories perform and the nature of the structure determines what these functions are. Finally, to the extent that a theory serves these functions, it can meet the needs of a particular field of inquiry by helping to solve both the research and action problems of that field. The field of inquiry that concerns us here is the activities associated with buying behavior: company marketing activities, government activities directed toward improving the welfare of society insofar as these activities impinge on buying behavior, and the teaching and research associated with the two types of activities. These taken together we shall call "the problem of buyer behavior."

First, the types of functions that a theory can serve are set forth to sensitize the reader to contributions that the theory might make and so prepare him for an evaluation of it in Chapter 10 after the structure and its application have been presented.

Second, the contribution of a theory to a particular field of inquiry can be assessed only in terms of the needs of the problems in that field. The second part of this chapter describes the field as a background so that the reader can better identify the needs of the field and so be prepared to assess in Chapter 10 the extent to which this structure, by serving the functions that it does, meets the current needs of the field.

Finally, our general discussion of describing a theoretical structure serves as an introduction to the rest of the book, which is largely devoted to the description of the structure of a particular theory and its application.

1.1 FUNCTIONS OF THEORY

In marketing, researchers have tended to limit the functions that a theory performs to two: description and prediction. Theorizing, however, can serve several additional functions (Rychlak, 1968). In this section, the various functions are classified into four categories: description, delimitation, generation, and integration. The task here is to briefly describe each of the functions as a criterion by which to evaluate the contribution of a theory in meeting the needs of a field.

1.1.1 Descriptive Function

To describe a phenomenon such as buying behavior, we use category—a construct—as the building block; empirical events can be placed into or assigned to a category. Then we develop a set of these categories—constructs—and link the constructs together to obtain propositions—statements of relations among the constructs. We design the constructs and their linkages in the best way that we can as a means to describe the phenomenon (buying *behavior*) and the forces that lie behind it—the forces that cause it—which will enable us to say that we have *explained* the phenomenon. The particular way that these forces cause the phenomenon is the explanation.

To explain a phenomenon, we give increasingly sophisticated descriptions of it. The need for explanation arises when describing a phenomenon because we wish to answer the question, "Why does the phenomenon occur?" In answering it, we come across new hypotheses based on information that surrounds the phenomenon and specifies the conditions of the explanation. For example, suppose that we wish to describe a housewife's choice of a brand of soup in the supermarket. After describing her physical movements near and around the shelf where soups are stocked, we wish to explain *why* she chose that particular brand. The immediate explanation, however inadequate, may come from our knowledge of the can's color, size, shape, or position on the shelf. A more adequate explanation may come from our knowledge of stored information in the housewife's mind about cans of soups. We could illustrate our point equally well with an industrial buyer. In any case, the more we know about conditions surrounding the choice, the better will be our explanation and prediction, provided, of course, that we can handle all of this information.

Thus the theory of buyer behavior serves the function of description to the extent that we not only describe the phenomenon to be explained—brand choice by the buyer—but explain it by specifying conditions that surround the phenomenon at the time of its manifestation. These conditions are both internal and external to the buyer. Attention, attitude, and intention, for example, are *internal* conditions, and the stimuli impinging on the buyer from his environment are *external* conditions.

1.1.2 Delimiting Function

Description must operate selectively. It does not include everything. A theory that does not delimit will break under its own overweight of explanation. The *purpose* of a theory dictates the nature of the selection. Our purpose is to describe buying behavior that has certain characteristics, as will be seen in the following chapters and some aspects of which are summarized in Chapters 8 and 9. Our purpose is not to attempt to describe and explain other behaviors such as insanity, marital relations, juvenile delinquency, and social mobility.

A central concept of theory is meaning. Meaning is associated with the delimiting function of theory, however, instead of the descriptive function because meaning is a relational concept. A relational concept is one that obtains its content from relations between and among things. It, therefore, finds its meaning only within a given theoretical context. When formulating constructs and propositions, we impose a structure, an intention to accomplish something, a *meaning* at the very beginning.

That we impose meaning at the very outset is a terribly important, nonobvious point that is often overlooked. It is illustrated in the self-designated practical man who says, "Don't bother me with the theory, just give me the facts." What he is really saying is, "Give me a set of facts so that I can fit them to *my* theory and so understand the phenomenon." What he does not realize is that if the facts had been collected in terms of his theory in the first place, they would probably have been much more useful.

Exactly how we view meaning depends on our position on the realism-idealism dimension. The realist tends to see the world as having an immutable existence, independent of the nature of the observer, and to think that the one-to-one mapping between reality and the abstractions (constructs and propositions) that he has imposed is always possible. The idealist, on the other hand, believes that the observer makes his own world and that to assume that his abstractions, though useful as labels, map anything having a clear-cut, literal, or unchanging existence adds nothing to our theoretical activity, to our understanding of the phenomenon.

If we are extreme realists, we tend to think that our meaning is derived from "hard data." But this is really not so. We are selective; we do admit that we overlook some variables and not others. Researchers using stochastic models in their attempt to understand buying behavior use "probabiliy of purchase" as an operational measure of habit (learning). For attempting to understand the buyer's search processes, for example, a better measure of learning is latency of purchase—the time elapsed between a given stimulus and purchase.

The point is that as realists we seldom talk about why we selected particular variables and omitted others; hence we are not quite so aware of the delimiting issues as are the more idealistically oriented scientists. We tend to hide behind the belief that operational definitions and measurements ensure that we have obtained the meanings that we want, that we need, that are inherent. The important but subtle point is that we must have some knowledge of a construct or proposition other than that given by a specific and concrete set of operations in order to know whether the operations are adequate to the task in the first place. For this knowledge, we must go back to the meaning that we originally imposed when we formulated the abstractions. This issue is seen most sharply, perhaps, if we think of the operations as being used in a laboratory experiment but intended for developing a construct for practical use, such as a construct that will yield easily collected data under field conditions and will predict purchase behavior. We must build into the experiment the necessary conditions, including controls, to really test the concept that we originally defined in a particular way before we ever thought about operational definitions and measurement, about how to test the truth of a proposition that incorporates the construct. This is the problem of *construct validation*.

If we shift to the idealist's point of view, the issue of meaning becomes much clearer, because it is obvious that we, as theorists, impose the meaning instead of its being imposed by the "hard data." To the idealistic theorist, operationism becomes a way of clarifying communication. If his ideas become too different, too unique for other theorists to understand, the theorists will demand some standard of measurement against which to judge the generality of his ideas; they will demand operational definitions.

It may be helpful in understanding the issue of meaning here to note the similarity between behaviorism in psychology, operationism (an emphasis on operational definitions), and the philosophical school of logical positivism that has had a profound influence on scientific thinking in the United States. A central principle of logical positivism as seen by the behaviorist is that of verifiability, which serves to delimit the scope of philosophical inquiry. To the behaviorist, unless a statement of fact can be verified in some way, it cannot be said to constitute a problem because it cannot be resolved. This also can be the distinction between ethical and scientific issues. As it is often said, "People can only fight about values because there is no rational solution." Therefore ethical issues are not problems to the behaviorist if he is also a logical positivist.

Thus by means of verification we transmute meaning into *knowledge*. Hence knowledge is a more abstract concept than meaning in that it subsumes *both* meaningful relations and the play of methodological evidence. Knowledge transcends meaning. When we say that we have an understanding of buying behavior, we mean that we have knowledge about this kind of behavior, that the meaning with which we endowed the behavior in formulating our abstractions has been verified.

To develop the idea of methodological evidence a bit further, it is helpful to distinguish between procedural evidence and validating evidence. This distinction has very great significance to those of us who are involved in the application of science to particular problems and therefore must work with the layman, the nonscientist, the pragmatist. Procedural evidence is shown when we believe a theoretical proposition because of its intelligibility, its consistency with commonsense knowledge, or its implicit self-evidence. Commonsense knowledge is the agreed-upon or accepted knowledge of a group, knowledge that is reflected in its culture and is no longer a source of contention among its members. Validating evidence, on the other hand, is obtained by what the scientist calls research. Unfortunately, procedural evidence probably carries a much greater sense of conviction to the layman than does validating evidence. This is one of the frustrations of the applied scientist.

The applied scientist must be heavily concerned with prediction and control. Here we use "prediction and control" in its methodological or theory-of-knowledge sense, rather than as a language of theoretical description or means of social control (Rychlak, 1968, pp. 134–136). In its methodological sense, the phrase refers to having the knowledge of the forces that bear upon an experimental situation so that they can be controlled enough to test the truth of the prediction implied in the proposition from the theory. If they are not controlled in some way, it will not be possible to test the prediction. Adequate control is especially difficult under field conditions. In summary, "Prediction is merely the test of understanding and control the practical reward " (MacLeod, 1947, p. 209).

We can illustrate our discussion of the means by which a field is delimited with the so-called "S-R bind." In their theorizing, behaviorists have developed a commitment to a certain procedure. This procedure consists of beginning with the stimulus (S) and always relating it to a response (R). They act as if all theorizing then must take place within these two limits. We believe, however, that R-R relations, and even S-S relations, may be equally productive.

The distinction between intervening variables and hypothetical constructs is useful in delimiting a field. Intervening variables are constructs that are derived directly from observable reality, whereas hypothetical constructs are not observable and must be inferred from the intervening variables. By working at the idealistic level and incorporating hypothetical constructs, we have greater freedom to mold our theory to meet our purposes, our needs. Our needs are to direct the understanding of buying behavior toward the practical ends of the company executive and the public policy maker. However, to ensure that the theory will contribute to empirical work, we can, by means of intervening variables, be operational and subscribe to the principle of verifiability. This can be partially illustrated from developments in psychology. A very realistic construct is *habit,* and it is typically defined in operational terms as "probability of response." This construct, however, does not carry us very far toward the understanding of human thinking. The limitation is serious because the buyer must be able to think in order to be affected by the symbols that constitute advertising, for example. Hull (1943), who did so much to build a structure around the construct of habit, clearly saw this limitation and proposed a construct that he called "fractional antedating goal responses." The essential point of the construct was that both animals and humans *learned* to look forward in time, to expect things to happen, to anticipate events. This much more idealistic construct was developed by others, especially Osgood as we shall see in Chapters 4 and 5, to connect up with the idealistic construct of attitude toward a brand and thus brought behaviorism and cognitive psychology into close contact.

The theory of buyer behavior does delimit the field as we shall see.

1.1.3 Generative Function

The generative function of theory—the capacity to generate testable hypotheses—is well known, being the most commonly accepted purpose of theory. It is what we usually mean when we speak of theoretical speculation, inventiveness, or even creativity. A theory must stimulate hypotheses, or it must provide essential notions, hunches, ideas, and so on, from which someone can create hypotheses that can be tested. When a theory is used to stimulate empirical investigation, we speak of using the theory heuristically. Heuristic use of theory, more often than not, is made by analogy or metaphor. For example, Freud used the physical concepts of hydraulic fluid to express mental states. In marketing, Howard (1963, 1965) has used stimulus-response learning theory to express buying behavior. Finally, the use of systems from physical objects to draw analogies with human behavior is common in most business fields.

The generative function and the delimitation principle are opposite tendencies. To delimit is to put constraints on or boundaries around speculation or hunches. This brings out the very important point that what we have generally called models (well-defined and operational bivariate or multivariate relationships) are lacking to a considerable extent in generative ability. The work in stochastic models can be cited as an example. As indicated above, the S-R theory in psychology, also, has been caught in this tendency to delimit, hence lacks generative capacity.

The theory of buyer behavior is probably high on the generative function. This comes from two aspects. First, the propositions and their relationships are numerous (truly multivariate), thus substantially increasing the combinatory possibilities. Second, there are a number of hypothetical constructs that contain surplus meaning because they are higher-ordered abstractions than the intervening variables, which add to the generative capabilities of the theory. On the other hand, a series of operational, well-defined intervening variables, which are less powerful in generative functions, tie the more generative, less operational system to reality. A series of doctoral dissertations (Sheth, 1966; Day 1967; Sethi, 1968; Campbell, 1969; Perry, 1968; Kerby, 1966) have carried out empirical investigations based on the propositions generated by the theory.

Propositions from the theory are largely summarized in the application section of the book, Chapters 8 and 9.

1.1.4 Integrative Function

The integrative function of theory has to do with bringing constructs and propositions together into a more or less consistent and useful whole. When theorists actively work to integrate and to pull together their theory explicitly and carefully into an interdependent unity, the result is called a formal theory. A good example of this is Hull's hypothetico-deductive theory of behavior (1943) in psychology. A number of "growth models" from economics are also good examples.

However, such formalization of all that is known in an area of investigation can have as side effects conflict, confusion, and inconsistency. For example, several independent researchers have attempted to construct complex cognitive consistency theories to explain attitude formation and change (McGuire, 1968c); some of these have created conflict and confusion.

The integrative function itself, however, is extremely important. What the theorist must do is to be aware of the dangers that are inherent. Psychology has gone through a period of emphasis on miniature theories, and we now see evidence of it in marketing (Haines, 1968). These need to be brought together. In marketing, it is probably the most central need today from all the three points of view: company practice, public policy, and teaching and research. Of late, the flow of good research has accelerated the need even further. This has been shown by Sheth (1966, 1967) with some preliminary attempts to integrate the existing knowledge in buying behavior.

The computer through simulation has vastly increased the possibilities of integrating constucts and propositions in a rigorous way, as Perry (1968) has shown in simulating some of the theory set forth in this book.

The structure described in this book, we believe, makes a major contribution in serving the integrative function in buyer behavior. It not only integrates empirical bits of evidence but also brings together theories and hypotheses of buying behavior and a significant part of the behavioral and cognitive traditions in psychology. A detailed statement of the integration is reserved for Chapter 10; by then the parts to be integrated will have become familiar to the reader.

1.2 THE PROBLEM OF BUYER BEHAVIOR

How can we describe the problem of buyer behavior to which the theory of buyer behavior is applicable in serving the usual functions of a theory? First, it is really many problems, so that we must talk about problem areas. Second, there is the usual distinction between practice and research. Although they can occur together such as in a company, their goals and methods tend to be different. Third, a large share of the issues involving the buyer have to do with the buyer-seller relation, and the seller is typically not a single person but an organization; in fact, "he" is an organization (marketing department) within an organization (the company). The buyer is also sometimes an organization, but for now we shall treat him as a single person to simplify. Fourth, there is often the sharp distinction between the private (company) and public (government) points of view. The issues can be pinpointed by focusing on marketing management.

1.2.1 *Marketing Management*

Let us consider marketing management as a system, as shown in Figure 1.1, in order to portray the nature of the buyer behavior problem. First, however, let us implicitly imbed this system into a much broader system—the national economy as a whole. The national economy from a company's point of view, consists of two subsystems: the company and the environment. A part of the environment not shown is, of course, the company's competitors. The part shown is the typical or representative buyer. Each subsystem has its own "settings" at any point in time.

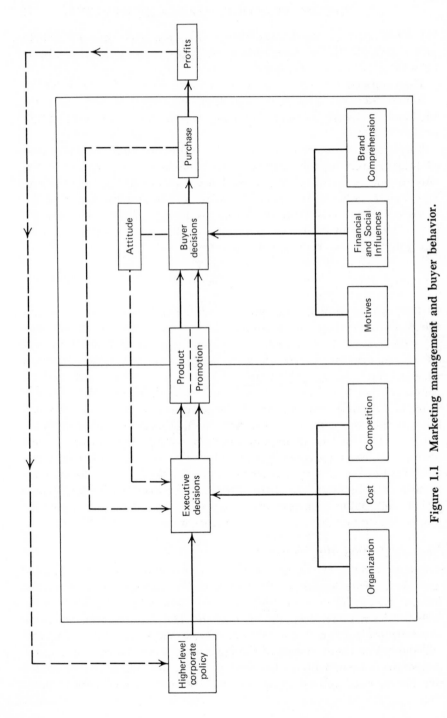

Figure 1.1 Marketing management and buyer behavior.

For example, the firm's settings may include its plant capacity, capital, and manpower. Each subsystem interacts with the other by offering something in exchange for something else.

Each subsystem's offering is an overt manifestation of goal-directed behavior: the firm offers certain products for sale because profit is one of its goals, and the buyer from the environment offers to buy the products because to do so will satisfy his wants. Marketing management's role as the interaction unit, or the exchange unit, can be said to consist of matching the two. This seems simple enough to accept at face value, but it is surprising how much it is ignored in actual practice. This failure comes about because matching the firm's output and the buyer's needs requires an understanding of both parties to the arrangement, not just that of the company's.

Now let us return to Figure 1.1 which is really a small system, a subsystem within the national economy where the seller and buyer come into contact, the *market*. On the left side is the company marketing operation (marketing management) and on the right is the buyer. The outputs from executive decisions are labeled as product and promotion. They represent communication between the seller and the buyer either through the physical product (the significate) or promotion such as advertising (symbols), respectively. The *content* of communication in either case is the attributes of the brand; for example, the buyer wants the brand only because it has *attributes* that meet his needs. We believe that the marketing mix decision should be conceptualized as the decision to appropriate money between these two channels of communication (product and promotion), rather than in the traditional way as price, distribution channel, product, promotion and advertising, and so forth. In the latter case, there is really an overlap: price decision can be communicated by advertising or by channel; price change can be conceived as promotion; product development or change can really mean communication through the product medium or by advertising; and so on.

On the surface this proposed way of looking at the problem may suggest that we are saying, "The company chooses between building a good product and spending its funds in telling the buyer what a good product its actual mediocre product is." However, the accelerated rate of technological change has greatly increased the futurity of executive decision making. Today the executive decides whether to devote R&D to producing a new product within five years or within ten years. Thus the time span and the nature of the decision have changed radically. Furthermore, buyers today need far more information, because the technological change is to a large extent product change. Finally, buyers purchasing different products vary greatly in their information requirements. All four factors cause this to be a meaningful way of conceptualizing the marketing decision.

The outputs from buyer decisions are called purchase and attitude. In fact information about the purchase output, or some internal state measure of the buyer such as comprehension becomes an input to executive decisions. Also, from purchase we show a link to profits and from profits to higher-level corporate policy to reduce the problem of suboptimization. The other output—attitude—is an input to executive decisions because many marketing decisions, particularly those related to advertising, can be more adequately evaluated or measured in terms of attitude than of purchase behavior as a practical matter. The use of purchase can introduce too many delays into the system.

Finally, a number of blocks are clustered around the two subsystems within the large box. These are the settings or the conditions of the wider system, the national economy within which the seller and buyer are subsystems. The decisions are made by each system in light of these conditions. For example, the marketing executive decides on a marketing strategy as reflected in product and promotion outputs taking into consideration cost, competition, and organizational constraints. Similarly, the buyer decides to buy a particular brand taking into consideration the content and level of his motivation, the financial and social influences that play upon him, and his understanding (brand comprehension) of the nature and availability of brands in the market.

1.2.2   Relevance of Theory

In showing the relevance of buyer behavior theory to the problem of buyer behavior, we focus first on the problem area of practice and then turn to research.

1.2.2.1   Relevance for Practice

There are, of course, two types of practice. The company wishes to make decisions, to follow a *company policy,* that will serve its goals. Also, the buyer desires to serve his goals. In the case of the buyer, the government, in its concern for social welfare, makes decisions intended to protect the buyer's interests. Hence we usually think of "practice," when applied to the buyer's interest, as being *public policy* instead of the buyer's policy per se.

The company policy maker at the marketing management level needs theory. In terms of Figure 1.1 the need for the theory is to help the marketing executive in making the decision that alters product and promotion, in collecting the data on which to base the decisions in the first place, and in interpreting the data once he has collected them.

The public policy maker can act in terms of Figure 1.1 in a number of ways, two in particular. First, it is hoped that by altering the environment of the company decision maker, the decision maker's behavior can be changed so as to be more in the social interest. The environment may be altered directly by directing the firm's decision maker to do or not do something. Also, it can be changed by altering the nature of the competition he faces, through an antimerger act, for example. Second, public policy can affect the buyer directly in such ways as providing him with information that he otherwise would not have. The Food and Drug Administration, for example, experimented in New York with making available a telephone number that could be called to obtain information about products.

Returning to the company point of view, the top-level company executive—the president or chairman of the board—is also concerned in two ways with company decisions about the buyer. First, as implied above, he is responsible for seeing to it that marketing management adequately carries out its task of serving the profit and growth goals of the firm. Second, he is concerned with potential and actual legislation affecting the buyer-seller relation, and this overlaps with the public policy maker's view. His interest in this regard takes the concrete form of such matters as testimony before legislative committees and participation in the legislative activities of his trade associations.

1.2.2.2 Relevance for Research

The growing interest in the problem areas of buyer behavior has stimulated a major increase in research in the past five years. The theory provides a way of rationalizing some of these past findings and of guiding future research. It can serve this guiding function because it specifies the constructs that are related and roughly how they are related. The task now confronting us for the years ahead is to specify more precisely the nature of these relationships and, in all cases, to estimate the parameters of these relationships under a variety of conditions. Also, because the theory set forth here provides a two-way street, it can be especially helpful in this task of specification and estimation of relationships. The researcher in buyer behavior can use it to find his way to the basic science. On the other hand, the basic scientist—for example, the psychologist—can use it to find his way to buyer behavior problems.

1.3 STRUCTURE OF THEORY

Having described the functions of a theory and the nature of the buyer behavior problem, so that we can better understand how these functions could serve the needs of the field, we now examine the general nature of theoretical structures, because the structure of a theory determines the functions that a theory can perform.

A theory is identified in terms of its structure: its parts and the relations among those parts. There are a number of dimensions on which the structure being set forth in this book can be objectively described in order to compare it with other theories in either related or quite distinct fields of knowledge. Such a comparison provides the reader with a carryover of understanding from his previous scientific training to the new theory and facilitates his comprehension of the theory.

The dimensions are (1) level of abstraction, (2) realism versus idealism, (3) objectivism versus subjectivism, (4) extrospection versus introspection, and (5) level of formality.

1.3.1 Level of Abstraction

Almost everyone would agree that theorizing is a process of abstraction based on observations of a phenomenon, however casual the observations may be. Here we are concerned with the level of that abstraction. Is the theory that is being set forth in this book very concrete and detailed or does it simplify immensely and include a large area of empirical phenomena in a few categories?

Abstraction from observable reality is a universal tendency and occurs in our daily behavior. For example, most of the mental images of objects that we form after learning about them from actual experience or information are first-ordered abstractions. When we label things with words and phrases, we indulge in abstraction. Abstraction, then, is a process of simplification and generalization which leaves out nonessential or less important details in describing a phenomenon. When we label an object as "apple," we remove specificity of exact color, shape, size, and weight and call by that name all objects that are similar but not identical. A second-order (higher-level) abstraction occurs when we call it a fruit and therefore remove still more detail of the various characteristics. However, enough detail is retained to exclude a host of other objects from being described as fruit. A still higher-order abstraction would be to call it vegetation. Another example of levels of abstraction would be to label an object as freeze-dried coffee, coffee, beverage, and so on.

In theory building, abstraction from observations leads to formulation of constructs. However, a construct is created from a particular point of view and to that extent is based on a selective or biased perspective. For example, a brand may be looked at from the point of view of a chemist or an engineer, a seller or a buyer.

Finally, the higher the abstraction, the greater the generality of the construct in a theory. As such, the construct is probably less operational and more hypothetical. However, at the more abstract level it possesses the power of showing relationships among more objects in existence.

The theory of buyer behavior described in this book is probably at a moderate level of abstraction. This is equivalent to the second-order level of abstraction to the extent that the theory encompasses description, explanation, and prediction of all types of buying behaviors and is not limited to either a given product class or even a type of product group such as consumer durables or industrial products. It is more abstract than many of the operations research models in marketing (Bass et al., 1961; Frank, Kuehn, and Massy, 1962; Buzzell, 1964). This higher level of abstraction has indicated to us, and the indication is supported by research to some extent (Howard and Moore, 1963; Strauss, 1964; Sheth, 1968), that industrial buying and consumer buying are not so different as has been suggested in the marketing literature (Dirksen, Kroeger, and Lockley, 1963; Alexander, Cross, and Cunningham, 1961). However, the theory is not so abstract as many of the personality theories (Hall and Lindzey, 1957) in psychology, for example, which attempt to explain and describe all behaviors, not just those exhibited in buying. At the same time, we concur with others (Miller et al., 1960, pp. 9–10) that a theory of behavior must be complex. We believe that this is particularly true of a detailed theory of buying behavior on which private and public policy is based. This complexity limits abstraction.

In addition, the theory of buyer behavior is moderately abstract to the extent that it is composed of a variety of constructs that vary in their level of abstraction: some are very abstract, whereas others are close to observable data. Broadly speaking, we have the two types of constructs discussed earlier—intervening and hypothetical (MacCorquodale and Meehl, 1948). Intervening constructs are the first-order abstractions of observable data. Therefore, they are abstracted the least. The hypothetical constructs are second- and higher-order abstractions. They are, as such, not directly linked to observable data, but are essentially abstractions of abstractions. They also contain greater meaning and are liable to misinterpretation, but this duolevel of abstraction provides greater power, as we shall argue later.

In this book, we differentiate the two types of constructs—intervening and hypothetical—by adding a prime to the word. Thus a construct called Attitude is a hypothetical construct, and another construct called Attitude′ is an intervening construct or variable. This is to indicate that the hypothetical construct is a further abstraction of the intervening construct, which itself is an abstraction of reality. The two constructs are different in their meanings in that the intervening variable captures only a part of the meaning contained in its counterpart hypothetical construct; hence the hypothetical construct is said to contain surplus meaning. Also, they serve different functions, which will be described later. We have chosen to label them in the same manner also for another reason. Many of the constructs have different meanings in their usage in psychology, social psychology, and marketing and therefore have been moved up and down the ladder of abstraction. This multiordinality of constructs (Korzybski, 1941) leads to serious confusion. Fortunately, we believe that most of this shifting has been limited between the two levels—first-order and second-order—of abstraction. Finally, to simplify there are some hypothetical constructs to which we have not assigned counterpart intervening constructs, and also four global intervening variables do not have hypothetical counterparts because they would be superfluous.

1.3.2 Realism versus Idealism

In addition to being more or less abstract, theories can be compared along a dimension known as realism versus idealism, which was discussed earlier in connection with the delimiting function of theory. The theorist who gravitates toward realism in his outlook takes the position that there actually exists structure in the world and that the scientist's job is only to discover it. He believes that whatever he perceives and cognizes really exists "out there" in the world. Behavioristic psychology is based on this type of view.

Skinner (1956) represents an extreme example of the realistic outlook. To him principles "in theory" are meaningless; he would say that as scientists we manipulate behavior in order to identify the parts and see the structure. The research in economics on intention to buy represents a highly realistic view. It has been kept very close to reality as though something physical were being measured, with little attempt to theorize about the nature of the process by which intentions are generated. In marketing, we quite frequently speak of a buyer's "preference map" as though his brain physically contained a transformed picture (in terms of a network of cells) of this map. There is some evidence from neurophysiology to suggest that this is possibly the case.

An extreme idealist, on the other hand, believes that there is no external world of reality apart from his own perception and cognition. According to him, it is not meaningful to speak of structure as actually existing because to theorize is to *create* (rather than discover) structure in the data that he collects. The psychoanalytic school of psychology is likely to be considered an idealistic approach because the theorizing has not been systematically tied to reality, although its practitioners have intimate, though not systematic, contact with reality.

The utility concept from economics tends to be used as an idealistic construct. Except for the very few instances where economists have attempted to measure it, it is used in a rather vague, ill-defined manner, with seemingly no great confidence that there is something like it in reality. Such natural scientists as James Conant (1952), too, fall into this category, however.

The more idealistic type of theoretical structure has the advantage of greater freedom in theorizing, in imaginatively postulating constructs and relations among constructs. It has the disadvantage, however, of removing the theorist from the disciplining effect of fitting his theory to the conventional wisdom about the nature of reality. By distinguishing between intervening variables and hypothetical constructs, we believe that it is possible to achieve the best of both possible worlds.

The theory of buyer behavior has a mixture of both realist and idealist constructs. We do not feel uncomfortable if our constructs do not correspond to neurophysiological or physical fact. If they happen to, that is a plus, but it is not a necessity, and here we part company with MacCorquodale and Meehl (1948, p. 105). In general it has a greater degree of realism than of idealism. However, we do have some constructs such as motives, perceptual bias, and attitudes that may not be justified as being existent in reality. Whether they are, remains to be seen. The intervening variables in our theory are realistic in outlook, whereas the hypothetical constructs are idealistic. As theorists, we admit that we are more biased toward realism following the tradition in psychology (Watson, 1913). However, with the somewhat primitive extent of our knowledge in buying behavior and related disciplines, we have tended to be idealistic in our attempt to explain and describe the buyer choice process.

1.3.3 Objectivism versus Subjectivism

Objectivism refers to the view that abstractions (constructs) and relationships among abstractions (propositions) transcend the individual theorist and that they may be grasped or understood by all individuals theorizing in that area. Objectivism is likely to occur when all of the theorists have had certain common experiences, so that abstractions have a common meaning to them. The common experience need not necessarily relate to reality, of course, but we would think of the common understanding as being on a firmer foundation if it does. In fact, in psychology, objectivism is taken to be the case where the scientist restricts himself to data subject to measurement in physical terms. "The criterion of truth must come from analysis, it must come from experience, and from that very special kind of objectivity which characterizes science, namely that we are quite sure we understand one another and that we can check up on one another" (Oppenheimer, 1956, p. 130). Behavioristic psychology represents this extreme.

Subjectivism, on the other hand, refers to the view that abstraction is a process that is unique to the theorist and that the relationships among constructs are somehow private, difficult to describe, and not easily communicated. One of the reasons for subjectivism is that the theorist introduces constructs which imply "getting inside the buyer's head". Psychoanalytic theories tend in this direction. The extreme subjective theorist takes the position that if at all possible to know what goes on in a buyer's head, one can only know if he has a detailed description of the buyer's abstractions from that buyer's unique point of view.

It is quite possible to bring objectivity to a theory by introducing arbitrary and new terminology, as has happened to some extent in psychoanalysis and S-R theories in psychology and in marginal analysis in economics. In marketing, this was true of the process of describing goods in terms of shopping, convenience, and specialty goods including recent modifications (Bucklin, 1963).

Objectivism is desirable in a theory if it is to contribute significantly to the development of a field. Some scientists implicitly take the position, however, that a theory must be realistic, and even extrospective as well, for it to be objective. This is not necessarily so.

When realism and objectivism overlap, we have the characteristic of a school of philosophic thought known as empiricism. Empiricism is simply the observation of facts apart from the principles that explain them. Empiricism has marked most of the academic research in buying behavior, perhaps in part because of the influence of operations research (e.g., Ehrenberg, 1959, 1964; Frank and Massy, 1963; Frank Massy and Morrison 1964; Frank, 1967b). Also, in the intellectual "revolution" that occurred in many business schools in the late fifties, the quantitative aspects of research were the easiest to be introduced systematically.

We believe that the theory of buyer behavior is characterized by objectivism in the sense that all intervening constructs can be grasped by all individuals. On the other hand, several of the hypothetical constructs are somewhat subjective in nature in that they are not easy to communicate.

1.3.4 Introspection versus Extrospection

Earlier we stated that the process of abstraction is from a certain perspective or point of view. Broadly these perspectives are classified as introspective versus extrospective. The introspective view refers to the formulation of constructs or theories from the perspective of the object of the study, such as the buyer in our case. The source of data is the object of the study itself, and the constructs developed are useful to the object. Freud's psychoanalytic theory of personality is introspective inasmuch as data were collected from the verbal reactions of the clients and analysis was meant for the benefit of the client. J. B. Watson objected to introspection on the grounds that it led to ideas being generated and confirmed on the basis of systematic self-reflection about their nature and consistency.

Extrospection refers to the formulation of constructs by a theorist from his vantage point as observer regardless of the point of view of the buyer. Operations research as well as normative model building are extrospective. They are more likely, in eliciting data from the buyer, to use scales that specify probabilities instead of the verbal counterparts that buyers find more comfortable. In psychology, Watson and others have steadfastly adhered to the principle of extrospection by borrowing analogic relations from physics. The extrospective view is conducive to testing the truth of ideas, but the introspective outlook may contribute immensely to new breakthroughs.

The buyer behavior theory described in this book is primarily an introspective point of view in that data are to large extent collected from a verbal or written statement by the buyer himself. There are exceptions, for example, sales data from the retail store, but for the most part data are gathered from verbal or written responses of the buyer. However, Watson's fear that an introspective perspective leads to metaphysics (a perspective that transcends reality) is not likely to be borne out in buying behavior because insofar as the constructs are subjective in nature, we can submit them to behavioral confirmation.

1.3.5 Degree of Formality

The final dimension in theory is well known to most researchers.

A majority of researchers may negate anything that is not formal as part of theorizing, and to that extent it is difficult to discuss the formal versus the informal dimension. We all know the ingredients that make a formal theory. Formal theory "is theory stated as specifically and uniformly as possible and written to bring together all the loosely joined tenets, hypotheses, and validated facts into a consistent interdependent unity" (Rychlak, 1968, p. 35). Margeneau (1950) and Royce (1963) call it a nomological network of constructs, preferably linked by mathematical relationships.

Informal theory, then, is theory that has not been stated explicitly, lacks a clear unifying abstraction, and, since it often goes unrecognized, does not have as its implicit goal the formulation of a logically consistent and mutually interdependent body of knowledge. If theorizing is thought of as involving conjecture, speculations, hunches, and guesses, then we must certainly hold open the possibility of informal theoretical influences.

The idea of informal theory can be carried further. Even the most formal theorizing is done in the context of a framework of less formal theory. Informal theory is often hidden in the unarticulated "guiding principles" of the formal theorist.

We hope that the theory of buyer behavior is considered a much more formal statement than conjecture or hunches as defined above. We think that it is relatively more formal than most theories, given the level of maturity of buyer behavior as a discipline and the extent of complexity of the area of investigation. Despite the fact that we have definitional (Chapters 3, 4, and 5) and operational (Chapters 6 and 7) statements that constitute one-third of the book, we have not found it easily possible nor have we striven to achieve a highly formalized theory. In general it is formalized, and we believe that progress can come from further formalizing it. A step was taken in this direction when some of it was described in a computer simulation (Perry, 1968). More recently, John U. Farley and Winston L. Ring have constructed a multiequation model of the theory, which they are now proceeding to test against empirical data.

1.4   SUMMARY AND CONCLUSIONS

The theory of buyer behavior is concerned with explaining brand choice and other aspects of buyer behavior.

In this chapter a philosophy-of-science view was taken of the theory, so that researchers of disparate scientific backgrounds would better appreciate the rationale for it. According to philosophy of science, theory performs a number of functions: description, delimitation, generation, and integration. Description includes explanation, hence prediction. By performing these functions a theory meets the needs of a field of inquiry.

The field of inquiry we know as buyer behavior was described by focusing on the marketing management operation of a company and its relation to the buyer. The marketing operation was set in the framework of the company, and the whole company was in turn set in the framework of the entire economy. Marketing management is looked upon as one in which the understanding of executive decisions and that of buyer decisions are considered to be equally important. This shows the separation between modern marketing and micro economics in two ways. First, marketing can no longer take refuge in the *ceteris paribus* notion of static economic theory in which consumers' tastes, preferences, and wants are held constant. It is essential to incorporate constructs, related to the buyer as an integral part of marketing, that explain changes in preferences. Second, by making product and promotion two *channels* of communication, we bring all nonprice variables in line with the price variable so dominant in the theory of the firm. Price is only one of a number of attributes that combined together form the content of market communication.

Finally, the structure of a theory determines the functions that it will serve. The dimensions for describing the structure of a theory were defined and explained to provide the reader with greater perspective on the nature of this particular theory. These dimensions are level of abstraction, realism versus idealism, introspection versus extrospection, objectivism versus subjectivism, and degree of formality.

CHAPTER 2

Summary of the Theory of Buyer Behavior

This chapter summarizes the theory of buyer behavior in order to facilitate the study of later chapters, particularly in Parts II and III. Some redundancy results, but, based on several revisions and comments from our colleagues, we find such repetition to be unavoidable for a meaningful communication of the theory.

The theory of buyer behavior consists of four sets of abstractions, interchangeably called constructs or variables: (1) input variables, (2) output variables, (3) hypothetical constructs, and (4) exogenous variables. The input and output variables are the least abstract, anchored directly to reality, and operationally well defined. They are called intervening variables, following MacCorquodale and Meehl (1948). They are more realistic and objective, and the links among them are more formal.

The hypothetical constructs in the theory are more abstract, only indirectly related to reality, and not operationally defined. They constitute the heart of the theory. Some of them are more realistic and objective than others, although quite formal because of linkages stated in the theory. Finally, they give a description of the buyer's mental state related to a buying decision and, therefore, map it by identifying, classifying, and labeling various conditions. They encourage speculative theorizing and to that extent serve the generative function.

The exogenous variables describe the contexts in which buying behavior occurs, and they are used for analysis and market segmentation. These contexts are not integral to the decision-making process, but they are powerful influences that the buyer takes into consideration. We isolate them, label them, and show their relations to hypothetical constructs, but do not explain changes in them.

In the sections that follow, a summary statement of the theory is presented. This includes discussion of the hypothetical constructs and, more importantly, the relationships among them by giving some popular examples of actual buying decisions. We reserve the exact definitions and discussion of principles underlying the hypothetical constructs for Chapters 4 and 5, however. In the same manner, the exact definitions and rationale for the relationships among the intervening variables and the exogenous variables are reserved for Chapter 3. In short, this chapter simply initiates the reader in the complexity of the theory.

2.1 BUYING PROCESS

Before describing the hypothetical constructs that constitute the theory, it may be helpful to summarize our way of looking at the buying process and the changes that occur in it over time.

Much of buying behavior is more or less repetitive brand choice decisions. During his life cycle, the buyer establishes purchase cycles for various products, which determine how often he will buy the products. For some products, this cycle is very lengthy, for example, the infrequent buying of durable appliances. Many other products have a short purchase cycle, for example, the constant replacement of many grocery and personal care items. There is, however, invariably the element of repeat buying whatever the purchase cycle. We must, therefore, present a theory that incorporates the dynamics of purchase behavior over a period of time if we wish to capture the central elements of the empirical phenomenon.

In the face of repetitive brand choice decisions, the consumer simplifies his decision process by storing relevant information and routinizing the decision process. What is crucial, therefore, is to identify the elements of decision making, to observe the structural or substantive changes in them, and to show how these decision elements affect search processes as well as incorporation of information from the buyer's commercial and social environments.

The buying process begins with the brand choice decision, given that the buyer is motivated to buy a product. The elements of his decision are (1) a set of motives, (2) alternative brands, and (3) choice criteria by which the motives are matched with the alternatives. Motives are relevant and sometimes specific to a product class, and they may combine to reflect some smaller number of higher-ordered motives. For example, motives related to nutrition and calories may be indications of a more fundamental motive, namely health. The alternative courses of actions are the various brands as well as their potential to satisfy the buyer's motives. The brands that become alternatives to the buyer's choice decision are generally a small number, collectively called his "evoked set." The size of the evoked set is at best a fraction of the brands that he is aware of and a still smaller fraction of the total number of brands that are actually available in the market (B. Campbell, 1969). The choice criteria match the buyer's motives and his means of satisfying the motives. They serve the function of ordering and structuring the motives. The choice criteria develop by a process of learning about the buying situation.

When the buyer is just beginning to purchase a product class, such as making a purchase required by a change in his life cycle, he lacks experience; he has neither well-defined choice criteria nor any knowledge of the various brands and their potential. He, therefore, *actively seeks information* from his commercial and social environments. The information that he either actively seeks or even accidentally receives is subjected to perceptual processes that not only limit the intake (magnitude) of information but modify it (change its meaning) to suit his own frame of reference. These modifications are significant to understand, since they distort the neat and simple "marketing stimulus–consumer response" relation (Nicosia, 1966).

Along with active search for information, the buyer may, to a considerable extent, generalize from similar experiences in the past. Such generalization can be due to physical similarity of the new product class to the old product class. For example, in the initial purchases of Scotch whiskey, the buyer may generalize his experiences in buying gin. Generalization can occur even when the two product classes are physically dissimilar, if they have a common meaning such as that derived from a company-wide brand name. For example, the buyer could generalize his experiences in buying a brand of refrigerator or range to his first purchase of a dishwasher of the same brand.

Whatever the source, the buyer develops sufficient choice criteria to enable him to choose a brand that seems to have the best potential for satisfying his motives. If the brand proves satisfactory, the potential of that brand is increased. Why this happens is described later. The result is that the probability of buying that brand is also increased. With repeated satisfactory purchases of one or more brands, the buyer learns about buying in that situation. It is even probable that he may manifest a routinized decision process whereby the sequential steps in buying are well structured so that some event that triggers the process may actually complete the choice decision. Routinized purchasing implies that the choice criteria are well established and that the buyer has strong brand preferences. For example, a housewife may discover, while serving meals, that her supply of coffee is exhausted and put down a brand of coffee on her shopping list. Similarly, an industrial buyer, as soon as he gets the requisition slip for bolts and nuts, puts the name of the supplier on it and mails a copy to that supplier.

The phase of repetitive decision making, in which the buyer reduces the complexity of a buying situation with the help of information and experience, is called the *psychology of simplification*. Decision making can be divided into three stages to illustrate the psychology of simplification: (1) Extensive Problem Solving, (2) Limited Problem Solving, and (3) Routinized Response Behavior. Extensive Problem Solving refers to the early stages of repetitive decision making, in which the buyer has not yet developed well-defined and structured choice criteria. The buyer has no strong predispositions toward any of the brands he is considering as alternatives. Limited Problem Solving is the next stage, in which the choice criteria are well-defined and structured but the buyer is undecided about which of a set of brands is the best for him. The buyer has moderately high predispositions toward a *number* of brands, but does not have very strong preference for any one brand. Routinized Response Behavior is the last stage, in which the buyer not only has well-defined and structured choice criteria, but also strong predisposition toward one brand. At this stage, although the buyer may consider several brands as possible alternatives, he has, in fact, only one or two brands in mind as the most probable choice alternatives.

The farther he is along in simplifying his environment, the less is his tendency toward active search behavior. Furthermore, the environmental stimuli related to the purchase situation become more meaningful and less ambiguous. Finally, the buyer establishes more cognitive consistency among the brands as he moves toward routinization, and the incoming information is then screened with regard to both its magnitude and its quality. He becomes less attentive to stimuli that do not fit his cognitive structure and he distorts those stimuli that are forced on him. These implied mechanisms explain a phenomenon for which there is growing evidence, such as that by Professor John Dollard at Yale: people can be exposed to a television commercial but not perceive it.

A surprising phenomenon, we believe, occurs in many instances of frequently purchased products, such as grocery and personal care items. The buyer, after attaining routinization of his decision process, may find himself in too simple a situation. He is likely to feel monotony or boredom associated with such repetitive decision making. It is also very likely that he is satiated with even the most preferred brand. In both cases, he may consider all existing alternatives including the preferred brand to be unacceptable. He, therefore, feels a need to *complicate* his buying situation by considering new brands, and this process can be called the *psychology of complication*. The new situation causes him to search for identity with a new brand, and so he begins again to simplify in the manner described earlier. Thus with a frequently purchased item, buying is a continuing process with its ups and downs in terms of information seeking, analogous to the familiar cyclical fluctuations in economic activity.

Identification of the stage at which the buyer is located at a point in time in terms of information-seeking effort is obviously important to the marketing manager. For example, if he knows that a substantial group of buyers are at a level of routinization where they feel satiated or their brand buying is monotonous, he can introduce a new brand (an innovation) that might provide the needed sources of change. Similarly, if buyers are in extensive problem solving, they are likely to actively seek information; hence mass media may prove very effective in communicating about a brand in the product class.

2.2 DESCRIPTION OF CONSTRUCTS

To describe buyer behavior is to explicitly state conditions under which either it is manifested or changes occur in the internal state of the buyer that will later cause overt purchase behavior. These conditions differ among buyers. For example, a commercial is broadcast during a television program. The whole family is watching the program, but when the commercial comes on, the housewife leaves the room to prepare and serve coffee. The husband and children stay in the viewing room, but while the children intently pay attention to the commercial, the husband shifts to reading the newspaper. It is obvious that the three groups of people faced with the stimulus emanating from the commercial have reacted differently. Why this variability in response to the same situation? Explanation will come if we know or hypothesize about the surrounding conditions, including any differences in the frame of reference of various viewers. For example, the housewife's attention is divided between watching the program and an equally well motivated competing activity. This creates an interfering force that prevents her from watching the commercial but is not strong enough to also disrupt the watching of the program. The husband would state, if asked, that he is bored to death with commercials and that, in any case, each commercial has an ax to grind. Besides, he is not interested in buying the product now or in the near future. The children, however, would state that they like commercials and, furthermore, are interested in the product advertised.

If all the conditions are described as above, we may abstract them and state that variability of behavior was caused by two constructs: attitudes toward advertisements and the product, and some situational barrier, say an inhibitor. The importance of this abstraction and theorizing, of course, is that the same two constructs may explain other people's behavior or the same person's behavior in another situation. To illustrate the latter case, suppose that the next week the family watches the same program in about the same manner. When the commercial comes on, the telephone rings. The housewife leaves the room to answer it and thus again manifests the behavior of not viewing the commercial. Again, we may think of the ringing of the telephone as a competing situation that demands her attention. Thus the process of abstraction has enabled us to generate other hypotheses and situations where the same phenomenon can be explained.

The constructs in our theory are similar abstractions. Some are more realistic, objective, and close to reality, whereas others are more idealistic, possibly subjective, and quite removed from observation. Because our aim is to describe and explain all types of buying behavior, we need more constructs and possibly more abstract constructs. However, an attempt has been made to use "Ockham's razor" in order to include only as many constructs as seem necessary.

Figure 2.1 represents the theory of buyer behavior. The central rectangular box isolates the various internal-state variables and processes that, combined together, show the state of the buyer. They constitute the hypothetical constructs. The inputs to the rectangular box are stimuli from the marketing and social environments of the buyer. The outputs are a variety of behaviors that the buyer manifests based on the interaction between the stimuli and his internal state. Stated differently, the output variables are the classification of buying behavior phenomenon that we want to describe and explain.

2.2.1   Input and Output Variables

2.2.1.1   Input Variables

At any point in time, the hypothetical constructs are affected by numerous stimuli from the buyer's environment. The environment is classified as Commercial or Social. The marketing activities of various firms by which they attempt to communicate to the buyer constitute the commercial environment. From the buyer's point of view, these communica-

30

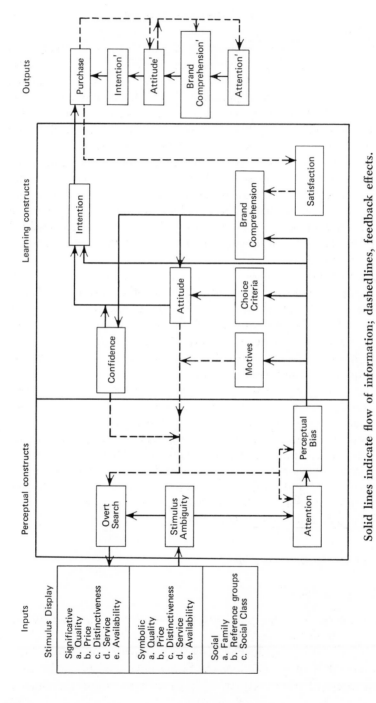

Solid lines indicate flow of information; dashedlines, feedback effects.

Figure 2.1 A simplified description of the theory of buyer behavior.

tions basically come by way of either the physical brands themselves (significative) or some linguistic or pictorial representations (symbolic) of the attributes of the brands. The two inputs are called Significative and Symbolic Stimuli. The third input variable is Social Stimuli. It refers to the information that the buyer's social environment provides regarding a purchase decision. The most obvious is word-of-mouth communication.

2.2.1.2   Output Variables

Behavior manifested by the buyer is quite varied and complex. For example, he reacts to the advertisements, the store, the display, and the brands. The most important (from the seller's point of view) is the purchase of a brand. It is the culmination of decision process and the one with which the theory is concerned. However, we think that there are several other behavioral manifestations that can be described, explained, and interrelated by the same constructs in our theory. Furthermore, they have been considered important by other practitioners and researchers (Adler, Greenberg, and Lucas, 1965; Lavidge and Steiner, 1961; Palda, 1966).

The five output variables are (1) Attention', (2) Brand Comprehension', (3) Attitude', (4) Intention', and (5) Purchase. All of them except Purchase are given the same labels as some of the hypothetical constructs described later, but are differentiated from them by the addition of primes. They are at least monotonically related to their counterpart hypothetical constructs. The essential difference is that hypothetical constructs are more inclusive in meaning, richer in speculation, and add considerably more than the output variables.

Attention' is a response of the buyer that indicates the magnitude of his information intake. There are several psychophysical methods of measuring Attention', such as pupil dilation (Hess, 1965; Krugman, 1964). *Brand Comprehension'* refers to buyer's verbal statement about his knowledge of brands in a product class. It could vary from the buyer's simply being aware of a brand's existence to a complete description of buyer's descriptive meaning of the brands. Some of the standard measures of advertising effectiveness such as awareness, aided and unaided recall, and recognition are different aspects of the buyer's comprehension of the brand. *Attitude'* is buyer's verbal evaluation of a brand's potential to satisfy his motives, his description of the connotative meaning of a brand. *Intention'* is buyer's expectation, expressed verbally, that, given his information about all the aspects of a buying situation and his predictions about the future states of the environment, he will buy the brand he likes most the next time he is motivated to buy. Finally, *Purchase* behavior refers to the overt act of purchasing a brand.

2.2.2   *Hypothetical Constructs*

The hypothetical constructs and their interrelationships are the result of an integration of Hull's (1943, 1952) learning theory, Osgood's (1957a, 1957b) cognitive theory, and Berlyne's (1963, 1964, 1966) theory of exploratory behavior, along with other ideas from the behavioral sciences. The process of integration is provided in Chapters 4 and 5.

We may classify the constructs into two classes: (1) those that have to do with perception and (2) those having to do with learning. Perceptual constructs serve the function of information processing, whereas the learning constructs serve the function of concept formation. We first describe the learning constructs, since they are the major components of the theory; the perceptual constructs that play the important role of obtaining and processing information are more complex and will be described later.

2.2.2.1   *Learning Constructs*

The learning constructs are labeled as (1) Motives, (2) Brand Comprehension, (3) Choice Criteria, (4) Attitude (toward the brands), (5) Intention (to buy the brands), (6) Confidence (in judging brands), and (7) Satisfaction (with the purchase of the brand).

1. *Motives* are the goals of the buyer impinging upon a buying situation. They are derived from the biogenic or psychogenic needs, wants, or desires of the buyer that are related to buying and consuming a product class (Bayton, 1958, Myers, 1968). Hence they are common across the brands that are treated as alternatives in a buying decision. Most of the motives, whether they are directly related to a product class or only indirectly impinge upon it, are based on buyer's expectations or anticipation of certain outcomes from the purchase of a brand in that product class (Cofer and Appley, 1964).

Motives are classified into two categories: (1) those that are relevant and specific to a product class and (2) those that are irrelevant. The *relevant motives* are very closely anchored to the attributes of a product class under consideration. For example, relevant motives in buying a dietary product, which includes brands such as Metrecal and Sego, may be calorie content, substitutability for a meal, nutritional strength, and taste. Similarly, relevant motives in buying an air-conditioner could be durability, quietness, cooling power, and design.

Some of the relevant motives may be very specific or unique to a product class. Such unique motives are likely to be more prevalent in industrial buying than in consumer buying, although it is possible to find examples of them in the latter case if thorough investigation is made. For example, elimination of headaches may be unique to the analgesics product class. Very often, however, a number of relevant motives are only indicators of some underlying general motive. In the previous example of dietary products, caloric content and nutritional strength may be derivatives of the general motive of good health. To the extent that relevant motives can be abstracted further, it is possible that a product class may be related to some other product class. We find, for example, that it is this type of abstraction that pulls together to some extent such brands as Metrecal (dietary product), Carnation Instant Breakfast (cereals), and Quick (milk additive).

The *irrelevant motives* are not directly related to a product class under consideration. However, they serve the important function of raising the buyer's total motivational state (intensity or arousal) and thereby "tune up" the buyer to attentively receive information or react to it.

Whether a motive is relevant or irrelevant in a product class is an empirical question. It is important to know the answer, however, because a relevant motive is both energizing (tuning up the buyer to buy) and directive (directing the buyer toward one specific brand) in its effect, whereas an irrelevant motive is only energizing. Examples of irrelevant motives are fear, anxiety, many of the personality variables such as authoritarianism, exhibitionism, and social motives such as power, status, and prestige. Although these motives are irrelevant, they are not innate but are learned, mostly in the process of acculturation.

2. *Brand Comprehension* is the second learning construct. It refers to knowledge about the existence and characteristics of those brands that form the buyer's evoked set of alternatives. As mentioned earlier, the evoked set is composed of only a few brands out of the many brands that are available in the market.

A brand is a first-ordered abstraction of objects that are either identical or very similar. The buyer attaches a word label to these objects such as Campbell's Tomato Soup. Whenever he sees a can of Campbell's Tomato Soup or hears the phrase, the image conveys to him certain specific and unique characteristics of these objects related to their appearance, buying and consuming procedures, and the extent of their potential to satisfy his motives. In short, it conveys certain meaning. In an advanced economy like ours where there are careful quality controls, the buyer can rest assured that any particular can with that label is just like another. If the quality control were not adequate, the buyer would not summarize various cans in one word or label, but instead would divide Campbell's Tomato Soup into subclasses. In fact, he has to some extent divided all Campbell's soups into subclasses by adding words such as tomato or chicken.

From the buyer's point of view—introspectively—the level of abstraction in Brand Comprehension is carried out to the extent that he can perform two functions. First, abstraction is carried out to that level where he can describe and communicate adequately to other people in his social environment. For example, when he wants to buy a brand, he often describes it to the salesgirl. This type of descriptive abstraction is called the *denotative meaning* of the brand. Second, abstraction is carried out to that level where he can perceive the brand as goal-object or an instrument of satisfying his motives. This type of abstraction is evaluative and is called the *connotative meaning* of the brand. The evaluative abstraction is *not* part of Brand Comprehension. Instead, it is stored in the hypothetical construct of Attitude, as discussed later. In Brand Comprehension, the buyer stores only the descriptive abstraction.

3. *Choice Criteria* is the third learning construct. Choice Criteria serve the function of organizing and structuring the buyer's motives so that motives that are relevant to this product class are interrelated and ordered in terms of their relative importance to him. Choice Criteria are the buyer's mental rules, which he utilizes to evaluate brands as goal-objects. Their function is to generate appropriate attitudes toward brands, so that the brand with the greatest favorable attitude is potentially most satisfactory to him. In short, they serve the function of permitting goal-directed behavior.

In view of the fact that Choice Criteria are learned, principles of learning become crucial in their development and change over time. There are two broad sources of learning: (*a*) actual experience and (*b*) information. Actual experience can be either with the *same* buying situation as in the past or with a *similar* buying situation. The latter is generally labeled as generalization, as discussed earlier. Similarly, information as a source of learning can be from (*a*) the buyer's commercial environment or (*b*) his social environment, as mentioned earlier.

4. *Attitude* refers to the buyer's relative preferences of brands in his evoked set based on his evaluative beliefs about these brands as goal-objects. It might be visualized as the place where the connotative meanings of the brands in buyer's evoked set are compared with Choice Criteria to yield a judgment on the relative contribution of the brands toward satisfaction of buyer's Motives. This judgment includes not only an estimate of the value of the brand to him, but also an estimate of the confidence with which he holds that position. This uncertainty aspect of Attitude can be called "brand ambiguity," since the more confidently he holds it, the less ambiguous is the connotative meaning of the brand to the buyer and the more likely he is to buy it (Day, 1967). Brand confidence is, however, an important concept, hence it is treated separately in the hypothetical construct called Confidence.

5. *Intention*, the fifth learning construct, refers to buy
as to when, where, and how he is likely to buy a brand. It .
possible modification of buyer's Attitude toward brands in terms oi
hibitory contingencies that may be present if the buyer bought a brand.
The buyer takes into account these contingencies as he perceives they
will arise within some specific time in the future. Consequently, he
may prefer brand A but may buy brand B because of some inhibitory
situation that prevents him from buying A *at the time* he decides to
buy. Intention, therefore, stores buyer's situational abstraction.

We postulate at least five types of inhibitory situations. They are
(*a*) high price of the brand, (*b*) lack of availability of the brand, (*c*)
time pressure on the buyer, (*d*) the buyer's financial status, and (*e*)
social influences.

An essential feature of all inhibitors is that they are *not internalized*
by the buyer because their occurrence is contingent and strictly situational. However, some of the inhibitors may persist systematically over
time as they concern a given buyer. If they persist long enough, the
buyer is likely to incorporate them as part of his decision criteria and
thus to internalize them. The consequence is that they may affect even
buyer's Attitude, Brand Comprehension, and Choice Criteria. A good
example of internalization by the learning process might be the constant
time pressure a housewife faces because she has taken a job. Continuation of time pressure may alter her evoked set as well as motive structure.
Convenience and saving of time may become an additional important
criterion, and her evoked set of brands may now include some timesaving
brands such as instant coffee. Similarly, as a result of a brand being
withdrawn by the company because of the brand's stage in the product
life cycle, its availability is permanently affected. The lack of availability
will then be learned and internalized, and the buyer will remove that
brand from his evoked set.

6. *Confidence* refers to the degree of certainty the buyer perceives
toward a brand. This certainty may relate to his Brand Comprehension
(denotative abstraction), his Attitude toward the brand (connotative
abstraction), his Intention to buy the brand (situational abstraction),
and his postpurchase evaluation of the brand (purchase experience
abstraction). Accordingly, Confidence is related to Brand Comprehension, Attitude, Intention, and Satisfaction. Its presence in several of the
hypothetical constructs has motivated us to treat it as a separate hypothetical construct. We think that it provides a good aggregate construct
that has great potential for empirical investigation. Confidence also has
a feedback effect on the motives in the sense that it affects information
seeking and processing, which are discussed later.

7. *Satisfaction*, the last of the learning constructs, refers to the degree

of congruence between the actual consequences from purchase and consumption of a brand and what was expected from it by the buyer at the time of purchase. It also includes nonevaluative other experiences from purchase of the brand. If the actual outcomes are adjudged by the buyer to be *at least* equal to those expected, the buyer will feel satisfied, that is, actual consequences are greater than or equal to expected consequences. If, on the other hand, he adjudges the actual outcomes to be less than what he expected, the buyer will feel dissatisfied, that is, actual consequences are less than expected consequences. Satisfaction or dissatisfaction with a brand can be with respect to any one of the different attributes. If the brand proves more satisfactory than he expected, the buyer has a tendency to enhance the attractiveness of the brand. If it proves less satisfactory than he expected, he is likely to diminish its attractiveness.

2.2.2.2   Perceptual Constructs

Another set of constructs serve the function of information procurement and processing relevant to a purchase decision. As mentioned earlier, information can come from any one of the three inputs—Significative Commercial Stimuli, Symbolic Commercial Stimuli, and Social Stimuli. The perceptual constructs in Figure 2.1 are labeled (*a*) Attention, (*b*) Stimulus Ambiguity, (*c*) Perceptual Bias, and (*d*) Overt Search.

A perceptual phenomenon implies ignoring a physical event, seeing it attentively, or sometimes imagining what is not present in reality. All perceptual phenomena essentially create some change in quantity or meaning of objective information.

1. *Attention* refers to the opening and closing of sensory receptors that control the intake of information. The manifestation of this phenomenon is generally called paying attention or ignoring the information. It suggests the extent to which the buyer is sensitive to information. Attention acts as a gatekeeper to information entering into the buyer's mental state. It thus controls the quantity of information input.

In Figure 2.1, Attention is a function of two other constructs: Stimulus Ambiguity and Attitude. In fact, however, several other constructs such as Confidence, goal conflict, and incomparability of alternatives are also its determinants. Most of these mediate their influence by way of Stimulus Ambiguity. They are discussed in Chapter 5.

2. *Stimulus Ambiguity* refers to the perceived uncertainty and lack of meaningfulness of information received from the environment. It affects Attention and Overt Search constructs.

Stimulus Ambiguity may change in a single communication, particularly if it is verbal as in radio and television commercials. The buyer may at first pay attention because of novelty or incongruence, but may find, as the commercial proceeds, that it is too simple and contains well-known facts about the brand or the product class. He may, therefore, ignore the message as the exposure continues. On the other hand, he may find that the ambiguity increases as the communication progresses. He will continue to pay attention so long as ambiguity does not exceed some tolerable level.

3. *Perceptual Bias* is the third perceptual construct. The buyer not only selectively attends to information, but actually distorts it once it enters his mental state. In other words, meaning of information is altered by the buyer. This aspect of the perceptual process is summarized in Perceptual Bias. The buyer may distort the cognitive elements contained in information to make them congruent with his own frame of reference as determined by the amount of information he already has stored. A series of cognitive consistency theories have been recently developed to explain how this congruency is established and what the consequences are in terms of the distortion of information that we might expect (R. Brown, 1965; Feldman, 1966). Most of the "qualitative" change in information arises because of feedback from various learning constructs such as Motives, Attitude, Brand Comprehension, and Choice Criteria. These relations are too complex, however, to be described in a summary. Accordingly, we have shown only the direct effects of Attitude and Motives in Figure 2.1.

The perceptual phenomena described above are likely to be less operative if the information is received from the buyer's social environment. This is because (a) the social source of information, such as a friend, is likely to be favorably regarded by the buyer, and therefore proper, undistorted reception of information will occur, and (b) the information itself is modified by the social environment (the friend) so that it conforms to the needs of the buyer, hence further modification is less essential.

4. *Overt Search* is the fourth perceptual construct. During the total buying phase, which extends over time and involves several repeat purchases of a product class, there are stages when the buyer *actively* seeks information. It is very important to distinguish between the situations when he passively receives information and those when he actively seeks it. We believe that the perceptual phenomena explained above are less operative in the latter instances, and that a commercial communication, therefore, at that stage has a high probability of influencing the buyer.

The active seeking of information occurs when the buyer senses ambiguity of the brands in his evoked set. This happens in the Extensive Problem Solving and Limited Problem Solving phase of the decision process. The ambiguity of brand exists because the buyer is not certain of the outcomes from each brand. In other words, he has not yet learned enough about the alternatives to establish an expectancy of potential of the brands to satisfy his motives or even fully comprehend their denotative meaning. He may also find that two brands are equally attractive and he is undecided which one to choose. In all such situations, the buyer will search for information.

This concludes our brief description of the hypothetical constructs. In the next section, we discuss their relationships by considering some common examples.

2.3 RELATIONSHIPS AMONG HYPOTHETICAL CONSTRUCTS

2.3.1 Some Examples

Figure 2.1 shows two types of lines: solid and dashed. All lines can be thought of as representing energy such as neural impulses. Solid lines represent the sequential paths by which cognitions (bits of knowledge) travel and lodge themselves in any of the hypothetical constructs. They also represent, in some cases, causal links among the constructs. Dashed lines represent the causal given conditions that act as feedbacks. They govern the quantity as well as meaning of cognitions as they are being lodged in the hypothetical constructs.

The easiest way to describe the relationships among the hypothetical constructs of the theory is to consider some common examples. We have chosen two elaborate examples. The first simply traces back the internal state of the buyer that he describes as causal in some specific purchase behavior. It is a static picture of the theory. The second example follows the paths that a commercial message takes within the buyer. It is a dynamic example.

Suppose that Mr. Jones is observed to purchase Winston filter cigarettes. This is incorporated in the output variable called Purchase in Figure 2.1. Our interest at this point is not in the quantity, the timing, or the place of his purchase. Rather, we wish to find out why he chose Winston over more than 60 major brands of filter cigarettes. When asked, Mr. Jones states that he regularly buys Winston and does so because he likes it. Pushed further, he states that he likes it because it has a combination of attributes that best provide what he is looking for in smoking cigarettes. Finally, being a patient and cooperative individual, he describes what he is looking for in cigarette buying and consuming: mildness, smooth draw, convenience in packaging and availability, and reasonable price. When further asked, he states that he knows of 16 brands of cigarettes, has himself tried 6 of them, and right now considers that Marlboro, Chesterfield, and Kent are other brands that he would consider buying and consuming.

The information can now be classified as related to several hypothetical constructs. Mr. Jones's liking and evaluation are part of Attitude. His purchase criteria are the Choice Criteria, and his brand awareness and consideration are part of Brand Comprehension. Mr. Jones also states that he does not *always* choose Winston because there are some occasions when he buys any of the other three brands. These occasions are quite varied: sometimes, for example, the store does not have Winston, sometimes his wife brings another brand because of a sale. The occasions are lumped together as inhibitors and are a part of Intention. Mr. Jones, however, is very confident of his evaluations of various brands of cigarettes. He is equally certain about his intention to buy Winston. This degree of certainty is captured in Confidence.

Next, there are a number of questions about why Mr. Jones is so confident, so certain of his evaluations, his criteria, and his knowledge of various brands. Based on several related questions, it turns out that Mr. Jones learned about these cognitions partly from personal experiences, partly from mass media, and partly from his friends and family. For example, when asked how he can be certain that Winston is the best brand for him, he states that he has tried several brands and, based on his postpurchase evaluations (Satisfaction), has decided that Winston is a very satisfactory brand. Similarly, he has also learned from personal experiences that he ought to look for the four criteria set out earlier. Finally, he admits that several years ago when he started smoking, he learned considerably about the brands and what to look for in them by word-of-mouth as well as mass media (Stimulus Display). He used to pay more attention to them then than he does now because he thinks he knows rather well how to evaluate brands of cigarettes. Furthermore, he does not actively seek any information now, although he did when he began smoking (Overt Search).

In our example, we have isolated enough information from Mr. Jones to be able to abstract from it most of the static storage constructs. These include the learning constructs of Attitude, Intention, Choice Criteria, Brand Comprehension, Confidence, and Satisfaction. Choice Criteria can be further abstracted to state that underlying Motives are really taste and economic value.

Now we turn to another situation. This concerns the newly introduced freeze-dried coffee. As the reader probably knows, there are two major brands of freeze-dried coffee: Maxim from General Foods and Taster's Choice from Nestle Company. In this example, we attempt to show the dynamics of a buying situation by bringing out changes that may occur in the learning constructs.

Suppose that we also have the cooperation of Mrs. Jones. We are fortunate to get in touch with her at a time when she has not yet heard of freeze-dried coffee. Mrs. Jones is a regular coffee drinker. She takes pride in making a good cup of coffee both for herself and for her husband, Mr. Jones. Her Brand Comprehension consists of the knowledge that there are two types of coffee: regular and instant. She is aware of several brands of regular and instant coffee. However, she is much more knowledgeable about regular coffee than about instant coffee because she herself seldom consumes the latter. Mrs. Jones does buy instant coffee because her son, who has just returned from Vietnam, prefers instant coffee to regular coffee.

Mrs. Jones's evoked set of regular coffee consists of only three brands: Maxwell House, Hills Brothers, and Savarin. Her Attitude is very strongly toward Maxwell House, and she would buy Hills Brothers or Savarin only occasionally because of some unforeseeable situation. This strong preference for Maxwell House is based on her Choice Criteria of strength, flavor, aroma, and economy, and the brand's ability to satisfy them. Her Confidence is also very high because she is quite certain of her evaluations of various brands.

One day, Maxim is introduced in her town. Mrs. Jones views a television commercial from General Foods that describes what freeze-dried coffee means and how it combines the flavor of regular coffee and the convenience of instant coffee. Although usually she ignores a large number of commercials, Mrs. Jones pays Attention to this particular commercial. She, in fact, diverts herself from her other activities and watches the commercial intently, suggesting that she is very interested in learning about the new coffee. A number of factors are responsible for her sensitivity to information. First, she is favorably predisposed to Maxwell House company. Second, she considers coffee an important product. Third, the freeze-dry concept is new and ambiguous to her. In particular, she does not know the difference between freeze-dried and instant coffee with respect to processing.

Mrs. Jones absorbs the following bits of information: (1) Maxim is a totally new kind of coffee, (2) which is based on freeze-dry process, (3) has flavor and taste of regular coffee, (4) but appears and is used like instant coffee. These bits of information are not congruent with her frame of reference, which has always kept regular and instant coffee in separate categories. After considerable mental reasoning, she concludes that (1) Maxim is a new brand of instant coffee, (2) perhaps better in taste than most other instant coffees, (3) because it is manufactured by a new process. This distortion in meaning is due to Perceptual Bias process. Finally, Mrs. Jones files away the distorted information as not relevant to her. However, this has added to her Brand Comprehension of instant coffee brands.

A few days later, Mrs. Jones is exposed to the same commercial. This time, she does not pay full attention, but she does listen and watch it. At the end, she concludes with greater firmness that Maxim is a new brand of instant coffee perhaps with improved taste over other instant coffees because of the new process.

Several days later, Mrs. Jones receives a sample can of Maxim. She would not have bought it nor served it, but the free sample generates enough motivation in her to prepare coffee using Maxim. However, she does this to serve only herself and her son. The actual experience proves that Maxim is surprisingly similar to regular coffee. Her son also praises it. With Satisfaction, Mrs. Jones reevaluates her Attitude toward Maxim and concludes that it is the most preferred brand of instant coffee.

Mrs. Jones then manifests some exploratory behavior. She talks with her friends about Maxim, trying to find out how they perceive it and whether they are using it at all. Her Overt Search is considerably high. Next time, she serves Maxim to her husband. He likes the taste and praises it. Her friends, in general, also consider it as a good product. Mrs. Jones now has such a high opinion of Maxim that she seriously considers it as a replacement for Maxwell House regular coffee. When the sample is exhausted, she buys a small jar of Maxim.

In our example, the perceptual constructs of Attention, Perceptual Bias, and Stimulus Ambiguity played central roles in the beginning. They were themselves governed by the buyer's Attitude. In fact, but for the free sample and the resultant consumption, the buyer would not have bought Maxim nor have considered it as an alternative. However, learning from significative communication not only enhanced her Brand Comprehension but also her evaluation of the brand, particularly when Maxim proved satisfactory to her and her family. Moreover, to comprehend the situation further and to be more confident, she sought more information. Overt Search process became active. Each additional bit of information added greater favorability to her evaluation of Maxim. Attitude constantly changed in a positive manner, so that she finally decided to buy Maxim. Presumably, Attitude was strong enough and there were no inhibitory factors, both of which lead to purchase.

In the examples, we have attempted to describe the interaction among the hypothetical constructs at the simplest and crudest level. In the next section, a more rigorous description is presented by focusing on changes in the learning constructs.

2.3.2 Dynamics of Buying Behavior

Over a period of time, the learning constructs in the theory of buyer behavior change in their content. Most of this change is due to learning of additional information. There are three broad sources of learning: (1) generalization from similar buying situations, (2) repeat buying of the same product class, and (3) Stimulus Display.

1. *Generalization from similar buying situations.* Not only is the buying process very similar across product classes, Choice Criteria involved in different product classes are also similar. This similarity in both the buyer's responses and the stimuli he faces from different brands enables him to transfer his past learning to new situations. The transfer of past learning is called generalization (Hovland, 1951; Osgood, 1949). Capacity to generalize provides the buyer with a truly enormous range of flexibility in adapting his purchase behavior to a myriad of varying market conditions.

Generalization can occur at any one of the several levels of buyer behavior suggested in the output variables in Figure 2.1. However, we are primarily interested in generalization of evaluative beliefs (Attitude) about brands which would allow a brand to become an alternative.

Broadly speaking, there are three types of generalization: (*a*) stimulus generalization, (*b*) response generalization, and (*c*) both stimulus and response generalization.

Stimulus generalization occurs when the buyer manifests the same response or considers manifesting the same response in the presence of a new stimulus that is physically or semantically similar to the old stimulus. For example, when *stainless steel* blades, *soft* margarines, or *diet* drinks are introduced, the buyer may transfer his buying behavior to these new products because of his past association with blades, margarines, or soft-drinks. If the buyer is loyal to a brand of blades, margarines, or soft drinks, he may generalize his buying to the new product but choosing the label of the old brand. For example, a Gillette Blue buyer may now buy or at least consider buying a Gillette Super stainless-steel blade.

Semantic stimulus generalization occurs when the new brand is equivalent in *meaning* to some old brand that the buyer prefers and consumes. There need not be any physical similarity. A good example is that of Carnation Instant Breakfast to which some buyers may generalize their breakfast cereal purchases and others their diet food purchases.

A second type of generalization is called the response generalization. Here, the buyer has some association between a stimulus and his buying behavior. Now, he manifests a new but similar buying behavior in the presence of the same stimulus. A common example is the in-store switching of the brand; the buyer has gone to the store to buy brand A because he reads its advertisement in the newspaper, but in the store he buys brand B. Similarly, "moving up" the quality in automobile buying (from Chevrolet to Pontiac or Buick) is another example of response generalization. Perhaps, the most adequate example is buying a *bigger-size* package of the same brand. These examples illustrate both physical and semantic response generalization.

A third type of generalization occurs when both the stimuli and the responses are similar to past learning. It is believed that, in such a situation, the amount of transfer is a function of the similarity among the old and the new responses, whereas the rate of transfer is a function of the similarity between the old and the new stimuli (Robinson, 1948). There are a large number of instances in which this type of generalization is likely to occur in buying behavior, since large companies today manufacture and sell a variety of brands and package sizes. For example, a cosmetic company such as Max Factor provides many shades of lipstick and other personal-care items.

2. *Purchase experiences.* Another source of change in the learning constructs is the repeated purchase of the same product class over a period of time.

Purchase of a brand entails two types of feedbacks. Both are summarized in Figure 2.1 in Satisfaction from which other constructs such as Attitude and Confidence are influenced. First, the experience of buying, with all its cognitive aspects of memory, reasoning, and so on, has a learning effect on the Choice Criteria. This occurs irrespective of which specific brand the buyer chooses in any one purchase decision because the criteria, like the motives, are product-specific and not limited to any one brand. Hence every purchase has an incremental effect in firmly establishing the Choice Criteria. This is easy to visualize if we remember that buying behavior is a series of mental and motor steps, whereas the actual choice is only its terminal act.

Purchase of a brand creates certain satisfactions for the buyer, which he compares with his expectation (Attitude) of the brand's potential. This expectation is the basis on which he made his decision in the first place. The comparison of expected and actual consequences causes him to be satisfied or dissatisfied with the brand. Hence the second feedback from Purchase behavior to Satisfaction changes the attractiveness of the brand purchased. If the buyer is satisfied with his consumption, he enhances the potential of the brand, which is likely to result in greater probability of its repeat purchase. If he is dissatisfied, the potential of the brand is diminished, and so is the probability of a repeat purchase.

If no inhibitory forces influence him, the buyer will continue to buy a brand that proves satisfactory. In the initial stages of decision making he may show some tendency to oscillate between brands in order to formulate his Choice Criteria. In other words, he may learn by trial and error at first, then settle on a brand, and thereafter buy the brand with a regularity to suggest that he is brand-loyal. Unless a product is of very high risk, however, there is a limit to how long this brand loyalty will continue: he may become bored with his preferred brand and look for something new.

3. *Information as a source of learning.* The third major source by which the learning constructs are changed is information from (*a*) the buyer's commercial environment, consisting of advertising, promotion, personal selling, and retail shelf display of the competing companies, and (*b*) his social environment, consisting of his family, friends, reference group, and social class.

We describe the influence of information at first as if the perceptual constructs were absent. In other words, we assume that the buyer receives information with perfect fidelity as it exists in the environment. Also, we discuss separately the information from commercial and social environments.

As mentioned before, the company communicates about its offerings to the buyers either by the physical brand (significates) or by symbols (pictorial or linguistic) that represent the brand. In Figure 2.1, the influence of information is shown on Motives, Choice Criteria, Intention and Brand Comprehension. Indirectly, it also influences Attitude and Confidence by way of Brand Comprehension. We also believe that the influence of commercial information on relevant motives is limited. The main effect is primarily to *intensify* whatever motives the buyer has rather than to create new ones. For example, physical display of the brand may intensify his motives to raise them above the threshold level, which, combined with strong Attitude, can result in impulse (unplanned) purchase. A similar reaction is possible when an advertisement creates sufficient intensity of motives to provide an impetus for the buyer to go to the store. A second way of influencing motives is to show the *perceived instrumentality* of the brand and thereby make it a part of the buyer's defined set of alternatives. Finally, to a very limited extent, marketing stimuli may change the *content of the motives*. This, we believe, is rare. The general conception both among marketing men and among laymen is that marketing stimuli change the buyer's motives. However, on a closer examination it would appear that what is changed is the *intensity* of buyer's motives already provided by the social environment. Many dormant or latent motives may become stimulated. The secret of success very often lies in identifying the change in motives created by social change and intensifying them, as seems to be the case in the recent introduction and success of dietary products.

Marketing stimuli are important in determining and changing the buyer's evoked set. Commercial information tells him of the existence of the brands (awareness), their identifying characteristics (Brand Comprehension), and their relevance to the satisfaction of the buyer's needs (Attitude).

Marketing stimuli are also significant in creating and changing the buyer's Choice Criteria. They become important sources when the buyer has no prior experience to rely on. Similarly, when the buyer actively seeks information because all the existing alternatives are unacceptable to him, marketing stimuli become important in *changing* his criteria.

Finally, marketing stimuli can unwittingly create inhibitors. For example, a company feels the need to emphasize price-quality association, but this may result in high-price inhibition in the mind of the buyer. Similarly, in emphasizing the details of usage and consumption of a product, the communication may create the inhibition related to time pressure. These inhibitory forces affect Intention.

The *social environment* of the buyer—family, friends, reference groups—is another major source of information in his buying behavior. Most of the inputs are likely to be symbolic (linguistic), although at times the physical product may be shown to the buyer.

Information from his social environment also affects all the learning constructs: Motives, Choice Criteria, and Brand Comprehension directly, and Attitude and Intention indirectly. However, the effect of social environment on these constructs is somewhat different from that of the commercial environment. First, the information about the brands will be considerably modified by the social environment before it reaches the buyer. Most of the modifications are apt to be in the nature of adding connotative meanings to brands and their attributes and of the biasing effects of the communicator's perceptual variables, such as Perceptual Bias. Second, the buyer's social environment will probably have a very strong influence on the content of his motives and their ordering to establish a goal structure. Several research studies have concentrated on such influences (Bourne, 1963; Bush and London, 1960; Gruen, 1960;

Laird, 1950; E. Katz and Lazarsfeld, 1955). Third, the social environment may also affect his evoked set. This will be particularly true when the buyer is ! .cking in experience. Furthermore, if the product class is important to the buyer and he is technically incompetent or uncertain in evaluating the consequences of the brand, he may rely more on the social than on the marketing environment for information. This is well documented by several studies using the perceived-risk hypothesis (Bauer, 1960, 1961; Bauer and Wortzel, 1966; Cox, 1962, 1967; S. Cunningham, 1966; Arndt, 1967b; Sheth and Venkatesan, 1968).

In describing the perceptual constructs—Attention, Perceptual Bias, Stimulus Ambiguity, and Overt Search—we mentioned that their function is to alter the quantity and meaning of objective information to suit the buyer's frame of reference as well as his needs. We wish to emphasize here that, between marketing and social stimuli, distortion is likely to be much greater for the marketing than for the social stimuli. This is essentially caused by the greater credibility—competence and trust—that the buyer attaches to social sources, as well as by the facility of two-way communication in social situations. Similarly, the buyer may actively seek information more from his social environment, particularly information that is evaluative in nature. Thus our discussion in the preceding two subsections must be qualified by the perceptual effects that are inevitable in any information processing.

2.3.3 Decision-Making Process

The dynamics of buying behavior can be put in decision-making framework to show aggregately what changes occur. We may accordingly classify a decision process as Extensive Problem Solving, Limited Problem Solving, or Routinized Response Behavior, depending on the strength of Attitude toward the brands (Howard, 1963; Sheth, 1966).

In Extensive Problem Solving, Attitude toward the brands is low. None of the brands is discriminated against enough to show strong preferences of one over others. In fact, the buyer may not even have a well-defined product class concept. At this stage of decision making, brand ambiguity is high, with the result that the buyer actively seeks information and there exists a greater *latency of response*—the time interval from the initiation of a decision to its completion. Similarly, *deliberation* or reasoning will be high, since the buyer lacks a well-defined product class concept. He is also apt to consider many brands as part of the evoked set, his Brand Comprehension will be extensive but shallow on any one particular brand, and stimuli coming from the commercial environment are less likely to trigger any immediate purchase reaction.

When Attitude toward brands is moderate, the buyer's decision process can be called Limited Problem Solving. There still exists brand ambiguity, since the buyer is not fully able to discriminate and compare brands so that he may prefer one brand over others. He is likely to seek information, but not to the extent that he seeks it in Extensive Problem Solving. More importantly, he seeks information more on a relative basis—to compare and discriminate various brands rather than to absolutely evaluate and comprehend each of the brands. His deliberation or thinking is much less, since Choice Criteria are tentatively well defined. Brand Comprehension will consist of a small number of brands, each having about the same degree of preference.

In Routinized Response Behavior, the buyer will have a high level of Attitude toward brands in his evoked set. Furthermore, he has now accumulated sufficient experience and information to have no brand ambiguity. He will in fact discriminate among brands enough to show a strong preference toward one or two brands in his evoked set. He is unlikely to actively seek any information from the environment, since such information is not needed. Also, whatever information he passively or accidentally receives, he will subject it to selective perceptual processes so that only congruent information is allowed. This may be seen in his tendency to pay attention to advertisements of brands he prefers and ignore those of other brands. Very often, the congruent information will act as "triggering cues" to motivate him to manifest purchase behavior. Much of impulse purchase is really the outcome of a strong predisposition and a facilitating commercial stimulus such as store display. The buyer's evoked set will consist of a few brands toward which he is highly predisposed. However, he will have greater preference toward one brand in his evoked set and lesser towards others.

As mentioned earlier, Attitude is a central construct in the theory. The greater the learning, the more favorable or unfavorable the Attitude toward the brand in the evoked set. In addition, two other aspects need to be examined.

First, although our focus is on brand choice behavior, the buyer also simplifies the total sequence of behavior necessary to make a purchase— going to the store, looking at the products, paying at the counter, and so forth—by reducing the number of steps and ordering them in a definite way. The greater the Attitude, the more the simplification of total buying behavior, hence the greater the routinization of his purchase.

Second, if the purchase cycle is very long, as is the case for automobiles and other durable appliances, the buyer may develop firm Choice Criteria and yet manifest exploratory behavior to a marked degree at each purchase decision because (1) market conditions invariably change and the buyer may find past experience insufficient, and (2) the Choice Criteria through forgetting and lack of use become fuzzy.

2.4   SUMMARY AND CONCLUSIONS

In this chapter, we have sketched a rough picture of the theory of buyer behavior. In the hope of adequately communicating the complexity inherent in the theory, a simple and, at times, crude description of the constructs is provided.

The theory of buyer behavior consists of two sets of hypothetical constructs: learning constructs and perceptual constructs. The learning constructs are (1) Motives, (2) Choice Criteria, (3) Brand Comprehension, (4) Attitude, (5) Confidence, (6) Intention, and (7) Satisfaction. They are interrelated as follows. Choice Criteria are derived from Motives as a process of learning. Attitude is a function of Choice Criteria and evaluative beliefs about a brand, the latter flowing from Brand Comprehension. Confidence affects Intention and input of information via Attention and Overt Search. Intention is a function of Attitude and Confidence plus situational inhibitory influences.

The perceptual constructs are (1) Stimulus Ambiguity, (2) Attention, (3) Perceptual Bias, and (4) Overt Search. Attention is a function of several variables, two of which are Stimulus Ambiguity and the buyer's Attitude. Perceptual Bias is a process that filters information to which the buyer pays Attention. Its function is to change the meaning of information absorbed by the buyer. It is also a function of a variety of factors, the most significant of which is the buyer's Attitude. Overt Search is active seeking of information. It is a function of Stimulus Ambiguity, Attitude, and Confidence. The latter exerts influence by way of the Motives construct, although in Figure 2.1 it is shown directly to simplify.

The hypothetical constructs are linked to form a network of constructs. This interrelationship is illustrated in two ways. First, two common examples of buying behavior are described and explained by the use of the hypothetical constructs. Second, the dynamics of change over time is elaborated using the decision-making framework. Decision making over time is classified into three phases: Extensive Problem Solving, Limited Problem Solving, and Routinized Response Behavior.

This concludes Part I, consisting of Chapters 1 and 2, which are respectively an introduction to philosophy of science and a summary of the theory. Part II, which contains Chapters 3, 4 and 5, presents the structure of the theory. Chapter 3 sets forth the general structure of the theory which consists of three elements: intervening variables (input and output), hypothetical constructs, and exogenous variables. It also describes the intervening variables and exogenous variables. The hypothetical constructs are divided into learning constructs and perceptual constructs. Chapter 4 deals with learning constructs, and Chapter 5 with perceptual constructs. Chapters 6 and 7 make up Part III, which is concerned with the measurement of two central output intervening variables, Attitude' and Purchase respectively. Part IV discusses application. Chapter 8 presents application of the theory to the problem of product innovation (significative communication), while Chapter 9 develops the application to mass communication (symbolic communication). Part V (Chapter 10) is concerned with conclusions as to the implications of the theory for basic research with regard to substance and method, and practice, both public and private.

PART II
Structure of the Theory

CHAPTER 3

Intervening and Exogenous Variables

Chapter 2 provided a simplified overview of the structure of the theory of buyer behavior as an introduction to the more detailed description here and in Chapters 4 and 5.

If the theory is to serve the functions and meet the needs described in Chapter 1, it must be related to the empirical phenomena that in some sense it is purported to represent. This relationship is shown by distinguishing in Figure 3.1, which is a complete representation of the theory, between the perceptual plane (*P* plane) which contains observable reality as viewed by the scientist—and the conceptual plane (*C* plane) which is the theory. Visualizing the *C* plane as lying above the *P* plane may help the reader to understand the distinction between the two planes, between theory and fact.

The contents of the conceptual plane are made up of two kinds of elements, as discussed in Chapter 1: intervening variables and hypothetical constructs. The intervening variables are constructs derived directly from observable reality, for example, Purchase. By taking certain measurements of acts having to do with actual buying, we derive a number that we say is Purchase. It is important for the reader to recognize, however, that intervening variables are not the objective data themselves; they are not the physical events; they are constructs but they are

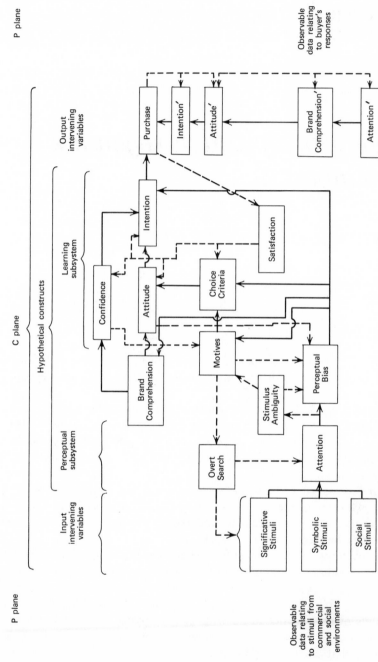

Figure 3.1 Theory of buyer behavior.

P plane

Observable
data relating
to buyer's
responses

C plane

Hypothetical constructs

Output
intervening
variables

Learning
subsystem

Perceptual
subsystem

Input
intervening
variables

P plane

Observable
data relating
to stimuli from
commercial
and social
environments

Purchase

Intention′

Attitude′

Brand
Comprehension′

Attention′

Intention

Satisfaction

Confidence

Attitude

Choice
Criteria

Brand
Comprehension

Motives

Perceptual
Bias

Stimulus
Ambiguity

Overt
Search

Attention

Significative
Stimuli

Symbolic
Stimuli

Social
Stimuli

54

first-order, not higher-order, abstractions. For some purposes, for example, it is better to use a measure such as the combination of three buying acts—three consecutive purchases of the brand—and label this construct "brand loyalty." The same argument can be made on the input side in dealing with stimuli. The important point is that intervening variables are one step removed from that which is observable by one or more of the scientist's five senses.

Hypothetical constructs, on the other hand, are not immediately based on observable reality. They are higher-order abstractions than are intervening variables. We can only infer their values indirectly from changes in the intervening variables; verification of the theory requires the formulation of intervening variables. Attitude toward a brand, for example, is a hypothetical construct; it is something that no one ever touched, smelled, saw, heard, or tasted. It must be inferred from something that is observable such as the written or verbal response to the question, "How much do you like this brand?"

In Figure 3.1 the lines can be thought of as a part of the buyer's nervous system. The solid lines indicate straightforward causal relations, which in themselves are complex enough. The dotted lines, however indicate feedback relations, which are still more complex and not as well documented. Referring to Figure 3.1, the reader will note that with the exception of Purchase the output intervening variables have the same names as some of the hypothetical constructs, but the intervening variable bears a prime symbol. In such cases the intervening variable is the more realistic counterpart of the corresponding hypothetical construct. The reason for this similarity in name is to simplify the exposition throughout the rest of the book. This approach is not completely comprehensive, however, since not all of the hypothetical constructs have counterpart intervening variables. We shall sometimes wish to measure these. If we do, counterpart intervening variables can be developed as we have in our empirical research. We have merely found the number of intervening variables as shown on the right side of Figure 3.1 to be convenient for purposes of exposition. Finally to simplify, a few of the relations postulated in the theory have been omitted from Figure 3.1.

3.1   CLASSIFICATION OF VARIABLES

3.1.1   Hypothetical Constructs and Intervening Variables

In Chapter 1, one dimension of a theoretical structure was said to be the realistic-idealistic one. Many behaviorists, including econometricians, are realistic in their theorizing and usually do not, or at least do not admit they do, make much use of hypothetical constructs. On the other hand, some are highly idealistic; for example, economists in dealing with the concept of utility are not much concerned with relating their construct to reality, hence with intervening variables. The evidence, however, is very persuasive to us that in the study of buying behavior we shall be seriously handicapped unless we are willing to become simultaneously idealistic and realistic in our theorizing, as suggested by MacCorquodale and Meehl (1948).

Let us illustrate the idealistic level. Two women are exposed to exactly the same television advertising, yet one of them later buys the brand but the other does not. This difference in purchase behavior must be explained. The piecemeal approach that characterizes most current buyer research appears to us to indicate that others believe, in a related way, that the whole of the purchase behavior process is too complex to be dealt with only in realistic terms. Still others may argue that we really need increasingly more abstract constructs, instead of more idealistic ones, which would then subsume the myriad of differences that cause us to think of the phenomenon as being complex. We are not at all optimistic about greater abstraction as a feasible alternative to hypothetical constructs.

The greater power of the idealistic approach comes about because we can define the hypothetical constructs somewhat more loosely, which releases our imagination to explore more fully new types of relationships. They are more generative. We can include in them more phenomena relative to the corresponding intervening variable; hence they contain *surplus meaning*. Much of the greater fertility of the hypothetical construct occurs also because if we are careful in our definitions, we can better communicate our comprehensive ideas about the phenomenon to our fellow scientists. We believe that this greater freedom to theorize will result in more progress, so long as we simultaneously try to verify the truth of the imaginatively derived hypotheses, for what we observe and measure is always less than what we infer.

Learning research with its atomistic nonintegrative tendencies is an example of the consequences of a rigidly realistic approach, although we see some evidence of change (Miller, Galanter, and Pribram, 1960). We believe that the use of hypothetical constructs will enable our theory to better serve the generative function, as discussed in Chapter 1, which in turn will help it to serve the integrative function and thus ultimately the descriptive function more adequately. Finally, even the delimiting function will be better fulfilled.

Consider one of the scientifically most respectable fields, physics. More than two thousand years ago the construct labeled "atom" was hypothesized. What scientist until recently had ever tasted, felt, heard, seen, or smelled an atom? Not long ago, we "split it," then "smashed it," and next "compressed it" as though it were as fully observable as a rubber ball; with quite recently developed techniques it is now possible to see it.

Although hypothetical constructs give free play to imagination, measurement is obviously essential at some point. We believe that it must play a central role now in systematic theory development. For this reason intervening variables are essential. They are intended to provide isomorphism between the hypothetical construct and reality. Let us illustrate. Attitude' can be said to reflect a part of the unobservable, and here we go beyond MacCorquodale and Meehl (1948) to Margenau (1950) and others. The point is that Attitude' is well enough defined that it can be connected to reality. It is *operationally* defined. The definitions of the hypothetical constructs are merely *constitutive*, that is, they are defined in terms of other constructs in the system, rather than in terms of reality. The *rules of correspondence* are the definitions and measurements of the intervening variables. These are rules whereby numbers are attached to objects, brands in this case, possessing the characteristic implied by the variable. Jones has an attitude of 3. This number is a measure of Attitude' which, in turn, is an *indicant* of Attitude because it is a part of Attitude. "At best, the two are *presumed* to be nonmonotonically related. At worst, merely a positive correlation of unknown magnitude is presumed to exist" (Torgerson, 1958, p. 7).

Some arrangements are needed to ensure an unambiguous and objective definition in the measurement process which is why we have "rules of correspondence." To the extent the rules are mathematical we can be more confident in using them. Because we believe that the rules are crucially important to success in developing knowledge in any field, Chapters 6 and 7 are devoted to these issues in connection with Attitude' and Purchase respectively.

The term "model" is often heard. We use it in its econometric sense of a relationship where the parameters of the functional relations are specified. A theory may be formal enough for the form but not the parameters of its functional relations to be specified. The task in the whole field of buyer behavior research is to develop models of the relationships among intervening variables: among input variables (S-S relationships), among output variables (R-R relationships), and between input and output variables (S-R relationships). As in psychology there will probably develop a tradition of miniature theories. We already see an example of this in Haines's work (1968) who presents an implicit S-R theory of consumer behavior. It is implicit in the sense that S is not specified, a limitation of all of the stochastic models developed in marketing.

3.1.2   Exogenous Variables

The hypothetical constructs and intervening variables are often put together in theory development and labeled "endogenous variables." These are variables the changes in which are explained by the theory. For a number of reasons elaborated below, it is also useful to postulate variables that influence the endogenous variables the changes in which are *not* explained by the theory. These are called "exogenous variables." The reader should bear this in mind because "exogenous" is sometimes used to refer to events outside the human body (Cattell 1, 1963, p. 191). Holtzman, on the other hand, uses essentially the same meaning that we do when he says that exogenous variables are independent of each other and endogenous variables are dependent on each other (1963, p. 206). Exogenous variables are outside the system of hypothetical constructs. Typically, we assume them to be *constant* during the period of *observation* of the buyer, but at times we may wish to focus directly on the consequences of change in them. They exert their effects *indirectly* on the output variables, since they operate by way of the hypothetical constructs. The specific relations will be described below and shown graphically at the end of the chapter.

There are three reasons for including them. The executive and the market researcher find it useful to divide the market into segments, each of which is more homogeneous than the market as a whole so that a more precisely appropriate marketing plan can be tailored to the particular segments. Also, we expect much of the fundamental research in buyer behavior to be done under field conditions where control is necessary. Finally, the effects of such marketing effort as advertising may be quite small, and so careful control is essential if its effects are to be identified. These reasons will be discussed at length below.

Now that we have perspective on the whole chapter, let us turn to a detailed discussion of the intervening variables and begin with the output variables, since these are more familiar to most of us.

3.2   OUTPUT VARIABLES

3.2.1   Introduction

The variables that link the hypothetical constructs to the real world on the output side of the theory are Purchase, Intention' (to Purchase), Attitude', Brand Comprehension', and Attention' (to the stimulus).

These intervening variables are sometimes referred to by communications researchers as "instrumental learning," to imply that they constitute a process by which the buyer learns such behavior as will enable him to reach his goals.

Executives view these variables as constituting a sequence of effects.* For example, referring back to Figure 3.1, Attention' leads to Brand Comprehension', Brand Comprehension' to Attitude', Attitude' to Intention', and Intention' to Purchase as though a change in one were a necessary *and* sufficient condition for change in the immediately subsequent variable. Practitioners of marketing, for example, often refer to "AIDA" (Attention, Interest, Desire, and Action) in discussing advertising and sales effects. Lavidge and Steiner (1961) proposed the response sequence as a useful concept in marketing. Finally, anthropologists and sociologists have established similar paradigms from their investigations of social innovation.

Facts are widely collected in terms of each of these sequential concepts, as Palda (1966) has so well shown, but empirical evidence on the nature of the relationships among them is sparse. The theory of buyer behavior, however, predicts that because of feedback conditions a change in a preceding variable is not even a necessary, much less a sufficient, condition for change in the subsequent variable.

The sequence of concepts, however, is extremely useful in marketing practice because each variable relates to a different hypothetical construct in the system, some of which may be relevant in some circumstances and others in other circumstances. Also, the intervening variables provide a fairly complete set of measurements in the attempt to understand the buyer.

In the past these sequential concepts have been used in marketing practice and research with almost no theoretical underpinnings. Our purpose here is to imbed them in the theory of buyer behavior. In this way the source and significance of each concept in the sequence can be shown, which will make the concepts more meaningful in research and practice. A key aspect here is that we must use the relations among the various elements of the sequence to infer the nature of the content and relations among the hypothetical constructs. One example that illustrates the nature of the research is the relation between Attitude and Purchase, which is currently of serious concern to market research directors because Attitude data are more useful in a number of ways. It is sometimes concluded from dissonance theoretic analysis that Purchase

---

* "Hierarchy of effects" has come to be the accepted term in the marketing literature, but this conflicts with the psychologist's use of hierarchy to imply a mutually exclusive set of alternatives.

causes Attitude change. From the analysis of attitude as a hypothetical construct, we view the relation as a feedback so that over time there is a two-way effect: at any point in time Attitude can cause Purchase, but Purchase, by way of the satisfaction that comes from it, can cause Attitude to change. We believe that more fruitful research is now possible in exploring the source, content, and relevance of the sequence.

We confine our list of output intervening variables to five—Attention', Brand Comprehension', Attitude', Intention', and Purchase—because these seem to meet the needs of many practical situations. If, as may often happen, a relationship is being tested that involves one of the other hypothetical constructs such as Motive, it can be added to the list of intervening variables and labeled by its construct name, with a prime sign to indicate that it is an intervening variable instead of a hypothetical construct. Also, it may appear strange to a psychologist to refer to Attention' and Brand Comprehension' as "output" variables. We do so because in marketing research practice they are often used as dependent variables, and in basic research we wish to understand the total process.

We now examine each of the intervening variables.

3.2.2   *Attention'*

Attention' is a continuous variable, but is measured at discrete times. It is a psychophysical measure that describes the opening and closing of the buyer's sensory receptors, such as pupil dilation, thus indicating concentration or the lack of it on a specified stimulus. Hence it is the magnitude of the flow of information into the buyer's nervous system, as contrasted with the much greater amount of information to which the buyer is actually *exposed*.

As Attention' is used in practice, the distinction between a flow at a point in time and the level of accumulation or stock of information from exposure over time is not always maintained. Attention' is sometimes said to be measured by eliciting awareness of a brand simply by asking the person, in terms of both unaided and aided recall, such questions as whether he is aware of the brand (or the advertisement). This method, however, measures a stock concept such as awareness, not a flow (Attention'). In discussions of "advertising principles," the term is used in the same sense in which we use it, but no theoretically supported measurement devices are offered.

Attention with its source in motivation is especially relevant in Product Innovation (Chapter 8) and Communication (Chapter 9). Since the buyer is constantly confronted with a plethora of environmental events, he must choose which ones he will attend to or perceive at any point in time. Of course, it matters greatly to the practitioner of marketing which events the buyer chooses to perceive: events emanating from his company or its products—and, if so, which particular one—or some other event. The practitioner devotes much of his time and financial resources to identifying and developing events that are more likely to catch the buyer's attention than many others the buyer might attend to. Furthermore, many products are probably not very ego-involving; hence stimuli representing them do not appear so important or relevant to the buyer.

3.2.3   Brand Comprehension'

There are literally four types of comprehension involved in buying: stimulus comprehension, brand comprehension, inhibitor comprehension, and product class comprehension. We deal here with Brand Comprehension. Stimulus comprehension is related to the hypothetical construct, Stimulus Ambiguity. Inhibitor comprehension is discussed below in connection with Intention' (to buy). Product Class Comprehension will be presented in Chapter 8.

Brand Comprehension' is the completeness of the buyer's verbal description of a brand, a product, or a service on a set of bipolar adjectival scales, which serve to communicate the denotative meaning of the brand to others. It has nothing to do with the buyer's evaluation of the brand, which constitutes the brand's connotative meaning to him. It includes all brands in the buyer's evoked set—the set of brands that he considers when he contemplates the purchase of a product class. Let us examine the concepts of denotative and connotative meanings because they will be useful in a number of ways.

The conventional semantic differential scales—particular bipolar adjectival scales such as pleasant-unpleasant, beautiful-ugly, or good-bad—seem to elicit connotative meaning. "Meaning" is used here in a semantic sense as being equal to behavioral reaction to symbols. This is what the brand connotes for the individual rating the brand on the scales. On the other hand, if objects are rated on psychophysical-type scales, for example, the absolute judgment, the denotative elements of meaning tend to be elicited. "Both of these biological systems—the affective energizing system [*connotative*] and the sensory-motor discrimination system [*denotative*]—are integrated in ordinary behavior . . ." (Osgood, 1962, p. 26, italics added). Now, let us fit this denotative or more physiological view into a broader framework, especially one that incorporates the social environment in which a buyer behaves, as well as making a more precise distinction between connotative and denotative (Diebold, 1965, p. 240).

"Denotative" applies to the descriptive aspects of a brand. It is these dimensions by which the buyer communicates the distinctions he uses in talking about brands in the same product class. They are socially prescribed meanings in the sense that the buyer is rewarded for their use with effective communication and social approval. Hence people do not differ greatly in their use of this referential or denotative meaning.

In connotative meaning, however, we expect large differences among buyers, because here we are dealing with what the brand connotes to the person, including the significance of the brand for his motives. Connotative meanings are said to be in part affective and emotional (Carroll, 1964, p. 83), and affect and emotion are related to motivation and preference.

3.2.4 Attitude' (toward Brand)

Attitude' is widely used empirically in marketing practice as an indicator of purchase. It has to do with the connotative meaning of a brand. It can be defined as a verbal expression of the consumer's evaluation of a brand or service on a set of bipolar adjectival scales defined in terms of the brand's potential to satisfy the buyer's motives that are relevant to the purchase of this product class.

3.2.5 Intention' (to Purchase)

Many marketing researchers wish to go beyond Attitude' and to secure some measure of future buying behavior, of intention.

Intention' is a verbal statement or combination of statements by the buyer in response to a question about the strength of his intention to buy a unit of the brand during some specified time period. We suspect, however, that a measure which incorporates inhibitors explicitly as well will be more fruitful.

3.2.6 Purchase

Purchase refers to the terminal act in the purchasing process which may not include consumption. This definition, even when confined to purchase alone, is not as unambiguous as it might at first seem. A housewife picks up a brand from the supermarket shelf, writes the name of a brand on her shopping list, pays for it at the checkout counter, and records the purchase in a purchase diary. Which of these constitute "purchase"? It is typically the case that each of a variety of indicators could be used to denote "purchase," but so long as we standardize on a particular overt movement and follow it consistently, this ambiguity presents no problems.

Let us now be more specific. Purchase is an overt, objectively discernible act that entails exchange of goods or services for some consideration and can be taken to reliably indicate a financial commitment to a certain brand in a specified unit amount. It need not necessarily be an irrevocable commitment, but can be some act that by custom and usage is accepted as a commitment. It refers only to a particular act or series of acts in the total purchase process.

3.3   INPUT VARIABLES

3.3.1   *Introduction*

Having defined and explained the output variables, we now turn to the input variables, since during the period of observation they are the causes of change in the values of the output variables where causality operates by way of the hypothetical constructs. We examine the idea of input variables at some length, because seldom in either practice or basic research are they well specified. Yet many conclusions are drawn as if they were. Also, they are complex and we do not discuss them systematically elsewhere.

The inputs can be thought of as mainly the sum of all the social influences and of the marketing effort to which the buyer is exposed. It is useful to classify them, as in Figure 3.1, into significative stimuli, symbolic stimuli, and social stimuli, because the psychological processes may often differ among the three. "Significative stimuli" refers to the stimuli that emanate from the physical brand itself, such as the buyer's noticing of it on the supermarket shelf. "Symbolic stimuli" are words, sentences and pictures disseminated by the seller; these, of course, necessarily involve thinking, whereas the significative need not imply thinking. They may be linguistic (spoken word), orthographic (printed word), or pictorial (picture or cartoon). "Social stimuli" emanate from other people in a face-to-face relation with the buyer. These may be linguistic or nonlinguistic, such as the other person's grimaces or other physical movements which transmit information. This classification is not exhaustive, and can be modified to meet specific needs, as we do in Chapter 8. For the moment, however, we summarize these forces into a single multidimensional variable called Stimulus Display, in order to discuss the input variables in a simplified way.

By Stimulus Display we mean essentially what the psychologist usually means by "stimulus," although even in psychology the term is variously used. It combines three basic ideas: (1) incitement, (2) external agent, and (3) relation to sensory process. It incites activity in the buyer, it is external to his physical being, and it is the input to his sensory processes. Stimulus Display is treated as an input variable instead of an exogenous variable because, as we shall see in Chapter 5, within the theory there is an explanation for changes in the variable.

The reason for using "display" to modify "stimulus" is to convey a sense of complexity to the physical event that characterizes most buying situations. A television commercial in terms of complexity is a far cry from such psychophysical events as electric shocks and puffs of air. Furthermore, "contextual cues" indicate objects or events that are not in the Stimulus Display directly but are located in the proximate area, since these also influence buying behavior. If a housewife is reading an advertisement that appears in the homemaking section of the newspaper, the homemaking articles can be contextual cues influencing her buying behavior. Newspaper readership studies, for example, indicate that placing an advertisement in its appropriate context, such as a sports equipment ad on the sports page, will considerably enhance its readership.

In some cases we must go further and specify elements of the social context, because social influences operate in much of purchasing and consumption. These, too, can be contextual cues. The exogenous variable—Social and Organizational Setting—is intended to specify the social effects on the hypothetical constructs up to the time the researcher begins his observation of the buyer. In many instances, however, especially with new products, social inputs will change during the observation period. These inputs, therefore, must be specified with care if we are to understand buying behavior.

Stimulus Display, because of its implication of complexity, conveys the notion that the buyers will selectively pay attention. There are "mechanisms which enable organisms (*buyers*) to respond selectively to important features of their environments while ignoring features which are of little or no importance" (Egeth, 1967, p. 41, italics added). We know from the unpublished work of John Dollard that this phenomenon operates in marketing. He has designed a procedure for computing a "cebued" rate for a company's television advertising, which we might call a crude measure of misperception. "Cebued" stands for "continuously exposed but unverified," which means that a person watched the *show* before and after the commercial, did not leave the room, did not engage in any other activity such as reading a magazine, and still cannot remember anything about the commercial. In a comparison of 21 commercials, the average "cebued" rate was 14 per cent for men and 13 per cent for women. In another comparison, this time of seven commercials, the range was 6 to 9 per cent for men and 1 to 8 per cent for women. These shows, however, were probably below the average of all shows in "cebued" rate.

The significance of this extreme selective perception—the viewer does not recall it in any way—is shown if we compare it with a careful British study (Nuttall, 1962) which found that *advertisement exposure* differed sharply among those who reported seeing the average weekday programs:

Not in room during commercial	24 per cent
Not sitting so as to see television set	10 per cent
Viewing something other than set such as a magazine	36 per cent
Viewing the set	30 per cent

Assume a "cebued" rate of 15 per cent of those viewing the *show;* 15 per cent were exposed to the commercial but cannot recall it. Also, assume the British experience is matched here: of those viewing the show only 30 per cent were viewing the set at the time of the commercial. Then, we can conclude that of those viewing the set at the time of the commercial 50 per cent tuned out the commercial.

We emphasize the perceptual effects now in order to prepare the reader for Chapter 5 which develops a theory of search. These effects, we believe, are often quite important in understanding the role of market communication. They also help to avoid taking an exaggerated view of the effects of advertising, such as could be inferred from Steiner's (1966) report that 80 per cent of the people sit through a television commercial and only 5 per cent show any signs of annoyance at the outset.

Stimuli are measured directly or indirectly (Logan et al, 1955). By direct measurement we mean the process of attaching numbers to physical characteristics of the advertisement or to dimensions of the meaning that an advertisement or a person's verbal statement objectively conveys about a brand. With indirect measures the observer infers the nature of the stimulus from some aspect of the buyer's psychological state, such as his answer to whether he recalled the advertisement, so that here the possibility is introduced of the buyer's own perceptual processes distorting the measurement. We first briefly investigate direct measurement.

3.3.2 Direct Measurement

Historically two kinds of direct measures have been used: apparatus-based and natural language. An apparatus-based definition involves physical instrumentation and a space-time framework for classifying stimuli, as in the laboratory. Even the psychophysicist, whom we think of as being highly realistic, still must use constructs that are not the physical reality itself. He speaks of "loudness" and measures the amplitude of the sound waves, and he uses "pitch" and measures the frequency of the sound waves. By and large, the psychophysical measurements have not been much used for specifying the stimulus in investigations of buyer behavior. Physical measures of sound, color, and light, for example, obviously have their role in package design and advertising, but it is safe to say that most of marketing communication involves meaning that is immensely more complex.

Meaning is transmitted mainly by human language. In principle, human language involves the second type of direct measure, natural language. A "natural language" definition is used when we classify three advertisements into, "not colorful," "colorful," and "very colorful," and thus define and measure them as stimuli. Specialists in speech instruction have gone further and specified the metaphor as a particular psychological input.

Content analysis is sometimes suggested as a natural-language measure of the stimulus. It has been defined as a research technique for the objective, systematic, and quantitative description of the manifest content of communication. Objective here refers to replicability; systematic, to exhaustiveness; quantitative, to counting; manifest, to observable, as contrasted with latent or nonobservable. Developments in psycholinguistics—the study of lawful relations *between* events in messages and the consequent or antecedent processes occurring in the individual who produces and receives them—are encouraging (Osgood, 1963b). Content analysis proceeds on the assumption of no structure and it develops a structure. For our purposes it would appear feasible to begin with the structure as described by the buyer's product class concept and then to apply content analysis within the framework of this structure.

Content analysis is appropriate for measuring stimuli represented by language, either linguistic or orthographic, such as advertising copy, salesmen's speech, and point-of-purchase advertisements. However, it does not deal with pictorial stimuli (pictures), pictorial representations (the Democratic donkey and the Republican elephant), or such physical stimuli as the speaker's grimaces and gesticulations. Also, it has been suggested that the systematic use of content analysis is appropriate only for messages of more than fifty words (Osgood, 1959).

Still another direct method growing out of information-theoretic notions has been proposed recently by Payne (Payne, 1966). There have been many attempts to apply information theory to measuring stimuli directly. Most of them have been unsuccessful, but a few interesting exceptions have occurred (Miller, 1956). Information-theoretic concepts are applicable only when the stimuli are *well defined* and measured in terms of *relative frequency*. The two conditions do not allow for "meaning," which is the relevant content of most marketing stimuli. Payne's method, which is related to information theory, is based on the idea that humans perceive in chunks and that in most situations perception is a compromise between precision (small chunks) and economy (large chunks). This analysis remains to be developed, so far having been applied only to pattern recognition, but it seems to have considerable potential.

Still more recently, McGuire (1966b) has proposed a measure of the stimulus which gets at one dimension of both its physical and its meaning aspects. He offers a way of computing the number of discriminations represented in the stimulus; hence he conceptualizes the complexity dimension of the stimulus, which, as we shall see in Chapter 5, has a number of significant psychological implications.

3.3.3 Indirect Measurement

An indirect approach to defining stimuli is the behavioral method. The individual buyer is asked to define a set of stimulus categories, and his definition is then used as the description of the input variable.

The perceptual effects discussed above imply one of the limitations of the method—there is a disparity between what the buyer is exposed to and what he perceives. However, this distinction can be conceptualized as a "stimulus-as-coded" (s-a-c) (Lawrence, 1963). In this view motives, attitudes, and contextual cues determine a coding strategy that operates on sensory input to produce an s-a-c that is associated with either overt behavior or something short of it, such as intention or even attitude. Also, it incorporates the buyer's tendency to bring together—to integrate—some aspects of a complex Stimulus Display, and not others.

There are two possible indirect approaches: (1) one set of buyers are used to define the stimulus, which is then applied to another set of people, and (2) the person whose behavior is being studied defines his own stimulus. With the first approach the analysis proceeds in two stages. First, the buyer, in effect, classifies the stimuli himself, which can be done either overtly or verbally. He is then presented with a number of stimuli and those to which he responds differently are put in different categories, whereas those to which he responds in the same manner are put in the same category. In analyzing selective perception, Egeth (1967) has summarized some studies that suggest how one might deal with this complex problem.

The second indirect approach is widely used in practice. It consists of merely asking people what stimulus they recall and then proceeding on the assumption that this in fact was the stimulus.

It would seem that, except for the complexity dimension of the stimulus, most of the stimulus displays that we must deal with in studying behavior can best be measured indirectly. Although perceptual problems make it a less precise approach, by using the stimulus-as-coded concept we may be able to make considerable progress, as we shall suggest in later chapters.

3.4   EXOGENOUS VARIABLES

3.4.1   *Purpose of Exogenous Variables*

One of the functions of theory is to delimit the area of discourse. To communicate effectively it is just as important that scientists and practitioners know what they are not talking about as it is to know what they are talking about. Exogenous variables serve this important delimiting function. They are postulated to be causally related to the output variables through their effect on the hypothetical constructs. Exogenous variables have implications for both research and practice, which we shall examine before proceeding to the individual variables.

3.4.1.1   *Research Purposes*

The hypothetical constructs are influenced by many environmental factors "outside" the theory, and for purposes of both research design and marketing practice it is helpful to provide some structure for these factors. To include them in the theory, hence to attempt to explain changes in them, would, however, widen the scope of the theory and render it unwieldy. Yet, we must somehow hold constant these outside factors in our investigations if we are to understand the effects of input intervening variables on the output intervening variables.

The effects of the history of the buyer—up to the beginning of the researcher's period of observation—can be thought of as being contained in his exogenous variables: the intensity of his valuation of the product class, his personality traits, his social class, his culture, and his reference groups, as well as more current factors, such as the amount of time he has to devote to purchasing his product and his financial status. On the other hand, effects that are admitted during the period of observation are treated as inputs (stimuli). Exogenous variables thus serve both an error-reducing function and the function of classifying people according to fairly permanent characteristics, as in market segmentation.

3.4.1.2   *Error Reduction*

Let us first discuss the error-reducing function. Buying behavior is complicated because the buyer's environment has many elements. If we hope to measure the relation between behavior and its causes, we must deal with this great variety of forces. It is the typical problem of multivariate experimental design. There may be so much error that it will swamp the observable effects of the stimuli we are concerned with. This possibility is particularly great in marketing where the variables of interest, such as advertising, exert relatively small influence in relation to the effects of variables beyond the company's control. The small change of 10 per cent in advertising effectiveness, however, can be very important in terms of company profits. Furthermore, most marketing studies are done under field conditions where the control of random effects is much more difficult than in the laboratory.

This error-reducing function of exogenous variables can be illustrated. In designing a study of housewives' acceptance of a new laborsaving food, early depth interviews indicated that about one-third of the housewives feared that the use of the food might impair the importance of their role in the home. Assuming that all housewives like convenience, we theorize that this would shape the relation between the level of advertising exposure and attitude toward new laborsaving foods because of the possible goal conflict. Let us assume that the variance for the sample as a whole is large. If we agree on the assumption that lower-class housewives are more fearful of losing their role than upper-class housewives, the introduction of the social-class variable should reduce the variance around the line of regression between advertising exposure and attitude and give us greater confidence that the posited relation is indeed true.

Now, we can see why there exist large interpersonal differences in buyer behavior (Anastasi, 1958). Not only does each buyer's exposure to current facts differ somewhat from that of other buyers, but, equally if not more important, because of his unique past history, his frame of reference will differ from that of others. Moreover through the feedback effects shown in Figure 3.1, his hypothetical constructs will significantly determine what facts he elects to perceive from the complex environment to which he is typically exposed.

Finally, neither the exogenous variables nor the contextual factors—forces specific to the situation—catch all the forces that affect a given buyer's behavior. Changes in a woman's marital status, for example, will change her purchasing behavior, but such effects are not included in the exogenous variables nor in the contextual factors. Instead they are called "random events." The reader may be asking, "How does one decide which is an exogenous variable and which is a contextual and a random event?" There are essentially four criteria for deciding whether to include a particular set of forces as an exogenous variable. (1) First and foremost, it contributes to the explanation of behavior. (2) Its inclusion is expected to reduce the error significantly in most situations. (3) It is efficiently measurable. (4) It is expected to be applicable over a wide range of product classes.

Although exogenous variables are important for reducing the error of measurement, they are also immediately useful in practice as the basis for dividing the market into relatively homogeneous segments, a technique called "market segmentation."

3.4.1.3 Market Segmentation

For a number of years the concept of market segmentation has frequently appeared in the marketing literature, both trade and academic. The idea is that since a company's market is made up of diverse buyers, the company should segment or divide the market in such a way as to achieve sets of buyers—segments of the market—the buyers within each segment tending to be alike. The company can then increase its effectiveness by developing a market plan for each segment. Furthermore—although this argument usually is left unstated—even if the company is not able for some reason to implement a plan for each of the segments, market segmentation will facilitate market analysis.

The idea of segmentation has been placed in a more dynamic framework and is now used to discuss the fact that as an economy's population and income grow, a market segment that was formerly too small to justify a product designed to fit its particular needs becomes large enough to justify the specifically tailored product and related marketing effort. Moreover, this increasing specialization of the market is the source of small new companies in the economy; for example, the Goya foods firm has grown primarily to serve Puerto Ricans. The products are developed to meet a more specific need.

Whatever the more general implications of the concept of market segmentation, executives always seem to believe that their company serves a heterogeneous set of buyers; if so, to increase the within-group homogeneity, it is necessary to classify the buyers in some way. A demographic variable may sometimes serve as a surrogate for an analytically relevant variable; it was reported recently that women over 45 are more inclined to try new things than are younger women (Advertising Age, October 30, 1967, p. 32). It could be that age here is a surrogate of sorts for Time Pressure because younger women with children simply do not have the time to collect the information to judge new products. Both socioeconomic and personality variables have in general been disappointing in their ability to tell us anything about purchase behavior (Frank, 1967a, 1967b; Frank, Green, and Sieber, 1967; but see Carman, 1968).

Also, we must ask when speaking of "within-group homogeneity," "Homogeneity with respect to what?" First, we are referring to *homogeneity in the nature of the buyer's response functions.* A response function is the functional relation between the buyer's purchasing responses and the policy variable being investigated, such as price and advertising. To the extent that a group of buyers are alike in this respect, the same marketing policy is desirable for all of them. Second, the group of buyers must be homogeneous with respect to some easily identifiable variables, so that by classifying them according to these variables we are simultaneously grouping them in terms of common response functions.

Assume that a matrix of two easily identifiable variables, each with five values, provides an adequate classification system. One optimum segmentation would be where the sum over cells of the matrix of the squared deviations from the mean of the predicted purchases in each cell is a minimum. To provide the data for this matrix—income and age—is not difficult, since in most market surveys such facts are collected as a matter of course. To test the validity of this method of segmenting a market, however, a third piece of information is needed—*the shape and position of the buyer's response curves.* This information is almost never available, so that we are forced to take market segmentation on faith and to *assume* that within-group homogeneity of response functions has been achieved.

The point is that though the concept of market segmentation is widely discussed, not much information is currently available on the potentialities of segmentation; research, however, is going forward, for example Carman (1968).

We believe that an optimum segmentation for one response curve as defined above is often something less than optimum for another; if so, management is faced with the task of deciding whether to have different classifications for different areas of marketing activity, such as one for price and one for advertising. What guides are there for forming these segments, these typologies? First, logic suggests that a set of categories must be mutually exclusive and exhaustive. The categories must be formulated so that each buyer will "fit" into some category and no buyers will be left over.

Second, either a pragmatic or analytic approach is possible. The executive can say, "I don't care according to what dimensions you classify the buyers as long as the resultant categories effectively meet my needs." The point is that it probably will not meet his needs, but he does not know this. From this pragmatic point of view, the traditional dimensions for classifying buyers are socioeconomic characteristics, personality characteristics, demographic characteristics, and product-specific characteristics. This is a "cut-and-try" or pragmatic kind of method, and to the best of our knowledge its validity has never been tested but is taken on faith, as already indicated.

Alternatively, an analytic approach can be used: the idea of a theory of buyer behavior—a logical system—with exogenous variables that are causally related to output variables by way of the hypothetical constructs. Here, buyers are classified according to dimensions specified by the exogenous variables. The key difference between the pragmatic and analytic approach is that with the analytic approach the theory specifies a causal relation between an exogenous variable and one or more of the hypothetical constructs and these constructs determine the nature of the response curve.

With the pragmatic approach the executive collects all kinds of information because he has no theory to tell him which is relevant and which is not. It leads to the executive being deluged with information, a condition encouraged by the computer. Much of the information will turn out to be useless. Many dimensions are attempted simultaneously, which limits the possibility of discovering the appropriate ones. If, for example, there are two categories on each of two dimensions, there are 2×2 or 4 classifications; with 3 dimensions there are 8 classifications; with 4 dimensions, there are 16; and so on. Thus we can see the limitations of the pragmatic approach.

Having described the purpose of exogenous variables generally and presented a particular application, we now turn to examine each of the exogenous variables that make up the theory: Importance of Purchase, Personality Traits, Time Pressure, Financial Status, Social and Organizational Setting, Social Class, and Culture. Each one will be defined, its effect on endogenous variables elaborated, the nature of change in it presented, and perhaps empirical evidence set forth. This detailed exposition, though necessary, may be somewhat heavy going, and the reader may find it useful to first turn to Figure 3.2 at the end of the chapter, which summarizes the relations and thus provides helpful perspective on the role of exogenous variables. Some readers, especially psychologists, may feel that to treat some of these as exogenous is at least unusual. We find it convenient for our purposes, however.

3.4.2 Importance of Purchase

3.4.2.1 Definition

Importance of Purchase is a variable in the buyer's frame of reference that corresponds to the *intensity* of motive(s), as discussed in Chapter 4. It includes the criteria by which the buyer orders a range of product classes in terms of his needs. It applies to the *product class* alone, and not to the brand, which is consistent with our general view of motivation. It is the saliency of one product class versus other product classes, and is variously labeled "degree of involvement," "importance of cognition," and "importance of the task." In fact, the construct grows out of the integration of the Lewinian view of motivation which postulates that motives are created by the situation and the behavioristic view which postulates motivation as an internal process (Cofer and Appley, 1963, esp. pp. 418, 782, 784–6). Further, "situation" can be thought of as consisting of two parts: the judgement task and the social setting of the task in interpersonal relations (Sherif, Sherif and Nebergal, 1965, p. 65). Importance or Purchase incorporates the former aspect and Social and Organizational Setting, the latter.

Importance of Purchase is one of the two central elements of perceived risk (Bauer, 1960) in which value and degree of uncertainty are combined to yield the degree of subjective risk. To illustrate, S. Cunningham (1967a), in pursuing the perceived-risk notion, asked the housewife to respond to a question involving the amount of "danger" she associates with trying a brand she had never used before: "We all know that not all products work as well as others. Compared to other products would you say there is: a great deal of danger, some danger, not much danger, or no danger, in trying a brand of headache remedy (or floor wax, or dry spaghetti), you have never used before?" The results were combined with an estimate of the buyer's certainty of the quality of each of the product classes to derive an estimate of perceived risk. Another measure of Importance of Purchase is simple rank ordering of the products (Sheth and Venkatesan, 1968).

The reason for having this separate variable is to suggest a way of classifying buyers that is useful in designing studies, since it makes a considerable difference in behavior in a number of ways. It appears that product classes are quite different with respect to this variable, which thus provides a general classificatory system for product classes.

3.4.2.2 Significance of Importance of Purchase

The buyer tries to be goal-directed, but has difficulty in obtaining adequate information on which to base his calculations in choosing a brand. Among other variables as well, Importance of Purchase influences how much effort he will expend to obtain the necessary information, as we shall see especially in Chapter 8. One way of saying this is that it influences his search for the information necessary to make his perceived environment correspond to his objective environment: to remove the gap between the two. He accomplishes this by exploratory behavior, which is defined to include a wide range of activity from (1) mere willingness to perceive information that is placed in direct contact with his sense organs to the other extreme of (2) extensive, overt effort toward searching for relevant information to expose his sense organs to. Attention, referred to in Chapter 2, adequately describes the lower range of this continuum, and change in Stimulus Display—Overt Search—describes the higher range of the continuum.

In addition to influencing exploratory behavior, Importance of Purchase also influences the magnitude of evoked set: the number of brands a buyer considers when he contemplates buying units of the product class which is an aspect of Brand Comprehension. This relation came out clearly in a study of industrial buying where amount of money spent annually for the item was a measure of Importance of Purchase (Howard and Moore, 1963).

3.4.2.3 Source of Change

Importance of Purchase for different product classes may change for an individual, to some extent, which is to say that the intensity hierarchy of his motives will be modified. In industrial buying it varies with changes in production technique. Generally, however, we expect this variable to be slow in changing, such as our response to long-run shifts in social values.

Its greatest significance is that differences will occur across products and among people, and if these differences are corrected for, the predictive power of the hypothetical constructs will be improved.

3.4.2.4 Empirical Evidence

Empirical research has not yet provided much evidence, but our current belief supports a linear relation between Importance of Purchase and Overt Search behavior. Yet, as in the case of a number of relations involving human behavior, we would expect this relation to be non-monotonic within the limits set by Time Pressure. As Importance of Purchase becomes too high, stereotyped behavior instead of information seeking would be expected. Probably few marketing situations involve such extremely high levels, however. Bogart in a study of newspaper advertising readership found "reported sighting of ads" to be positively correlated with "enjoyment from using the product" (Bogart, 1964) and it is reasonable to interpret this result as indicating that "greater satisfaction" reflects differences in intensity of motivation among product classes. In contexts other than buying there is empirical evidence on the effects of the intensity of motivation on perception (McGuire, 1968b), and Sherif especially has developed the idea that high ego involvement leads to a tendency to distort judgments on attitude scales in particular ways (Sherif, Sherif, and Nebergall, 1965).

3.4.3 Personality Traits

Still another element of a buyer's frame of reference is his personality traits; like Importance of Purchase, this element too is related to motivation in that the *content* and intensity of a person's motives detremine the nature of the personality that he is. Personality is defined as an enduring disposition or quality of a person that accounts for his relative consistency in emotional, temperamental, and social behavior. By personality *trait* we mean those characteristics that account for differences among people and that are predictive of their behavior.

To grasp the comprehensiveness of this definition, we must recognize that personality theories such as those by Freud, Jung, Murray, and Rogers are viewed at least by their creators as general theories of behavior, as capable of explaining all behavior. To convey some idea of what is thought of as personality in its more technical senses, we can refer to the standard personality measures, for example, the Edwards Personal Preference Schedule which identifies such traits as aggressiveness, dominance, achievement, exhibitionism, autonomy, and affiliation.

Personality theory from psychology served as the intellectual foundation of the Motivation Research movement in marketing practice which developed in the mid-fifties and became very much a fad. Because it held the center of the marketing stage for some years, it may be helpful to compare it with the framework we are proposing. Motivation Researchers treated personality traits as intervening variables. The hypothetical constructs were left implicit, and the rules of correspondence were ignored. Whether treating personality traits as an exogenous variable is the best procedure for capturing these forces is an empirical question yet to be answered. Although the movement contributed a considerable amount of confusion and nonsense, it had two very beneficial effects on operating research practice. First, it sensitized researchers to the possibility that human behavior could be subtle, which was a welcome contrast to the mechanistic, survey view that had earlier held sway in market research. Second, it introduced into marketing the long-standing social research practice of preceding a large-scale study with a pilot survey to formulate hypotheses to be tested by the larger study.

One of the principles underlying the Motivation Research view was the belief that a company could segment its market according to the personality types of its buyers. The belief was that after the different need segments had been identified, it would be found that the image held by each segment was consistent with the particular needs of the buyers in that segment. A second premise was that each brand has an "image" made up of attributes that extend beyond the physical attributes of the brand. The significance of this premise for market planning was that the company should develop a market plan that would build the image of its brand so as to be still more consistent with the needs of the segment it had decided to serve. In this way the buyer's preference for the brand would be increased. The belief came to have a wide following, but to our knowledge it has never been tested.

Using automobile buyers Evans tested the validity of the first idea of Motivation Research: there is a relation between the needs of a buyer and the brand he buys (Evans, 1959). Evans found some slight evidence, and in a reanalysis of Evans' data Kuehn found a little more evidence but still not enough to follow Motivation Research principles (Kuehn, 1963). Westfall studied compact, convertible and standard cars, using a different test, and found differences only between standard and convertible and between compact and convertible (Westfall, 1962). Larger differences may be found among brands of other products, but that remains to be seen. Market researchers are becoming more and more dubious of this simple Motivation Research approach, probably because psychologists have become skeptical of the validity of the traditional instruments for measuring human needs and because the few strictly buyer behavior studies have not been encouraging. The belief now is that the problem is too complex to be handled in this way.

In addition to the simplistic ad hoc Motivation Research approach to personality traits which not long ago captured most of the attention in marketing circles, personality traits are significant in other ways. First, a stimulus may have a strong effect on behavior either because it is effective in getting through the buyer's perceptual processes (search) or because it changes his view once it has been perceived. By recognizing this, McGuire through his "compensatory principle" has been able to reconcile some of the contradictory evidence that has been found in laboratory studies, such as the relation between self-esteem and influenceability (McGuire, 1968b). The person with low esteem is more likely to "tune out" a stimulus, and more likely to be affected by it if it gets through, than is a person of high esteem. Alternatively, a person of high esteem is less likely to "tune out" the message and also less likely be persuaded by the information. The specific perceptual mechanism by which this "tuning out" is accomplished is described in Chapter 5. Also, McGuire suggests that sex differences in influenceability are due to women perceiving messages more easily rather than being more persuasible.

Second, personality traits having to do with mental capacity also make a difference—chronological age, for example (McGuire, 1968a). Eight or nine years of age is the peak period of suggestibility; it then declines up to adolescence, when it levels off. As for mental age, intelligence, with simple messages there is probably a negative relation between age and influenceability, because perception is not a serious problem for any one and more intelligent people are less persuasible. With complex messages, however, perception is a problem for the lower intelligence, and there may be even a positive relation between mental age and influenceability. Thus, because of these effects on influenceability, we postulate that personality traits affect search effort as reflected in Overt Search, and whenever Overt Search is affected we expect attention to be affected for reasons set forth in Chapter 5.

A third personality characteristic—anxiety—has been shown to be related to breadth of categorization (Kogan and Wallach, 1964), which we view as similar to the number of brands in evoked set, an aspect of Brand Comprehension. However, the phenomenon seems to be truer of women than of men.

Fourth, "venturesomeness" was found to be related to the tendency to accept new products, although the specific psychological mechanisms that might account for it were not spelled out (Robertson and Rossiter, undated, p. 15).

Finally, personality traits represent motive content and so we postulate that personality traits affect motives.

The opportunity to identify underlying relationships even in a naturalistic setting with all of its attendant "noise" would seem to be improved when personality variables are controlled and we distinguish between the perceptual and the learning effects of stimuli.

3.4.4 Time Pressure

3.4.4.1 Definition

Time Pressure is the inverse of the amount of time the buyer has available to perform the behavior required for the acts of purchasing and consumption. It is the amount of time required to perform these acts in relation to the time he has allocated to himself for doing them. It incorporates momentary instead of long-term changes in the time available for purchasing.

Not much is known about it generally. A large international study of time utilization now under way, however, may help in providing a foundation of facts on which to build. Also, other less comprehensive studies have been made (De Grazia, 1962).

3.4.4.2 *Source of Change*

Variations in the nonbuying demands on a person's time are the primary source of change in Time Pressure. Historically, this pressure on the housewife has probably increased. True enough, she now has many labor-saving devices, but as her real income has risen, she buys more, and as technological change has created a flow of new products, she must spend more time buying.

The momentary changes with which we are concerned here, however, are due to shifts in other demands on the buyer's time, thus altering the amount of time he has available for purchasing.

3.4.4.3 *Significance*

Time Pressure exerts an effect on overt Purchasing behavior by way of one of the learning constructs, Intention (to purchase) in the sense that some effort is usually required to carry out the purchase act, which thus tends to inhibit the act. Insofar as Time Pressure varies among brands, it is postulated *ceteris paribus* to cause the buyer to favor the brand that takes the least time. We also postulate that Time Pressure will cause search to be more vigorous, but that it serves to limit the things to which attention is paid: span of attention is reduced (March and Simon, 1958, pp. 116, 154). Thus it limits overt search and forces the buyer to make his choice based on less complete information.

3.4.5 Financial Status

3.4.5.1 *Definition*

Financial Status is more exterior and perhaps less stable than most of the exogenous variables. It can be defined as the funds available for purchasing goods and services during some specified time period. We assume that the funds normally arise from current income or saved past income (assets). Earned income is probably an appropriate measure for most people, except those with an independent income.

3.4.5.2 *Changes in Financial Status*

Economic theory provides an elaborate explanation of how an individual's or a firm's income changes as a result of the business cycle. In addition, it gives a number of other reasons such as temporary loss of employment, rising standard of living, and success in professional life.

People from a less-developed country would be expected to differ on this variable from people from a more-developed country. It thus becomes relevant in making international comparisons, although its effects could be confounded with those of culture.

3.4.5.3 Significance

Analytically, Financial Status affects Intention as an inhibiting factor, which causes a buyer to behave contrary to some of his attitudes. We find it useful to conceptualize as inhibitors all effects on behavior except those that are internalized, that is, exert their influence through Attitude. These noninternalized effects always cause behavior to differ from the behavior that would be dictated by Attitude alone. The buyer prefers A but buys B because of inhibitor effects, just as in the case of Time Pressure. Financial Status could deter purchasing a brand because of its high price.

Perhaps Financial Status is not so important in the choice within a given product class as in the choice among product classes. As income levels change, the product classes that people buy change correspondingly; for example, as income goes down, consumers buy less expensive cuts of meats, because they are attempting to maintain the same food value with more limited funds. Simultaneously, however, the influence of price as a variable in the buyer's choice within the product class probably increases.

Does the buyer respond to an increase in the income constraint with the emotional response of *frustration?* If motivation is at a high level, logically this could occur. Our guess is that it does, in fact, occur. When one stops to consider the central role that material wealth plays in our society, a consumer's income and asset position would be expected to have a great amount of motivational significance (J. Brown, 1961). Income not only sets a limit on one's total purchasing, but has an important influence on a buyer's social status; hence a decline in it would create anxiety in the individual. This lack or deficiency is, of course, a subjective matter, and it has been dealt with by the economist as a part of the "permanent income" hypothesis (Ferber, 1962).

The hypothesis states that a person comes to adopt a certain acceptable standard of living and as his income falls below that level, he will "dissave," that is, consume his assets. As his income exceeds that necessary to provide this standard, he will save more of his income. How this level of saving is determined can be explained by Lewin's level of aspiration concept. As people's incomes go up and exceed their expectations in regard to the amount of money they will have available, their expectations (aspirations) will correspondingly increase but at a slower rate than their incomes increase. Over a long period people's aspirations tend to conform to their performance. The adjustment of the "permanent level" for an individual is presumably a slow process.

Because of the relatively slower rate of decline in aspiration level, frustration would seem to be highly probable as incomes decline over the downswing of the business cycle. Fortunately, the business cycle has become less of a problem, but its significance for behavior probably still exists to some extent and is deeply felt among the generation of people who were reared—that is, who acquired their basic outlook— during the Great Depression of the thirties.

What the consequences of this frustration might be are not clear. The usual prediction is that frustration intensifies motivation. Up to a point this could heighten arousal and cause the buyer to perceive more relevant data. Presumably, "price" would be comparatively more relevant, for example. If motivation becomes too great, the buyer will supposedly close off information and tend to ignore the economic consequences of his purchasing, which would approach the type of stereotyped behavior that is sometimes popularly labeled as "irrational."

The formal organization also imposes analogous constraints on the industrial buyer. It has been reported that changing cash and income levels in a company will cause top management to shift the criteria to be used in selecting suppliers; for example, as cash levels decline, price will become a more important criterion, whereas such criteria as delivery time will become less important.

3.4.5.4 Empirical Evidence

Economists in pursuing the measurement of income elasticity— changes in a consumer's total consumption in relation to changes in his income—have provided ample evidence that changes in income do change the total amount of goods purchased. As indicated by the permanent income hypothesis, the income-consumption relation holds across product classes and across income groups. Furthermore, there is evidence, although not nearly so much, that consumers change their purchases of closely related product classes in response to income changes; for example, as incomes go down, individuals buy cheaper product classes.

Historically, economists have been less interested in income as a determinant of behavior than in price, and they have sometimes concluded that there is an interaction between the two. Stigler (1952, p. 45), for example, states: "There is a presumption that commodities with high income elasticity have high price elasticity." We have seen no empirical evidence on his contention; a rough analysis that we did of some of Richard Stone's data on the American economy failed to support it. This contention can be interpreted in more cognitive terms, however, as implying that as people's incomes decline, they become more sensitive to price. Cassady and Jones (1951) state that this was found to be true in the retail gasoline market. In this form, the assertion is consistent, for example, with the prediction made above that decreasing income will cause the person to weight price more heavily, which, in turn, will cause him to be more likely to perceive price information. Hence it is perhaps mainly a perceptual phenomenon, although it may also imply a heavier weighting in the choice process. Frustration with its consequent effect on arousal as discussed in Chapter 4 could be the source.

There is evidence, also, that buyers become less receptive to new products when incomes decline over the business cycle (Mueller, 1958). Perhaps this can be explained by increased concern with risk, a lower level of Confidence inhibits the buyers' purchase of new alternatives. Correspondingly, we would expect a reduction in impulse (unplanned) purchasing as discretionary income declines even more than total income.

Finally, in a study of 150 shoppers in the Boston area, it was found that lower-income consumers are less susceptible to the frustration of finding dissatisfaction in a store from stock shortages and poor clerk service than are higher-income consumers (Callazo, 1966). Our guess, however, is that Social Class would explain more of the variance here than income (Financial Status).

3.4.6   Social and Organizational Setting

3.4.6.1   Introduction

Let us now examine the first of the three social variables: Social and Organizational Setting, Social Class, and Culture. We can think of it as being more immediate in its influence than the social aggregates of Social Class and Culture.

Before going ahead to examine the nature and effects of social influence, one complication must be emphasized. For many purposes social influences can be treated as exogenous variables as we are suggesting. Often, however, they operate to change the situation, to provide new information during the period of observation, and must then be dealt with explicitly as a part of the Stimulus Display or as contextual cues. This point is important because often a chain of people are involved, the effect being triggered by an advertisement, then passing through a number of people, and being exerted on the buyer. Arndt (1967) in his word-of-mouth communication documents the role of social influences in *consumer* behavior. If the task is one of attempting to understand the process by which an *industrial* buyer comes to accept a new product, casual observation suggests that the current inputs of information from the organization, such as discussions with the design engineer and the production manager, usually are quite important as a source of influence on his behavior. When this is so, these current effects from the social environment must be built into a structure that partially represents the stimulus situation. Social influences defined as an exogenous variable alone will not suffice under these conditions.

To distinguish between the two broad kinds of buyers—consumers and organizational (distributive, industrial, and institutional)—in terms of the role of social expectations we can use the two concepts of reference group and formal organization.

3.4.6.2 Reference Group

A useful definition of a social group is to say that "the minimum properties of a group are that it consists of a number of individuals who, at a given time, stand in more or less definite status and role relationships to one another (organization, leader-follower relations) and who share a set of values or norms" (Sherif and Koslin, 1960, p. 12). This broad definition can incorporate the reference group, the family, *and* the formal organization.

The formal organization—for example, the company—is large, is specialized with respect to purpose, and does not depend particularly on face-to-face relations for its communications. The reference group is distinguished from the family and the formal organization in that it is small, unspecialized with respect to purpose, and relies on face-to-face interaction. Also, past and anticipated reference groups influence a buyer's behavior, as do his current groups. The family is small and specialized and, though using face-to-face relations, does not depend solely on them. The reference group and family are the major means by which the influence of social class and culture is transmitted.

The family, too, can be a well structured social grouping, hence more structured than the "social group" that we have in mind. Without question, family influences are felt in purchases made for the family in the sense that one person is buying for others in the family. The role of the family in influencing buying decisions has been studied (Wolgast, 1958; Sharp and Mott, 1956; Wilkening, 1958; Young, 1952; Lansing and Kish, 1957; E. Katz and Lazarsfeld, 1955). None of these studies systematically get at the detailed influence process, but deal more at the aggregate level. Some advertisers feel that this tendency for family influence to operate is becoming increasingly sharp which suggests that a part of the advertising effort should be directed toward other members of the family. It is reported, for example, that more husbands are helping their wives do the grocery shopping, hence are entering directly into the purchase decisions about grocery items.

Just how useful "social setting" can be in classifying the consumer-buyer in some meaningful sense is not well established at the moment. An illustration of how it might make a difference will add meaning to the construct. A man working on a construction job probably would buy for use in this social setting a completely different Thermos jug than he would if he planned to take it regularly on Sunday School picnics dominated by women. He would use quite different criteria, that is, quite different product attributes (and verbal descriptions of attributes) will create favorable anticipations in him and cause him to buy. Part of the reason is functional in that the physiological demands are different, but the social setting would also differentiate the purchasing criteria. On the job his self-concept would be that of a "he-man"—coarse and crude, for example. Color could reflect this, as well as shape. For the picnic, his self-concept would be much more in tune with that setting.

Self-concept, or self-image as it is more popularly known, is one construct that is close in meaning to what we have in mind and one that has received some attention in the marketing literature (Grubb and Grothwohl, 1967). The general idea of self-concept is that an individual's behavior cannot be understood and predicted without a knowledge of how *he* views *himself* in relation to that environment (Wylie, 1961, p. 6). Operationally, for example, a buyer is asked to rate himself on a number of bipolar adjectival scales, such as deliberate-impulsive, simple-complex, or robust-fragile. Then he is asked to rate his most preferred brand and his least preferred brand on the same set of scales. The prediction is made that his self-image so measured will correlate more closely with his most preferred brand ratings than with his least preferred brand ratings (Dolich, 1967). Sheth has found, however, that the congruence between a preferred brand and self concept is at least partly spurious because of the tendency of a respondent to rate himself higher which then matches better with the higher rating of the preferred brand than with less preferred brands.

This methodological view implied here smacks of the simplistic approach earlier ascribed to Motivation Research as it was defined a decade ago. The self-image construct, however, appears also to attempt to incorporate two substantive phenomena. First, social interaction is a central issue; the case where the environment is other people is incorporated. Second, and related to the first, it attempts to deal with expressive meaning, which seems often to be a fact in buyer behavior. Expressive meaning applies to the case where symbols are used by a human to express something about himself in addition to the usual purpose of symbols, which is for him to name something of relevance to him (Brown, 1965, p. 567). One way that a person uses expressive symbols may be in his purchasing and consuming activity. It is a way of describing at least one source of the nonfunctional purchasing criteria that we seem to observe in advertising: a man buys Salem cigarettes because he likes to think of himself as (his self-concept is) a virile, handsome young man attractive to beautiful young ladies capering through an open field as pictured in the Salem ads. Presumably, the purchase of a brand that carries this association can be satisfying for a reason that has nothing to do with any physical attributes of the brand itself. It is satisfying only because it is associated with something else. Both of these substantive ideas will be used in Chapter 8.

How useful the self-image construct turns out to be to describe "social setting" is at the moment a matter for conjecture. In summarizing a splendid review of the area in psychology, Wylie states:

On the whole, we found that there are enough positive trends to be tantalizing. On the other hand, there is a good deal of ambiguity in the results, considerable apparent contradiction among the findings of various studies, and a tendency for different methods to produce different results. In short, the total accumulation of substantive findings is disappointing, especially in proportion to the great amount of effort which obviously has been expended [Wylie, 1961, p. 317].

Although there have been no careful reviews of work in the buying area and not a great amount of effort has been devoted to it, our impression is that a similar conclusion would apply.

One of the major problems has been that "these constructs have been stretched to cover so many inferred cognitive and motivational processes that their utility for analytic and predictive purposes has been greatly diminished" (Wylie, 1961, p. 318). Our belief is that a more restricted definition used more realistically and less subjectively (see Chapter 1) would be useful in classifying consumers into groups. We know that some constructs that attempt to incorporate smaller units of behavior, such as self-esteem, have been quite useful. Perhaps there is some halfway house between the global concept and the more restricted concept of personality trait that will be more fruitful.

We postulate that a consumer's reference group will influence Motive, Brand Comprehension, and Attitude. To the extent that these social pressures are not internalized but are treated by the consumer as constraints, the reference group will influence Intention.

3.4.6.3   *Formal Organization*

Organizational buying has not been studied nearly so extensively as consumer buying. When studied, it tends to be treated in quite a different way. In general, it is not done systematically, but Wind offers an interesting exception (Wind, 1966).

Organizational change is typically brought about only at a slow rate; hence organization as an exogenous variable becomes relevant mainly when the researcher compares behavior across organizations. In fact, because of its inability to predict the consequences, top management is typically quite reluctant to attempt to change the organization. On the other hand, in a company that is in serious trouble financially, radical changes are sometimes made. It is surprising how similar the rules of behavior may be across organizations for people engaged in the same *function* (Howard and Morgenroth, 1968) but how they differ across different functions of the same company.

Organization conditions buying behavior in two ways:

1. It influences the amount and nature of the information that the buyer is exposed to at any point in time.
2. Because it has shaped the buyer's hypothetical constructs in the past, it influences the amount and nature of the information that he actually perceives and the way in which he processes that information.

A great amount of the organization literature in recent years has been addressed to the issue of conflict between the behavior that the individual member desires and the behavior demanded of him by the organization. This conflict is part of what we mean by inhibitors contained in Intention. The buyer likes Supplier A but management directs that the purchase be made from Supplier B, so that the buyer is inhibited in following his own preferences. In industrial and institutional buying it is very difficult, however, to evaluate a buyer's performance, that is, it is difficult to know whether the buyer is serving the organization's goals (Strauss 1964). This leaves the buyer with considerable freedom to use his own goals and to feel less need to change his motives to conform to organizational requirements, although our experience has been that he can seldom articulate this fact in this way. He often looks at it in another way: he complains that management does not know how good a job he is doing.

In addition to its effect on his inhibitors underlying Intention, presumably the organization will in time shape the buyer's Motives, and in this way Choice Criteria for the product class, then the number and content of the suppliers in his evoked set, which constitute Brand Comprehension, and finally his Attitude will be influenced.

The formal organization represents a particular kind of environment in at least three senses. First, the amount of influence from it is great. Obviously, the effect of a formal organization on behavior varies according to the extent it is *decentralized,* the amount of freedom that it permits the buyer. At one extreme the conditions of purchase may be specified in much detail from elsewhere in the company; for example, the user in the plant can be the real buying decision maker and then the buyer is free only to write out an order to a user-specified supplier for the user-specified product. At the other extreme, the buyer may have wide latitude. Our research experience has been that purchasing executives at the vice-presidential level believe that the degree of decentralization is perhaps the most important consideration in attempting to understand industrial buying.

Second, organizational rules, especially the goal aspects, may not be well delineated and stable—there is little policy—which leads to a great amount of implicit bargaining between a buyer and his counterparts elsewhere in the organization, such as engineers and production managers, as well as between the boss (purchasing agent) and the buyer himself. This is further complicated by the fact that, as indicated above, it is both difficult to judge a buyer and difficult for him to relate his behavior to the organization's goals, that is, to judge *himself* against what the organization expects of him.

Third, if a new product is involved, other people in the company—especially the design engineer and the production manager—become "buyers," too. If so, it is better to conceptualize the problem as "a group of buyers." Under these conditions, what the buyer does is determined partly by what he thinks the production manager will do, and the production manager's behavior is partially determined by what he thinks the buyer will do, and so on. When this is true, more elements in the situation must be specified by the researcher if he is to understand the behavior. This is analogous to the oligopoly problem about which economists have written so much. This kind of indeterminate interdependence undoubtedly characterizes consumer buying for the family to some extent, but we think that usually it can safely be assumed away. We believe that it is the most typical situation in industrial buying of *new* products but the extent of it varies much among the products being purchased (Strauss, 1964).

To predict the behavior of a buyer when he is in this highly interdependent situation, two types of studies are necessary: (1) mapping the communication and decision-making network within the organization that shapes the behavior of the buyer, the behavior that we as researchers are trying to predict, and (2) "mapping the heads" of the participants in the decision-making process. The first type of study requires an understanding of modern organization theory. The second type of study is identical to that necessary for predicting the behavior of the buyer such as a consumer who can often be viewed as not being in an interdependent situation. When there is more than one person but the interdependence is determinate, one person's premises about the others' behavior become part of the data for the mapping process, and so we still have the second case. The first type of study, however, can involve both interdependence and indeterminateness, as already indicated.

3.4.7 Social Class

Social Class is the second social variable. The concept describes the condition that a society is divided into classes, that some of these classes are viewed by the members of the society as being more important than others, and that in a society the classes can be ranked in a hierarchy based on the views of its members about the value of each class in terms of its contribution to the society as a whole. Technically, not only is the status of each class relevant, but the status must be perceived by each individual and endowed with a corporate interest.

If "social class" is interpreted to mean that the classes are clearly demarcated instead of being arbitrary cuts across a continuum of status positions, the empirical facts do not correspond to the concept (Brown, 1965, pp. 101–140). "Social class" is being used here, however, in a broad sense. If we think of social class or "style of life" as the form or quality of behavior manifest in occupation, possessions, recreation, manners, and similar factors, we know that different styles of life are valued differently. We know that some occupations are valued more highly than others, and this evaluation can be looked upon as a continuum.

We postulate that a person's social class influences his Motives, and Attitude. Also, it may well be that some social class sanctions are not internalized and instead are viewed by the buyer as a constraint upon his behavior, thus affecting inhibitors and Intention. Finally, evoked set is influenced, and so Brand Comprehension is affected.

Changes in social class are slow. The study of the differences in *purchasing habits* between the upwardly mobile and the downwardly mobile, however, offers a fascinating field of endeavor. We have seen no significant evidence on this issue (Reissman, 1959), although there have been mobility studies (R. Brown, 1965). It would be fascinating to use the concept of *status consistency* to analyze differences in purchasing patterns and specifically, for example, its implications for word-of-mouth communication in transmitting product information.

Published evidence to support the implication that preferences (Attitude) vary among social classes is not plentiful although there is a wide variety of fairly systematic evidence that motives vary among classes (Cofer and Appley, 1964, pp. 570–571). One reason for the limited evidence is perhaps that income data are much more easily collected, but Social Class, since it is defined in terms of values, is more appropriate for marketing. Yet there is probably considerable overlap in effects on buying behavior between income and social class.

A study of attitudes and sense of frustration toward stock shortages and poor clerk service in retail stores reports that higher-income shoppers were much more likely to change stores in response to these two attributes than were low-income shoppers (Callazo, 1966).

The middle class is generally believed to shop with the greatest intensity. Bauer (1960), using the perceived-risk notion, argues that the middle class deliberates and plans more than either the upper or the lower class. Katona and Mueller (1954) using income categories as their criterion of class, found in the early 1950's that people with incomes of $5000 to $7500 per year shopped with the greatest vigor. This study was recently replicated and supported for furniture and television (LeGrand and Udell, 1964).

Some evidence indicates that the rate of acceptance of new products may vary considerably among social classes, but that the pattern of differences varies from product to product, as can be seen in Table 3.1. Also, the rate of adoption of television was almost completely in inverse relation to income, which contradicts the prediction from naïve application of economic analysis that people with higher incomes are

TABLE 3.1 Social Class and Three Consumer Innovations

| | Proportion Accepting | | |
Class	Television (%)	Canasta (%)	Supermarket (%)
I	24	72	52
II	44	72	80
III	48	44	56
IV	52	20	80
V	84	32	52
VI	72	12	48

more likely to direct their purchases toward expensive items. Here occupation was used as the indicator (Graham, 1951).

Also, there may be a relationship among the social classes in the temporal order in which they accept changes in purchase patterns, such as major style changes. The "trickle down" theory, for example—that new fashions are accepted at the top, each lower class then adopting them from the class above—has long been believed. Katz and Lazarsfeld (1955) have provided contrary evidence, however.

As for variations within a given class, it has been hypothesized that people who are close to moving into the next class are more likely to be innovators, except on issues that determine their acceptance into the next class (R. Coleman, 1960).

Finally, it is sometimes alleged that the social class hierarchy is becoming less distinct in the United States, but no satisfactory evidence is available to support this belief (Reissman, 1959). There is evidence that the mobility rate has not changed in the past half century (R. Brown, 1965).

3.4.8 Culture

The third social variable is the buyer's culture. Briefly, Culture is a selective, man-made way of responding to experience, a set of behavior patterns. More generally, Culture consists of *patterns of behavior*, transmitted from member to member by *symbols* and constituting the distinctive achievement of human groups. The essential core of culture consists of traditional *ideas* and especially their attached *values*; culture systems may, on the one hand, be considered as products of action and, on the other, as conditioning further elements of action.

At the individual level, culture refers to attitude, beliefs, and customary behavior. Hence we postulate that Culture affects Motives, Brand Comprehension, Attitude, and Intention. These in turn, influence the searching for and perception of information. In more conversational language, Culture is a set of social influences, and, in general, social influences have four effects: to provide the buyer with socially appropriate motives that have a variety of implications for his behavior, to tell him that brands are available, to provide him with facts about the merits of the brands before the purchase, and, after the purchase, to provide him with reassurances that his purchase was a good one.

What is the relevance of culture for marketing practice? Many speeches have been made on this topic by marketing practitioners, particularly in the last ten years as American firms have rapidly expanded abroad and encountered new cultures. A perusal of the trade literature, however, will show remarkable differences of opinion among executives about the consequences of culture for marketing plans.

One way to think about culture is to ask whether people in different cultures would use the same set of attributes to evaluate a brand, the empirical counterpart of Choice Criteria. Osgood has presented considerable evidence that the adjectival scales used to describe a concept, such as the *dimensions* of preference space for a given brand, are very similar across cultures, whereas the evaluations of a concept differ markedly (Osgood, 1962):

> . . . the semantic framework within which these affective judgments are made is constant; the modes of qualifying concepts display the same correlational structure, despite real differences in location of particular concepts within the common framework [Osgood, 1964, p. 174].

The extent to which these conclusions carry over to purchasing, where fairly specific criteria tend to be used, is yet to be determined because Osgood employed very general adjectives in his work.

The phenomenon of subculture—such as Irish, Jewish, Negro, Puerto Rican,—is often helpful in understanding buyer behavior. Each subculture has its peculiar preferences, hence it often should be examined separately, although the differences tend to disappear as people become absorbed, acculturated. Under the heading of ethnicity it is a variable in social-class determination.

Acculturation is a slow process, so that by and large investigators of buying behavior are concerned with cultural differences across people instead of over time. Studies of buyers at different stages of the acculturation process would be interesting, along the lines of the "assimilation" studies of how groups of people from one culture are absorbed into another culture, as were the Irish in Boston. The concepts and methods that have evolved from these studies may be useful in understanding the process of social change brought about by marketing innovations such as the introduction of new products.

Kluckhon has nicely summarized many of the intercultural differences that have been documented (Kluckhon, 1954). Culture makes a difference in the way that one perceives things, for example, sounds in foreign language are misheard; orientation in space is culturally determined as is behavior with respect to time, perception of color, and remembering and forgetting. Cognitive or thinking processes are also influenced. Thus classification schemes are different, some cultures making finer discriminations than others and making them in different areas. The expression of emotion and the circumstances giving rise to emotion vary. Evaluative behavior is different, that is, the essence of a culture is its selectivity and the essence of that selectivity depends on the distinctive values of each culture and their configuration. There is fairly systematic evidence that learned motives, too, vary among cultures (Cofer and Appley, 1964, pp. 568–569). Only now, however, are studies being made that show the direct relation between values and behavior (Moscovici, 1963). Brown, for example, asserts that *achieved* instead of *ascribed* attributes are given greater emphasis in fixing social status in the more highly industrialized countries (R. Brown, 1965, pp. 104–105).

Graham, in studying social class differences in the acceptance of innovations, found large variations between Italians and others in their rate of adopting the supermarket as the place of purchase (Graham, 1951). The Italians were much slower, for largely cultural reasons having to do with the manner of purchasing and preparing food. In Guatemala, the purchasing habits of the Indians differed sharply from those of the natives of European descent (Tax, 1958).

3.5 SUMMARY

A basic philosophical position was taken that to carefully separate hypothetical constructs and intervening variables will lead to greater progress in the field. In this way the hypothetical constructs are set out as constituting a broadly defined program of research. The need for correct rules of correspondence between reality and the intervening variables was emphasized.

The boundaries of the theory of buyer behavior—the intervening and exogenous variables—were set out. The intervening variables are of two types: input and output. Here, the description of the input was kept very simple: the Stimulus Display. The measurement problem was dealt with in order to add concreteness to the discussion. The output intervening variables are Attention', Brand Comprehension', Attitude', Intention', and Purchase.

To provide perspective, the variety of effects of the seven exogenous variables are summarized in Figure 3.2. This perspective is essential to an appreciation of the important role that we expect exogenous variables to play in explaining buying behavior.

In discussing the exogenous variables, we have by no means included all of the available evidence in each case (Carman, 1965b; Rotzoll, 1967), nor have we attempted to describe the precise nature of the relationship. Also, we expect these relationships to be more complex than shown here. To fully develop the pertinent relations, each variable would require a separate research project. Our purpose here was, first, to indicate the relevance of exogenous variables and thus to delimit the structure

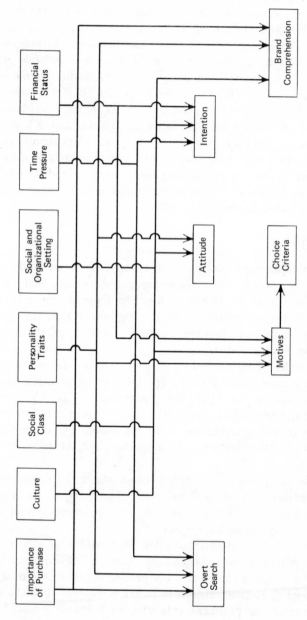

Figure 3.2 Effects of exogenous variables.

of the theory that we are presenting, so that we will know what we are not talking about in discussing the theory. Second, we wished to offer suggestions to researchers about the nature of the controls needed in identifying fundamental relations in the study of buying behavior. Third, we intended to provide a more systematic approach in the efforts to segment markets in terms of management's needs, and of the public policy maker's need in evaluating marketing practices.

CHAPTER 4

Learning Subsystem

We now turn to the heart of the structure of the theory: the hypothetical constructs. These constructs are more idealistic than their intervening counterparts and have surplus meaning that gives us leverage and imagination in thinking about the nature of the system and particularly in communicating its relevance to reality.

The task of Chapters 4 and 5 is to present the hypothetical constructs and their interactions that take place within the framework of the exogenous and intervening variables and in response to changes in the Stimulus Display during the period of observation. More specifically, we wish to develop systematically a number of elements of behavior that were merely touched upon in Chapter 2. Complex stimuli are everywhere, hence the concept of stimulus integration must be introduced. Furthermore, the stimuli are typically not the brand but symbols that stand for the brand, and this condition requires considerably more intellectual effort from the buyer. It involves language and thinking. Also, sequential behavior is central to buying. Stimuli must be learned; the buyer must learn to look for information. Motives must be learned, brands must be learned, and, finally, a series of motor acts having to do with purchase and consumption must be learned. In sum, infinitely *more* learning is involved than in typically simple laboratory learning situations.

Because of the amount of variation in the learning that may occur from situation to situation, let us make two simplifications to facilitate exposition. First, buying situations can be classified to form a typology or set of global intervening variables according to whether the buyer must learn a lot, learn somewhat less, or learn very little (J. Howard, 1963). In the first case he does not even know the product class concept: he has never heard of instant coffee and is confronted with Sanka, a brand of instant coffee. This is called Extensive Problem Solving. In the second case he knows the product class concept, but not the particular brand concept. He has bought instant coffee for years but he is confronted with a new brand of instant coffee with which he is unfamiliar. Limited Problem Solving is the term applied to this type of decision situation. In the third case, he knows the product class and has a preferred brand in that product class, but changing market conditions, such as alterations in price, may cause him to learn about the changing factor each time he goes to buy his favorite brand. This situation we label Routinized Response Behavior.

Extensive Problem Solving occurs when there is a radical product innovation in the market—television, electronic kitchen ranges, computers, and so forth—and so we deal with this case and Limited Problem Solving in Chapter 8 on product innovation. Chapters 4 and 5 will be confined mainly to Limited Problem Solving. Finally, Routinized Response Behavior will be sketched out explicitly at the end of this chapter, since we can probably ignore perceptual variables in this type of decision, at least they loom much less important than they do in Limited Problem Solving and Extensive Problem Solving.

A second simplification is to separate the hypothetical constructs into two groups, perceptual and learning. True enough, learning occurs in the perceptual processes, too, as we indicated above, but the overt act of purchase is more intimately connected to the other constructs: Motives, Choice Criteria, Brand Comprehension, Attitude, Intention, Confidence, and Satisfaction. These learning constructs we call the learning subsystem, as shown in Figure 4.1. Chapter 5 is devoted to the perceptual subsystem made up of the four perceptual constructs: Attention, Stimulus Ambiguity, Overt Search, and Perceptual Bias.

The learning constructs are related to each other as shown in Figure 4.1. The solid arrows are straighforward flows and effects, and the dashed segments represent a feedback relation. Purchase is the output, but the input can be the Achilles' heel of the learning subsystem when it stands alone. Let us see why this is so.

We are implicitly assuming in Figure 4.1, as does most current buyer research, that the stimulus-as-coded (s-a-c)—the stimulus actually perceived by the buyer—is identical with the Stimulus Display, the physical

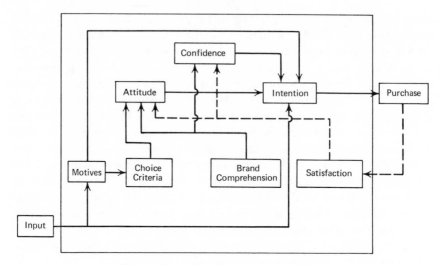

Figure 4.1   The learning subsystem.

events in the buyer's environment that stir or prod him. That is, the human is assumed to be a perceiving system of perfect fidelity. Under some conditions—under fairly uncommon conditions, we believe—this may be a safe operating assumption. Under other conditions, which we think are more typical, the s-a-c is a modified version of the real Stimulus Display. If so, consideration should be given to making the s-a-c an intervening variable, hence thinking of the buyer as responding to the thing he perceived instead of to the thing that is really "out there." Also, the mechanisms by which the Stimulus Display is modified to yield the s-a-c must then be understood. This is the province of Chapter 5.

Let us now turn to the learning subsystem, bearing in mind (1) the perceptual simplification we have made, (2) that a number of the hypothetical constructs have counterpart intervening variables, as shown in Figure 3.1, and (3) that the exogenous variables constitute a vehicle for relating a number of forces that bear on the buyer to shape his hypothetical constructs. We take each of the constructs, one at a time, and examine its theoretical underpinnings.

4.1 BRAND COMPREHENSION

Brand Comprehension is a cognitive state of the buyer that reflects the extent to which he has sufficient knowledge to establish well-defined criteria for identifying the brands he encounters and to have available the words for discussing a particular brand, but not for evaluating it. Information affects Attitude through Brand Comprehension.

4.1.1 The Brand Concept and Language

The brand is merely another class concept and, like all class concepts, has both a denotative meaning and a connotative meaning. The denotative elements of its meaning are those socially designated attributes by which the buyer identifies one brand as being different from another and in terms of which he discusses it with other people. The connotative meaning, on the other hand, includes those attributes by which the buyer evaluates the brand in terms of his motives and, more specifically, those attributes that constitute his Choice Criteria. This aspect of brand meaning will be elaborated later when we discuss Motive, Choice Criteria, and Attitude.

When we speak of the buyer as having sufficient knowledge, we think partly of the denotative meaning of the brand. This meaning is the criterial attributes—the attributes that the buyer and his speech community use for inferring a brand's membership in a category and concluding that brand A is in product class X. It implies the language (1) for identifying, (2) for thinking about, and (3) for talking with others about the brand. Coca Cola for the older generation, for example, is a bottle of a certain shape, containing a tangy, gingery dark liquid that fizzes. Its sensory characteristics are emphasized.

This denotative meaning links the concept of a brand to the whole gamut of the role of language in an organized society and enables us to conceive of buying behavior as simply one aspect of the total culturally patterned behavior exhibited by a human. An object with four wheels is an automobile. If it possesses certain other criterial attributes that we associate with sports cars, it is "sports car." All objects with these attributes have a linguistic equivalence: they are called "sports cars." However, this *linguistic* equivalence is matched in every case by some sort of *nonlinguistic* equivalence. First, as we have just indicated, sports cars are equivalent in terms of their criterial attributes. Second, and here the implications are profound indeed, the term "sports cars" carries much connotative meaning. We associate the word with the pleasures of a holiday, a rapid run down a mountain road, perhaps even a sexual experience, and so forth. Thus there is an isomorphism between naming behavior and its nonlinguistic equivalent of other sorts of culturally patterned behavior (R. Brown, 1965) involving our Motives, Choice Criteria, and Attitudes. In a technologically advanced society where mass communication plays a central role, a linkage between denotative meaning and the connotative meaning of the concept of brand could have significant implications for buying behavior. These inferences are discussed in Chapters 8 and 9; here we merely develop the basic concepts as a part of the theoretical structure.

Having examined the basic idea of brand, we see that Brand Comprehension does not stand by itself but is meaningful only in relation to the product class concept of which the brand is a member. Because we take the product class concept as given in this chapter and deal with it in Chapter 8, we shall not carry further here the analysis of the relationship between the two, except for the concept of the buyer's evoked set. The evoked set concept is too central an element in buyer choice for us not to develop it at some length here.

4.1.2 Nature of Evoked Set

We begin with evoked set because we must first specify what it is that we are explaining. The not so obvious point here is that the buyer does not choose among all of the available brands in the product class, if their number happens to be large, for example, more than seven or eight. The brands that the buyer considers as acceptable for his next purchase constitute his *evoked set*. We have hypothesized for some time (J. Howard, 1963) the existence of such a phenomenon. Since then we have found other evidence to support it (G. Miller, 1956; Wallace, 1961), but only recently has systematic empirical evidence of it been found in consumer buying, although we were able to document it in industrial buying some years ago (J. Howard and Moore, 1963). Campbell (1968) found that for toothpastes and detergents no buyer had an evoked set larger than seven, with the mean numbers being 3.1 and 5 respectively. Also, a buyer who has a small evoked set in one product class, has small evoked sets in other product classes.

What are the determinants of the magnitude of evoked set? What decides the number of brands among which a buyer will choose? We postulate that the exogenous variable of Importance of Purchase is positively related to it. Social and Organizational Setting also influences it, but probably in various ways. Also, Personality Traits make a difference, as indicated by the research on width of categories that people use (Pettigrew, 1958). Campbell's empirical work did not support the role of Importance of Purchase, but there was a serious question about his measure of that variable. He did find that brand loyalty and size of set were inversely related and that price sensitivity and size of set were positively related.

The magnitude of the evoked set clearly sets a limit on choice at any moment in time. Consequently, in comparing buyers' responses it may be useful to standardize on evoked sets, to classify buyers according to their evoked sets. If a buyer does not have A in his evoked set but does have B, we would predict that he will respond much more sensitively to a change in the price of B than he will to a change in the price of A.

The concept has still more subtle implications. It is sometimes alleged that voters, as well as others, presumably including buyers, can be inconsistent in their choices without feeling any particular conflict if the choice is not very important (Abelson, 1968). This possibility weakens our capacity to make sense of behavior. Intransitivity, which plagues economists and decision theorists, is a special case of inconsistency. Our belief is that if the analysis is confined to brands in the buyer's evoked set, less intransitivity will be encountered.

The fact of the set and its size is also relevant in thinking about public policy with respect to proliferation. Many critics allege that the number of brands available to the buyer places too great a burden on him and thus confuses him. However, the concept of evoked set suggests that the buyer simplifies his choice process by choosing from only among a few. When the known brands are not numerous, the number in the buyer's evoked set probably bears some relationship to the known number of brands, but when they are numerous, it probably bears no relationship to the number of brands known.

4.2 MOTIVES

Motives are the second of the three elements—Brand Comprehension, Motives, and Choice Criteria—in the buyer's decision process, which combine to yield Attitude, the evaluation of a brand's quality. We use the plural form because we expect that in most buying situations more than one motive is operative. In one sense, Motives are the most important of these in that they play a central role not only in learning and behavior but also in regulating the input of information.

"Motive," "goal," "need," "drive," and "want" will be used interchangeably here—even though these terms tend to be used in slightly different ways in the psychological literature—because treating them as synonyms facilitates discussion and does not result in serious ambiguity (English and English, 1958). Goal, however, must be distinguished from the goal-object, the brand.

Motives are the biogenic or psychogenic needs, wants, or desires of the buyer in purchasing and consuming an item in a product class. They include the consciously sought goal, which is considered to determine behavior.

Motives have two aspects. First, they are the impetus, the "push" to behavior, an energizing or arousing instead of a directive effect on behavior (Osgood, 1957b, pp. 367ff). A sated man confronted by a table heavy with food makes no choice because he is not hungry, he has no need, he is not motivated to make a choice that leads to action but he knows with confidence which dishes he would choose if he were hungry.

Second, through Choice Criteria, Motives are also directive, directing the buyer toward the purchase of a particular product class. This effect is the source of the man's knowing which type of dish he would choose if he were hungry. A motive becomes associated with some brand of a particular *product class* and endows that product class with its connotative characteristics; thus Choice Criteria are derived. In this sense Motives have a directive effect in causing a person to buy a brand in this product class, but not a particular brand. In other words, this aspect of a motive is "product-class specific," but not "brand-specific." A motive is associated with a particular *brand* only in the sense that one brand may serve the need represented by that motive better than other brands. When we speak of a nonspecific motive, we are referring to a motive that is satisfied by other product classes, too.

Motives serve an essential role in explaining overt purchase behavior. The reader will recall from Figure 4.1 that Motives serve a threefold function. First, they affect Choice Criteria and in this way exert an influence on Attitude. Second, there are short-term fluctuations in their intensity which affect Intention. Evidence of the short-term fluctuations is shown, for example, in the data collected by William Yoell. Housewives who had not eaten for two hours are reported to have bought $2.20 more groceries than "usual," Those who had not eaten for five hours bought $7.50 more. The relationship is presumably nonmonotonic, since there is good evidence that this functional form characterizes the relation between Motives and behavior (Berlyne, 1965). Finally, Motives affect the perceptual process via Attention, Perceptual Bias, and Overt Search, but these perceptual effects are multifaceted and complex, and we shall delay discussion of them until we deal with the information input in Chapter 5.

4.2.1 Specific Definition of Motives

A brief historical background of developments in the process of motivation will provide the reader with helpful perspective and a quick clue as to the point of view expressed here. In the past two decades it has become more and more apparent that the Hullian and Freudian theories of motivation are not sufficiently congruent with the empirical facts. For many types of behavior the Hullian drive-reduction view has been found to be insufficient. It holds that behavior is learned only when drive is reduced, that is, roughly speaking, when "a need is satisfied" as a result of that specific behavior. The buyer does learn in this way but he learns in other ways too.

Freud's theory of instincts is equally inadequate when it is stretched to account for the development of the effective ego. The human personality is too complex to be explained by this simple instinctual theory. Perhaps the one type of behavior that has increasingly raised the most questions for both of these orthodox theories is exploratory behavior about which more and more empirical evidence has accumulated (Berlyne, 1966). This fact is especially important because we believe that many of the subtle, complex, and little understood aspects of purchasing behavior, such as the role of advertising, fit snugly under the rubric of exploratory behavior.

Let us set out one view of the motivation process that seems to capture most of the crucial distinctions contained in the extant motivation theories, so that we shall have a foundation on which to build in attempting to understand buyer behavior (Cofer and Appley, 1964). First, the concept of a stable equilibrium model is either stated or implied in all of the theories. A disequilibrium in the motivational system occurs, for example, when some need arises and elicits certain equilibrating responses such as some course of action expected to satisfy the need and these responses cease when equilibrium is restored as a result of the need being met. This simple equilibrium model is later modified by the introduction of concept of level of aspiration and exploratory behavior.

Second, the system can incorporate not only innate motives, but also such learned motives as affiliation and achievement. Innate motives do require the reduction of bodily needs for behavior to be learned, but learned motives do not. The *sensitization-invigoration* process underlies innate motivation: behavior energized by the biological needs of sex, hunger, thirst, and pain. The *anticipation-invigoration* process, on the other hand, underlies learned motivation which does not require drive reduction. "Invigoration" is used instead of "arousal" to avoid implying that arousal necessarily intervenes between the stimulation of anticipation and its consequences in the latter mechanism, although in most cases it probably does. Let us examine these two concepts.

Sensitization-invigoration refers to the stimulation that comes from the operation of the physiological or innate needs. These are simple, mechanistic effects, largely common to both men and animals. The motivation process operates because the internal state of the buyer's body—a biological need—*sensitizes* him to stimuli, and in the presence of these stimuli the buyer is excited or aroused. The reduction of this biological need causes him to learn a habit, a mode of behavior. This has been demonstrated by a great number of experiments.

The question is whether in an advanced economy buying derives directly from these needs or whether its source is learned motives. Most researchers believe that some buying behavior is motivated by the biological needs. How many times have you been motivated to buy a cake for dessert when you by chance walked past a bakery on your way home and were assailed by the enticing odors emanating from it? We have already cited data suggesting that food deprivation influences a housewife's total purchases of food on a given shopping trip. We know of little systematic evidence on the issue, but learned motives are probably much more important.

The anticipation-invigoration mechanism which is applicable to learned motives is based on the observation that both man and animals come to *anticipate* the occurrence of a reward or a punishment. Presumably these anticipations are elicited by stimuli associated with the reward or punishment.

Let us examine how these stimuli which constitute a part of the anticipation-invigoration mechanism become learned, and thus also observe the relation between this mechanism and related concepts. To do this, we make use of the construct of mediator (Osgood, 1957b), which is based on Hull's (1943, 1952) concept of the anticipatory goal response. We elaborate the concept to develop our Choice Criteria, Brand Comprehension, Attitude, and Intention. It is a solid foundation on which to build a more elaborate set of constructs that we believe to be necessary for the research required to meet our needs.

Osgood's mediator involving responses and stimuli internal to the buyer's body has the motivational properties of both arousing and directing the behavior of the buyer toward a product class. How it is derived can be illustrated with a child learning to use language through the motive of fear (Osgood, 1957b). To begin with, the child has no fear of an open flame. After experiencing the pain from contact with the open flame, he comes to *anticipate* pain, having acquired a *conditioned fear* of it. The acquisition of this fear is shown in the upper portion of Figure 4.2.

In the figure, S is the open flame; from being burned by it, the child learns to anticipate the pain, hence to avoid it, as shown by the solid arrow from S to R_T, where R_T is total behavior. In the typical situation, when the child experiences the fire, he hears the word "Fire" uttered by a parent or some other adult. This new stimulus, which is verbal, is represented by $\boxed{S}$. Hearing only the *word* comes to have the *similar*

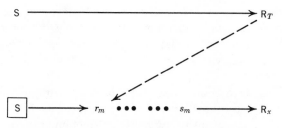

Figure 4.2   Acquisition of mediator.

effect of causing him to anticipate the pain and so to respond in a particular way, R_x.

The response (R_x), however, is not identical to the total effect (R_T) that occurs when the child physically contacts the flame instead of merely hearing the word. The child may, for example, move away from a neutral object that he is touching when he hears the word, but he may not spring away as he does when he touches a hot object itself. Responding to the word is rewarded, however, because the child avoids being burned when he pays attention to it. Consequently, with experience the *word* acquires more and more the capacity to elicit the total behavior (R_T) of springing away when he hears "Fire!" It is now an instrumental response; that is, the child uses the response to avoid a problem.

The motivating effect of the word "Fire" arises from the *anticipation* of pain, the internal response being caused by the association between the fire and pain developed in the past. This internal response, if it is strong, can as an internal stimulus motivate other responses, internal or external. In discussing Choice Criteria we shall spell out these internal stimuli and responses, but for the moment we wish merely to show their motivational relevance.

The motivation of the external responses of *buying* by these internal stimuli and responses that represent this anticipation is the feature of most immediate interest to us. Also, we must try to understand how words and other symbols trigger the long sequences of acts—a housewife hears a television advertisement, drives a distance to a food shop, walks into the store, and inspects items at length—that culminate in the purchase act and continue afterward in carrying out the consumption process as well. The invigorating element of this learned complex response—the total sequence of internal responses—is the *anticipation-invigoration* mechanism.

With this view of the motivation process we are able to move to the much more complex behavior that, we believe, characterizes most purchasing situations. We can now, for example, better explain how the exogenous variable of Social and Organizational Setting which implies learned motives can differentiate among buyers in terms of their purchasing criteria.

Now that we have shown how certain events, or qualities (stimuli) of objects such as the attributes of a brand, come to have the capacity to elicit in the buyer anticipation of satisfaction, the question arises how the underlying motive(s) is learned, since we believe along with others "that most of the motivational characteristics of the adult human are learned or acquired" (Cofer and Appley, 1964, p. 572). We have already illustrated how fear might be learned. That there are differences in learned motives among social classes and cultures, hence also among individuals, is clear. McClelland's pioneering work with the achievement, affiliation, and power motives has shown effective ways of measuring interpersonal differences in learned motives and of manipulating their intensities. But to induce a motive into an individual in order to gain further understanding of the process by which motives are learned, such as in an experimental situation, is quite another matter. Such induction has been accomplished with fear, as we shall see, but it has not been possible to go much further than this (Cofer and Appley, 1964, pp. 566–588; R. Brown, 1965, pp. 419ff; J. Brown, 1961, Chapter 5). We must recognize, however, that systematic study has come late to the area of motivation and our limited capacity to induce learned motives by experimental means is a serious handicap.

Before proceeding to related topics—an overall structure of Motives, the close and complex relation between motive and the learning of both preference and the overt behavior required to provide the satisfaction indicated by that preference—let us briefly consider how the learning of a motive differs from the learning of other elements in behavior. Three chief criteria are used to determine whether a given process is a learned motive, as opposed to a habit. One criterion is its capacity to activate or accentuate other responses, for example, to cause a person to buy more of a given brand. A second identifying feature is the rewarding or reinforcing value of its reduction or removal as indicated by the learning of new responses, for example, a buyer's choice of a different brand after he has learned a new motive. The third criterion is the presence of stereotyped behavior, which is the ability of the motivation process, under such conditions as extremely intense motives, to suppress or inhibit other responses; for example, if motive intensity is increased, the person buys nothing but vacillates between the three brands in his evoked set.

4.2.2 Structure of Motives

Let us use the concepts of sensitization-invigoration mechanism and anticipation-invigoration mechanism to obtain a more detailed grasp of the elements that make up this exceedingly complex but important process of motivation. We can now use the concept of motive structure to make a transition in our thinking from these simple ideas to a much more sophisticated set of notions.

First, there is the dominance hierarchy of motives. At any point in time a buyer is beset with a number of motives demanding satisfaction, but he cannot satisfy all of them simultaneously. Therefore, a hierarchy of motives—motives arranged in ascending order according to their intensity—becomes established. The most urgent motive, that is, the one at the "top" of the hierarchy, is satisfied first. The exogenous variable, Importance of Purchase, is intended to identify the "average" position over time of a product class in this hierarchy and enable us to make interproduct comparisons of modes of purchasing behavior. Other goals lower in the hierarchy go unsatisfied at least temporarily. The issue here is central to all behavior. For example, imagine a housewife's total activity during the week. How does she allocate her time and how much of it to buying? In simplest terms, at each point in time she allocates her time to the activity that will satisfy the motive that is dominant at the moment in her hierarchy. This purchasing activity when completed will satisfy that motive enough so that it drops to a subordinate position in the hierarchy. There are some complications, which we shall omit here, such as "what happens if she is interrupted to turn to some other activity before she completes the current purchasing?" This has been well worked out theoretically (Atkinson, 1964, pp. 308–316).

Once a goal has been satisfied, the question is whether the buyer will return to the activity, which was interrupted to serve the most important goal. Whether he does depends on the presence of cues to define the path back to the original activity (Atkinson, 1964). Also, if the goal currently being satisfied is very intense, he will persist unduly with the activity even though another goal "comes up."

For the rest of the discussion of motive structure let us assume that our buyer has at the top of his hierarchy a motive that requires for its satisfaction the purchase of any brand in a particular product class. Also, for the moment let us assume that a single motive is operating.

With this background, let us refer to the second dimension of motive structure—the *arousal-directive* distinction, which we have already discussed very generally. What is the relation between arousal and direction? Consider a housewife, for example. To satisfy her achievement need, she must have the high regard of her peers. To obtain it, she must buy well, so as to both take good care of the family and have extra money to spend on hairdos and similar items that will enhance her status with her neighbors. Such attempts to satisfy the achievement need are very general, however: there are many products to be bought each of which will contribute to the housewife's sense of achievement.

This generalized need not only gives direction to the housewife's behavior but, like any intense motive, also represents an increase in the arousal aspect of motive. A higher level of arousal makes her more sensitive to information as she sees a television advertisement describing a refrigerator. The advertisement creates an anticipation of satisfaction of achievement by offering a means of better meeting the needs of her family through replacing the worn-out refrigerator with a new one. The anticipation also adds to arousal. In addition, however, the advertisement serves as a cue and directs her to buying refrigerators as one avenue of satisfying the generalized achievement need. Further this high arousal state also precipitates action, and the directional or cue effects give direction to that action: buy refrigerators instead of a myriad of other things she might devote her time and money to buying. To go beyond the product class choice to explain how she chooses a particular brand within the product class of refrigerators, we must incorporate additional variables in the system, especially Attitude, Confidence and Intention. These will be discussed later.

Third, there is the source of the motive, whether innate or learned, which was also discussed earlier in terms of the sensitivation-invigoration mechanism and the anticipation-invigoration mechanism. As we indicated there, the distinction is important because a different motivational process operates in each case.

Let us move now to the fourth dimension of motive structure, which is one of the most useful contrasts: the means-end chain as shown in Figure 4.3. Terminology for this important idea is varied. Inclusiveness hierarchy means the same thing (English and English, 1958, pp. 240–41, Cofer and Appley, 1964, p. 684), as does personality hierarchy, where "hierarchy" is used in a sequential sense instead of a mutually exclusive sense. Which goals does another goal include? One goal or motive can be the means to satisfying a more general goal. The achievement motive, for example, is believed to be a means of satisfying the more general negative goal of anxiety. The term "subgoal" is sometimes used to describe these more specific goals.

At the top of the hypothetical means-end chain of Figure 4.3 are shown three innate motives. The next lower level is the learned motive of

Figure 4.3   Means-end chain.

anxiety, and we might postulate that the learned motives of affiliation and achievement are linked to it. Correspondingly, we could postulate that the very specific elements, convenience and taste, are Choice Criteria and are linked to the specific motive of achievement. A person is striving for recognition in a social group that places a high value on good wine, for example. These very specific criteria, convenience and taste, by existing in his Choice Criteria in turn give rise to the still more specific content that we attempt to identify in deriving attitude scales. Here we see how Motives, Choice Criteria, and Attitude are intimately linked.

Presumably, the more specific the motives in the means-end chain, the more they tend to be influenced by the social exogenous variables of Culture, Social Class, and Social and Organizational Setting. These social effects, we believe, are essential to an understanding of buyer behavior, especially in an advanced economy where the variety of products probably forces sharper discriminations.

A fifth distinction of the structure of motives is so obvious that it may seem unnecessary, yet we find that it often causes trouble in analysis because it is left ambiguous. It is the actual *content* of each position in the structure, which is simply a verbalized description of what the motive is versus the intensity of the motive. To discuss motives in a comprehensive manner, we must be concrete; for example, it is often helpful to use the categories from such standard personality tests as the Edwards Personal Preference Schedule: achievement, deference, exhibition, affiliation, dominance, aggression, and so forth.

A sixth characteristic is whether the goal is positive or negative, as mentioned earlier. Does the buyer in his purchasing activity attempt to achieve a desirable goal ("approach") or to avoid an undesirable goal ("avoidance"). The two learned high-level goals that have been researched—fear and anxiety—are negative, a fact that hampers our understanding of the role of motivation in behavior because we believe that most buying is motivated by positive goals. From his own experience in buying, the reader can probably recall instances of negative goals—

toothpaste to prevent decay—but most buying goals seem to be positive. Katona cites some evidence that people are more likely to buy when positive instead of negative goals operate (Katona, 1963).

A seventh characteristic is the absolute *intensity* of motive (arousal) as contrasted with its weighting *relative* to other motives.. Its relative weighting places it in the dominance hierarchy that we mentioned earlier, but this tells us nothing about its *absolute* intensity which also has significance for behavior. Short-term shifts in this dimension are the source of the equilibrating role of motivation discussed previously. These short-term fluctuations in the absolute intensity of a motive are not reflected in Attitude, but instead bypass Attitude and exert their effect on Intention. Also, as we shall see in Chapter 5, they affect the buyer's tendency to take in information.

The eighth dimension of motive structure is their *number*. As the number of motives increases, their structure becomes wider. The task of buying can be viewed as one of matching a multidimensional goal set with a multidimensional brand, by which we mean a brand that has several relevant attributes. This way of looking at buyer motivation highlights the learning process: the buyer must learn both the dimensions of the goals—especially the dominance hierarchy—and those of the brands. It also explains the difficulty he encounters in comparing widely different brands, since each brand may be related to a slightly different set of goals. In learning a product class concept, the buyer reconciles all those motives that he thinks apply to all of the brands that he views as being in that product class.

A ninth dimension is the degree of consistency of the motives at a particular level in the buyer's inclusiveness hierarchy: the amount of conflict that exists in a goal structure as a result of the particular configuration of that structure. Goal conflict can be illustrated by the housewife who likes instant breakfast foods because they are convenient and free her time for other activities but dislikes them because they make her less essential in the home.

Finally, a tenth dimension is relevant versus irrelevant motives. A relevant motive is one that is satisfied by brands in the produce class under investigation whereas an irrelevant motive is one that is operative in the situation but is not satisfied by brands in the class. This distinction is especially important in examining perceptual effects on purchase. Further, a relevant motive may be specific or non-specific. If it is specific, it is uniquely satisfied by brands in the product class. If not, it can be satisfied by brands in other product classes as well.

After this general introduction to the structure of motives, we now proceed to examine more specifically the nature of the means-end chain.

We emphasize learned goals, although we have no doubt that innate goals often operate. We begin with the most general kinds of learned goals and then proceed to the less general, the more specific and these correspond to levels in the means-end chain.

4.2.2.1 Very General Motives

Two very general learned motives—fear and anxiety—have been sufficiently researched to be discussed with some confidence.

Fear has been well investigated (J. Brown, 1961). An experiment by N. Miller illustrates the process of learning a fear under laboratory conditions and is one of the few studies in which a new motive is induced, which, of course, is a powerful tool of investigation (Dollard and Miller, 1950, p. 65). Miller used a box consisting of a white compartment where shock could be given to a rat and a black box to which the rat could escape after having been shocked in the white compartment. The rat could open the escape door in the white compartment either by turning a wheel or by pressing a bar. Before any shock was administered, the rats showed no preference for one compartment over the other; that is, they did not try to escape from the white to the black compartment. However, as soon as the shocks were administered in the white compartment, they ran to the black compartment. Later on, they ran to the black compartment even when shocks were not administered.

Miller interprets this behavior to suggest that the surrounding cues of the white compartment acquired the capacity to stimulate the responses that originally were elicited by the shock. Later on, the cues *even without the shock* made the rats run, bite the grid, and claw the door because of fear that they would be shocked—an *anticipation* that they learned. As a result of the fear motive, the rats learned to turn the wheel that would open the door; furthermore, when the experiment was changed so that the wheel no longer opened the door, they learned to press the bar. Thus the rats acquired a new habit, which testifies that the motive was indeed learned by reducing the fear motive. It will be recalled that earlier we said this capacity to induce a habit is one criterion for distinguishing motive from habit.

Some psychologists have attempted to produce acquired motives based on positive instead of negative anticipation. Dashiell and Myers, as well as Miller, have attempted to use hunger as the basis of an acquired motive, but results have not been satisfactory (J. Brown, 1961). The fact that hunger and the other primary appetitional motives are much slower in their onsets than is shock may be the reason for the difficulty of establishing acquired drives from hunger.

It is worth noting that so far the experiments with fear as an acquired motive seem to suggest that such motives are largely situation-bound; specific situational cues (like the white compartment where the rat was shocked) become the causative factors for acquired motives, and these are not transferred to the other situations. One possible exception to this nontransferability is suggested by Dollard and Miller (1950) and also by J. Brown (1961) when they emphasize the role of *self-administered* verbal commands in arousing motivational states. For example fire as a stimulus to create the fear motive is found to be situation-bound for the animal; for example, a rat must feel the presence of fire from such stimuli as the visible flames and the hot air. Hence the rat is capable of being conditioned only to a given situation like the cage or the room; the surrounding stimuli of the cage or the room alone can, even in the absence of fire, create fear drive. On the other hand, for a human, the word "Fire!" either self-uttered or received from another person, is sufficient to arouse the fear motive in any situation. These verbal processes can in man easily become independent of specific situations.

Fear is widely used in marketing (Anastasi, 1964). Drugs and safety equipment, for example, seem to rely heavily on fear as the motivating force for their purchase. Fear appeals are common in advertising copy that speaks of "halitosis," "B.O.," "coffee nerves," and "tired blood." More dramatic are the current American Cancer Society's advertisements against smoking.

Anxiety is the second of the two very general learned motives. Among the motives peculiar to humans are the social motives of achievement, affiliation, and power. However, some psychologists believe that as a consequence of social conditioning, for example, Social and Organizational Setting, Social Class, and Culture, these motives derive from the more basic condition of anxiety, hence constitute lower links in the inclusiveness hierarchy than fear and anxiety, as we have indicated in Figure 4.3. Anxiety is the *fear of an unknown future*. To illustrate, if a buyer is subject to anxiety—an unpleasant emotional state, a present drive with a future reference—he may seek success (achievement) as a means of obtaining security which he expects to relieve his anxiety.

J. Brown (1961, pp. 171–176), for example, holds that anxiety is the basis of what might be called "the drive for money" that seems to characterize much of our striving and would seem to be relevant for buyer behavior. To him, the process runs as follows. Certain cues such as an empty pocketbook or overdrawn bank statement come to elicit anxiety. These cues have this effect because of verbal statements received, particularly from parents, about the consequence of having inadequate funds. Also, our experience with the effects of innate motives such as hunger could be a source of reward. With experience a wide variety of cues such as observing people's differing attitudes toward those who are wealthy and those not so wealthy come to cause anxiety. The state of having money rewards or reinforces the activity of getting money because it allays the anxiety. Freud elaborated the idea of anxiety much further, and his work is highly relevant here (Cofer and Appley, 1964).

4.2.2.2 General Motives

The conventional measures of motives that psychologists use are at somewhat of an intermediate or middle level in the inclusiveness hierarchy dimension of goal structure, which is illustrated by the third level in Figure 4.3. These measures, for example, the Edwards Personal Preference Schedule, deal with such needs as those for achievement, dominance (the desire to be a leader), and exhibition (the desire to be clever and talk about personal achievement). As scientists analyzing a problem of buying, we are free to operate at any level in the buyer's goal structure, are though, we believe, that the middle-level motives are less useful for understanding buyer behavior than the more specific ones. The middle-level motives however, may be useful by helping us to better understand the total structure; for example, we may be more effective in working with the lower level if we know the level above it.

The most systematic and comprehensive research effort has probably been applied to the achievement motive and the techniques developed here have also been used for identifying the affiliation and power motives although not nearly so extensively. David McClelland and his associates have worked consistently in developing the concept and testing it over a period of more than ten years (McClelland et al., 1953; McClelland, 1955; Atkinson, 1958; McClelland, 1961). The key hypothesis is that a person holding certain religious values—those associated with the Protestant ethic—is more likely to have a strong desire to succeed, to achieve, than is a person with the opposite values. The operational measure of the achievement motive is a technique associated with the Thematic Apperception Test (TAT) in which the person is asked to write a story about a picture. The empirical support for the achievement motive is impressive (R. Brown, 1965), especially since it has to do with the complex area of motivation where knowledge is skimpy.

So far as we know, the relevance of this test for buying behavior has not been developed. It would seem to hold promise, particularly because of its high operationality, but there are some problems. One of the most serious is that it has proved to be more applicable to men than women. Women have been found not to differ much on it, probably because they tend not to expect to be evaluated so much upon their economic achievement as upon their beauty.

On the other hand, the husband's influence may be strong enough for his achieving characteristics to be reflected in the criteria that his wife uses in purchasing the product. Most importantly, however, the methodology used for developing the achievement motive would seem to be just as applicable to motives on which women do differ. Another problem is that the evidence favors economic achievement instead of general achievement, but this specificity could have arisen because one of the four original TAT pictures used to measure the motive was of a man standing over a machine (R. Brown, 1965, p. 474).

In the past two decades there have been a few serious attempts to apply the conventional need (personality) measures from psychology to buying behavior. One of the most carefully designed investigations was by Evans, which was discussed in Chapter 3 in connection with personality traits as an exogenous variable. He applied the Edwards Personal Preference Schedule to a sample of Ford and Chevrolet owners to see if it were possible to discriminate between the owners of these two brands of cars in terms of their personality traits (Evans, 1959). Of the eleven traits used only four were significant at the 10 per cent or higher level: dominance (the desire to be a leader), exhibition (the desire to be clever and talk about personal achievement), autonomy (the desire to be independent in thought and action), and affiliation (the desire to be friendly and loyal to friends). Yet these limited results must not be disregarded as unimportant. Buyer behavior is complex, and small contributions to explanation should be appreciated.

Other studies came to similar conclusions. Koponen also applied the Edwards Personal Preference Schedule to a 5000-family consumer panel (Koponen, 1960). Only cigarette data were made available on the relation between the test scores and usage of the product class; no data were offered on brand choice. Heavy smokers were found to score higher in expressed need for sex, aggression, and achievement than the average smoker. Tucker and Painter used the Gordon Personal Profile to relate scores on ascendance, responsibility, emotional stability, and sociability to usage of chewing gums, headache remedies, cigarettes, mouth wash, and deodorants. Some slight relationship was found (Tucker and Painter, 1961). For a splendid brief view of the value of personality traits in understanding buyer behavior and a thoughtful rationale for this view, see Wells (1966).

4.2.2.3 Less General Motives

There seems to be a growing belief in market research practice that to understand buying behavior the investigator can more fruitfully research the lower end of the inclusiveness dimension of motive structure by means of so-called "depth studies." These *ad hoc* descriptions are only a little more abstract, not much higher in the hierarchy, than the brand dimensions represented by attitude scales.

Most of the current work in operating market research seems to have taken its inspiration from the Haire study which dealt with more general motives (Haire, 1950). Haire, in about 1948, presented two groups of housewives with identical grocery lists, except that one group's list contained Nescafé instant coffee and the other's Maxwell House regular gound coffee. Instant coffee was a radically new product at that time. The housewives were asked to describe the kind of a person that they believed would buy the products on each list. In general, the person shopping with the Maxwell House list was described as thrifty and a good housewife; the one buying the Nescafé was described as lazy, poor planner, spendthrift, and generally not a good wife.

This is a projective type of personality test such as the TAT mentioned above. The principle of the test is that the buyer is asked to tell a story about an ambiguous stimulus (a picture) and given no more direction than this. Since his responses are thus in no manner specified, it is assumed that he will through the process of projection go beyond the recognition of the events and objects in the picture to a full interpretation based on his own life experience.

It is further assumed that in so doing he reveals himself more accurately than if he were asked directly how he personally views the picture, or, in this case, the grocery list. He "projects" (ascribes) his own beliefs into the stimulus, hence reveals them, whereas he might not reveal them in response to a direct question. In the Haire study it was assumed that if the other person used Nescafé and our buyer did not like Nescafé, our buyer was likely to state or imply that the other person was not a desirable person. The specific interpretation here is that housewives generally wish to be thrifty, good planners, and good housewives, hence will buy those brands that they see as reflecting these qualities. A pantry check supported the interpretation, in that housewives who did not ascribe the unfavorable characteristics to Nescafé buyers were much more likely to have Nescafé in their pantries.

In current practice these measures tend to be subjective and qualitative, but imaginative, careful, highly trained interviewers can with lengthy systematic effort elicit usefully informative descriptions of the buyer's motive structure. The descriptions are useful in rationalizing data and deciding what other data to collect, particularly when used in the way personality measures have tended to be used in psychology, that is, to explain interpersonl differences.

4.2.3 Goal Conflict

The dimension of motive structure that obtains when several conflicting motives are operating simultaneously may be quite relevant to the understanding of buyer behavior. We believe that goal conflict often arises as the buyer goes through the process of developing Choice Criteria which we postulate as being the foundation of Attitude, the source of the content that is required in Attitude scales. How does the buyer add, summate, or reconcile these conflicting effects in purchasing? In the area of complex social behavior, money is the focus of many needs and its possession the means to many rewards, which suggests that the goal summation problem may at times be quite sharp (Hull, 1952, Chapter 8). Hence the lack of reconciliation of somewhat incompatible motives is one source of uncertainty, which leads to conflict, which in turn leads to information seeking. The experimental literature has scarcely begun to tackle the problem of goal summation. A related problem develops when different brands serve slightly different goals—a reconciliation that must be accomplished if Choice Criteria are to develop. Still another related problem occurs when the contributions of the brands to the Choice Criteria are not clear, but are ambiguous. Neal Miller's work is the most advanced in this area and will be presented in Chapter 8.

In line with this problem of conflict, we believe that the housewife is more ego-involved—her goals are more intense—in purchasing than is often implied by such terms as "learning without involvement." One cannot read Cox's comprehensive, systematic interviews of two housewives, for example, without concluding that much buying behavior is significantly important to the buyer (Cox, 1967). As a consequence we would speculate that there is always a general latent conflict in purchasing by housewives which may have analogues among nonhousewife buyers.

First, a family's wants are insatiable, but a housewife's buying behavior is seriously constrained (inhibited) by her husband's income (Financial Status). Second, society demands that she provide for the needs of her family, thus lending a flavor of urgency to her purchases. Third, she also has a number of strong personal desires, especially that of maintaining her personal appearance, which influences her position in her peer group—her bridge club, for example—and motivates the purchase of hairdos, cosmetics, and clothing. Scattered, unsystematic interview evidence suggests that the housewife tends to buy such personal items with "residual" funds after first meeting her family needs.

We believe that often there is a sharp *conflict* between the family needs and the "residual" needs and that this conflict has significance for purchasing behavior. It would tend to elicit the energizing or arousal effect of motivation mentioned earlier which is essential to learning and has many other implications; for example, on these grounds we postulate that the exogenous variable of Financial Status influences Motives. With experience, the housewife probably develops rules for allocating available funds between the two major expenditures—for her family's needs and for her personal needs—but any disturbance such as a downward shift in the family income or the appearance on the market of a medium- or high-priced new product may force her to revise the rules, which would, in turn, recreate conflict. The housewife may find brand loyalty to be one way in which to avoid the recurrence of this unpleasant conflict in her purchasing decisions.

An interesting case of this conflict appears to exist in the purchase of food. Bauer (1965b) in a study of attitudes toward food costs and values that he conducted for the grocery industry found that housewives were very concerned about the cost of food. Yet more of them (40%) felt that they were getting more of their money's worth in their food purchases than in buying any of the other items that they considered important: medical care (22%), clothing (30%), housing (23%), home furnishings (18%), automobile (17%), recreation and leisure (14%), and personal service (6%). Further questions revealed, however, that this concern about cost did not carry over to specific foods. Also, not many thought that food costs were anything that something should be done about. In other words, it seems that the housewives were concerned only about the total budget for food.

Bauer's conclusions are consistent with the hypothesis speculatively advanced above that the housewife has two broad groups of conflicting goals—those of serving her family and those of serving her own needs. We would interpret both groups of goals, for example, as being means to the more general goals of status and position (achievement). Unfortunately, money spent for food to serve the first group of goals subtracts from the housewife's ability to serve the second group of goals through buying cosmetics or hairdos.

This conclusion is consistent with further findings of the Bauer study—food was both the most talked about item in the BLS consumer product groupings and the item that housewives enjoyed most complaining about, but they did not take their complaints very seriously. "It would appear that while most people take their opinions about food costs seriously, they in turn convert it [their concern about food costs] into a popular topic which people who do not take their opinions seriously can find an opportunity for diffuse griping" (Bauer, 1965b, p. 127). It could be inferred that the people who griped about the cost without taking their opinions too seriously did so only as a means of relieving their frustration in trying to meet both goals.

Our guess is that goal conflict is quite common in buying new products, since their purchase and use often require significant behavior change, until the appropriate goals are fully learned by the buyer, that is, until he develops Choice Criteria for the particular product class. Furthermore, goal conflict is only one of a number of sources of uncertainty, all of which have an arousing effect (arousal).

Also, the traditional convenience-shopping distinction can be viewed as conflict between convenience and range of choice (variety of alternative brands) (Mertes, 1964). Convenience goods are those which the buyer wants generally available, for which he is unwilling to shop, and from which he does not demand variety. With shopping goods, he does want greater variety and is willing to expend the time and effort to shop.

4.2.4   Marketing Effort as an Influence on Motives

To what extent can marketing effort make a difference in behavior by its effect on the buyer's goal? Since systematic empirical evidence is almost nonexistent, we are largely confined to conjecture in answering this question. Logically, marketing effort could affect buying behavior in one or more of three ways: (1) by causing the buyer to perceive the product as a means of satisfying a given motive, that is, by making a brand a "perceived instrumentality," (2) by intensifying the motive, and (3) by changing the content of the motive.

Most marketing effort is intended, it seems, to cause the buyer to see a brand as a perceived instrumentality. Advertising studies show rather clearly, for example, that advertising can cause a person to perceive a brand as having certain satisfying attributes that he had not before perceived in the brand.

Casual observation suggests that companies believe that the less general criteria (Choice Criteria) can be influenced by salesmen—that the buyer's goal *content* can be changed—a belief that is commonly reflected in sales management discussions of industrial purchasing. In buying new products, in particular, the buyer is believed to be influenced by the salesman to choose more on the basis of speed and color than on that of durability and economy, for example. Advertising a brand of coffee as a "friendly" drink might cause the buyer to evaluate *all competing beve-*

ages on a "friendliness" basis. In fact, a great amount of marketing effort seems to be devoted to getting the buyer to evaluate the product class by criteria on which the advertiser's brand rates particularly well. This practice is obvious in industrial marketing. The effectiveness of the practice may be enhanced by what seems to be the tendency of the buyer to apply criteria in sequence—once he encounters a brand that does not meet the criterion, that brand is eliminated from the range of choice, even though a simultaneous evaluation of all its attributes would place it higher in his preference hierarchy. There are not many systematic data but a lot of persuasive casual evidence is available suggesting that advertising will cause people to *say* that they use different criteria as a consequence. What is lacking is evidence that this shift in stated criteria is in fact associated with a shift in purchasing behavior.

If we accept Shepard's view that the motive structure is quite flexible, we would expect marketing effort to play a major role in changing goal content (Shepard, 1964, p. 277). He says that "Salesmen are probably among those principal beneficiaries of this human weakness"; by "weakness" he means that buyers seem to make their choices based on cognitive expediency—finding the frame of mind that makes one alternative better—and not as a part of some optimal rational strategy. He concludes this because of the clear evidence that people are not always transitive in their choices. If they prefer A to B and B to C, they do not prefer A to C which is the meaning of intransitivity. He goes on to illustrate. "As a colleague of mine remarked: How many sets of encyclopedias have been sold by encouraging, in the prospective buyer, an unusual state of mind in which he temporarily convinces himself that, yes, he is going to become the scholar and astonish his acquaintances with his range of knowledge?" an intention that is seldom fulfilled. Face-to-face interaction is much more likely to have this effect, we believe, than the usual forms of commercial communication with the consumer. Also, we believe that there are great differences among people and among face-to-face situations in their effects.

Turning to the intensity dimension of goals—the case where a given set of goals exist but their relative weighting can be changed—we expect it to be manipulatable. It is believed, for example, that the desire for good health can be used as the basis for advertising that certain diseases are prevalent. The information about the disease creates anxiety in the buyer, which is a stimulus that leads him to act, that is, to buy a remedy; at the same time, the advertisement shows a direction in which to act, a course of action that will reduce the anxiety.

The concept of *relative deprivation* perhaps can be used as one specific mechanism. By showing the buyer the attractive clothing that members of his peer group wear, his anxiety can be aroused, because he comes to believe that relative to other people that count, he is not so well off in terms of his clothing as he had thought, which could violate his achievement motive. Buyers are probably looking for such information much of the time in order to maintain status in their peer group and in their social class. Again, empirical evidence is limited, but an ad-testing firm, using the psychogalvanometer, reports that in general drugs receive relatively low scores; foods, higher scores; and automobiles, still higher scores. This evidence, if valid, suggests that buyers generally pay more attention to advertising about some product classes than about others.

4.3   CHOICE CRITERIA

Motives is the source of Choice Criteria, as we see in the definition of Choice Criteria: a cognitive state of the buyer which reflects those attributes of the brands in the product class that are salient in the buyer's evaluation of a brand and are related to the buyer's motives that are relevant to this product class in the sense that the brands in the product class have the potential for satisfying those motives. Thus Choice Criteria link Motives to brands via Attitude.

In Part II of this book we take the product class concept as given and do not explain how it forms and changes. The concept is important for all that follows in the rest of this chapter, however, because it serves as a framework for explaining much of the complex behavior exhibited in buying and consuming. All of the constructs that make up the learning subsystem are inextricably linked to it, as we shall see later.

With this dynamic interdependence of the constructs in mind, let us turn to the particular way in which the product class concept with Choice Criteria as its connotative elements serves as a foundation of buying behavior.

4.3.1   *Representational Mediation as Complex Behavior*

By comparing the levels of complexity of behavior it is possible to see more clearly what, specifically, complicates the understanding of human behavior. In Figure 4.4 the least complex behavior is illustrated at the bottom, with additional complications being incorporated at each level and the most complex behavior shown at the top. At the bottom is the simple stimulus-response situation: the stimulus is a simple blow or sound, the response is a very simple act, and no thinking is involved. The intermediate level incorporates complex *stimuli* and complex *responses*, but still no thinking. The highest level incorporates symbol

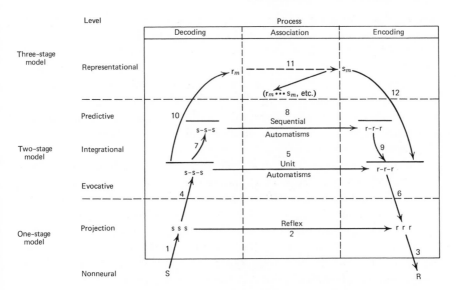

Figure 4.4   Three-stage mediation model.

manipulation (thinking), and it invokes the representational mediation process which generates both denotative and connotative positions in mediators. The concept of mediator was introduced in discussing how motives and their anticipations are learned. The connotative aspects of the mediator level can be represented empirically by the idea of semantic space where the axes are the dimensions on which the buyer conceptualizes a brand. In a sense, as a buyer "zeros in" on a brand and his purchasing of it becomes more habitual, his buying behavior in acquiring this brand is also simplified and corresponds to lower and lower levels in the diagram. This is an example of the psychology of simplification referred to in Chapter 2; we shall discuss the psychology of complication in Chapter 5.

Let us begin, in Figure 4.4, with the simplest form of behavior. The S (stimulus) and R (response) are external to the body (nonneural), and s and r are their internal or neural counterparts. Path 1-2-3, the projection level, is the reflex behavior that requires no learning at all. The doctor when he taps below the kneecap with his little rubber mallet in a physical examination causing the toe to kick out illustrates the operation of reflex behavior. An important point is that the nature of the stimulus is very simple—the sensation arising from the light blow of the mallet. Contrast this exceedingly simple stimulus with that represented by a package of rice on the supermarket shelf. A little reflection will disclose the great number of dimensions by which the package, its surroundings, and its contents could influence behavior.

Reflex behavior is represented by a simple input-output arrangement, the *one-stage model*. The input process of this stage is called *sensation*, as contrasted with *perception* which is used to describe the input process to the two higher, more complex stages. We do not emphasize sensation because of its relatively minor role in the complex problems we are concerned with. Hence the one-stage model is a simplifying expositional device and has little relevance to buying.

The second, integrational level, incorporates three complications: complex stimuli, complex responses, and sequential behavior (time dimension). It is a *two-stage model* in the sense that it deals with (1) the learning of complex stimuli and the analogous learning of complex responses and (2) learning to associate a complex stimulus *with* a complex response. Many stimuli encountered in the world are complex, and the buyer must learn to deal with them. At a minimum, he must learn to discriminate between a box of Uncle Ben's rice, a box of Carolina rice, and a box of River rice. Two or three dimensions such as color, size, and configuration of printing may suffice. On the other hand, several dimensions may be required. Hence we must understand how the buyer learns to integrate these stimuli so as to make the necessary discriminations to be able to identify his preferred brand. Knowledge of how stimulus integrations develop can play a role in package design, advertising, and similar areas. The reader must bear in mind, however, that we are assuming away many perceptual problems in this discussion. These are introduced in Chapter 5.

The buyer must also learn to integrate the various overt behaviors required in purchasing and consuming the product. Behaviors associated with consuming a product have tended to be ignored in the buyer behavior literature, even though to "consume" a Polaroid camera, for example, the user must go through a number of acts. In other words, we probably do not concern ourselves nearly enough with the responses marked r-r-r- in Figure 4.4 as we attempt to understand buyer behavior.

There are two principles of learning: contiguity and reinforcement. First, the buyer integrates—*learns* to integrate—the elements of a complex S, according to the contiguity learning principle, the number of times these elements have been paired in the past: the more frequently they have been paired, the more likely the buyer is to make the integrations, hence to discriminate accurately among the brands this time. Second, and correspondingly, the reinforcement of these pairings does not seem to facilitate integration. The same two statements apply equally well to the integration of responses.

Reinforcement, however, does play an essential role in the second complication introduced at the integrational level in the figure—the buyer learns to associate the complex stimulus that is the brand (not symbols that stand for the brand) with the response that is a series of acts required in buying and consuming the brand. Here behavior is of the operant or instrumental variety, and reinforcement is more essential (Osgood, 1957b, p. 371). Behavior at the *evocative* integrational level, however, is still unthinking (automatic) and is performed as a unit, that is, stimulus and response occur together in time. The contiguity principle of learning operates here. Path 1-4-5-6-3 represents this simpler level of integrational behavior (unit automatons). We can say that this behavior is evocative, because as the association between S and R is learned, the S will evoke R with a very high probability.

Now let us take the more complex case of the *predictive* integrational level of behavior. Path 1-4-7-8-9-6-3 incorporates the time dimension illustrated in *sequential* behavior. That is, there can be a time lag between the appearance of S and the resultant R, but S will evoke R with a lower probability than it would at the evocative level. Hence we say that the behavior is predictive. As in the evocative type of integrational behavior, this behavior is still the unthinking (automatic) kind that occurs in animals as well as man.

Finally, the representational level, the nonautomatic, thinking kind of behavior, incorporates the one characteristic that truly distinguishes man from animals—the capacity to use *language*. It is the total relationship, path 1-4-10-11-12-6-3 in Figure 4.4. Dotted line 11 is the mediator generated by the representational mediation process and symbolized by $r_m \cdot \cdot \cdot s_m$. This describes the behavior exhibited by a housewife when she begins to think about purchasing a brand after seeing a television advertisement, which merely "represents" the brand but is not the brand in fact (symbolic information instead of significative information). She has begun to integrate the stimuli emitted by the picture of the brand's package on the television screen, and a part of her thought process has to do with the acts that must be integrated in order to purchase and consume the product. In information-theoretic terminology, she must take in and comprehend (decode) the external message (the advertisement) by transforming it into an internal message, she must decide which brand to buy, hence at some later time she must transform (encode) the internal message into a complex external response (purchase and consumption).

We assume the advertisement was seen at home rather than at the point of purchase, hence that we are dealing with sequential behavior, which is not shown in Figure 4.4 at the representational level. To portray sequential behavior, we would extend a line from the predictive part of the integrational level to the stimulus side of the representational level and, correspondingly, from the representational level to the predictive portion of the response side of the integrational level.

A key point, however, is that the response to the advertisement (the symbol), for example, purchase, is asserted by Osgood to be typically less than would be the response to the brand itself (the significate). We mentioned the principle that incorporates this difference in responses earlier when we discussed the formation of a mediator in connection with the learning of motives. The anticipation-invigoration mechanism is important in explaining the differing effects on the buyer, for example, of a merchandising policy (significate) versus that of an advertising policy (symbols). What can we say about the conditions that determine the amount of discrepancy between (1) the behavior elicited by the brand and (2) the behavior elicited by an advertisement about the brand? ". . . the mediating reaction to the sign is not the same as the mediating reaction to the significate but rather consists of those most *readily conditionable, least effortful,* and *least interfering* components of the total original reaction" (Osgood, 1963a). This should not be confused with inhibition, which is a part of Intention and where we distinguish between internalized and noninternalized influences on behavior.

In summary, the three-stage model incorporates the two-stage model and adds another crucially important aspect to the individual's buying process—*thinking* and the use of *language.*

4.3.2   Mediator and the Learning Process

We now examine a simplified way in which complete behavior can be learned, that is, we focus on learning at the representational mediation level of Figure 4.4. The central questions in learning are "What is the probability of a given S evoking a given R?" and "What is the role of learning in determining this probability?" To answer the first question is to describe change in behavior, and to answer the second is to explain a large part of all behavior. Figure 4.5 shows the relation between stimulus integration, response integration, and stimulus-response association.

The SI represents stimulus integration, and three possible integrations are shown in the figure, SI_1, SI_2, and SI_3. These could be integrations of the different elements of a complex newspaper advertisement, for example; the probability of each of these occurring is shown at the left.

Given a particular stimulus integration, the next question is which mediator it is likely to evoke, to call to the buyer's mind. That is, of which product class is the buyer likely to think as a result of perceiving that particular stimulus integration? The second column of probabilities in Figure 4.5 illustrates how likely each SI is to call up the particular mediator, the particular product class. To simplify, only one mediator has been shown. In reality, it is crucially important which mediator is evoked, because it sets the stage for the rest of the process. If Mediator 2 were called up instead of Mediator 1, for example, an entirely different array of brands would be brought to the buyer's mind.

The RI in the figure indicates response integration—the pattern (a series of steps) of behavior required to purchase and consume a particular brand. The RI_1, RI_2, and RI_3 indicate that this buyer has three brands in his evoked set, all of which, of course, are contained in a particular product class concept; for example, the three integrations may represent three brands of tomato soup. The probabilities for these integrations are shown in the extreme right column of numbers.

Finally, given that a particular response integration will be made, the question remains which integration is likely to be associated with Mediator 1. Which brand is the buyer likely to purchase? These probabilities are shown in the third column from the left.

Now, let us bring together the parts of the whole decision process—the stimulus, the mediator, and the response—and introduce some complications. First, one important determinant of the extent to which S evokes R is the ambiguity of the Stimulus Display, since it influences one of the perceptual constructs, the buyer's Attention. Figure 4.5 is a behavioristic way of describing Stimulus Ambiguity. The stimulus integration SI is the extent to which the buyer brings together—integrates—the various elements of a complex stimulus. There is only a .40 probability that SI_1 would be made. Perhaps S is not clear; for example, the printing is smudged. Whether the probabilities should add up to 1 depends upon the particular assumptions made.

Second, Choice Criteria may not be well formed (product class concept is not well defined), so that even a well-integrated stimulus would not call up that mediator but some other mediator. This might occur

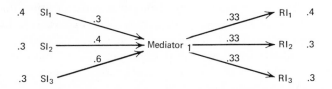

Figure 4.5   Stimulus integration, mediator, and response integration.

when more than one motive is being served by a product class and these motives conflict. The probability that SI_1 would elicit Mediator$_1$, could, for example, be no more than chance, as shown in Figure 4.5, assuming that we were sure it would call up one of three mediators.

Third, even though the probability is high that SI_1 will be made and that the display will be associated with a given mediator, it could be that none of the alternative brands, each represented by an RI (the sequence of acts required to complete the total purchasing act of that brand) are well enough known for that mediator to be associated with that brand. The buyer is not sure how well each of the brands in evoked set measures up against Choice Criteria. We refer to this as brand ambiguity (Confidence) by which we mean that the buyer lacks confidence in evaluating the brand. This relationship, too, might be close to equiprobable, as shown in Figure 4.5.

The ideal case, if you are the seller of the brand represented by RI_1, is when the probability of a given integration upon seeing an advertisement for any brand in the product class (SI_1) is 1.0, the probability of SI_1, being associated with this mediator, is 1.0, this mediator with RI_1 is also 1.0, and the probability of RI_1 is 1.0.

This way of structuring the integration and association aspects can be useful not only in thinking about the problem but also in quantitatively analyzing buyer behavior. Measuring instruments can be designed to reveal the probabilities, and each stage can be viewed as conditional probabilities for the succeeding stage; for example, the probabilities that certain stimulus integrations will be made become conditional probabilities in computing the probability of certain mediators being called up.

What is the role of learning in changing these probabilities? First, there is a source of increased probability which is a result of previous learning but not tied to current learning. This source is *generalization*. Every day we observe enormous variety in human behavior. One of the mechanisms contributing to this variety is stimulus generalization where the basis of generalization—transferring past experience to new situations—is the physical similarity between the new object and the object previously experienced. In addition, however, we are able to extend this already large potential of physical generalization for variety in behavior to a far larger range of variety. The extension is by means of the concept of *mediated generalization* in which generalization operates at the symbolic level and the person generalizes from one stimulus to another according to the similarity of *meaning* between the two stimuli instead of their physical similarity.

The concept of mediated generalization has particular significance for the use of a brand name that covers more than one product. Much institutional advertising, for example, is justified on the grounds that it builds a company brand name, thus causing the buyer to endow the company's new brand with the qualities that he has come to associate with the company. To test the idea of mediated or semantic (as it is sometimes called) generalization, Kerby (1966) asked 99 housewives whether General Electric vacuum cleaners, automatic washers, portable television sets, and refrigerators were more alike in meaning than were Sunbeam vacuum cleaners, Philco automatic washers, Admiral television sets, and Norge refrigerators. "Meaning" was elicited here by having the housewives rate each brand and product on a seven-point scale for each of a number of dimensions. An analysis of the data indicated that ten of the respondents showed a reliable indication that they perceived the different products with the same General Electric brand to be more similar in meaning than they did the same products under different brand names.

Second, given the intensity of Motives and generalization tendencies, any other changes in these probabilities are a result of the learning of stimulus integrations, response integrations, and stimulus-response associations. These three types of relationships can be pursued more usefully for our purposes, however, by relating them to the learning constructs of the theory of buyer behavior. In this way, we show how the concept of product class, especially with its connotative elements of Choice Criteria, serves as a means for connecting the learning constructs of the theory of buyer behavior to the neobehavioristic view set forth by Osgood. These relations (Figure 4.5) not only show some of the intellectual roots of the theory of buyer behavior, but also have the practical advantage of making available to the buyer behavior researcher a far more elaborate body of theory and empirical research than is given or even cited in this book.

By postulating Brand Comprehension and Attitude, we, in effect, break mediator into its denotative and connotative elements, respectively. In addition, Brand Comprehension also incorporates the phenomenon of evoked set.

Intention is the buyer's *anticipated* association between the mediator and a response integration. It is implied by the probabilities in the third column from the left of Figure 4.5. We postulate that Intention is underlain by a plan that is the sequence of anticipated internal and external stimuli and responses, suggested by the integrational predictive level of Figure 4.3 which yields sequential behavior. Although Osgood does not develop it, he implies the intention concept and even goes so far as to use the term occasionally (Osgood, 1957b).

Satisfaction is related to mediator in the sense that the feedback from Purchase, including consumption, is one of the sources, probably the dominant source, of the strength of the association between the mediator and the various integrated response patterns of Figure 4.5. This strength as indicated above is shown by the probabilities in the third column from the left.

Osgood does not concern himself directly with the ambiguity of the brand, the person's subjective capacity to evaluate the significate that is our Confidence, but he does extensively develop the problem of the ambiguity of the stimulus. He does this by way of his concept of hint. He distinguishes between the symbolic and significative stimuli elsewhere, but he does not make this distinction in discussing ambiguity of stimuli and he assumes that the stimulus is the significate. Hence for the role of stimulus ambiguity (Stimulus Ambiguity) and especially significative ambiguity (Confidence) in influencing perception and search we turn mainly to D. E. Berlyne. For the effects of significative ambiguity on overt behavior we make use of Lewin and others (Atkinson, 1964, Chapter 10).

Implicit in all of this discussion of the learning constructs are the arousing and directive forces of Motives. Earlier in this section we said that Choice Criteria link Motives to brands through Attitude. Let us now be explicit about this linking process and thus anchor Choice Criteria firmly into the theory of buyer behavior.

In using the mediator concept to show how a child might acquire the learned motive of fear, we said that the mediator has both arousing and directive effects. By means of it buyers learn to anticipate rewarding and punishing experiences. Thus mediator implies Motives. One dimension of Motives is means-end, as illustrated in Figure 4.2. The lower end of the means-end structure contains Choice Criteria. Choice Criteria represent dimensions of anticipated means of achieving reward and means of avoiding punishment that will be available to a buyer if he purchases any brand in a given product class. These brands are closely substitutable in terms of the motives served.

Thus Choice Criteria are associated with a particular product class and represent latent dimensions on which the buyer evaluates each brand in order to form his Attitude toward that brand. He then buys a particular brand because the brand's attributes evoke the necessary internal and external responses and stimuli, the buyer having come to associate anticipated reward or avoidance of punishment with these attributes.

To elaborate, Choice Criteria are the connotative elements of the product class concept. The product class concept is, of course, the meaning of "product" to the buyer, from which he derives the meaning of a particular brand in that class. This meaning develops through the representational mediation process by which man through the thinking process links such linguistic events as advertising and word-of-mouth discussion to such nonlinguistic events as buying a brand. It is representational in the sense that the process is at the symbolic, not the significative, level of behavior (Figure 4.4); symbols are used to identify, think about, and discuss significative objects such as brands. It is mediational in the sense that it links the symbol and the significative levels of behavior. This mediation process obtains an isomorphism between naming behavior—it is "Campbell's Tomato Soup"—and other culturally conditioned behavior such as the purchase and consumption of Campbell's tomato soup.

This meaning of product class (Choice Criteria) can be empirically measured by the idea of semantic space where the dimensions of the space are the factors derived by factor-analytic techniques from the scores on attitude scales that are relevant for the product class. This view of behavior is largely Osgood's imaginative extension of Hull's theory of "fractional antedating goal-responses," which was advanced to explain the tendency of both animals and humans to anticipate events especially those that have been rewarding or punishing (Hull, 1943; Osgood, 1957a, 1957b; Osgood, Suci, and Tannenbaum, 1957).

In summary, these learning constructs elaborate the response side of Figures 4.4 and 4.5. In Chapter 5 we do the same with the stimulus side. In this way we see a major line of the intellectual development that is involved in the theory of buyer behavior.

4.4 ATTITUDE

Motives give rise to Choice Criteria. Brands in the buyer's evoked set, as identified and denotatively described by Brand Comprehension, are evaluated according to Choice Criteria to yield Attitude. Hence in Attitude these brands are ordered in terms of their potential to satisfy the buyer's motives.*

---

* The buyer's uncertainty in judging a brand against his Choice Criteria is clearly an influence on behavior. It is a moot point at the moment, however, whether it is more productive to treat it as an element of Attitude or as a separate construct. One of the authors prefers to treat it in the first manner and to assume that uncertainty is reflected in the extremity of the buyer's attitude ratings of the brand, since additional information and experience (certainty) make the buyer firmer in his attitude statements. The other author prefers to treat it as a separate construct because this and other uncertainty exert a pivotal influence both on search and on overt purchase behavior as we shall see. In this book we have chosen the latter course.

4.4.1 Definition of Attitude

Attitude is a cognitive state that on a number of dimensions reflects the extent to which the buyer prefers in terms of Motives each brand in his evoked set in relation to other brands in the set. It has only a directive effect and not an arousal or energizing role. Finally, Attitude contains only evaluative information regarding a brand. An example may clarify the definition. Suppose that a buyer wants to satisfy certain motives in buying a convenience food item. He evaluates the brands in that product class in terms of the three purchase criteria that each brand must provide nutrition, must have a low calorie content and, must be moderately priced. The purchase criteria presumably represent the buyer's relevant motives. It is the function of the Choice Criteria, as discussed earlier, to structure the relevant motives, and thereby order as well as aggregate or summate them according to their importance to the buyer. It is by a process of learning that structure is obtained. For example, Choice Criteria may aggregate nutrition and low calories as both representing the health motive and reasonable price as representing the economic value motive. Furthermore, it will state whether the health motive or the economic value motive is more important to the buyer.

Our definition of Attitude differs from several other definitions or descriptions given in cognitive psychology. We shall contrast some of them to show the difference.

The first such conceptualization is Allport's definition of attitudes that he developed after reviewing the literature in 1935. According to Allport, an attitude is (1) a mental or neural state (2) of readiness (3) organized (4) through experience, (5) exerting a directive or dynamic influence upon individual's response to all objects and situations with which it is related. Our definition of Attitude is definitely a mental state and, therefore, uses linguistic encoding and decoding. Second, Attitude is not a readiness to respond in our definition but is the basis for directing the buying response toward a particular brand. Third, Attitude is an *organized* mental state, and we agree with Allport on that aspect. The organization, however, is limited only to the *evaluative* characteristics of the brand, and these are governed by the buyer's motives. Attitude toward a brand is a multidimensional phenomenon. Organization of evaluative characteristics is in terms of these dimensions. Furthermore, Attitude toward one brand is related to Attitude toward other brands in the buyer's evoked set, as well as toward brands that have some broader common connotative significance as in durable appliances that often have one common brand name for several product classes. The relationships between the Attitudes toward various objects of consumption implicitly argue for the relevance of the various cognitive consistency theories. Fourth, we take a broader view of the learning of Attitude than Allport suggests. Allport limits his theory to learning from experience, just as do Doob (1947) and Chein (1948). We have earlier in the chapter presented an extensive description of learning from *information*. In fact, the latter is more crucial in today's society because of mass communication.

A second framework within which to contrast our definition of Attitude with others is the functional approach to the study of attitudes (D. Katz, 1960; D. Katz and Stotland, 1959; Sarnoff and D. Katz, 1954; Smith, Bruner, and White, 1956). In this view, attitudes are formed and undergo change in accordance with the needs they serve, and an understanding of these needs (motivations) may enable us to understand attitudes in their functional role. D. Katz (1960), for example, broadly classifies attitudes into four components: (1) those that serve the instrumental, adjustive, or utilitarian function, (2) those that serve the ego-defensive function, (3) those that serve the value-expressive function, and (4) those that serve the knowledge function. Our definition of Attitude definitely serves the adjustive, utilitarian function. This function is congruent with economic theory as well as learning theory, both of which we have used in our discussion of buyer behavior. Attitude also may serve the knowledge function but only with respect to the structure of evaluative aspects (connotative meanings) of various objects of goal satisfaction.

Attitude, as defined here, incorporates both ego-defensive and value-expressive functions, whereas we interpret Katz as treating all motives associated with purchase as utilitarian. We postulate that whenever the motives implied by these two functions are relevant to a product class, they influence the content of Choice Criteria, which are the dimensions according to which Attitude is formed. Ego-defensive needs are dealt with at some length in Chapter 5, and value-expressive needs are discussed in Chapter 8. Furthermore, both types of motives can operate in the search behavior process as well as in Purchase, but in this book we have left the nature of search behavior largely implicit, current research not being sufficient to easily render it explicit.

A third framework is the cognitive, affective, and conative paradigm. Cognitive elements are the knowledge about the brands and the product class. Affective elements are emotions or feelings toward objects, such as like-dislike. Finally, the conative elements refer to action toward the objects and thus include specific motivations. Our definition of Attitude—an index of the perceived instrumentality of a brand to satisfy a set of motives in terms of purchase criteria—has some characteristics that do not fit into the trichotomy of cognitive-affective-conative elements. We include only those cognitive elements (knowledge) of a brand in the buyer's Attitude that he uses for evaluative purposes. Other cognitive elements that he uses to describe the brand or the product class are part of Brand Comprehension. Also, the affective elements in our definition are not of the general like-dislike type, but represent more specific dimensions. We believe that in the attitude scales described in Chapter 6 affective elements (feelings toward a brand) are implicit in the buyer's evaluation. In other words, in his evaluation of a brand's potential to satisfy his motives, the buyer also generates feelings that are evaluative in nature. Indeed, the broader connotation of the term "affect" when applied to a realm of emotions such as love, hatred and anxiety suggests that affective elements are part of a person's motivational makeup. The conative elements occur because of anchorage of evaluation of a brand in terms of purchase criteria, which presumably represent relevant motives. Again, however, only the directive effects are included, the energizing effects being incorporated in Intention.

In a sense our definition of Attitude, therefore, consists of all the three elements of cognition, affect, and conation but only in a restricted way. Several researchers (D. Campbell, 1947; Kahn, 1951; D. Campbell and Fiske, 1959) have also found the three components to be highly correlated. A high degree of correlation between two components is more commonly obtained by the Michigan researchers represented by Rosenberg (1956), Carlson (1956), and Fishbein (1967). On the other hand, Osgood, Suci, and Tannenbaum (1957), using the semantic differential, obtain orthogonal (independent) factors of evaluation (affective type) and potency and activity (cognitive type), which suggests that possibly there is no correlation. In fact, they restrict the definition of attitude to the evaluative factor. Lavidge and Steiner (1961) also limit preference toward a brand to the affective component. Since their model was presented in order to measure advertising effectiveness, a discussion of the differences between our definition of Attitude and their definition of preference is reserved to Chapters 6 and 9.

A last comment on the definition of Attitude is related to the means-end analysis of attitudes. Several researchers (M. Smith, 1949; DiVesta and Merwin, 1960; Fishbein, 1967; Anderson and Fishbein, 1965; Rosenberg, 1960; Carlson, 1956; Peak, 1955) have considered attitudes toward an object as a composite of the perceived instrumentality of that object to the person's goals, weighted by his saliency of those goals. A common multiplicative formula has been given by Rosenberg (1956), Hovland and Rosenberg (1960), Zajonc (1954), and Fishbein (1967). Our definition of Attitude is closest to this kind of analysis, but there are some important differences. First, the valences of various motives are derived analytically, rather than by directly questioning the consumer, which may be difficult, especially where social inhibitions are active (D. Campbell and Fiske, 1959). Second, only those cognitions of the brand enter into attitude measurement that are *evaluative* in nature.

4.4.2   Attitude Formation and Change

From a marketing point of view, there are two major questions about attitude formation and change: what is the process of change and what are the general determinants in this process? The first is essentially a theory of attitude change, and the second includes the forces specified in the theory, as well as other forces that operate in a field context but are not specified by the theory. For a review see Myers (1968) and Adler and Crespi (1966).

Cognitive consistency is perhaps the most generally accepted explanation of attitude change. The basic principle is that a buyer has a strong need for consistency and attitudes are generally changed in order to eliminate some inconsistency. A buyer sees an advertisement about a new brand which states directly or by implication that the brand is better than the one he is now buying. Thus the buyer is confronted with an inconsistency, which he must reconcile. This is a special case of the general problem of conflict.

There are three versions of the application of the consistency principle—congruity, balance, and dissonance—with congruity being the best worked out. R. Brown (1965) has carefully developed an example of the application of the congruity model, discusses the model in terms of advertising and salesmanship, and evaluates the model.

The buyer can reduce his inconsistency, as we have indicated, by changing his attitude. Hence if the information is unambiguous and credible, the attitude toward the old brand is not related to a number of other cognitions, such as the additional functions discussed above, and the product class is not too important, we would expect attitude change to be the typical mode of reducing inconsistency. There are other modes of reduction, however. The buyer can, for instance, change his perception of the information, especially if the information is ambiguous. The mechanisms that operate here will be discussed in Chapter 5. Also, he can reevaluate or reinterpret particular dimensions of the attitude. Moreover, he can question the credibility of the source of the information. Brehm and Cohen (1962, pp. 306–309) have summarized a considerable body of evidence with respect to modes of inconsistency resolution, but with an emphasis on the dissonance version.

McGuire (1968d) has splendidly compared the formulations from psychology that subsume, supplement, supplant, or oppose the consistency explanation.

In marketing we are concerned primarily with feedback from use of the brand (Satisfaction) and with commercial information as determinants of attitude formation and change. The role of feedback from consumption was emphasized when we discussed the importance of reinforcement in relating the stimulus and the response. The role of commercial information will be examined in Chapters 8 and 9. We must recognize, however, that many other influences operate. Recent buyer research has shown that social communication also makes a considerable difference, hence it, too, will be considered in Chapter 8. Enduring psychological characteristics make a difference, and so we postulate that the exogenous variable of Personality Traits influences Attitude. In addition, there are a number of genetic and physiological factors and, finally, factors emanating from total institutions, all entering into attitude formation and change (McGuire, 1968b, pp. 62–90). We discussed total institutions earlier within the framework of the exogenous variables of Social and Organizational Setting, Social Class, and Culture. It is important to understand the nature of these variables, because so much buyer research is done in a naturalistic setting where, since control is difficult, we need to identify as many sources of variation as possible.

4.5 INTENTION (TO BUY)

Attitude gives direction to purchase behavior—the tendency to buy one brand instead of another—but it does not incorporate a number of other forces that bear upon purchase. Hence there are discrepancies between Attitude and Purchase, and we would expect these to be much greater in naturalistic settings than in the laboratory. *Intention* is postulated to incorporate these additional forces to the extent that the buyer anticipates them. Thus Intention links Attitude to Purchase.

Intention is defined as a cognitive state that reflects the buyer's *plan* to buy units of a particular brand in some specified time period. Intention reflects his Attitude, his Confidence, and his anticipations about certain constraints which inhibit the effects of Attitude and Confidence. These constraints are elements of his plan, and Intention is the uncompleted portion of the plan. Hence, Intention carries us up to the point of choice and so we avoid the necessity for purchase as a hypothetical construct.

The ex ante–ex post distinction is useful in discussing these constraints. A buyer with a firm favorable Attitude toward a brand and looking forward in time to buying this brand has from his information and experience come to expect certain events in his environment that will tend to constrain his purchase. These constraints are called inhibitors, because they inhibit the buyer from making the choice indicated by his Attitude. The buyer also expects these events or inhibitors to have certain values or intensities. This ex ante situation is reflected in his statement of Intention. After he has bought—the ex post situation—he may well find that he encountered constraining events he had not anticipated or that the events were of different values than anticipated. This ex post information is not relevant to his Intention. Like Attitude, Intention has a great amount of surplus meaning, as we shall see in the discussion that follows.

To make the meaning of Intention more specific, we assume Intention and Purchase to be perfectly consistent at the time of Purchase. One of the reasons for using the construct is the availability of data—data about Intention, not only are easier to collect, but, more importantly, can be taken at a different and earlier point in time than purchase data. In one case the buyer fixes the time, and in the other the researcher fixes it. To the extent, however, that the lag is greater between the measure of Intention and the act of Purchase, greater discrepancies between Intention and Purchase would be expected, because the buyer must *anticipate* environmental changes that will occur after the Intention measure and before Purchase. The longer the period of anticipation, the greater we would expect the anticipation to err. That humans do learn to anticipate events we learned in the discussion of Motive and Choice Criteria. Also, technically, Intention is the uncompleted portion of a plan *whose execution has begun.* How serious this condition is in complicating measurement remains to be discovered.

The simple example of a buyer's plan shown in Figure 4.6 will make clear the construct of Intention. This description of a buyer's plan was developed by repeated interviewing of a person living in New London, New Hampshire, but its truth has not been tested because of lack of data. Box 1 is the triggering device, which prompts Box 2, where a comparison is made between the actual and desired levels of gas in the tank. If the tank is more than one-fourth full, the buyer proceeds on his intended trip; if it is not, he proceeds to Box 3. The reader can follow through the diagram with ease and identify each of the conditions (inhibitors) that this buyer viewed as relevant in his gasoline purchasing.

The diagram also clearly reveals the difference between information-processing rules and decision rules. Except for the initial and terminal boxes and Boxes 5 and 11, each box represents an information-processing

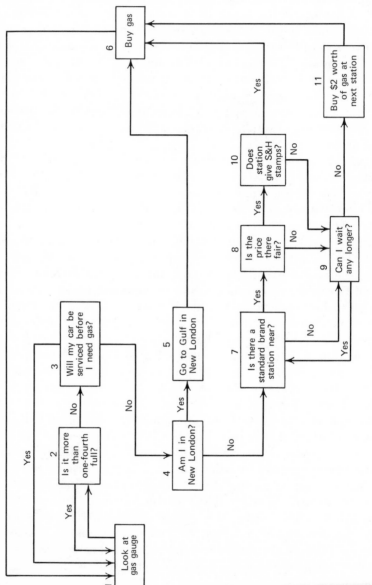

Figure 4.6 Plan of motorist buying gasoline.

rule; for example, in Box 2 the buyer must have information about both the required minimum level and the actual level of gas in the tank and must compare the two in a particular way. Each box is connected with another box, however, by an implicit decision rule, such as "If my tank is less than one-fourth full, I ask myself whether my car will be serviced before I need gas."

Also, we can see the implicit role of Attitude. This buyer prefers Gulf gasoline, as shown in the relation between Box 4 and Box 5, but he may or may not buy Gulf, depending on the conditions described by the other boxes. These conditions are inhibitors on Attitude toward Gulf.

Finally, we can see the relation between the plan and Intention. Intention is the uncompleted portion of the plan. If the buyer were asked, at Box 2, whether he intended to buy Gulf gasoline, he would, we presume, answer in the affirmative. If asked at Box 7, however, we suspect that his intention would be less positive.

Having briefly examined an example of a plan that underlies Intention, let us relate the concept of a plan to mediator. As we said in discussing Choice Criteria, a mediator can be viewed as a structured sequence of internal stimuli and responses and may be thought of as information-processing rules and decision rules in which the elements—stimuli and responses—become associated through either experience or information. The internal stimuli and responses link any external stimulus and response and thus also the initiating stimulus (S) and ultimate response (R). The S is a complex sign for the significate instead of the significate itself, whereas the R is some fractional portion of the total complex behavior that would have been elicited had the buyer been exposed to the significate instead of the sign, that is, to the physical brand instead of the advertisement. Mediators *mediate* or link the responses made to the relevant significate with those made to the symbol, and they are some form of nervous system response (Diebold, 1965). The use of language (symbols) and thinking are intimately bound together.

A mediator representing sequential behavior, such as that involved in the purchase of a new brand, can be shown graphically as follows, S and R being external and s and r internal:

$$S–r–s–R–S–r–s–R$$

The first S might be an advertisement, for example, and the final R, a purchase. The length of this chain is defined in an arbitrary manner, depending on the needs of the study, because *buying* like any other act is merely a portion of an ongoing stream of acts that together constitute *total behavior*. The middle R could be a question that the buyer put to his friend about the merit of the brand, and the middle S could be the friend's reply. The final R could be an act required in consuming the product, as is the case when the consumption behavior itself affects the choice of a particular brand.

With this linkage of the concept of Intention to mediator as an underlying rationale, let us turn to a model of executive decision that has been tested and found to be a true description. We think it provides a sounder foundation for speculating about the nature of Intention. Figure 4.7 charts the sequence of steps that occurred in an executive's pricing decision process (Howard and Morgenroth, 1968). The initating external S in this case was the report from the district sales office (Box 1) of the price per unit being charged at a competing retail establishment. This S triggered an internal response (r) in the form of the question, "Has my price changed?" implied in Box 2. This internal response became an internal stimulus (s), which triggered an answer, "yes" or "no." An examination of the figure will reveal that the boxes represent the buyer's information-processing rules; for example, Box 2 represents two pieces of information compared in a particular way. Furthermore, the relation between two boxes implies a decision rule; for example, the relation between Box 3 and Box 4 implies "If the price is an increase, I ask myself whether it is an increase or a decrease."

What is the relation between Intention and Attitude in Figure 4.7? Although Attitude is not shown, it can be easily inferred by the nature of the situation. The market demand for this product is highly inelastic, variable costs are constant over a very wide range of changes in volume, and the executive is largely evaluated by short-term profits. Hence if the initiating competitor had increased the price (see Box 3), our executive strongly prefers a higher price. If the initiator had lowered the price, our executive strongly prefers the old price. In other words, except for the effects of the inhibitors represented in Intention, our executive always prefers the highest possible price.

Where is Intention in Figure 4.7? If the executive whose thought processes are represented in the figure were asked, "Do you intend to change price in Detroit next week?" presumably he would run through the model and, in the boxes requiring data that will develop between now and next week, would estimate future values and state his intention. His estimates of future values would be *anticipations* about his environment. Intention is defined as the uncompleted portion of a plan. In terms of Figure 4.7, Intention depends, of course, on when the Intention measure is taken. If taken at the time of Box 1, Intention is the whole process. Here we see the possibility that Intention may not lead to Purchase, because the executive's anticipations about environmental variables can be wrong even in a well-planned decision, as the one repre-

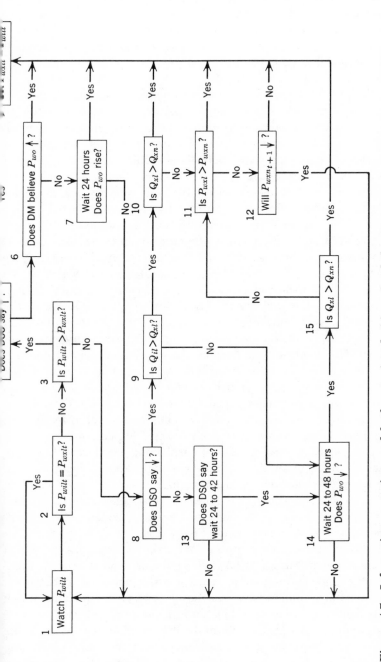

Figure 4.7 Information-processing model of executive decision. *Symbols:* P, price; w, wholesale; i, initiator; l, local market; n, nearby market; t, time; DSO, district sales office; DM, decision maker; x, decision-maker's company; o, other major competitors (neither i nor x); and Q, expected physical volume of sales.

sented here happens to be. Thus this plan represents a *strategy:* the outcome depends on the information that exists at the moment. In simpler situations, such as a more stable environment, we would expect a *fixed-response* plan, where Intention would be a better predictor of Purchase, although even here social pressures, for example, could operate as inhibitors.

Also, the plan of Figure 4.7 includes *stop rules.* These are provisions for no-purchase situations, for example. All of the lines terminating in Box 1 represent stop rules. It is important to bear in mind that no choice is not a special case of choice, because it requires no allocation of resources. Stop rules are especially important in explaining why no purchase occurs even though Attitude is favorable to a brand.

In terms of historical development, the rule concept may seem far removed from the concept of mediation. As we have indicated earlier, mediation was developed particularly by Osgood out of Hull's work, in an effort to extend the principles of simple stimulus-response analysis to the complex behavior described by the representational level of Figure 4.4. As Campbell has shown, the $_sH_r$ of Hull's model, which is the basis of neobehavioristic thinking, is the counterpart of Lewin's "structured pathways to the goal region" (D. Campbell, 1963). Lewin's work is a foundation stone of cognitive psychology, and Reitman has integrated the concept of the information-processing rule into cognitive psychology (Reitman, 1965). One of the prominent neo-behaviorists, Berlyne, treats "rule" analysis of behavior as an alternative to stimulus-response, as, we suspect, most behaviorists would (Berlyne, 1966, pp. 166–168). However, Reitman correctly points out that to use the information-processing or rule approach implies no intellectual commitment: "You can be a Hullian, a Lewinian, or a Freudian" (Reitman, 1966 1, p. 5).

It is possible to go still further in explaining the logic of a plan. Following G. Miller et al. (1960), but continuing explicitly with the consistency hypothesis referred to in discussing attitude change, which in turn is an aspect of conflict, we postulate, first, that there is a basic building block of human behavior that can be called the TOTE unit (test-operate-test-exit); it is shown in Figure 4.8.

The principle is that the activity that a buyer performs is guided by the outcomes of various tests. If the test yields no difference (consistency), he does nothing. If it yields a discrepancy (inconsistency), he does something, and here we use the general term "operate," which can apply to asking questions, as here, or to some overtly physical activity, such as driving a nail. Let us illustrate the latter. A man is repairing his boat dock by driving down those nails that over the years have "worked out." He "tests" each nail to see if it should be driven in.

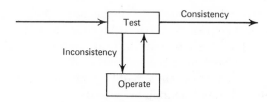

Figure 4.8 TOTE unit.

If it is not flush with the board, he "operates" by hitting it with the hammer, then "tests" again to see if it is flush with the board now, and so on. The stimulus thus is not an absolute value but a difference.

Returning to our information-processing model, in Box 2 of Figure 4.7 the executive "tests" by asking himself, "Is the wholesale price of the initiator in the local market at time t different from my price in that market?" If the answer is negative, there is no inconsistency, hence no "operation" and no change. The test has revealed consistency. If the answer were affirmative, when the executive "tested," he would "operate," that is, he would go to Box 3. In this way we can trace through the entire diagram of Figure 4.7 in terms of the TOTE unit pictured in Figure 4.8.

Second, we postulate that plans for action are arranged in hierarchical order. Plans for very specific behavior are triggered and guided by more general or higher-order plans. We know that many housewives do not, on a given shopping trip, plan to buy a particular item, as suggested by Kollat and Willett (1967). By strict definition, buying this item would then be impulse purchase. On the other hand, we suspect that these housewives have a more general plan of shopping, which triggers and guides the specific plan for purchasing a given item at a given time. For example, on every third trip to the supermarket the housewife may deliberately walk past every display so as to be reminded of items that she needs. If so, the definition of planned shopping used by Kollat and Willett is too restrictive for companies studying the effects of their advertising. A longer time period of possible purchase should be specified in the question of when buying occurs, perhaps one that covers the regular purchase cycle.

We suspect that the higher-order plans also affect many buying-related decision processes, such as deciding from which store to buy.

4.5.1 *Inhibitors*

Intention incorporates constraints or inhibitors. One distinguishing feature of inhibitors is that they are noninternalized forces. This characterization is warranted by research on dissonance which suggests that a person can exhibit behavior contrary to his attitude and still not experience dissonance if he feels that he has no control over the event: he then treats it as a constraint (Cohen, 1964). We expect, however, that with time some of these constraints may become internalized, hence their effect may be shifted from Intention to Attitude.

In discussing inhibitors, a sharp distinction must be made between inhibiting the buyer's behavior and inhibiting his preference as reflected in his Attitude. We are concerned only with the latter. These events limit or inhibit the power of Attitude to shape behavior. True enough an inhibitor such as a low price can supplement the effect of high Attitude to increase the probability of purchase. In this sense an inhibitor would seem to be supportive of Attitude. Nevertheless, the power or capacity of Attitude to shape behavior is still being limited by it. We use "inhibitor" to emphasize the void between Attitude and overt behavior seldom discussed in the literature of cognitive psychology although of late it has received somewhat greater attention.

What is the source of the noninternalized constraints—the inhibitors—that are contained in Intention? We can think of them as being divided into two classes: those currently emanating from the buyer's environment and those carried over from past environments and contained in his exogenous variables.

The first group of inhibitors can be further divided into commercial and social. Price is one of the commercial influences, but it has two meanings to a buyer. It can be a constraint, but it can also signify quality (McConnell, 1968). Using price as a measure of quality is quite rational behavior in the sense that the buyer learns that brand price and brand quality are associated, in fact, on more than a chance basis. Consequently, when his information about the varieties of alternative brands is very poor, price becomes a valid cue. Our concern with price here, however, is entirely as a constraint, not as a quality cue.

Price is a central variable in partial equilibrium analysis of economic theory, and economists have extensively theorized about it. The empirical work, however, has been largely limited to situations where all alternatives in the product class are highly similar and even identical, so that price becomes very important to the buyer in discriminating among alternatives, and, correspondingly, the differences among sellers' prices are negligible. More recently, researchers of marketing have studied price effects in situations where "brands are differentiated" and major interbrand price differences sometimes exist. To the best of our knowledge, these diverse marketing-oriented studies have not been summarized and generalizations are lacking. One safe generalization is that the effects of price on purchase behavior vary enormously according to whether the price difference is advertised. We have seen no empirical attempts to relate price to Intention directly.

Another commercial inhibitor is the availability of the brand in the retail store. For many low-price items, perhaps even for most, the buyer is not inclined to shop or to go outside his regular shopping routine in one or two stores to find a preferred brand. Under these conditions, the brand's availability in the store makes a great difference, so that whether the buyer thinks that it is available makes a difference in his Intention. Obviously, not all cases are so black and white; for example, the brand can be made available by the store manager if the buyer will wait a few days. Moreover, location within the store—whether the brand is displayed at eye level or is "hidden" by the retailer in an obscure place—can affect purchase.

Not only price and availability, but other "in-store" influences can be incorporated into the plan. We can then see the intimate connection that exists between the plan to buy a brand and the higher-order plan that involves, in the first place, the decision at which retail store to shop. Relating the higher- and lower-order plans should be a fruitful area of research.

Social influences on behavior operate by way of internalization, identification, or compliance (Kelman, 1961). These processes will be examined at length in Chapters 8 and 9 and here we mention them only briefly. Internalization occurs when as a consequence of information from the other person, the buyer perceives the brand as serving his needs. Identification occurs when someone whom the buyer admires and likes suggests, for example, that he buy a particular brand. Compliance occurs when someone, who has social power over the buyer, suggests that the buyer use a particular brand. We think of the compliance process as generating inhibitors for the buyer and thus affecting his Intention. Internalization and identification are predicted to affect Attitude but they have differential effects.

As for the role of exogenous influences in changing Intention, we postulate that the social variables—Social and Organization Setting, Social Class, and Culture—as well as Financial Status and Time Pressure serve as inhibiting effects that are captured in Intention.

4.5.2   Plan Formation

The process by which a plan is formed and extinguished is not well understood. As Modigliani and Cohen have stated in describing the role of intention data in predicting the level of economic activity, "Actually, the problem of how anticipations are formed and revised falls on the borderline of traditional economics, and it may well be that advances in this area will require closer cooperation between economists, psychologists, and other social scientists" (Modigliani and Cohen, 1961, p. 152). "Anticipations" as used here is really an expectation about the value of an inhibitor.

Generalization, both physical and mediated, it is our guess, is one of the dominant processes by which plans are acquired. Technically, it is response generalization, and it is well illustrated in the supermarket. A housewife on her regular shopping trip buys many items, some of which are probably very similar in terms of operative inhibitors, and this may be true even of the new product class for which she yet has no plan. The transfer of an old plan used for a similar product class to the new product class could easily take place. A favorable condition to the transfer would be some intensity of motive but not too much.

For new purchase situations that are quite different so that generalization of the total plan does not occur, a higher level of thinking is required. The housewife may ask herself whether she has seen analogous problems; for example, to identify relevant inhibitors in buying a television set she may call upon some electronics experience. We know that people use a number of heuristics in solving complex problems (Newell, Shaw, and Simon, 1958).

If she has solved the problem once and made a purchase, the strength of the plan in guiding her succeeding purchase behavior will be determined, to a great extent, by the number of times the plan is repeated. The reader will recall from the discussion of Choice Criteria that Osgood hypothesizes that reinforcement is not necessary for learning response integrations, and this suggests that contiguity will suffice to bring the various individual acts together to form a well-structured plan.

The intensity of Motives also presumably makes a difference. If the intensity is too low, the housewife is less likely to develop a plan. Correspondingly, too high an intensity would impede learning. Once performance is well learned, however, increased Motives should be related linearly to intensity of Intention, to the anticipated performance of the purchase-associated acts implied in the plan that underlies Intention.

Also, it may be fruitful to think about differences among buyers in their purchase plans as a basis for identifying individual differences. It may well be that research on the structure of plans will cause us to view plans as a part of human personality just as we now view need structure. There has already been some effort in that direction (Kollat and Willett, 1968), although it is not conceptualized in this way.

4.5.3   Empirical Evidence

Is there empirical evidence that supports our postulate that Intention is positively related to Purchase? Economists, who in attempting to predict the level of sales of consumer durable items such as television, washing machines, and houses have researched the construct more than anyone else, but have approached it primarily from the realistic end of the realism-ideal continuum presented in Chapter 1, and have done little theorizing. To predict the purchase of a product class is quite a different matter, however, from predicting brand choice, given the purchase of the product class. Controversy still exists as to the usefulness of intentions for predicting product choice in consumer durables (Ferber, 1966; Juster, 1966). Such difference of opinion is consistent with our theory for two reasons. First, in the case of consumer durables a time interval could elapse between the measurement of the intention variable and the purchase act itself. In the interim the buyer could have received new information to cause him to change his expectations or his needs, hence his Intention. Second, the buyer is more likely to receive information in the case of consumer durables because he exerts more shopping effort on them than on nondurables, hence is more apt to obtain new information before buying.

Dulany (1968), in an experimental context involving verbal behavior, has developed a sophisticated and rigorous way of conceptualizing intention which logically relates his measuring instruments to the construct. By manipulating intention and related variables, he has typically obtained correlation coefficients greater than 0.9 between intention and overt behavior.

The effects of intention on brand choice have been studied (Rothman, 1964; Wells, 1961), with Ehrenberg (1966) doing the most extensive analysis, but unfortunately mostly at the aggregate level, which weakens its contribution for our purposes. After having investigating twenty product fields, each of which was apparently broader than a product class, he concludes that the relationship $I = K/U$, where I is Intention, U is Purchase (Usage), and K is a constant, fits most of the products with a mean deviation $(I - K/U)$ of about 3 percentage points. For new products, however, the error was systematically much larger: K varied between 6 and 17.

4.6   CONFIDENCE (IN CHOICE)

Confidence plays a major role in the buyer behavior system. It is postulated to be positively related to Intention and negatively related to Motives (arousal), which in turn affects the buyer's information input by way of Attention and Overt Search. The second aspect will be developed in Chapter 5.

Because of its dual role, Confidence is the central equilibrating construct of the system. When Confidence is low, the buyer seeks information and is less likely to Purchase. As information is acquired, Confidence rises and the probability of Purchase increases. As Confidence increases, however, the buyer's tendency to take in information declines. When a satisfactory purchase is made, Confidence increases still further. Eventually brand loyalty is achieved and information is closed out. Underlying the equilibrating role of Confidence is, of course, the equilibrating role of Motive—Purchase probability increases as Confidence increases because Motives is freed from the restraining effect of uncertainty.

Confidence is the inverse of brand ambiguity, and brand ambiguity has to do with the significate. Stimulus ambiguity has to do with the symbol. Confidence is the extent to which the buyer believes that he can estimate the net payoff, that is, the reward from buying a given brand. "Net" refers to the difference between the total reward and the deterring effects of inhibitors and negative Motives.

Confidence is similar to the expectancy concept of both cognitive psychology, summarized by Atkinson (1964), and decision theory. It differs from expectancy, however. The value of the brand to which it relates is much more elaborated. The cognitive theorists think of attitude toward the brand as being the value of the alternative, whereas the decision theorists think of the value as being the expected utility of the brand as measured by the standard gamble. It is our belief that both of these views omit the role of inhibitors as reflected in Intention which are probably quite important in many purchases. The incorporation of the inhibitors provides us with a more elaborated concept of expectancy or probability. Included in this more global concept of Confidence is the buyer's uncertainty about the state of the inhibitors that are operative in the actual choice and purchase acts. Also, it includes the uncertainty about aspects of the consumption of the brand.

The effect of high Confidence is to free the buyer to follow the dictates of his Attitude as modified by Intention, instead of experiencing the "drag," the expenditure of nervous energy that occurs when acting in the face of great doubt and high stakes.

Is the relationship between Confidence and Purchase additive or multiplicative? It is usually postulated to be multiplicative, as Atkinson (1964, pp. 274–277) has shown in his summary.

What support can be assembled for the idea that Confidence and Purchase are positively related? Atkinson summarizes the a priori evidence well, but does not give empirical support (Atkinson, 1964, pp. 274–276). Juster (1966), however, found that consumers who were more confident in the intention to buy a consumer durable were more likely to carry out their intention than were those who were not confident. Johnson found that those who were more confident in their ability to judge a brand were more likely to buy it (Johnson, 1968).

4.7 SATISFACTION

Satisfaction does not affect Purchase directly, as do Attitude and Intention, but instead is our first case of a servomechanistic relation—a purchase and consumption feedback relation—which has more complex consequences than the straightforward relations discussed so far. We set it out here as a hypothetical construct because we think it desirable to have some such construct short of the reduction of motive intensity.

Some may question the use of Satisfaction on the grounds that it is implied in the reduction of Motives intensity. We believe that especially for field research it is essential to set out an explicit link and to develop empirical content of this link, as we recently found that D. Katz (1967), too, has argued. We believe that this content could greatly strengthen our understanding of product design. It could improve our grasp of which particular dimensions of our product cause the purchase of it.

Satisfaction is defined as the buyer's cognitive state of being adequately or inadequately rewarded in a buying situation for the sacrifice he has undergone. The adequacy is a consequence of matching actual past purchase and consumption experience with the reward that was expected from the brand in terms of its anticipated potential to satisfy the Motives served by the particular product class. Most of the reinforcement will be derived from consuming the brand, but occasionally the mere act of purchase may also be rewarding, such as shopping in a high-prestige store. We must recognize that Satisfaction is not necessarily the same as some objective evaluation of reward; for example, the satisfaction derived from a gift of $10 can vary among people and for a given person over time (Homans, 1961).

We have emphasized the reinforcement effects of feedback—greater satisfaction causes increased Attitude for the respective brand in evoked set—but, as Spence has postulated, feedback from experience with the brand also affects habit. Hence we extend our formulation and postulate that feedback also affects Choice Criteria and the motor habits of purchase and consumption. The effect on Choice Criteria and motor habits is postulated to vary directly with the *number* of purchases instead of the amount of reinforcement from those purchases.

Satisfaction enables us to deal directly with the often discussed issue of whether Attitude causes Purchase or Purchase causes Attitude. As we see here, Purchase can indirectly affect Attitude through Satisfaction. Directly, however, the direction of causation is from Attitude to Purchase.

A number of elements determine the amount of the effect of Satisfaction on Attitude: its intensity, the relation between anticipated and actual Satisfaction, its certainty, its latency, and its periodicity.

4.7.1 Intensity of Satisfaction

It is clear that the amount of reinforcement, measured indirectly by the reduction of the intensity of the Motives that the goal object satisfies, in terms of hours of food deprivation, for example, affects behavior. This fact has been thoroughly documented in the laboratory with simple, nonchoice, nonpurchasing behavior. The relation between reward and behavior, however, has not been nearly so well studied under conditions of choice. Most of the laboratory studies pose simple one-alternative situations with "behavior" and "nonbehavior," instead of the choice situation that involves choosing between two or more closely similar alternatives. The nature of the general relation between reinforcement and behavior in the multiple-alternative case is not known, except that it is positive. Yet the few studies that have been done under choice conditions are reasonably consistent with the experiments done in simpler situations (Bush and Mosteller, 1955). To our knowledge, there have been no systematic field studies of this central influence in buying behavior, but it is implicit in all marketing research studies. For an interesting laboratory study see Lo Sciuto, Strassmann, and Wells (1967).

Only recently has evidence been found to support the proposition that Attitude can be learned in the same way as habit, that is, by reinforcement (J. Howard, 1963). Classical conditioning techniques have been used to instill attitudes toward the socially significant verbal stimuli of nationality names and familiar masculine names (Staats and Staats, 1958). Two other experiments in the same vein are reported where it is argued that attitudes are learned as concepts (Rhine, 1958). Furthermore, attitudes toward unfamiliar social objects were learned through conditioning. It was also found that attitudes generalize from one object to a similar one (Rhine and Silun, 1958). Both of these characteristics of Attitude—they are learned and they generalize—cause us to think of Attitude as responding to Satisfaction in the same way in which, according to laboratory experiments, overt behavior responds to reinforcement.

4.7.2 Expected versus Actual Satisfaction

Attitude involves an expectation or anticipation of satisfaction from buying a given brand. Some laboratory evidence from a nonbuying context suggests that if the buyer's expected satisfaction has been greater than his actual satisfaction turns out to be, his final satisfaction will be smaller as a result. Let us see how this might occur.

Before the purchase of a brand, the buyer has an expectation represented in Attitude (A_t). After purchasing the brand, he proceeds to consume it and thus to derive certain actual satisfaction, which is Satisfaction (S_{t+1}). $(S_{t+1} - A_t)$ depends on the difference between his anticipated satisfaction (A_t) and his actual satisfaction (S_{t+1}) and f is a mathematical operator of some kind which preserves the sign. If $S_{t+1} > A_t$, the effect of Satisfaction on Attitude will be greater than if $S_{t+1} < A_t$. Thus we can now state the equation that reflects the effect of the relation between Attitude (expected satisfaction) and actual Satisfaction on Attitude:

$$A_{t+2} = f(S_{t+1} - A_t) + A_t$$

The final outcome is A_{t+2}, which is Attitude after all effects of Satisfaction from this purchase upon Attitude have been worked out.

The problem is more complex when there are many inhibitors. We predict that the greater the inhibitory effects, the less will be the net satisfaction; for example, a buyer normally enjoys a brand less if he pays more for it. Cordoza has presented contrary evidence in laboratory study of buying which indicates that *more* shopping effort by the buyer can increase his evaluation of the amount of satisfaction he receives from the purchase (Cordoza, 1965). Whether this interpretation is correct for these types of circumstances is currently a matter of debate (McGuire, 1966a).

This principle of disappointment—an emotional response that occurs when actual Satisfaction is less than expected Satisfaction—suggests that for a marketer to build too high an expectation for a brand can be undesirable. One of the manufacturers of a high-quality shampoo maintains that it has difficulty introducing new products because consumers expect the quality to be much higher than that of competitors and are disapppoined if this is not always so.

The principle also helps to explain the content of evoked set. If there is extreme disappointment in the quality of the satisfaction received from purchase and consumption, the brand, we postulate, will be dropped from the buyer's evoked set because the buyer admits into his evoked set only those brands that offer him adequate expected satisfaction, as we saw at the beginning of the chapter. As we did there, we postulate again that adequacy is determined by the buyer's level of aspiration. Level of aspiration is a useful concept in a market where information is less than perfect, which is of course by all odds the most typical situation. The buyer expects the level of performance to be acceptable to his image of himself, his ego, his self-concept (Lewin, Dembo, Festinger, and Sears, 1944; Atkinson, 1964, pp. 96–101).

Let us now relate the concept of evoked set to the discussion here. In Section 4.3 it was said that motivation can be viewed as a self-equilibrating system: tension arises because a need exists (an unsatisfied state), the need leads to action that is intended to satisfy the need, the action satisfies the need, and the tension declines (a satisfied state). However, the boundary between the satisfied and unsatisfied states of the buyer (the level of aspiration) is also variable. As the buyer purchases and is repeatedly satisfied, his level of aspiration rises and may render a brand in his evoked set unacceptable. If so, this brand is dropped from his evoked set, and a new brand is chosen to replace it.

On the other hand, if a buyer has difficulty in finding adequate brands after extensive search, his level of aspiration will decline, and henceforth he will admit brands of a lower quality to his evoked set than he would have before.

The concept of level of satisfaction provides, via its effect on evoked set, a dynamic framework for understanding a number of aspects of the buyer's purchasing pattern.

4.7.3 Ambiguity of Satisfaction

When the reinforcement is received from Purchase, it can still be ambiguous. Ambiguity arises either because the buyer's Motives are not clear—not well summated—or because the contribution of brands to given goals is not clear. This lack of clear-cut evaluation can be illustrated in an actual industrial buying situation.

An industrial purchasing agent had been buying welding rods from Supplier A for a number of years and had been receiving satisfactory statements from his company's plants about the quality of the rods. For internal reasons Supplier A changed the numbering system by which the rods were identified, and the purchasing agent of the buying company immediately began to receive complaints from the welders in the plants about the quality of the rods. The welders thought that it was a different kind of rod than they had been using. The functional or technical contribution of the rod was not discriminable enough for the workers to use the rod's quality as a means of identifying it, and so they resorted to using the numbering system. At the purchasing agent's suggestion, the selling company went back to its old numbering system, and the complaints ceased.

This example also illustrates a second kind of ambiguity that often arises in practice. The buyer is purchasing for consumption by someone else—someone in the plant, in our example of industrial purchasing—and this consumer may not report his satisfaction in an adequate manner. In fact, in industrial purchasing the user will commonly report no feedback at all to the buyer, unless a product fails badly.

The more ambiguous the satisfaction, the less it will affect Attitude. This relation can be conceptualized in terms of expected value: the greater the uncertainty, the less the expected payoff.

4.7.4 Latency of Receipt of Satisfaction

Still another dimension of reinforcement that influences Satisfaction is the period of time that elapses between purchase and the receipt of reinforcement from that purchase. In many products, for example, consumer durables, the period is quite long between the purchase and the final reinforcement. The greater the latency of reward, the less the satisfaction. Nonreinforcement is, of course, merely the extreme case of delay in reinforcement.

4.7.5 Periodicity of Satisfaction

Periodicity has to do with the temporal pattern in which satisfaction is obtained. Latency of reinforcement discussed above is merely a special case of the general problem of periodicity. Considerable research has been done on this dimension of Satisfaction under the rubric of "partial reinforcement." Studies of partial reinforcement seem to give results contrary to the general principle that greater Satisfaction increases Attitude. In partial reinforcement studies it has been found, for example, that intermittent instead of regular reward has a greater effect on learning than does regular reinforcement. A more careful explanation suggests that the reason is that, in line with the discussion of disappointment, partial reinforcement leads to disappointed expectations of Satisfaction and the disappointment gives rise to frustrations. These frustrations, in turn, increase the intensity of Motives and so the probability of action is enhanced via the effect of arousal on intention, but it does not increase learning (Attitude) (Spence, 1960).

Five general patterns of reinforcement have been investigated: continuous, variable ratio, fixed ratio, variable interval, and fixed interval (Ferster and Skinner, 1957). Continuous reinforcement—each buyer is rewarded as soon as he buys—has been found to be the most effective. Variable ratio refers to the case where a buyer is reinforced after a given *average* number of purchases but the actual number varies from time to time. It is less effective than the first but more effective than the following three. Fixed ratio applies where the buyer is rewarded according to a fixed number of purchases; variable interval, according to varied periods of time after the purchase; and fixed interval, according to a given period after the purchase. None of these patterns so far as we know have been studied in a buying context, and their significance remains to be worked out.

4.8 PURCHASE DECISION

The three subprocesses that make up what we globally call "the decision process" are: Extensive Problem Solving, Limited Problem Solving, and Routinized Response Behavior. We define them as intervening variables and in this way formulate a typology of decision situations (J. Howard, 1963). First, the buyer is unfamiliar with the product class of the brand with which he is first being confronted. This process is Extensive Problem Solving. Second, the buyer is familiar with the product class of the brand with which he is confronted, but he is unfamiliar with the brand. This less complex process is Limited Problem Solving. Third, there is the case of the buyer who is familiar with both the product class and the brand. Both Attitude and Confidence are high with respect to the preferred brand in his evoked set. It is called Routinized Response Behavior. Let us examine it here, since it is needed to complete the picture of the total purchasing process. The first case will be dealt with in Chapter 8 and the second case, though implied in this chapter will be developed in Chapter 5.

The beginning point of this third process is usually an increase in the buyer's Motives in response to some external event. Motivational equilibrium is disturbed. A particular motive or set of motives has risen in the dominance hierarchy of the buyer's motive structure to a point where it demands satisfaction at the expense of all other activities if need be and here as usual Motives are associated with a particular product class.

Given this relative intensity of motive strength and given that preference (Attitude) among the brands in the product class is clear and unambiguous, two other hypothetical constructs come into play. First, the absolute intensity of Motives must be great enough to overcome the inhibitors that interfere with the action. Second, whether Motives are intense enough depends not only on the inhibitors but also on Confidence. If Confidence is high, the buyer's motives that are relevant to this product class are free to energize action and so overcome inhibitors. If Confidence is low, action will be impeded.

When the values of the three constructs—Attitude, Confidence, and Intention—are not such as to yield action, the stop rule that we mentioned in discussing Intention is said to operate.

This type of decision process can be described as being in purchase equilibrium. Except for the situation variables represented as inhibitors in his purchase plan, he will exhibit a high probability of buying his preferred brand.

Routinized Response Behavior is the stage envisioned in most of the economic and decision-theoretic literature. The economist describes it as the case where "tastes are given." For us it is the least interesting stage. We are more concerned with the dynamics of the path by which the buyer achieves this equilibrium, which will be further discussed in Chapter 5. From the standpoint of the seller, however, it is very important. As one executive put it, "A loyal buyer is worth seven times as much to us as an occasional buyer."

In purchase equilibrium, brand choice is not a fixed response, however, but a strategy, its outcome depending on the ex post state of the buyer's inhibitors in his plan to buy that underlies his Intention. Thus the probability of choosing the preferred brand from among the other brands in his evoked set is someting less than 1.0.

Finally, we see here how the motivational equilibrating process occurs within the framework of the purchase equilibrium. In the next chapter we discuss information equilibrium, which is an essential element in purchase equilibrium.

4.9 SUMMARY OF LEARNING CONSTRUCTS

Each of the seven learning constructs has been defined and its role in the structure of the theory described. This description assumed that the stimulus-as-coded was a perfect counterpart of the physical stimulus. In the next chapter we drop this assumption and proceed to define and describe variables that explain why and how the stimulus-as-coded may differ considerably from the physical stimulus.

CHAPTER 5

Perceptual Subsystem

We have emphasized repeatedly that buyers learn from both experience and information. The effects of *experience* as a feedback from Satisfaction upon Attitude shape the expected values of the brands in the buyer's evoked set. *Information* in the form of both significative and symbolic cues is the means by which the buyer learns Motives, Choice Criteria, Brand Comprehension, the value of each brand (Attitude) within his evoked set, and Confidence in judging each brand, as well as Intention to buy each brand. These cues may be either social or commercial. Hence we now focus on the perceptual subsystem (Attention, Overt Search, Stimulus Ambiguity, and Perceptual Bias) which, as described in Chapter 3, converts the external event—the stimulus—into a stimulus-as-coded (Lawrence, 1963; Egeth, 1967). The s-a-c becomes an input in the learning subsystem and is converted into an influence on Purchase.

The s-a-c can differ sharply from the objective stimulus, which hampers the attempt to understand buying behavior, especially under field conditions where the Stimulus Display and contextual cues are often quite ambiguous. We are concerned here with explaining the nature of the perceptual coding response, the mechanisms by which the raw stimulus is transformed into an s-a-c.

The effect of information on the variables that make up the learning subsystem is not a unilateral one. The learning variables, for their part, also affect the *quantity* and *quality* or meaning of the information, because there are a number of feedbacks into the perceptual process from Motives, Attitude, and Confidence which influence the effects of the incoming information. These hypothetical constructs and their interac-

152

tions explain why an advertisement is "seen" by some people and not by others even though all are exposed to it (Chapter 3) and why a given person "sees" it today but not next week even though he is exposed to it at both times. Also, the constructs explain why some new products fail and others do not. The full significance of this bilateral relation between information and learning will be examined in Chapters 8 and 9, since here we are concerned only with the pure theory of buyer behavior.

A new type of element is encountered in the perceptual subsystem. So far all of our elements have been entities or state constructs—usually the hypothetical counterparts of variables. Here, however, we encounter two elements that are processes instead of entities. Perceptual Bias is one. A number of entities or state descriptions can be identified in the processes that constitute Perceptual Bias. Its constituent parts will be described later in the chapter, but the task is too great to be done systematically in this book. Correspondingly, we formulate Overt Search for information as a process, not an entity. It involves a whole new range of subsidiary behaviors that are generated by this process, such as the behaviors involved in reading advertisements, talking with friends, or consulting technical reports such as *Consumer Reports*. The other two hypothetical constructs, Attention and Stimulus Ambiguity, that complete the perceptual subsystem are entities instead of processes.

It is convenient to break this process of receiving facts or search for facts into two parts: (1) the quantity of the information content received and (2) the quality or meaning of that information content. This distinction is a very crude one; for example, Attention is concerned solely with regulating the flow, that is, the *quantity* of input, but Perceptual Bias, in addition to distorting the information, also seems to regulate the flow to some extent. Nevertheless, the quantity versus quality distinction is a useful expositional device when discussing exceedingly complex relations. Perceptual Bias determines the meaning of the information and will be discussed in Section 5.2. Let us first examine the three variables in the perceptual process that determine the amount of information.

5.1 INFLUENCES ON QUANTITY OF INFORMATION

Since a number of factors influence the quantity of information that a buyer receives, we summarize them and their consequences to provide perspective on the buying process.

First, the *content* of the object or event which is serving as the Stimulus Display—both its psychophysical and semantic properties—

will make a difference in its consequences for the response variables. Second, the Stimulus Display to which the buyer is exposed is partially under his own control. By "exposed" we mean he has had the physical opportunity to perceive it. He seeks out one advertisement instead of another. This activity is captured in Overt Search.

Third, given the buyer's previous exposure to the object or event which has been a Stimulus Display and given the nature of that event, another influence on the information flow is Attention. It sits astride the flow of information through the buyer's receptors located in his eyes, ears, nose, mouth, and skin and regulates this flow as though it were a gate valve being lowered or raised in accordance with the information needs of the buyer. If its regulatory effect is not sufficient to provide the buyer with adequate information, Overt Search is called upon to supplement Attention by providing the buyer with new exposure until his information requirements are met.

Attention is in turn influenced by the arousal element of Motives, and the level of arousal is influenced by Stimulus Ambiguity, which in turn is partially caused by the ambiguity of Stimulus Display. Stimulus Ambiguity captures previous exposures to the ad as well as its inherent complexity in the sense that Stimulus Ambiguity refers to the buyer's inability to make sense of it at the moment. The ambiguity of the brand (Confidence) operates in a fashion parallel to that of Stimulus Ambiguity. Thus there is a feedback effect on Attention from arousal. There are also other feedback influences on arousal, but they are too complicated for our simple summary.

In the following pages the term "search" will be used to describe in a broad, loose sense the efforts by the buyer to do something about his information input. It includes mainly the consequences of Attention and Overt Search, and it can be called the psychology of complication.

Search effort is a central but not well understood process in human behavior. Its implications will be developed in Part IV in connection with product innovation where its effects are very obvious, whereas in less radical changes in behavior its role is more subtle and correspondingly more difficult to observe and understand. The purpose here is to present the mechanisms that underlie the process so that in Part IV the reader will come to it with a fuller understanding of its nature. We shall first discuss the mechanisms having to do with Attention and then deal with Overt Search. Finally, we shall discuss Stimulus Ambiguity because of its effect on Attention.

5.1.1 *Attention*

Attention refers to the degree of "openness" of the buyer's sensory receptors for a particular feature of a specified stimulus display and a consequent narrowing of the range of objects to which the buyer is responding, in relation to the range to which he is exposed. It is one of the three methods by which the buyer controls the flow of information into his nervous system. The other two methods are Overt Search and Perceptual Bias.

Attention can best be illustrated by using its visual aspect, but the receptors for the other senses operate in a roughly analogous way. The eye camera that has been used recently in advertising provides a concrete way of thinking specifically about visual effects. Still more interesting work is now going forward in some of the advertising agencies. It is known that a person's visual intake capacity can change through pupil dilation from 2 to 8 mm, which provides a 17-fold change in the area of the opening of the eye (Geldard, 1953, p. 23). The purpose of the eye camera as developed by Hess and others is to measure the degree of pupil dilation as it varies in response to different advertisements, packages, and the like.

It so happens that the visual system is affected also when the stimulus is, in fact, being received through other, for example, auditory, receptors (Geldard, 1953, p. 23). Hence measures used for the visual sense may be equally applicable to auditory effects; for example, a buyer's auditory response to a radio commercial might be measured through his eyes.

5.1.2   Overt Search

Attention is the first method of control used by the buyer to satisfy his information requirements but it is limited to the stimuli to which he is exposed. There are times when this amount of control is not adequate in the sense that he is motivated to look at, to be exposed to, other stimuli. It is this additional information to which the second source of control, Overt Search, is directed.

Overt Search is the *process* by which the buyer selects a particular element of his environment as the Stimulus Display in order to clarify the descriptive and evaluative cognitions related to a brand or to the product class as well as to satisfy motives such as novelty or to clarify the saliency of motives in a given situation. It involves at the least the buyer shifting his head, for example, and extends, in the other extreme, to seeking out and talking with particular people in order to obtain the information wanted, as well as to formal search effort. Hence it extends to extensive thinking, to manipulating the symbols received in the process of exerting the physical movement to acquire the information. It manifests itself in the form of looking for additional advertisements, talking with other people such as friends and neighbors, and reading technical reports on particular product classes and their brands.

It is especially relevant in new products when often a great amount of information is required, as we shall see in Part IV.

An intermediate stage of search between Attention and Overt Search could be conceptualized. Krugman (1967), in a thinking-looking-feeling paradigm for evaluating the effects of advertising, refers to *looking* as the tendency for the buyer to focus on a specific element of the Stimulus Display or to scan the entire display where this scanning behavior is measured by a mechanical eye-movement recorder. We mention the paradigm here because "looking" could be considered to be an intermediate stage between Attention and Overt Search. To simplify, we shall incorporate eye movement into Overt Search.

Overt Search involves us in a whole new range of behaviors that are central to buying, behaviors that are influenced by all of the factors bearing on the arousal aspect of Motives and by exogenous variables. The significance of Overt Search for buying, however, can best be developed in Part IV and the discussion here confined to the mechanisms that underlie it.

5.1.3 Stimulus Ambiguity

The ambiguity of the Stimulus Display is another influence on the flow of information into the buyer's mental process. It is the lack of clarity of the neural messages incited by the physical object or event (Stimulus Display) and which are permitted to enter the buyer's body via Attention. In summary, we discuss here the process by which Stimulus Ambiguity leads to increased Attention and to change in Stimulus Display (Overt Search). Also, the effects of brand ambiguity will be incorporated.

It has long been observed that higher animals—both man and other animals—spend a substantial portion of their time in bringing their sense organs into contact with biologically neutral stimulus patterns, that is, with objects or events that do not seem to be inherently beneficial or noxious. In human societies such activities are often called "recreation," "entertainment," "art," or "science." Until about fifteen years ago these activities were hardly noted in the theoretical and experimental literature in psychology. Since then, however, considerable and growing attention has been paid to these problems in Eastern Europe as well as in the West under such headings as "exploratory behavior," "curiosity," and "orienting response" (Berlyne, 1960, 1965).

Because of this research we can say that information is sought to meet two specific needs: to solve purchasing problems and to maintain a satisfactory level of stimulation. Such information seeking is called exploratory behavior. The function of seeking information for solving purchasing problems—*specific* exploratory behavior—can be further subdivided. First, it may deal with sensory ambiguity, the mere physical nature of the advertisement, for example, or the fuzziness of a picture such as "snow" in television. The purpose of seeking this type of information is to solve *perceptual* conflict. Second, information seeking can be directed toward reducing the ambiguity of the *meaning* of the stimulus and is then devoted to solving *conceptual* conflict, that is, ". . . conflict between mutually discrepant symbolic response-tendencies—thoughts, beliefs, attitudes, conceptions" (Berlyne, 1966, p. 31).

Diversive exploratory behavior, on the other hand, serves the function of maintaining a satisfactory level of stimulation for the buyer. It sets a framework within which specific information seeking takes place. Diversive behavior is directed toward maintaining something like an optimum amount of novelty, surprisingness, complexity, change, or variety to ensure the buyer's sense of well-being. Experiments have shown that people, though disliking too much variety, also dislike too little stimulation, hence try to avoid an environment that is informationally barren. Furthermore, there is evidence that prolonged subjection to an inordinately monotonous or unstimulating environment is detrimental to a variety of psychological functions.

Diverse exploratory behavior has nothing to do with obtaining information about a brand in order to make a choice and is motivated by factors quite different from specific exploratory behavior. The role of diversive behavior as an aspect of buying has become increasingly important as the tempo of technological change has quickened and has fantastically increased the flow of new products. Imagine the situation of a toy manufacturer whose product becomes obsolescent within weeks and even days as children tire of it and look for something new to hold their attention. Child boredom is not new, but our capacity to quickly make available new products on a nationwide basis is new.

Central to the understanding of buyer behavior is what motivates both specific and diversive exploratory behavior. For the answer to this we turn to the Stimulus Ambiguity–arousal relation.

5.1.3.1 *Stimulus Ambiguity-Arousal Relation*

We postulate that Stimulus Ambiguity elicits arousal and that arousal causes exploratory behavior, which is the search effort that buyers are known to exhibit. First let us examine the concept of Stimulus Ambiguity, and then discuss arousal.

What do we mean by "ambiguity"? It is the lack of clarity of the Stimulus Display in communicating the descriptive and evaluative aspects of the brand, product class and the nature of Motives. This lack of clarity can in itself satisfy such motives as the need for novelty. It refers to the collative properties of Stimulus Display: novelty, surprisingness, change, ambiguity, blurredness, incongruity, complexity, puzzlingness, and power to induce uncertainty. We call all of these collative properties "ambiguity" in order to simplify the exposition. Someone doing research on the topic would wish to be more specific. Ambiguity is probably an important influence, especially in an advanced economy where products are more complex and symbols are more used to transmit information about the products.

How is Stimulus Ambiguity related to arousal? What the collative properties have in common to create this effect of exploratory behavior is not completely clear as yet (Berlyne, 1966). The best evidence seems to suggest that it is conflict, and following Berlyne we accept conflict as our working assumption.

To relate the discussion to another body of analysis, we note that conflict is not exactly the same as the information-theoretic concept of uncertainty, although it is similar. Both increase as the number of alternatives (stimuli or brands) increase and also as the alternatives approach equiprobability. Uncertainty, however, does not reflect differences in absolute strength, and the concept can be applied only where the alternatives are altogether mutually exclusive.

Arousal refers to "wide-awakeness," "alertness," or "excitedness" and has grown out of several developments in neurophysiology and psychology in the past fifteen years. "Fluctuations in arousal are reflected by changes in the electrical activity of the brain, in electrical and thermal properties of the skin, in muscular tension, in the circulatory system, in the respiratory system, and in the diameter of the pupil, all of which can be recorded and precisely measured" (Berlyne, 1966, p. 31). It extends all the way from deep sleep to frenzied excitement. There is increasing evidence that arousal can be equated with the concept of drive used in the behavioristic view of motivation.

Accepting the idea that Stimulus Ambiguity causes arousal, the question is, "How do we know that arousal leads to exploratory behavior?" There are two justifications for connecting increases in arousal to exploratory responses. First, considerable research, particularly in Russia, has shown experimentally that some forms of exploratory behavior are associated with changes in arousal. There seems to be a network of processes by which the animal mobilizes his capacities to absorb information through its sense organs, transmits the information through its central nervous system, and acts promptly and energetically. Second, there is growing evidence that the collative properties of a stimulus display that serve to elicit exploratory behavior are capable of increasing arousal.

Having acquired a general understanding of arousal and its source, let us be specific about the way in which it operates in the theory of buyer behavior. Its first effect is on Attention. We postulate that there is a positive relation between the two over the relevant range. Arousal causes the sensory receptors to open and thus increase Attention. This opening of receptors requires little effort, and no conscious effort, and therefore the effect of arousal is felt on Attention first. If opening his receptors does not provide adequate information to the buyer, however, he proceeds to the more effortful activity of changing his Stimulus Display, by exerting active Overt Search or, in psychological terms, exhibiting an "orienting response." This search effort on the part of the buyer obviously involves highly complex behavior. Moreover, the nature of the stimuli—symbolic instead of significative—also requires complex behavior, as defined by the three-stage mediational model discussed in Chapter 4 where we learned that symbolic stimuli can be handled only at the mediational level of mental activity (see Figure 4.4). This complexity is emphasized here because it must be recognized in designing research to test propositions about buyer search.

Usually objects or events which typically serve as Stimulus Displays in a modern, highly advanced economy are signs instead of the significates, and symbols are never innately rewarding. With the high rate of technological change in distributing products, the buyer gets more of his information by advertising. Also, when he shops for the brand, he is likely to find it in packages which makes it difficult for him to physically see it. The way of the future may be a store in which the items are hung on the wall, with no intention that they be handled. The buyer orders by number, and his order is assembled in the warehouse as he shops. Hence the buyer tends more and more to be removed from the physical product itself until after he actually purchases it. In this way the product cues operate only after the purchase and then in the form of feedback from consumption. In anticipation of the purchase, product cues to the extent that they matter at all probably operate largely for those products with which the buyer is familiar.

For the new and unfamiliar brand, however, the cues represented in the package are really denotative instead of connotative in nature. They serve primarily a sensory function, the basis for identifying, discussing, and thinking about the brand. The buyer can identify his brand by the cues, but he cannot evaluate it through the cues in terms of his needs. The evaluative or connotative meaning conveyed by the brand name is largely acquired from symbolic cues representing the brand or from the generalization that is made from buying a related product.

There remain important exceptions to the general rule that relevant stimuli are symbolic in nature, such as the sample or model in industrial buying and the sales kit of the Fuller Brush representative. More and more in American marketing, however, the weight of telling people about the product has shifted to the package, mass media, and word-of-mouth. These objects and events, of course, all represent signs instead of the significate, and since signs are never innately rewarding, one of the central problems is to get the buyer to use the product in the first place so that he can be rewarded (Skinner, 1953).

Most of the signs are words—elements of human language that are *ambiguous* and *laden with social meanings*, hence not easily comprehended. The exceptions are such factors as the level of sound in radio and television and size of type in print advertising, which resemble the psychophysical stimuli historically studied in psychology and are probably not very important elements in buying.

Earlier we stated that if changing receptors does not suffice to reduce Stimulus Ambiguity, the buyer changes Stimulus Display. What evidence have we that buyers do, in fact, deliberately change the array of complex stimuli to which they are exposed? We all have experienced the tendency to change Stimulus Display. One of the earliest systematic studies of buying (Katona and Mueller, 1954) by incorporating the concept of the extent of deliberation dealt with the tendency of the buyer to change his Stimulus Display, although ths study did not distinguish between the ambiguity of the stimulus and ambiguity of the brand. There it was found that a buyer uses advertising and other impersonal sources, as well as the personal source of word-of-mouth. This study has been replicated (LeGrand and Udell, 1964). It is useful to distinguish between the two sources—the personal and the impersonal—because personal sources are believed to be more effective. In recent years, word-of-mouth has been getting considerable attention (Arndt, 1967), and systematic evidence on this source is now available and will be presented in Part IV.

In their empirical study of personal influence which dealt with impersonal sources as well, Katz and Lazarsfeld present an interesting idea that might be related to the distinction between diversive and problem-solving exploratory behavior. They differentiate between women who bought a new product because they merely wanted a change, which we would term an act that occurred as a result of diversive exploratory behavior, and those who did so because they were dissatisfied with their present brand, which we would say sprang from problem-solving behavior. For dissatisfaction to occur, the buyer presumably had received favorable information about competing brands, and this was accidental, whereas the first was what we might call buyer-initiated. The buyer-initiated type of change has been supported in a number of studies done in India. Whether the Katz and Lazarsfeld question, "When you made the change, were you dissatisfied with the product you used before, or did you just want to make a change?" really elicited this subtle but important difference is, however, an open question (Katz and Lazarsfeld, 1955, p. 209).

Katz and Lazarsfeld found that in marketing activity, dissatisfied women reported both more exposure and more susceptibility to advice and influence than did the respondents who were satisfied with their brands. This finding suggests that the buyer-initiated change does not cause so much exposure to information as does problem-solving behavior. A further interesting finding was that this difference in exposure between the two types of women did not exist in fashions. Perhaps on fashion issues women are always on the alert, but are in general less alert in regard to consumer goods. At present we must consider these extensions from Katz and Lazarsfeld as being speculative.

A more precise statement of the Stimulus Ambiguity-arousal relation is shown graphically in Figure 5.1. Because the relation is the foundation of the theory of search, we shall examine it in detail: first those aspects to the right of X_1 of Figure 5.1 and then those to the left of X_1. The

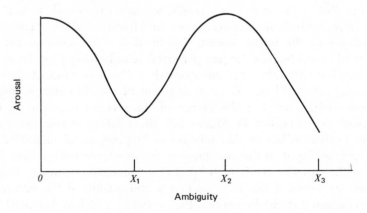

Figure 5.1   Stimulus Ambiguity-arousal relation. (After Koch, 1963, Figure 16, p. 319.)

first can be described as leading to search for information about the brand being considered, and the second, to the search for interesting stimuli.

1. *Search for information about the brand being considered.* The search effort implied in positions to the right of X_1 in Figure 5.1 represent specific or problem-solving exploration: the search for information about a brand. "Specific exploration occurs when something is perceived in unfavorable conditions (e.g., briefly, in dim light, in the distance), affording too little information to identify its attributes" (Berlyne, 1964, p. 24).

Presumably what happens in this X_1 to X_2 range of Stimulus Ambiguity is that a buyer learns more and more about a stimulus and so moves to the left on the Stimulus Ambiguity axis, and consequently arousal is decreased, assuming that his initial position was somewhere to the left of X_2 but to the right of X_1 in Figure 5.1. To support this hypothesis there is considerable evidence which indicates that as buyers become more loyal, they are less susceptible to information generally (Arndt, 1966). Automobile buyers who have bought the same brand twice in a row are less apt to shop than are those who bought another brand on their previous car purchase (Evans, 1959, p. 363; Engel, 1965).

There is also evidence, however, that buyers will become increasingly attentive to information about the particular brand to which they are loyal. These two contradictory conclusions can be reconciled by recognizing that two different mechanisms are at work. As the buyer becomes more familiar with his brand, he does tend to close off information about the product class as implied in the Stimulus Ambiguity-arousal relation. But at the same time, as will be shown below, there is a feedback from Attitude to Motives, hence to Attention, which increases the probability of the buyer "seeing" information that relates to his most preferred brand but not his less preferred brands. Therefore, he is more sensitive, but only *relative to other brands* in the same product class.

Having examined the X_1 to X_2 segment of the Stimulus Ambiguity-arousal relation, what is the nature of the relation over the X_2 to X_3 segment? As indicated in Figure 5.1, the relation is negative in this range. Berlyne refers to this relation as "supramaximal inhibition" but does not develop it. If the ambiguity is this great, we believe that distortion of the stimulus is often the probable immediate solution. This distortion we would define as a change in the *quality* of the information that is captured in the Perceptual Bias variable, which is discussed later. The long-run solution in this range, however, is for the buyer to tolerate the ambiguity of the situation long enough to absorb more information from the available sources and in this way reduce the ambiguity instead of misperceiving the information (Berlyne, 1963, p. 231).

2. *Search for interesting stimuli.* Here the analysis of the Stimulus Ambiguity-arousal relation and its consequences is completed by examining the X_0 to X_1 range of the ambiguity axis in Figure 5.1.

Obviously, a major change in the buyer's environment, such as the appearance of a much better new product, or any other object can cause the buyer to perceive new stimuli. In addition, however, the stimuli confronting a buyer can change even though his environment is constant in terms of the objects and events it presents to the buyer. This is the more interesting case. It occurs when the stimulus is so unambiguous that it falls to the left of the X_1 position, which motivates the buyer to look for something new to relieve his boredom.

Thus those positions to the left of X_1 represent diversive exploration, the escape from boredom, where the ambiguity is deficient and where the exploration is aimed at stimulation from any source that is sufficiently interesting.

For any given buyer, what is it that fixes X_1 where it is, since this position plays such a crucial role? First, it differs much among individuals. Hence this difference is a personality characteristic (Berlyne, 1963, pp. 344–347), and we postulate that the exogenous variable of Personality Traits influences search effort. Second, it varies according to the general experience of the individual. If he is typically exposed to a great variety of stimuli in his daily life, as is a person living in a large urban area, his X_1 position will be more to the right. He becomes bored at a higher level of ambiguity than does a person who typically is subjected to fewer stimuli, as is one living in an isolated rural area.

Zajonc (1965, pp. 34–35) raises a question about exploratory behavior. After a careful survey of the literature, particularly of studies of verbal behavior including comments on advertising practice, he concludes that people like a stimulus the more they are exposed to it and questions whether it is correct to say, as Berlyne does, that organisms "prefer" novelty. Zajonc argues that they look at the familiar because they think that as a result of their past experience they will be rewarded by so doing.

In addition to Zajonc's question, the view expressed here that people seek the unfamiliar may seem inconsistent with the consistency theory used in analyzing change in Attitude and Intention in Chapter 4. If the reader will recall the argument implied in Figure 5.1, however, he will see that it is perfectly consistent with the consistency principle that a buyer strives toward a harmonious, stable, and balanced confirmation in his information-seeking behavior. The only difference is that here the process by which a buyer achieves consistency is seen as being somewhat more complex. Under certain circumstances the buyer does seek the unfamiliar, but it is only a part of his total behavior on the way to achieving consistency with his environment. In this total process he may periodically review his environment to ensure that he is not missing a better brand than the one he is now buying.

3. *Epistemic behavior.* To complete the motivational basis for explaining search effort, it is necessary to broaden the discussion to include a third type of exploratory behavior. It is epistemic behavior, which is directed toward the acquisition of general knowledge useful to future behavior instead of the immediately useful search effort exhibited in specific and diversive exploratory behaviors. Its identifying characteristic is that it is directed toward the acquisition of knowledge for *future* use. The information so acquired becomes *stored up* knowledge. It has been implicit in the earlier discussion, but we have considered it wise to avoid introducing it until now to simplify the exposition. In all of the psychological research bearing on the search process that we have seen, the stimulus has been the significate, which, of course, simplifies the description of the process. In much buying, however, the stimulus and significate are separate since most of the information is received from symbols. Also, even when the two are the same, as when a housewife looks at a brand on the shelf in the supermarket, there is thinking involved, hence conceptual as well as perceptual conflict exists. Conceptual conflict can motivate epistemic exploratory behavior but perceptual conflict does not.

Epistemic behavior is important to the understanding of buying in at least three ways. First, conceptual conflict enables us to incorporate *brand* ambiguity as indicated by Confidence. Even though Stimulus Display is perfectly unambiguous, the brand concept being represented by the Stimulus Display can be unclear. Although this Stimulus Display is clear he has not yet received enough information for an adequate understanding of the brand concept. Brand ambiguity will be dealt with in the next section.

Second, we casually observe women shopping merely to be well informed so that when the need arises for a product, they can buy it with a minimum of effort. As the flow of new products into the market has accelerated, the need for this type of effort has rapidly increased. Industrial buyers sometimes spend considerable time reading trade magazines for the same reason. Earlier we mentioned that women are alert with regard to information about fashion products.

Thus we are led to the third purpose of epistemic behavior—to be a well-informed buyer in fulfilling a social role, in maintaining a social position. One is valued according to how much he knows with regard to the availability and value of products, a characteristic of advanced societies which David Riesman (1950) has so well described with his concept of "other-directed" people. We deal with this aspect of search behavior under "opinion leadership" in Part IV.

5.1.3.2 Level of Stimulus Ambiguity-Arousal Relation

Another set of feedback effects also influence the amount of search effort. These can be visualized as operating by affecting the *level* instead of the shape of the Stimulus Ambiguity-arousal relation of Figure 5.1 and thereby influencing Attention and Overt Search. Specifically, the higher the level of the curve in terms of the vertical axis—the greater the absolute level of arousal—the greater the attention given to the Stimulus Display, although at some level we expect this relation to become nonmonotonic. We shall discuss three factors that influence the level of the relation: Confidence, Attitude, and conflict in Motives.

Here we are able to show the pivotal role of Confidence—conflict due to the buyer's uncertainty in judging the brand—in the total system that is the theory of buyer behavior. In Chapter 4 its function in causing overt behavior was developed. Here we emphasize its function in increasing Attention and Overt Search. When the buyer's Confidence is low, he is motivated to look for information (Berlyne, 1963; Lanzetta, 1967), and at that point Confidence has little or no effect on overt purchase behavior. As he acquires information about the brand, his Confidence builds and becomes a force behind overt purchase. Once the buyer has acquired enough information, Confidence no longer stimulates information acquisition but now becomes quite important in motivating purchase.

We treat Confidence as the inverse of brand ambiguity. Also, we postulate that the relation between brand ambiguity and arousal has the same shape as the Stimulus Ambiguity relation shown in Figure 5.1. Thus when brand ambiguity is at the X_2 position, Confidence is fairly low, which by way of arousal stimulates Attention and also Overt Search if opening of receptors is not adequate to meet the information needs. As the buyer acquires information, brand ambiguity declines (his Confidence increases), and he approaches the X_1 position.

The positions to the left of X_1 are important. They represent diversive exploratory behavior. The buyer searches for information, but this time he searches for information about new alternatives to put into his evoked set to replace his current ones. The existing brand becomes less acceptable. Whether the motive behind this change in the buyer's evaluation of the brand is boredom, as we alleged when discussing the stimulus, is an open question, however.

Cognitive theorists would describe the X_0 to X_1 stage as arising because of an increase in the level of aspiration, rather than because of boredom. Simon, for example, speaks of a rising aspiration level as the source of search effort. The aspiration level concept does not imply a change in the intensity of motivation itself, as discussed in Chapter 4, but a change in the *conditions of motivation*. That is, as a buyer finds that his Satisfaction can be achieved less effortfully (and Stimulus Ambiguity declines because of his learning of the stimulus), his standards of what is adequate in the way of Satisfaction increase. The buyer's level of aspiration will continue to rise until his expectations of Satisfaction are disappointed, which will cause Attitude toward Brand A to lower. Because of the lowered Attitude, he will try other brands. In this process he may find a new one that is superior. Also, Satisfaction from A may continue to decline until it is unacceptable and is therefore dropped from evoked set.

What is important is that these changes in the buyer's evoked set arise (1) from internally generated sources as well as (2) from having a new product appear in his environment. The internally generated effects must be recognized in explaining buyer behavior.

For our purposes this third stage of the Stimulus Ambiguity-arousal relation is crucially important because it suggests a condition under which the buyer, for internal reasons alone, having anything to do with whether a new brand is being introduced to the market, comes to be aware of a brand that is new to him. We postulate that a buyer may repeatedly pass through a cycle of loyalty and disloyalty. He tries a brand, likes it and becomes loyal. After a period of consuming it either he becomes bored or his aspiration level rises and he looks around for another brand. Executives in the detergent industry report that they observe this happening among consumers of detergents.

It is doubtful that behavior in this stage can be manipulated in any way by marketing effort, but its prediction would be of immense value in planning the introduction of a new product, because a market where most people had reached this stage would be ripe for new product introduction. The significance of this point is further developed in Chapter 8.

With regard to this diversive exploration, it would appear that the rate at which brands attain it—the rate at which buyers will fully learn about their current product—varies remarkably according to the innate complexity of the product class (brand ambiguity) and the importance of the product class (Importance of Purchase), hence the willingness of the buyer to risk trying something new. The exogenous variable of Importance of Purchase was incorporated into the theory largely to enable us to improve our prediction in this way. If the product is difficult to evaluate and important, the buyer may never reach X_1 stage and thus will remain permanently brand-loyal. Hence the conditions of the speed of the movement toward the X_1 range are similar to but probably not identical with those determining brand loyalty.

The second influence on the level of the Stimulus Ambiguity-arousal relation is the value of the buyer's Attitude. The relation is positive: the more he likes the brand, the greater will be the level of arousal.

The role of the value of Attitude in influencing Attention has perhaps best been shown by the work of Hess. Earlier it was mentioned that pupil dilation is one of the measures of arousal. Hess, however, treats pupil dilation as a measure of Attitude, not of Attention. He has found close agreement between the person's stated attitude and that indicated by the pupil-measure for food products (Hess, 1965). There was lack of agreement in areas involving social values and social pressures. This might suggest that the pupil dilation is unaffected by social pressures and that when social effects are present, the pupil-measure can be more accurate than the person's stated attitudes. There is some evidence that the principle of attitude affecting Attention applies not only to vision but to taste and smell as well.

Also, at the low end of the liking scale—disliking—there is probably an increase in arousal, because people are aroused to approach situations they like and to avoid situations they dislike. This is contrary to Hess's implied position. Nevertheless, it may be that like-dislike are asymmetrical, which is what we find on attitude scales. Buyers tend to distribute themselves more on the positive side than on the negative. Hence for purposes of buying behavior this deficiency may not be too serious.

A third influence on the level of the Stimulus Ambiguity-arousal relation is conflict among motives which serves to increase arousal. This is behavioral conflict, the problem of competing responses; when a buyer is confronted with choosing a brand that serves two conflicting goals, arousal will tend to increase. We expect this phenomenon to be particularly obvious when a buyer is contemplating the purchase of a brand of a new product class, a situation where he has not yet reconciled his conflicting goals. A related case, and with the same consequences, occurs when brands are judged on slightly different criteria, which can be referred to as incomparability. It, too, would be especially applicable, we believe, with new products.

5.1.4   Summary of Influences on Quantity of Information

The nature and source of some of the influences on the stimulus-as-coded operating through the quantity of information have been examined. Overt Search exerts its influence directly by partially determining the particular environment of a buyer and the particular portion of that environment which the buyer will select as the Stimulus Display. Attention is the other direct influence upon the s-a-c. Lying behind these two constructs, however, are four indirect influences that operate through arousal: Stimulus Ambiguity, feedback from Attitude, feedback from Confidence, and goal conflict.

5.2   PERCEPTUAL BIAS

The quality or meaning of the information the buyer receives is the subject of interest here. This is obviously a very important practical issue. Advertisements often leave the impression that their writers believe that their sole function is to create attention, "to get the ad into the buyer's head." The consequences may sometimes be like those of the advertisement run by a cereal manufacturer which reportedly doubled its *competitor's* sales. It received the attention wanted, but the message actually imparted was, in effect, "Buy my competitor's brand."

The quality of the message is determined by Perceptual Bias, the fourth and last hypothetical construct in the perceptual subsystem and in the total system that constitutes the theory of buyer behavior. It can be defined as a complex process consisting of the perceptual and cognitive devices by which the buyer qualitatively distorts or selects information that he has already taken into his nervous system. It is a process, not a state construct. It is made up of a number of subprocesses, each consisting of a set of relations, but current research does not permit us to develop these subconstructs quite so fully as we have most of the rest of the theory.

These combined mechanisms that make up Perceptual Bias operate on the quantity of neural signals received to generate a stimulus-as-coded. This s-a-c is the output of the perceptual subsystem which becomes an input to the learning subsystem. A part of what we are dealing with here is, in communications terminology, "selective exposure," and "selection retention."

A more complete picture of the perceptual processes can be drawn if we begin from a behavioral base: the way in which the various dimensions of the typical multidimensional Stimulus Display and contextual cues that confront the buyer are *integrated* in the buyer's mind to yield the s-a-c. To put it another way, we wish to obtain a better understanding of the coding response. To do this, we draw upon the three-level view of behavior set forth in Chapter 4 where some of the principles of stimulus and response integrations were first discussed.

5.2.1 Integration of Stimulus Dimensions

Before proceeding to examine the influences on the buyer's stimulus integrations and therefore those forces that help shape his s-a-c, let us discuss more fully what it is that we mean by stimulus integration and so provide perspective on the complex relations involved.

Integrating stimulus dimensions is the manifestation of stimuli being learned; hence the process partially determines where the buyer is located on the OX axis of the Stimulus Ambiguity-arousal relation of Figure 5.1. When we say that the elements of a stimulus display are well integrated—the integration is evocative instead of predictive as described in the three-stage mediation model of Figure 4.4—we are implying that the stimulus has low ambiguity or high certainty; for example, as a result of being exposed to only a part of an advertisement the buyer may perceive the entire advertisement. Hence the process of stimulus integration explains how, through the process of learning, the stimulus causes the buyer to move to the left on the OX axis of Figure 5.1.

When Stimulus Display is complex, as it typically is, the buyer can perceive some part of it or its entirety. The extent to which he does perceive all of the elements is called the "degree of integration." An example will make the concept more meaningful. The Scott Paper Company, some ten years ago, ran a series of advertisements on toilet tissue. Although the particular arrangement varied, all advertisements in the series contained four elements: a picture of a baby (S_1), a picture of a young lady who was ostensibly the baby's mother (S_2), some copy devoted to health and indirectly to the health aspects of using toilet tissue (S_3), and a picture of a roll of ScotTissue (S_4). Let us assume the elements could be integrated as follows: S_1 to form SI_1; S_1 and S_2 to form SI_2; S_1, S_2, and S_3 to form SI_3; and S_1, S_2, S_3, and S_4 to form SI_4, and that SI_1 is the most probable, SI_2 less probable, SI_3 still less probable and SI_4 is the least probable.

Integration can have either a facilitating or an actual distorting effect, both being systematic or nonrandom. It has a facilitating effect when after having integrated the dimensions of a stimulus display and having been exposed to only one element of that display, the buyer perceives the missing elements of the integration as though they were "out there"

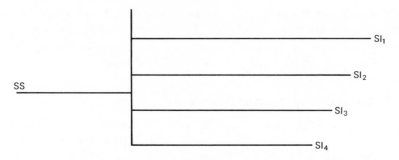

Figure 5.2   Stimulus integration.

in fact. Distortion comes about when the integration contains (he perceives) elements that *do not exist* in fact in the Stimulus Display. One element that is actually there calls up elements that are not there but in another context have become associated with that element. Also, distortion occurs when the buyer systematically omits elements that are there.

The actual extent of integration, as explained earlier, is determined by the number of times the elements have been paired in the past, not by reinforcement as we learned in Chapter 4. The stimulus integration hierarchy and its relation to attitude and response integration were shown in Figure 4.5. They are shown in more detail in Figure 5.2. The SS indicates some antecedent event, such as the buyer being exposed to the magazine that contains the advertisement. The lengths of the stimulus integration lines correspond to their respective probabilities as determined by the amount of previous pairing. We assume that SI_1 is most likely to occur because it requires the minimum of integration.

From the principles of the integration of stimulus dimensions, it is clear that (1) the complexity of the Stimulus Display (the number of dimensions to be integrated) and (2) a buyer's previous experience with that Display—his previous exposure—will both make a difference in the perceived stimulus, the stimulus-as-coded.

In addition to the complexity of the Stimulus Display and the number of past pairing of the elements of the Stimulus Display and contextual cues, other factors shape the nature of the stimulus integrations that a buyer makes: feedback from the content and intensity of his Motives and from Attitude upon his sensory integration processes. The Attitude effects are especially complex in the sense that the attitude first called up by a given stimulus sets into motion a train of effects unique to that particular attitude.

5.2.2   Effect of Motives on Stimulus Integration

Is there a feedback from Motives to Perceptual Bias? If so, what is its effect on the s-a-c? What is the effect of the content and intensity of Motives on the stimulus integration made by the buyer? This is an important question because in many purchase-influencing situations there are contextual cues—events outside the Stimulus Display but proximate to it—that operate and so influence the buyer's motive intensity and content. In automobile advertisements, often a very sexy young lady is perched on the hood of a new-model automobile. An analgesia buyer is exposed to an analgesic advertisement on the medical page of the local newspaper. Again, a sexy young lady is shown draped around a piece of heavy industrial equipment.

In Chapter 4 the number of times the elements of a stimulus display have been paired in the past was said to influence which stimulus integration (SI) will be made. This rule remains true, but a number of complicating conditions having to do with Motives and the motivation process modify it, as shown in Figure 5.3.

The left-hand side of Figure 5.3—an elaboration of Figure 5.2—

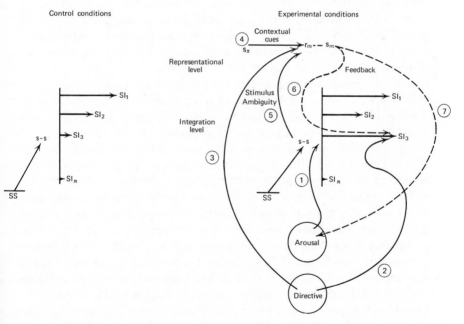

Figure 5.3   Attitude and integration of stimulus dimensions. (From Osgood, 1957b, p. 389.)

presents the typical situation: the pairing of elements of Stimulus Display that has occurred most often in the past is most likely to occur now, as shown by the longer line for SI_1. In an experiment this situation would represent the control conditions. The right-hand side illustrates the variety of experimental variables that can be manipulated, hence is called the experimental conditions. The SS is the external stimulus, such as the Scott Paper advertisement mentioned above, and s-s is the internal sensory stimulus, which internally represents the external physical advertisement.

At the bottom of the right-hand sketch are two circles, arousal and directive. These refer to the two aspects of Motives discussed in Chapter 4 in connection with the motivation process. Every motive has an arousal effect, and it is common to all motives and transposable from one motive to another (Osgood, 1957b, p. 369). Also, let us bring in another motivational distinction made in Chapter 4 that is essential here. A relevant motive serves a given product class. An irrelevant motive is one that is not satisfied by the given product class at all (N. Miller, 1959, pp. 253–354; Osgood, 1957b, p. 383).

An irrelevant motive has only the first effect, that of stimulating arousal. The sexy young lady draped around an industrial product, we presume, is a good example of this, as is the use of a high-quality store to buy a product of no great significance (status motive). As suggested by Path 1 of Figure 5.3, experimentally increasing arousal would merely make the most probable integration SI_1 more probable. As a consequence, the existence of the young lady might cause the buyer to *perceive* only the young lady and not the product itself.

Increasing a relevant motive—such as stimulating the achievement motive in the industrial advertisement—will have a directive effect in addition to its arousing effect. It will cause the buyer to make the integration that was associated with that motive—as shown by Path 2 in Figure 5.3, the SI_3 integration. The buyer will perceive something related to the industrial product.

To examine the arousal effect of increasing the intensity of motivation, let us look at a study in which a sample of people was divided into two groups, one "threatened" and the other "unthreatened." The threatened group was made "threatened" by being told they might have a neurotic personality, which would be revealed by this perceptual test. "Threat" was an irrelevant motive, that is, it was presumed not to be associated with any of the alternative sensory integrations of Stimulus Display. Both groups were presented with a completed square figure, which was alternated with various incomplete versions of that figure. The threatened subjects were significantly more inclined to report closure—"seeing" the *incomplete* squares as complete—than were the unthreatened subjects.

Hence the most probable integrations were made more probable by an irrelevant drive (Moffitt and Stagner, 1956). It can be inferred from this not only that there is a feedback from Motives to Perceptual Bias, but that it operates in a particular way.

To examine the directive effect of increasing the intensity of motivation, we take a relevant drive in the context of the Scott Paper example and use it with the concept of stimulus integration in Figure 5.2. Assume that the housewife has a strong learned drive to preserve her health, a drive that has been stimulated by certain contextual cues such as a very recent discussion with a neighbor about matters of health. Since the advertising copy (S_3) discusses health, she associates the health drive with integration SI_3, as in Figure 5.2. However, if we assume that health is associated with toilet tissue as a product class—toilet tissue serves the health need—the learned drive relevant to maintaining health elicits integration SI_4, which includes a brand in the product class and is what Scott Paper Company intended the reader to do. This particular integration occurs because SI_4 includes the health copy, and any brand in the product class serves the health motive. Hence we see the directive effect of motivation in influencing stimulus integration, that is, in influencing what buyers perceive.

In the extreme case, the buyer could perceive the roll of ScotTissue even though she were in fact exposed only to one element of the advertisement, such as the picture of the baby observed as she casually thumbs through a magazine. The more intense are Motives, the more likely she is to make these misperceptions. In summary, the directive or relevant motives are those that are served by the product class under consideration. They influence the choice of particular *brands* only in the sense that some dimensions of the given brand will satisfy a motive more than will the same dimensions of other brands in that product class. Thus Scott Paper would have had to persuade the buyer that ScotTissue served the health motive better than other brands.

Some evidence is available to test the proposition that Motives can have a directive effect. In an experiment, a state of felt success was induced in one group of people by having them manipulate the easy part of a level-of-aspiration task. In another group a state of felt failure was induced by having them manipulate the difficult part of the task. Then two sets of words—one set being success-related and the other set, failure-related—were presented to both groups for tachistoscopic recognition. The success-experiencing subjects had the lowest thresholds, that is, they perceived the success-related words at the fastest tachistoscopic speeds. The failure-experiencing subjects had the lowest thresholds for failure-related words (Postman and Brown, 1952).

If the relevant motive and the irrelevant motive are equally strong, presumably conflict and still greater arousal will result, but only if the two individually have opposite effects on behavior.

5.2.3   Attitude Feedback upon Sensory Integration

To be more realistic, the role of Attitude in the motivational-perceptual effects must be incorporated. So far we have taken as given the fact that a particular complex of product class, evoked set, and brand was called to mind. Obviously, this too is an influence, and which one is called to mind makes a lot of difference. Thus we see the interaction of Motives and Attitude in affecting perception.

Since here the issue of the feedback effects has to do with which mediator is called up, we specifically assume that what is called up (brought to the buyer's mind) is the product class–evoked set–brand complex, which is the product class, the buyer's evoked set in that class, and the dominant brand in that set. The one study on evoked set (B. Campbell, 1969) indicates that at least in the two product classes investigated, one brand in the buyer's evoked set had a considerably higher probability of repeat purchase than the other brands and thus gives us support for assuming that *only* one brand will be called up. The assumption is an oversimplification, but it will make the exposition easier. Furthermore, we are assuming that all of the associations with the product class—both its denotative and connotative attributes—are called up. Later, in discussing vigilance and defense, we drop this assumption.

Going ahead with the main theme of the effect of motivation on the integration of stimulus dimensions, let us examine the process by which Attitude "gets called up" or comes into play, since each particular attitude when it is evoked will set into motion a whole train of perceptual effects. As shown at the top of Figure 5.3, there are three means by which a particular Attitude (r_m . . . s_m) is called up. First, it is called up by Motives if the motive, assuming a single motive is operative, has previously been associated with the meaning inherent in that particular Attitude, as indicated by Path 3. This could occur if it is a relevant motive—if it is served by the product class represented by this attitude—which is presumably much the most common way.

Second, surrounding events to the situation but outside the Stimulus Display—contextual cues—can tend to call up a particular meaning, such as a discussion of health, which is associated with a particular brand. Here contextual cues are indicated by S_x, and Path 4 is involved. There is a good evidence that an advertisement for medicine appearing on the health page of a local newspaper will be seen by more people than if it appeared on some other page of the same newspaper. This evidence suggests the important role of contextual cues in market communication if we stop to consider two things. First, the buyer is confronted with a plethora of stimuli; he simply cannot take them all in. He must be *selective*. Second, one of the major tasks of market communication is to convey the proper context of the product, the set of contextual cues that will call up or evoke the appropriate Attitude, that is, the appropriate product class concept. These ideas begin to indicate the central role of editorial content in influencing printed communication effects and of the show in influencing the effect of television communication. The concept of contextual cues opens up a systematic way of developing this area of knowledge.

Third, if the Stimulus Display (SS) is ambiguous and provides incomplete information to the buyer, as it usually does, it can have a selective effect on which Attitude is called up. This is represented by Path 5, Stimulus Ambiguity. There is a clear distinction in principle between contextual cues and Stimulus Ambiguity, although operationally this distinction may be less clear-cut. Stimulus Ambiguity pertains to phenomena that are within whatever is defined as Stimulus Display. Contextual cues have to do with events that are outside Stimulus Display but are proximate in space and time.

High Stimulus Ambiguity obviously describes a large proportion of marketing communication situations. Consider a television commercial; it may exist for no longer than twenty seconds, and the buyer may, in fact, only see the latter portion of it because his attention is not immediately called to it when it first appears. No imagination is required to appreciate the ambiguity of such a stimulus. Furthermore, a systematic theory of visual illusions that is applicable to a wide range of esthetic problems—perspective in paintings—and commercial work has been developed out of essentially the Stimulus Ambiguity concept by drawing upon the well-recognized psychological phenomenon of constancy scaling (Gregory, 1966).

These three sources of Attitude tune-up—Motives, contextual cues, and Stimulus Ambiguity—suggest the great variety of behavior that can emerge with only a single Stimulus Display (SS) when contextual cues exist, the motive structure is complex, and the Stimulus Display ambiguous. It is not surprising that the measurement of advertising effects should be difficult, since all of these conditions prevail in a typical marketing situation. The variety indicates the complexity of the problem we are dealing with when attempting to explain real-world purchasing.

Now that we know the various ways in which Attitude can be evoked, let us examine the feedback effects from Attitude upon perception. By way of perspective, however, let us remember that Figure 5.2 indicated that of all the elements in Stimulus Display (SS) that a buyer might perceive, one is most probable, which was SI_1 in the figure. This probability was determined by the contiguity principle: the more often that elements of the Stimulus Display have been paired in the past, the more likely they are to be perceived together in the future. Now, we are saying that the feedback from Attitude too can modify what is perceived by having both the energizing effect and a directive effect shown in Paths 1 and 2 of Figure 5.3, which were discussed earlier. In fact, when discussing Paths 1 and 2 we were implicitly asuming that a given Attitude had been called up. By making this assumption explicit, Paths 6 and 7 become the counterparts of Paths 1 and 2, respectively, although Motives (Paths 1 and 2) continue to operate along with the Attitude effects.

As a technical point, Attitude per se is not energizing but instead stimulates Motives. To simplify the exposition, we describe the process as though the energizing effect of Attitude on Perceptual Bias was direct instead of indirect through Motives.

5.2.3.1 *Certain Consequences of Feedback from Attitude for Perception*

Let us separate all of the other feedback consequences of Attitude for perception from those that we ordinarily associate with perceptual vigilance and perceptual defense, two widely recognized phenomena in psychology. We first discuss the other consequences and then examine vigilance and defense in the next section.

The feedback from Attitude has two kinds of effects, which are Paths 6 and 7 respectively shown in Figure 5.3. First, let us examine the effect of contextual cues upon which sensory integration is made and begin with Path 6 which represents a directive or selective effect.

If a relevant drive (Path 2) is combined with contextual cues, cues external to the stimulus display (Path 4), such as the nature of the television show during which the advertisement appears, we predict complicated interactions between the feedback from Attitude (Path 6) and the effects of the relevant components of Motives (Path 2). Both the feedback from the contextual cues (Path 6) and the effects of the relevant drive (Path 2) should serve to select out associated stimulus integrations. The television show could cause the housewife to expect a cosmetics advertisement, and the relevant drive could be affiliation, the woman's desire to associate with men and women. In Figure 5.3, as in the example, they both happen to select out the *same* stimulus, although this need not always be the case.

Now we examine the effect of contextual cues on perception via Path 7. The energizing effect of Attitude (Path 7), in contrast to its directive effect via Path 6, should merely strengthen the most probable sensory integration (SI_1). If the dominant integration is *not* the same as that facilitated by the combined contextual cues *and* relevant drive (Paths 2 and 6), however, competition among the possible stimulus integrations and consequent interference with each other should result.

Let us now turn to the effects of Stimulus Ambiguity. Attitude can be called up (Path 5) by the ambiguity of the stimulus (SS), and that attitude will in turn select out a certain integration (Path 6) which may not be the the one that carries the appropriate information to the buyer. Consequently, he can be looking at one stimulus but, in fact, be perceiving another. In examining this phenomenon, we consider whether the ambiguity is sensory or semantic. This distinction is important because in measuring advertising effects, the buyer's learning of the stimulus per se must be separated from his learning of the meaning that the advertisement imparts about the denotative or connotative attributes of the brand. This subtle but real difference tends to be swept under the rug in many laboratory studies where the stimulus is typically the significate: the stimulus *is* the goal-object, the brand.

First, let us take the case where the ambiguity is with respect to the sensory characteristics, rather than in terms of the meaning of those characteristics. Some supporting evidence is available to suggest how Perceptual Bias can occur and affect the buyer's response to an advertisement. Subjects were required to match the apparent colors of cutout shapes with a color wheel made up of yellow and red segments. The color of all the test objects—the cutout shapes—was actually an *identical* brownish orange. Their shapes, however, were cut to represent different meaningful objects of known color such as a tomato and a lemon or a lobster claw and a banana. Despite the fact that the subjects thought they were making identical matches, their actual matches deviated toward yellow for objects known to be yellow and toward red for objects known to be red (Bruner, Postman, and Rodriques, 1951).

We interpret this experiment as indicating that the shape cues as an ambiguous stimulus evoked their appropriate attitude, that is, an object shaped like a tomato evoked the product class "tomato" and the subject's preferred brand with all of its meaning. The attitude that was thus evoked caused the feedback to the sensory cortex. This feedback served to selectively modify choices at the sensory integration level among the color alternatives in the color wheel. When the person attempted to match that brownish-orange tomato with the color wheel, he perceived the physical object (the brownish-orange tomato shape) as being redder than it actually was.

Second, let us turn to the case where the stimulus integration is ambiguous as to *meaning* (semantically ambiguous). A black three of diamonds presented in the tachistoscope may be interpreted as either a black three of spades or a red three of diamonds, depending on whether the color or shape cues happen to be dominant in the buyer's mind. But whichever way it is perceived, the feedback from this interpretation—from the Attitude called up—selectively modifies the sensory integration of the display toward congruence between the color and shape. If the buyer is exposed *too long* to the stimulus, however, he will correctly identify the card as incorrectly designed (Bruner and Postman, 1949). The reader can imagine the consequences of ambiguous advertisements for the quality of perception when, as in the typical case, the buyer looks at the advertisement in a casual manner and for just a brief interval of time.

5.2.3.2 Effects of Vigilance and Defense

Having discussed both the selective and energizing effects (Paths 6 and 7) of contextual cues through the feedback from Attitude and the selective effect (Path 6) of high Stimulus Ambiguity, let us examine the energizing effect (Path 7) of high Stimulus Ambiguity. The attempt to deal with this aspect of high Stimulus Ambiguity permits us to incorporate two widely recognized perceptual phenomena: vigilance and defense.

Given Attitude and an ambiguous stimulus, the feedback effect can be still more complex than has been indicated so far and has to do with what is called "perceptual vigilance" and "perceptual defense." These phenomena are well-documented in the psychological literature, and here the task is to explain both the mechanisms that underlie the phenomena and their relevance to buyer behavior. Vigilance is said to exist when the buyer "sees" the stimulus more distinctly than is justified by the nature of the stimulus itself. Perceptual defense is the opposite: the buyer "sees" the stimulus less well than would be expected from the nature of the stimulus alone.

The effect provided by an ambiguous Stimulus Display (Path 5) can be sufficient to excite the dominant *evaluative* component of the complex of product class, evoked set, and Attitude without being sufficient to excite the total reaction pattern of the entire product class concept, its denotative as well as its connotative (Choice Criteria) characteristics. Thus we drop the assumption made in the preceding section that all of the product class denotations and connotations are necessarily called up and accept the notion that only parts of the complex become operative.

Three results could be expected under this condition of incomplete information. First, the direct feedback (the broadly evaluative component of the brand concept, Attitude) should "tune up" the integration of coevaluative terms (Path 6). By "coevaluative" terms we mean those elements of the stimulus display that have the same evaluative meaning for the buyer as Attitude. This would result in "vigilance."

Second, the feedback from the denotative or nonevaluative aspects of the brand concept can, however, stimulate irrelevant motives, which have an arousal or energizing effect (Path 7). If the energizing effect is mild, it will merely add to vigilance. Third, the energizing effect (Path 7) may be intense; for example, a former beauty queen's deep concern about the loss of her appeal as a result of advancing years might be stimulated by some unintended comment in a cosmetics advertisement. If so, it will lead to fixation of the most probable integration, as shown in Figure 5.3, where probability is determined by the number of past pairings of the stimulus elements. This is perceptual defense, such as occurs when buyers are located in the X_3 position of the Stimulus Ambiguity-arousal relation, only here it is further complicated by an irrelevant motive. If the motivation is very intense, even disorganization or disintegration of stimulus-integrative mechanisms can occur.

The research supporting the ideas on vigilance and perception have been in terms of negative motives, but there appears to be no reason why it should not apply to positive motives as well. If so, we are dealing with a much more general behavioral mechanism here than is usually implied by "defense" (Osgood, 1957b, p. 397). Furthermore, the term "defense" would not be appropriate because "defense" has a specific and more restrictive meaning: a buyer selectively perceives so that he is protected from perceiving something unpleasant or threatening to his ego.

5.2.4 Summary of Perceptual Bias

The interactions between Motives (content and intensity), product class, and Attitude with each other and with the nature of the Stimulus Display—its ambiguity and the presence of contextual cues—have been examined to show how a number of perceptual mechanisms operate to modify the input that is admitted into the buyer's body by the joint action of Attention and Overt Search. These mechanisms make up the hypothetical construct, Perceptual Bias, the output of which is a stimulus-as-coded. We believe that the mechanisms can be used to explain a number of things that we see happening in marketing generally and in advertising in particular. They also point up the enormous complications involved in evaluating advertising, for example, under field conditions. But they also make constructive suggestions: how to control for more of the variability.

5.2.5   Quality of Information and Mass Communication

Let us relate the foregoing ideas on perception to the broader issues of communication in preparation for Chapters 8 and 9. A functional view of mass media often espoused by the mass communications researchers (E. Katz, 1968) holds that people can and do use mass media for different purposes: (1) to help them solve problems, (2) as a source of evidence that supports their existing views, and (3) because of interests.

In the earlier discussion of the Stimulus Ambiguity-arousal relation, it was assumed that buyers use the media for the first function—to help them solve their buying problems, to give them answers to their informational questions, to provide information as the basis for a buying decision.

Is there evidence for the second function, however? Do buyers use information to support their current views which logically could occur either in the processes of Perceptual Bias and Attention or in Overt Search? This function is expressed in the concept of "supportive exposure," and that people do seek support for their preconceptions is a widely accepted proposition in the mass communications research field (E. Katz, 1968). There is experimental evidence to support "supportive exposure," and this will be discussed.

However, to avoid confusion we must first dispose of a further extension of supportive exposure which is also widely accepted in communications research—"selective avoidance." By "selective avoidance" is meant the tendency to avoid information that contradicts the buyer's existing views. Here there is no supporting evidence, but some contradiction, hence no reason to believe that it is so (McGuire, 1968b). This conclusion about selective avoidance might seem to contradict the earlier comments on perceptual defense. It does not, however, because there we are referring to degree of ambiguity, not to contradictory information. The stimulus is too complex (ambiguous) to try to make sense of it.

To return to the phenomenon of supportive exposure, the rationale usually advanced to explain it is dissonance theory and, more specifically, "discrepant information." Typically the buyer is being confronted with competitive advertising that is "discrepant," information that contradicts what he now believes about the connotative attributes of his preferred brand (Attitude). He develops a preference for Brand A and then sees advertising that praises the merits of a competing Brand B. By implication Brand B appears better than A and yet he is loyal to A.

How does the buyer respond in this situation which characterizes almost all buying in an advanced economy with mass advertising? Let us first analyze the situation in terms of the principles of defense and stimulus integration instead of dissonance theory. Assume that the appropriate product class—the one containing A and B—does get called up by B's advertisement. The advertisement for Brand B is less likely to contain so many coevaluative elements as A's, because B is a brand different from A and he prefers A. Insofar as B's advertisement does not contain these elements, the buyer is less likely to make the integration appropriate to B's advertisement. In terms of Figure 5.3, Path 6 will not be favorable to Brand B.

Thus to the extent that B's advertisement is ambiguous, even though it contains coevaluative elements, the buyer is less likely to make the integrations appropriate to it. If it were a particularly attractive advertisement (have high Attention value), however, the attractiveness combined with ambiguity will have a high energizing effect, which can cause disintegration of any tendency to make integrations. As a consequence, the buyer is not likely to "see" the advertisement for B.

There has been considerable research on and theorizing about this issue in dissonance theory (Brehm and Cohen, 1962, pp. 51–60), which predicts that the buyer when confronted with a competing advertisement would normally find it unpleasant and would "avoid" it. As we said above, there is little evidence supporting "selective avoidance" and some contradicting it. Dissonance research has not been directed to those cases where the buyer is free to avoid this discrepant information but to instances where ". . . the nature of the information is impossible to predict completely (as on news broadcasts), because indications about the nature of the information are misleading (as newspaper headlines sometimes are), because the information may be 'forced' on one by a friend, and so on" (Brehm and Cohen, 1962, p. 50). What does seem to happen instead of "avoidance" is that discrepant information is misinterpreted. Perceptual Bias operates instead of Attention or Overt Search. "The more discrepant communication is perceived as less fair, less informed, less logical, less grammatical, less interesting, etc. . . . Besides affecting how the message is perceived as regards evaluation *of the information* [italics added], the discrepancy also affects where the message is perceived to lie on the attitude dimension" (McGuire, 1968b, pp. 215–216). Thus not only the quality of the message, for example, its credibility, but what it is thought to suggest about where the brand lies on the brand-evaluative dimension is also distorted.

This distortion of the attitude position on the evaluative dimension of the brand is the basis for Sherif's theory that when the buyer's involvement in the product class (Importance of Purchase) is high, the individual will distort his evaluative judgment of a brand when it falls in the "zone of acceptance" by making it *closer* to his desired position than it really is. When it falls in his "zone of rejection," he will make it still *further* away from his desired position (Sherif, Sherif, and Nebergall, 1965). Sherif's ideas appear to be very relevant to buying in cases of high motivation. This distortion, for example, would have a double effect: (1) the buyer would perceive the brand in a less favorable light, (2) hence would be less likely to perceive information about it.

Interest in the topic is the third reason for selecting some stimuli instead of others that is discussed in mass communications. For example, if interest were the motive, the buyer would be indifferent to which side of the argument he heard concerning the topic. Interest and supportive motivations are difficult to separate empirically (E. Katz, 1968). "Interest" is used by Katz, however, to refer to a wide range of ego-involving instances, whereas we have used "diversive exploratory behavior" to mean the need to maintain a satisfactory level of stimulation, which, in an interesting series of experiments, Berlyne calls "interest" in the stimulus (Berlyne and Peckham, 1966).

5.2.6   Dissonance Effects on Perception

The effects of "discrepant information" as viewed from the vantage point of dissonance theory have been set forth, and it seems appropriate to refer briefly here to dissonance in general because it has received considerable attention in the marketing literature.

Dissonance theory is one application of the consistency principle used in explaining Attitude formation and change (Chapter 4), and it has been applied to a wide range of problems other than those of discrepant information. Unfortunately, its predictions have to do mainly with behavior after the decision (Bruner, 1957), and this characteristic greatly weakens its usefulness for our purposes. True enough, the buyer's psychological state soon after the decision presumably will have some influence on his next purchase, and we are very much interested in the stream of purchasing acts, not just a single act. Furthermore, we do need in buying research a much better understanding of the *consumption* behavior as an influence on future purchase. However, this linkage between the immediate postdecision state of the buyer and his behavior leading up to the current decision, a repetition of the same overt act (purchase), has not been investigated by the dissonance researchers and still constitutes a gap in our knowledge. Moreover, we are not certain that dissonance effects are not merely postdecision behavior rationalizations with little behavioral significance. Because of the more limited coverage of its predictions, we touch only briefly on dissonance analysis as an aid in understanding Perceptual Bias.

Dissonance theory in general predicts that whenever cognitions are dissonant or in conflict with each other or with behavior (or with information), tension is created, which motivates the person to a certain course of action directed toward reducing the tension. The similarity of this proposition to the phenomena of vigilance and defense is obvious.

We would expect dissonance to arise, for example, with "disappointed expectations" as described earlier, that is, where the fact of Satisfaction is less than the buyer expected as indicated by the value of Attitude prior to his purchase. The extent of other situations in buying that give rise to dissonance is not known. Furthermore, there is currently lack of agreement, theoretically, on whether dissonance is more appropriate for viewing many of these issues than are two other possible precepts: the principle of congruity (Osgood, Suci and Tannenbaum, 1957) and the balance model (Rosenberg and Abelson, 1960; Cohen, 1964, Chapter 5).

A number of ways in which a person might reduce dissonance have been tested, and some of these fit into our category of "affecting the quality of the buyer's information." One avenue is *opinion change* (the buyer changes his perceived facts), the cognitive aspect of attitude. Another is *perceptual distortion,* and a third is *recall of information.* In communications terminology the first two would be "selective perception" and the latter, "selective recall."

5.3 SUMMARY AND CONCLUSIONS

We have shown in this chapter that the stimulus-as-coded is typically a modified version of the buyer's environment, where the nature of the environment is influenced by Overt Search. How much of what he is exposed to actually enters his nervous system is determined by Attention. The nature of the modification of that which is admitted by Attention is determined by Perceptual Bias.

The determinants of the quantity of the input information to the buyer have been formulated in this chapter: Attention, Overt Search, Stimulus Ambiguity, Conflict in Motives and feedback to Motives from Confidence, and Attitude. This input is the transformed by Perceptual Bias, a complex process construct made up of a number of mechanisms, into the output, which is the stimulus-as-coded. Here, too, are a number of feedbacks that show the complex relations between the two subsystems, as illustrated in Figure 5.4.

In the figure the central connecting link between the perceptual and learning subsystems could be the stimulus-as-coded which, from Perceptual Bias, feeds all of the learning process during the period the buyer is being studied. The ambiguity of Stimulus Display (Stimulus Ambi-

184

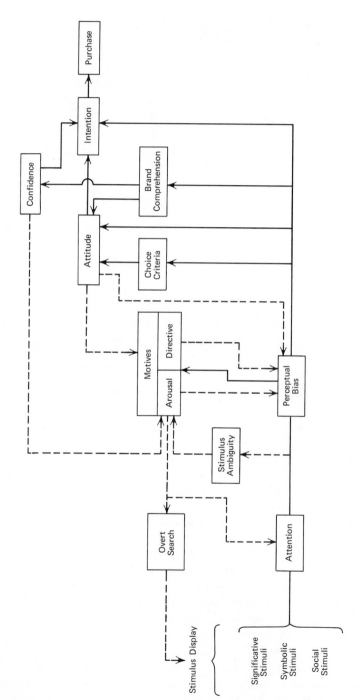

Figure 5.4 Interconnections between perception and learning. Solid lines indicate flow of information; dashed lines, feedback.

guity) acts as a feedback to arousal, which influences Attention and Overt Search. Feedback from Confidence, and Attitude, have corresponding effects.

A number of mechanisms operate in Perceptual Bias serving to modify the flow of information that gets through Attention. They operate on the stimulus integration process. There is feedback from arousal to Perceptual Bias irrespective of whether motive is relevant or irrelevant to the particular product class. If motive is relevant, however, there is also a directional feedback to Perceptual Bias. Finally, there is the question of which Attitude gets called up—becomes operative—and it has two effects. Depending on the conditions, there is, first, a feedback from Attitude to arousal and from it, in turn, to Perceptual Bias. Second, there is a feedback directly on Perceptual Bias.

These interconnectives between the two subsystems show us the difficulty of doing research on one independently of the other. The stimulus-as-coded concept, however, if operationally defined, makes possible treating them as separate systems.

5.3.1 Stimulus-as-Coded as a Hypothetical Construct

Clearly, the use of the s-a-c construct, if it can be made operational, will permit much better control, especially in the field studies that will probably continue to characterize most research in marketing. The construct will aid in relating the two separate research areas—perception and learning—distinctively separate areas that are also likely to characterize buyer research such as advertising and brand loyalty.

Some ideas that will help in operationalizing the construct—converting it into an intervening variable—are set out by Lawrence (1963). For our purposes it will be necessary to distinguish between the denotative and connotative aspects of the s-a-c—what it is that the buyer discriminates by and what it is that the s-a-c suggests in terms of his needs. Also, s-a-c will incoporate more than one sense, such as both seeing and hearing a television advertisement. There would be a structure within each of the two general dimensions. Krugman's (1967) thinking-looking-feeling paradigm is suggestive and particularly his way of measuring "thinking." "*Thinking* will be defined in terms of thoughts which come spontaneously to mind while an ad was being viewed." These thoughts are then analyzed for their connections "which link some content of the ad to some content in the personal life of the respondent." He does not, however, attempt to describe the s-a-c denotatively.

5.3.2 Exogenous Variables

At least three exogenous variables influence the quantity of information. Greater Importance of Purchase will cause a greater tendency to change Stimulus Display. High values of Time Pressure will, on the other hand, decrease it.

Finally, Personality Traits make a difference. In fact, we suspect that they make a greater difference in perception than in learning. Such personality traits as self-esteem and anxiety constitute an influence. People with low self-confidence or high anxiety are less likely to seek information, especially women. The role of personality traits was referred to as one of the determinants of the OX_1 range of the Stimulus Ambiguity-arousal relation for the individual buyer, in connection with perceived risk.

Personality Traits probably become even more significant in influencing the quality of the information (Perceptual Bias), as suggested by some of the experiments briefly described in this chapter. This is a well-researched area, and we have not in any way attempted to summarize the available findings (Berlyne, 1963, pp. 344–347). One of the very interesting conclusions, for example, is that people of low esteem appear to make decisions by closing out information, whereas high-esteem people take in the information but are able to process it meaningfully (McGuire, 1968c).

5.4 HYPOTHETICAL CONSTRUCTS AND INTERVENING VARIABLES

The hypothetical constructs that make up the main part of the theory of buyer behavior have been developed here and in Chapter 4. Let us now relate these constructs to the output intervening variables. It is possible to show why it is not necessarily true that a change in one variable is a necessary and sufficient condition for change in the successive one, though most practitioners believe in this Response Sequence. We use "Response Sequence" to give more precise definition to the traditional notion of hierarchy of effects, however, we do not require that a change in one variable is a sufficient much less a necessary condition to change in a subsequent variable. It is the network of relations among the output intervening variables such as Attention', Brand Comprehension', Attitude', Intention' and Purchase although we do not exclude the intervening counterparts of the other hypothetical constructs. It is a process operating over time and summarizing the functional relations among these intervening variables. We think of it as being quantitatively described by a set of simultaneous equations that represent the network.

Attention' is the intervening counterpart of Attention, but supplementing this construct are the vigilance and defense effects of Perceptual Bias which are not captured in Attention. Brand Comprehension' refers only to the denotative aspects of the brand element in evoked set. Attitude' refers to the connotative aspects of the brand concept and so is the intervening counterpart of Attitude. Intention' to buy is the cognitive counterpart of another intervening variable—Purchase—and captures the effects of inhibitors on brand purchase. We assume that Intention' and Purchase measures, if taken simultaneously, would yield the same results in terms of brand choice.

The simple, unilateral view of causation, often assumed by the users of the Response Sequence of marketing effects and implied in the output intervening variables, is seriously vitiated by the great variety of feedbacks that have been postulated in Chapters 4 and 5. Although Attention' was found to be more sensitive to the *content* of the stimulus than might be expected, we would expect Brand Comprehension' to be still more sensitive because the need to endow a piece of information with meaning probably forces a more complex process. In Chapter 9 other examples will be shown.

We emphasize these particular intervening variables because they tend to be employed in practice and are found to be useful. For purposes of fundamental research, however, one may wish to use others.

5.5 THEORY OF SEARCH

We have attempted to set forth the elements of a theory of search. Confidence, the inverse of brand ambiguity, acts on arousal, which in turn stimulates Attention and Overt Search until adequate information is obtained. Thus we can speak of an information equilibrium when the buyer has acquired the information he needs. At the same time he has achieved a purchase equilibrium in which Confidence exerts a strong influence. Hence confidence plays a pivotal role in explaining behavior. It is a determinant of both search behavior and overt purchase until an information-purchase equilibrium is achieved when it affects only overt purchase. Chapter 8 in particular calls upon these ideas.

Going further in developing search concepts, we can think of overt search activity as being the output of the learning subsystem in place of Purchase, with the alternatives being various sources of information such as word-of-mouth and advertising. An information source instead of a brand then becomes the goal object toward which the motivation process is directed. Intention becomes the intention to use one source instead of another, Attitude is the preference for one source over another, and Confidence is the buyer's confidence in judging the subjective quality of various sources. In this way the whole gamut of concepts and relationships of the buyer behavior theory can be focused on information seeking. Hence we see how the process construct of Overt Search can be broken down into its state components.

5.6 ROUTINIZED RESPONSE BEHAVIOR

To provide a simple way of looking at the complex process of learning to buy, we have postulated the three types of decision processes or situations: Extensive Problem Solving (the buyer knows neither the brand nor the product class), Limited Problem Solving (he knows the product class but not the brand), and Routinized Response Behavior (he knows both the brand and product class). At the end of Chapter 4, buyer behavior as exhibited in Routinized Response Behavior was described. In Chapter 5, the nature of the perceptual process was developed to show how the buyer receives his information for moving from Limited Problem Solving to Routinized Response Behavior. The same perceptual processes operate, of course, when the buyer moves from Extensive Problem Solving to Limited Problem Solving, but we deal with that topic in Chapter 8.

The Theory and Its Measurement

CHAPTER 6

Attitude' as an Intervening Variable

In Part II, we presented the theory of buyer behavior and gave detailed descriptions of its hypothetical constructs. The latter, as mentioned earlier, are comparatively more abstract and richer in meaning. Some of them could be generalized to other economic contexts, just as they have been generalized to buying behavior from clinical and experimental psychology and social psychology in general.

However, the generality of hypothetical constructs necessarily leaves out the details involved in a specific buying situation or decision. Therefore, to apply the theory of buyer behavior to a specific product class, we must have operationally defined, less abstract constructs that will be counterparts of many of the hypothetical constructs. These are the response intervening variables, whose interrelationships were described in Chapter 3. They serve the function of bridging the gap between the specific reality of a buying situation and the theory of buyer behavior.

Part III of the book, consisting of Chapters 6 and 7, is concerned with the response intervening variables. However, we limit a detailed discussion to only two such variables: Attitude' and Purchase. First, some of the response variables in the sequence are relatively less important to the description of brand choice behavior, which is the topic of concern here. Attention' to a specific bit of information is an example.

Second, some of the other variables are well-defined, and considerable objective research on them already exists in the literature on buying behavior. To that extent, we feel that a description and discussion in detail of those variables would have been a rehash of what is already known. Intention' is, to some extent, one such variable. Finally, the two output variables of Attitude' and Purchase are more fully discussed because we define and measure them in ways that differ to a considerable extent from many similarly labeled concepts both in behavioral sciences and in marketing (Sheth, 1969b; Sheth and Ring, 1968). This is elaborated in Chapters 6 and 7.

In Section 6.1, we discuss rules of correspondence for Attitude' which entail definition and measurement. Our definition of Attitude' is very specific, compared to what is discussed in social psychology in the area of attitude formation and change. Measurement of Attitude', on the other hand, is more complex than most existing procedures.

Section 6.2 describes, in broad terms, what is meant by measurement and scaling. This is followed by description of procedures related to measurement of Attitude' in section 6.3. Finally, we discuss measurement of attitude change over time in Section 6.4.

6.1   RULES OF CORRESPONDENCE

An intervening variable is linked to observable data by rules of correspondence (Margenau, 1950; Torgerson, 1958; Royce, 1963). Rules of correspondence refer to definition and measurement of the construct so that observable data can be isomorphically transformed into an intervening variable. Attitude' is accordingly given an operational (as opposed to constitutive) definition, and measurement procedures are also described later in the chapter.

6.1.1   Definition of Attitude'

In Part II, we pointed out that attitude is a construct that suffers from multiordinality, as discussed in Chapter 1. Multiordinality denotes the quality of a construct having several meanings, depending on the level of abstraction. Attitude has, in the past, been moved up and down the ladder of abstraction: some researchers have treated it as an observable, operational variable, which itself is a function of more fundamental processes such as the tendency for congruence, balance, consistency, or equilibrium among cognitions (DeFleur and Westie, 1963). Others have considered attitude to be a hypothetical variable (and richer in meaning), similar to motivation or learning. According to them, attitude itself is the cause of behavior or behavioral intentions (D. Campbell 1963).

In the theory of buyer behavior, we have separated attitude into two constructs in order to clarify the multiordinality: (1) Attitude, which is more abstract and hypothetical, and (2) Attitude', which is less abstract and operational. Attitude as a hypothetical construct was described and compared with other similar points of view in Chapter 4. Now we define Attitude' as an intervening variable and, in the process, compare it with other definitions of a similar viewpoint.

Attitude' is defined as buyer's evaluation of a brand or service as measured (either verbal or self-administered) on a set of bipolar scales reflecting salient purchase criteria common to the product class in which the brand is one element of the set. More abstractly, Attitude' is the buyer's belief about the brand or the supplier as a perceived instrument of his goal satisfaction.

The bipolar scales are the salient purchase criteria that the buyer uses in making choices among brands. They are not specific to a brand, but are common to all the brands in a product class. The scales are *indicants* of Choice Criteria, and by the procedures described in this chapter, we show how to derive Choice Criteria from these indicants. The evaluation of a brand on these scales brings out connotative meanings that the buyer has learned about a brand from either experience or information. In short, Attitude' is much more restrictive than most of the definitions given in social psychology. As such, it is less abstract, more realistic, more formal, more introspective, and possibly more objective. For a meaningful comparison, it may be useful to look at various definitions from certain points of view.

First is Allport's (1935) definition of attitude as a mental or neural state of readiness, organized through experience, exciting a directive or dynamic influence on individual's response to all objects and situations with which it is related. This definition is more appropriate for Attitude, the hypothetical construct, than for Attitude', the intervening variable. Since it was discussed in Chapter 4, we shall not compare it here with Attitude'.

Second, the functional approach to attitudes (D. Katz, 1960; D. Katz and Stotland, 1959; Sarnoff and D. Katz, 1954) considers that attitudes could be classified as serving four separate functions. Attitude', the intervening variable, serves the instrumental utilitarian function, as can be seen from the definition. Attitude, the hypothetical construct, in addition serves the ego-defensive and the value-expressive functions. However, the knowledge function is served by Brand Comprehension because of the descriptive rather than evaluative nature of cognitions involved in it.

Third, a major framework of defining attitudes is in terms of the cognition-affect-conation paradigm so common in psychology. In all the definitions of attitudes, affect (liking, preference, etc.) is considered an essential element. We, however, think that affect as measured in terms of a single liking scale is really an aggregate index or summary which itself is a function of the evaluative beliefs about the brand (Rosenberg, 1956, 1960). As an index, affect may have good predictive power for subsequent behavior, but it is lacking in explanation as to *why* it would predict behavior. In our first study based on the theory of buyer behavior, we find that a significant correlation (.40 or above in a sample of 954 households) exists between affect and many of the evaluative beliefs relevant to a convenience food product. It is more meaningful, however, to the marketing manager to know the extent of the buyer's evaluative beliefs than the extent of his general liking. This is because he can communicate accordingly on some beliefs and not on others. For example, in the same study, we find that liking is highly correlated with "delicious taste" and "real flavor" in the case of an instant breakfast, but also with "easy to use" and "good for a snack" in the case of a milk additive. The theory of buyer behavior is more useful to the marketing manager when it shows these evaluative beliefs. Lavidge and Steiner (1961) limit the definition of attitude to the affect component in their hierarchy of responses for advertising effectiveness. We, on the other hand, obtain the evaluative beliefs that are presumed to be the cause of the affect component.

The conative elements or behavioral intentions are included by some researchers in their definition of attitude in addition to the affective elements. We separate the conative elements in another intervening variable (Intention'), however, and exclude them from the definition of Attitude'. The theory of buyer behavior then posits that behavioral intention measured by Intention' is due to Attitude toward a brand, Confidence in its judgment, and situational contingencies which act as inhibitors. To that extent, Attitude' is causal to Intention' but itself does not contain conative elements. However, it is possible to conceive that conative elements are implicit in our definition of Attitude' to the extent that bipolar scales reflect purchase criteria which themselves are based on buyer's motives.

The cognitive elements (knowledge, beliefs, etc.) are present in our definition of Attitude'. In fact, from the discusion above we may state that Attitude' explicitly includes only cognitive elements, whereas affect and conation are derivatives and so only implicitly present. However, we include only those beliefs about a brand that are *evaluative* and serve the instrumental, utilitarian function. Other beliefs about the brand are part of Brand Comprehension, particularly those that are descriptive of the brand and its relation to other objects.

Finally, our definition of Attitude' is probably closest to that of the Michigan researchers and their means-end analysis of attitude change (M. Smith, 1949; DiVesta and Merwin, 1960; Rosenberg, 1956, 1960; Carlson, 1956; Peak, 1955; and Fishbein, 1963, 1967). They define attitude toward an object as a composite of the perceived instrumentality of that object to the person's values or goals, weighted by his saliency of those values or goals. In other words, attitude is the product of potential of various characteristics of an object times the valence of the individual's values. (For this multiplicative relation, see Rosenberg, 1960; Fishbein, 1967; Zajonc, 1954.) However, Attitude' as defined here differs from the means-end approach to the extent that we only include salient motives by limiting the evaluation on those purchase criteria that are important to the consumers, as found from preliminary pilot studies in each case. Thus the weighting procedure is considered unnecessary. Some support for this comes from Rosenberg's study (1956) where valence or saliency itself was much less important in explaining correlation between beliefs and general affect. Furthermore, the first ten or fifteen values ranked according to their importance did not produce greater correlation when compared to the last fifteen values. In fact, it would appear that including a total of 35 values for evaluation is itself less meaningful when salient values ranged from zero to six at best for any one subject in the sample; and for a majority of the subjects, it amounted to only two or three. A closer look at the results in Rosenberg's study clearly show that inclusion of nonsalient values in fact suppresses the correlation between evaluative beliefs and general affect because the chi-squared value of association between affect and perceived instrumentality for the first 20 salient values was 35.51 ($p < .001$), but it was divided as chi-squared value of only 20.82 ($p < .01$) for the first more important 10 values and that of 38.47 ($p < .001$) for the less important last 10 values (Rosenberg 1956, Table 3).

Although we do not separate saliency of motives from evaluative beliefs in Attitude', there may be product classes in which the degree of importance of salient motives varies from one individual to another. We, therefore, suggest that, in general, the researcher must also obtain the extent of saliency of each salient purchase criterion, and when individual variability is found in analysis, it may improve the correlation between general affect, behavioral intention (Intention'), or buying (Purchase) on the one hand and evaluative beliefs (Attitude') on the other hand, by multiplying evaluations with saliency. A more important influence, however, seems to come from the buyer's Confidence in making the evaluations. The theoretical explanation may be that there are differences in sources of learning. A consumer who has learned from commercial sources of information may evaluate the brand the same as a consumer who has learned from buying experience, but the former may be less confident in his judgment. The lack of confidence then enables competing stimuli to change the buyer's behavioral intentions or actual buying behavior.

6.1.2   Measurement of Attitude'

The second aspect of rules of correspondence is measurement of Attitude' toward a brand in terms of the observable data. The rest of the chapter is devoted to procedures related to this, and here we only point out some broad generalizations. First, measurement of Attitude' is, by the definition of intervening variables, limited to operationally defined and measurable properties of a brand. A brand may possess a complex attribute, such as a technical or chemical component, which is an important evaluative criterion for the buyer. But if it cannot be operationally defined or quantified, *from the buyer's point of view,* we must either ignore it or have some approximate measure for it. With increasing commercialization of technical breakthroughs, this may become a serious methodological problem in years to come. Second, what we measure are the *properties* of the brand from the *introspective perspective of the buyer.* Furthermore, these properties are limited to the evaluative beliefs. In other words, we consider neither the brand itself (as an object) nor all its properties. Also, it can possess a set of attributes from a chemist's point of view or the seller's point of view, but we are only concerned with properties that are meaningful to the buyer. We think that this perspective should be emphasized, because many measurements of attitudes in buying behavior are based on a variety of perspectives, which results in contradictory findings. Third, Attitude' is a vector (or a matrix if there are more dimensions than one) consisting of scores of a buyer for various brands belonging to the same product class. The same purchase criteria are used for evaluating several brands, all presumably the elements of buyer's evoked set. This is a further limitation in our measurement, because the same brands may not belong to evoked sets of all the consumers (B. Campbell, 1969) or a product class definition may not be the same across all consumers (J. Howard, 1963). A careful investigation and knowledge of the product class is, therefore, mandatory before we use the theory of buyer behavior, so that a meaningful explanation can be provided.

In summary, Attitude' is defined and, more importantly, measured in a very specific way, and to that extent it is delimiting. It will stimulate empirical investigation, but any speculative theorizing may come only from its counterpart, Attitude, which is not so delimiting as a construct.

6.2   MEASUREMENT AND SCALING

6.2.1   Scaling of Attitude toward a Brand

Scaling is a procedure by which a measurement standard or a scale is developed. Its subsequent use in specific situations is not scaling but simply using a scale. A good example is the temperature scale (thermometer)—there scaling is the process by which a thermometer is calibrated. It could be used in a variety of situations by modifying its physical shape, size, or gradations. In other words, we do not focus on the procedures of administering and scoring of an attitude scale, but rather on the process involved in the construction of a scale.

Development of a scale is intimately connected with the measurement of properties of an object. Measurement is the assignment of numerals to represent properties of an object according to the laws of the real number system (N. Campbell, 1920). Similar definitions are provided by Stevens (1939), Coombs (1952), and Ellis (1966). The important point in measurement is the isomorphic (one-to-one) representation of the property by the real number system. The characteristics of the number system then should be adequate enough to isomorphically transform a property into numbers.

The three important characteristics of the real number system are *order* (numbers are ordered), *distance* (difference between pairs of numbers are ordered), and *origin* (the number series has a unique origin indicated by zero). It is possible to give empirical meanings to the properties of an object such as a brand in terms of these number characteristics. For example, the property of pleasantness of taste of several brands in an edible product category can be represented by order characteristic of the number system. Similarly, the property of nutrition can be represented by the distance characteristic of the number system. In short, an isomorphic transformation of the property into the numbers is a necessary condition in establishing a scale of measurement.

6.2.2   Types of Scales

The three characteristics of numbers enable us to classify the *types of scales* available to measure properties of an object. Stevens (1951), for example, distinguishes among nominal, ordinal, interval, and ratio-type scales. The *nominal scale* is one that has none of the characteristics of the number system. Instead, numbers are used to represent the objects themselves (as opposed to any property of the object) for verification, identification, and classification. Numbering all the brands of beer sold in a given region is a good example of nominal scaling. If it is a nominal scale, the permissible statistics for analysis are set theory, mode, and contingency analysis (Stevens, 1951).

Recently, however, more complex statistical analysis has been performed on data that are essentially nominally scaled. For example, Burt (1950) has suggested the use of factor analysis for classificatory, qualitative data. Sheth (1966, 1969e) has provided a cumulative measure of brand loyalty based on nominal (purchase or no-purchase of a brand) type of data. This is elaborated in the next chapter when we discuss Purchase as an intervening variable. Sheth (1968e) also shows how, in many multivariate analyses, classifactory data can be used. A variety of complex stochastic models of consumer behavior are available which essentially start with nominally scaled data (Sheth, 1967; Montgomery, 1967).

The second type of scale is called an *ordinal scale* which enables the researcher to (rank) order the objects in terms of the magnitude of a *property* they possess. We can then state whether one object is greater than or less than any of the other objects with regard to a property they commonly possess. The ordinal scale incorporates the order characteristic of the number system. Then all objects which have a common property that could be ordered can be put on an ordinal scale by isomorphic transformation of the property into the numbers. Rank-ordering several brands of beer in terms of perceived quality would be a good example of ordinal scale.

Stevens (1951) suggests that permissible statistics are median, percentile, and rank correlations. Both the nominal and ordinal scales, however, suffer from lack of metric information. Recently, several nonparametric scaling techniques (Coombs and Kao, 1955; Coombs, 1964; Shepard, 1962, 1963; Kruskal, 1964; Guttman, 1944, 1950, 1958; Lingoes and Guttman, 1967) have emerged which distill metric information from nonmetric ordered data.

Incorporation of each of the characteristics of the number system takes away a great deal of freedom in assigning numerals to represent a property. For example, the inclusion of an order characteristic in ordinal scale requires that the order of numbers assigned agree with that of the property. However, compared to other types of scales, discussed later, which incorporate other characteristics as well, a great deal of freedom still remains in the ordinal scale. In fact, any order-preserving (monotonic) transformation from one set of numbers to another set is permissible in the ordinal scale.

The third type of scale is called an *interval scale*. It incorporates the first two characteristics of order and distance. In addition to the order of the numbers corresponding to the order of the magnitude of various amounts of a property, the size of the difference between pairs of numbers has meaning and corresponds to the distance between the corresponding pairs of objects with regard to the magnitude of property. Comparison of nutritive property possessed by various brands is a good example of using an interval scale. Inclusion of distance characteristic further reduces the freedom of arbitrarily assigning numbers. However, the freedom remaining amounts to linear transformation of one set of numbers into any other set of numbers. The possibility of linear transformation, therefore, still leaves a good deal of freedom. The permissible statistics are the quantitative statistics that include mean, dispersion, and correlation.

The fourth type of scale is called the *ratio scale*. It incorporates all three characteristics—order, distance, and origin. Inclusion of natural origin limits the use of ratio scale to those properties of objects that possess a unique starting position. The distances between pairs of objects are then uniquely determined as ratios of the magnitudes of the property. Price of a brand is a good example of measurement of economic value by the use of ratio scale: price has unique zero, and distances are ordered.

Ratio scale is the most rigorous of all types of scales. By incorporating all characteristics of numbers, it removes the maximum amount of arbitrariness in assigning numbers to represent a property. By the same token, the freedom is now limited to arbitrarily assigning only one number, and the remaining numbers are all determined by the scale.

Both interval and ratio scales are limited to linear transformation. Furthermore, the ratio scale is limited to linear transformation, which has the form $y = ax$.

Torgerson (1958) has provided a slightly different classification of types of scales, although the underlying theory is similar to Stevens' (1951). Table 6.1 is based on Torgerson's scheme of classification.

Table 6.1   Types of Scales of Measurement

	No Natural Origin	Natural Origin
No Distance	Ordinal scale	Ordinal scale with natural origin
Distance	Interval scale	Ratio scale

It will be noted, first, that Torgerson has omitted nominal scale in his classification. This follows from the argument that it is the property of an object and not the object itself that is involved in scaling, and all properties possess at least ordinal characteristics. N. Campbell (1920) concurs in this argument. Both, of course, differ from Stevens. Second, another type of scale is added—ordinal scale with natural origin. This is to separate the properties that are ordinal but seem to possess a unique zero position from those that do not possess a unique starting point. Preference for a brand may be classified as one such property that has a natural origin (no preference).

6.2.3 Approaches to Scaling

Any theory is from a perspective or point of view. The theory of buyer behavior is introspective to the extent that it is from the buyer's point of view that we abstract constructs. Scaling of properties of an object such as a brand has a delimiting function in the sense that it is from a perspective. Although a variety of perspectives may exist, we find that in behavioral sciences most of the approaches can be classified into three categories. These categories are derived from the S-O-R paradigm, so commonly known and used in psychology (Torgerson, 1958). The basic assumption is that response (R) can be explained by the stimulus (S), or organism (O), or the interaction of stimulus and organism (S-O).

In the *stimulus-centered approach,* the systematic variations in the reactions of the individuals to stimuli are attributed to differences in the stimuli themselves with respect to a designated property. In the process, respondents are treated as replications or observations: adding respondents at random from the same population or deleting them would have no effect on the scale. Thurstone's (1928) attitude scale construction would fall into this category. The general procedure is to select a set of statements that vary in their favorableness to an object such as church, company, or brand. The statements are classified into separate piles by a sample of respondents in terms of the degree of favorability or unfavorability that the statements possess *toward the object.* From the frequency of respondents, some statements are discarded and others are rearranged, so that the final scale possesses the complete range of statements from being extremely unfavorable to being extremely favorable toward the object. This scale, once developed, is used as a standard to measure attitudes of a group of people of interest to the researcher.

The *subject-centered approach* assumes that systematic variations in the reactions of the respondents to the stimuli are due to individual differences among the respondents. Here the stimuli or the statements are treated as replications, and adding or deleting a statement from the same stimulus population at random would have no effect. The scaling technique presented by Likert (1932) would be subject-centered. The procedure is to take a large number of statements and ask the respondents whether *they* agree with them and to what extent. The scores (generally ranging from −2 to +2 or 1 to 5) on various statements are added together. Then item analysis is carried out, whereby each statement's score is correlated with the battery score. Any statement that shows no correlation with the battery is considered to be undifferentiating and is generally removed from the battery. Also, internal consistency is performed on the statements. The pruning of the original number of statements into fewer numbers is the process of scaling and is based on the respondent's reactions or agreements. Once the final scale is made up, it can be used as a standard to measure attitudes of people belonging to a group in which the researcher is interested.

Finally, there is the *response approach,* in which variability in reactions to stimuli is attributed to both variations in the respondents and in the stimuli. Here the freedom of adding or deleting at random either a stimulus statement or a respondent is limited. In the response approach, then, both the respondents and the stimuli are scaled. Guttman's scalogram analysis (1944) would be an example of response approach despite the fact that it resembles the subject-centered approach of Likert. A good example is also the semantic differential technique proposed by Osgood, Suci, and Tannenbaum (1957). Generally, it resembles a subject-centered approach in that it is the respondents who are scaled or ordered by their scores on a set of bipolar seven-point scales. However, if several concepts are evaluated by the respondents, then it is possible to scale or order the concepts as if they were the stimuli.

In summary, the stimulus-centered approach of scaling ignores individual differences, and its objective is to scale or order various stimulus statements. In the subject-centered approach of scaling, the variability in the stimulus statements is ignored, and the objective is to scale or order the respondents. In the response approach of scaling, both the subjects and the stimuli are scaled or ordered.

The theory of buyer behavior states that a buyer possesses strengths of Attitude' toward various brands in his evoked set. Each brand has to be scaled for a comparative analysis. However, our interest, from the marketing manager's point of view, is not in one buyer but in comparisons among several buyers. Each buyer is likely to differ in his Attitude' toward a brand, and he should be scaled or ordered for classification and segmentation. Hence it is the response approach of scaling that is appropriate to measurement of Attitude'. In fact, we have chosen a procedure (to be described in the next section) that closely resembles the semantic differential.

6.3 A MULTIVARIATE APPROACH TO ATTITUDE' MEASUREMENT

Within the broad framework of response approach to Attitude' measurement, we present a multivariate method of obtaining Attitude' scores for buyers. The basic approach is to obtain the dimensionality of purchase criteria which will define Choice Criteria and use these dimensions to create a "preference" space for the buyer. A brand is then evaluated and placed as a point in this space. Similarly, all other brands in which the researcher has interest or which are part of the buyer's evoked set are so evaluated and placed as points in the same space. The similarity of two brands can be derived from the inverse of the distance between them in their locations in the space.

The mathematical procedure involved in the measurement of Attitude' is similar to the multidimensional scaling procedures (Torgerson, 1958). However, from our point of view, there exist several problems with multidimensional scaling in general that we think must be elaborated before we discuss our own procedure. It is our belief that the multivariate procedure suggested in this section is not only theoretically sound, but is also devoid of the problems of multidimensional scaling.

Then we suggest ways in which a researcher can obtain salient purchase criteria for the development of scales on which to acquire a buyer's evaluative beliefs about a brand.

Next, Attitude' scores of buyers are obtained using factor analysis. Finally, interbrand similarities are found for a comparative statement about brands under analysis.

6.3.1 Limitations of Multidimensional Scaling

Several limitations are brought to our attention in the use of multidimensional scaling techniques despite their importance and diffusion in several areas including attitude measurement. Most of these limitations can be attributed to the direct extension of unidimensional methods of scaling (paired comparisons, equal-appearing intervals, etc.) to multidimensional phenomena without relevant justifications.

6.3.1.1 Dimensionality and Attributes of a Concept

One of the fundamental problems with the existing multidimensional approaches has been limiting the technique to finding the dimensionality of a *single attribute* of a concept or a brand. For example, research has been limited to obtaining the dimensions of color, shape, or size of a set of concepts. Since each of these attributes actually is one of the several properties that a concept can and does possess, the analysis is limited. If the researcher is interested in only one such attribute because his theory dictates that he so limit himself, there is no real problem with existing multidimensional approaches. However, more often than not, the theory demands that several concepts be compared or adjudged in terms of similarity based not on one common attribute across the concepts, but on *several common attributes*. This is particularly true in the case of buying behavior where the several brands (concepts) are compared for similarities in terms of a variety of attributes, such as price, taste, and convenience, contained in the quality of a brand. In the measurement of attitudes, instead of meeting the limitation by proper measures of similarities (distances) between the concepts based on several specific attributes, an easy exit has been resorted to through utilization of single gross attributes like preference or liking. In fact, utilization of preference or liking as a single attribute has enabled the researchers to extend the unidimensional methods of scaling to multidimensional methods. In stimulus-centered methods, we find that all the unidimensional approaches such as paired comparisons, equal-appearing intervals, successive intervals, and triadic combinations, can be extended by simply asking the respondent to answer the preference or liking of a *pair of stimuli as compared to another pair of stimuli* in place of each stimulus separately (Messick, 1956). Thus the distance measures for multidimensional scaling are obtained by making *paired comparison* of *pairs of stimuli*, or by asking to differentiate between a *pair* of stimuli on a 9- or 11-point scale of similarity.

To us it appears that the purpose for which multidimensional scaling came into being has been defeated by such extensions. The purpose was to cope with the *complexity* of the interrelations among concepts by utilizing multivariate procedures. This is clearly not done. What is really needed is a procedure, based on theoretical reasoning and relevant for a specific situation, that will enable the researcher to take into account the complexity of concepts by incorporating and aggregating several attributes present in them. In buying behavior, for example, the buyer chooses brand A over brand B because of several purchase criteria each reflecting a property (attribute) of the brands. Since this aggregation procedure is subject to individual differences, we find that a simple preference (affect) measure may not tell us much as to why the buyer prefers brand A over other brands: *The "why" aspect has to be built into the rule of correspondence to provide any connection between the hypothetical constructs and intervening variables.* Thus, unless the "why" aspect is incorporated, we may easily find two buyers, for example, both preferring brand A over other brands but for entirely different attributes possessed by brand A as compared to other brands. In summary, then, we must at first provide an index of similarity between the concepts which incorporates the underlying complexity of the concepts.

6.3.1.2 Lack of Conceptual Foundations

A problem related to the complexity of concepts in terms of the multi-attributes discussed above is the theoretical appropriateness of the desired properties of investigation. In this respect our remarks will be primarily in terms of multidimensional approaches to *attitude measurement*. It should be noted that despite a variety of definitions of attitudes, complex theories of attitude change, and a definite recognition of the complexity that attitudes possess, the scaling of attitudes has been mostly in terms of liking-disliking, favorableness-unfavorableness, and so forth (McGuire, 1966a). The only exceptions are the semantic-differential (Osgood, Suci, and Tannenbaum, 1957) and instrumentality-valence methods of the Michigan group (Fishbein, 1967). The result is that in both unidimensional and multidimensional scaling, there exists a common attitude measurement as an indicant for a variety of theoretical postulates. In social psychology, for example, several separate consistency theories can all explain the same measures of attitude change (Feldman, 1966).

It will be evident from Part II that in a complex theory of buyer behavior, a simple like-dislike comparison of brands would result in inappropriate rules of correspondence. We must have measures of similarity between brands on more specific and theoretically dictated attributes of the brands. It is possible to obtain good predictive indication in gross liking or preference (affect) scales in terms of overt subsequent buying of a brand. However, we do not know *why* that liking or preference exists and *why* the buyer subsequently buys the brand, hence cannot communicate adequately and appropriately to different segments of the market either by significative or symbolic means. In other words, it is not sufficient that a system works; we must know how or why it works. It is precisely for this reason that we attempt theory building.

6.3.1.3 Problem of Additive Constant

As already mentioned, most of the multidimensional scaling techniques are extensions of traditional unidimensional ones where judgments of similarity are obtained between the members of *pairs* of stimuli rather than about a single stimulus. The resultant scale values represent the distance between two stimuli on a distance continuum, rather than the position of one stimulus on an attribute continuum. Now, in all of the unidimensional scaling methods the choice of an origin and a unit is arbitrary; hence the distance estimates are all *relative*, being based on an arbitrary origin. The relative or comparative distances must first be converted to *absolute* distances to utilize some powerful mathematical techniques related to interpoint distances among real points in Euclidian space. The conversion of relative distances to absolute distances requires estimating a constant. "Inherent in this approach is the danger of considering distances which actually represent non-Euclidean relationships as being Euclidean" (Messick, 1956, pp. 93–94). However, several estimation procedures have been developed that enable the researcher to convert relative distances to absolute distances and mathematically justify a Euclidian space (Messick and Ableson, 1956; Torgerson, 1958). The resulting constant may nevertheless entail a large number of dimensions, which will throw suspicion on either its accuracy or the Euclidian properties of the data. "If a distance function could be found which did involve an arbitrary constant but still retained the interval properties of some of the scaling methods discussed above, many of the criticisms of the relative distance approach could be avoided" (Messick, 1956, p. 95).

The problem of additive constant is mentioned here to point out that standard extensions of unidimensional techniques may be inappropriate not only because of complexity of the problem or lack of theory, but also because there are some real mathematical problems in multidimensional analysis. The particular approaches provided later in the chapter circumvent these problems by obtaining absolute scale values from which distances are then created between two brands for each buyer.

6.3.1.4 Aggregate Approach of Stimulus-Centered Methods

Finally, the existing multidimensional methods, particularly in the stimulus-centered approach to scaling, have ignored individual differences by averaging over individuals and obtaining average values of relative distances. The theory of buyer behavior, on the other hand, suggests definite individual differences on the hypothetical constructs, and, therefore, a strict judgmental method (stimulus-centered) is not appropriate. On the other side, of course, the marketing practitioner is not interested in a single buyer; he must cater to the mass in the advanced economy. He wants to know the individual differences in order that he may *segment* the total market into components and then hope to communicate individually with each segment. Thus what is really needed is a method where both the stimulus and the organism are influential in the differential responses.

Very recently, Tucker and Messick (1963) have provided an individual difference model for multidimensional scaling to remove this problem of aggregation. The model* permits the determination of separate multidimensional spaces for individuals having different viewpoints about stimulus interrelationships. We shall utilize their quantitative system for our purposes later on.

To summarize, existing multidimensional scaling methods suffer from lack of incorporating complexity of interconcept relationships, from theoretical foundations, from the additive constant problem, and from the aggregate analysis. These limitations make it inappropriate to adopt the techniques as they are in buying behavior. This is particularly true in our case where we begin with an explicit statement of the theory of buyer behavior. What we need is some approach to Attitude' measurement that is anchored to the theory.

6.3.2   Scaling Procedures to Measure Attitude'

To obtain Attitude' score for an individual buyer as he perceives a brand, a three-step scaling procedure is followed. First, the salient purchase criteria that are implicitly related to the buyer's relevant motives are obtained. In fact, these criteria may be considered as the operational indicants of Choice Criteria. Second, a sample of buyers are asked to evaluate a brand in terms of the attitude scales. Finally, the evaluations are aggregated analytically to obtain independent dimensions of the buyers' evaluative beliefs about the brand. The resultant Attitude' scores (uni- or multidimensional) will then scale the buyers.

The procedure is repeated for all the brands in the product class. The purchase criteria from which the bipolar scales are generated remain the same, but the buyers now evaluate another brand. Finally, various brands can be scaled based on Attitude' scores of the buyers.

6.3.2.1   Development of Scales Anchored to Relevant Motives

The first step toward construction of an Attitude' scale is to ascertain which attributes of the product class have goal-satisfying capabilities. This can be done in several ways.

1. First, an investigator who has considerable experience with the product class (the marketing manager of a well-established product, for example), can use this experience as a valuable guide in choosing the relevant attributes to create the scales. A good example of this is Mitchell's analysis of a well-known drug (1967). Of course, these at-

---

* In this and the next chapter, "model" is also used to refer to a method in some cases because often methods are called models in the published literature.

tributes are salient from the buyer's point of view, but the marketing manager knows them.

2. Second, it is advisable to conduct a pilot depth study *explicitly* to obtain the want-satisfying properties of a product class. The depth study is not necessarily limited to the psychoanalytic depth interviews so widely used in motivation research. In fact, psychoanalytic emphasis is inappropriate because we wish to obtain the relevant Motives, not the more abstract, very general motives discussed in Chapter 4. What is emphasized is the technique of open-ended (nondirected) interviews with a small group of heterogeneous buyers. Similarly, the purpose is to explicitly obtain those properties of a product class that are pertinent to relevant Motives.

Stefflre (1965) uses a somewhat similar technique to create a product usage matrix that provides buyers' perceptions about the uses to which products can be put. For example, both pickles and potato chips may be used for snacks and would, therefore, belong to the same cluster. Furthermore, pickles and potato chips may be complimentary rather than competitive or substitute products, which can also be seen from their usage. We mention Stefflre's work because it is a preliminary step toward classifying, hence defining, a product class.

However, our interest is in measurement of attitude toward *brands* in that product class, which is the next step in the scaling procedure. In a depth interview, the buyer is asked only to enumerate *properties* of the brands in a product class that have the potential to satisfy the buyer's relevant Motives.

3. A third approach is word association. Recently, Deese (1965) has pointed out several advantages of the word-association method over the usual semantic-differential technique in obtaining connotative meanings of a concept. Word association refers to the association of words, phrases, adjectives, and so forth, that come to the mind of the buyer as soon as he is confronted with the product, or more specifically, the brand. For example, given the concept "automobile," the buyer may respond with "Cadillac," "blond girl," "carefree," and so on. Similarly, given the concept "Tab" he may respond with "Coca-Cola," "diet drink," "tabulating machines," or "IBM."

Word association is widely used as a projective technique in motivation research. Once again, we emphasize that *what is of interest to us is the technique and not the theory of psychoanalysis.* Furthermore, we utilize the technique for a purpose quite different from that which it serves in motivation research and other areas. For example, Deese uses it to obtain meanings and structure of linguistic thought process. Our goal is to extract only those properties of the brands in a product class that have potential to satisfy buyers' motives. We can easily use the word-association technique for our purposes by appropriate instructions to the respondents. For example, we may ask for associations of properties toward a brand of soft drinks, say Tab. A respondent may give associations of (1) low calories, (2) cola taste, (3) reasonable price, (4) suitable size, and so on. It is also possible to obtain word associations at the product-class level rather than for each brand separately in the same fashion.

4. In certain situations, a direct interviewing or word association may not be appropriate because the buyer is unwilling to express himself directly. For example, in the early fifties, a housewife would intentionally give incorrect answers about liking of instant coffee because of social taboos. Similarly, buyers would overtly express a liking for light beer, but would purchase regular beer (Haire, 1950). We are all too familiar with the half-serious crack about buyers rebottling private-label liquors in the empty bottles of "prestige" brands. D. Campbell (1950) provides several indirect ways of measuring attitudes. The most common approach is to use projective techniques. The buyer, by commenting on someone else's buying behavior, in fact, projects himself and his own buying behavior. A good example of the relevance of projective technique is in obtaining properties of a brand of tampons.

We have described various methods of identifying scale contents which reflect the salient Motives as indicated by purchase criteria. What the content of the salient Motives will be and which method is best suited to extract it are empirical questions. The theory of buyer behavior tells only what to look for based on the interrelationships of constructs. Once the salient criteria are identified, the next step is the construction of a scale to measure them.

Based on a pilot depth study, we found that seven criteria* were salient in the purchase of a convenience food product. This was the first study at Columbia Business School as a part of testing the theory of buyer behavior on a number of new products. The salient criteria were found to be (1) taste, (2) substitute for meal, (3) nutrition, (4) filling (substantiveness), (5) snack, (6) protein content, and (7) economic value. Presumably, each of these characteristics of the product is related to some underlying motives specific to the product class. For example, nutrition and protein are likely to be derivatives of health

---

* In fact, a total of 13 salient criteria were obtained and used in a mail questionnaire at the beginning of the study. From among these, only seven were used for three telephone interviews spread over five months.

motive. Similarly, substantiveness, snack, substitute for meal, and taste are likely to be derivatives of appetite motive.

Each of the characteristics is considered to be an evaluative criterion by the buyer. It is possible, then, to construct bipolar scales, one for each of the criteria. The bipolar scales can be graded on a 5, 7, 9, or 11-point basis, with a neutral position in the middle. On the ample evidence that a 7-point scale is most satisfactory (Osgood, Suci, and Tannenbaum, 1957), we prepared the following 7 scales:

	+3	0	−3	
1. Delicious Tasting				Not Delicious Tasting
2. Good Substitute for a Meal				Not a Substitute for a Meal
3. Very Nutritious				Somewhat Nutritious
4. Very Filling				Not Very Filling
5. Very Good for a Snack				Not Good for a Snack
6. Good Buy for the Money				Not a Good Buy for the Money
7. Good Source of Protein				Not a Good Source of Protein

We may assign the numerals +3 to −3 or 7 to 1 so that the least satisfying degree of an attribute is on one side (either −3 or 1). A buyer who checks the midpoint (0 or 4) is assumed to be just adequately satisfied with the brand in terms of that characteristic on which he evaluates it. It is the minimum degree of potential that the brand has for him. Any evaluation below that is not positively satisfactory.

A number of assumptions related to the type of scaling are present in the scale construction as described above. First, the graded scale (from +3 to −3) is assumed to have equal intervals. Thus the distance between +3 and +2 is assumed to be the same as that between +2 and +1 or −3 and −2. A look at the various purchase criteria to which the scales are anchored may seem to make this an unreasonable assumption. For example, taste could at best possess ordinal characteristic, but not the interval characteristic. However, we wish to emphasize that the buyer, based on his general education, has probably acquired sophistication as to what the numbers and the distances among numbers mean so that when we ask him to evaluate the brand on an interval scale, he is very likely to perceive the potential accordingly. In other words, we believe that to the extent that we are dealing with *human perception of a property* (and not property from some other point of view), it is possible to obtain interval measures. Second, the neutral point (0 to 4) on the scale is assumed to reflect several things. If we follow the learning theory explanation (Osgood, 1957a), the neutral point assumes that the buyer has no idea or knowledge to evaluate the brand in terms of that characteristic. It is to that extent a "don't know" category. On the other hand, it could be a genuine midpoint in the sense that it is just enough for the brand to be evaluated as satisfactory. There are at least two possible refinements that would remove this multiple meaning of the neutral point. First is the explicit statement elicited from the buyer that he does not know. Second is to ask him how confident he feels in his evaluation on that characteristic. It is presumed that the greater the learning, the more confident the buyer will be.

The scales so constructed are very similar to the semantic differential. However, there are several important differences.

1. The first and the major difference is that the bipolar anchored descriptions (adjectives, nouns, phrases, or adverbs) are dictated by the theory of buyer behavior. Unlike deducing both denotative and connotative meanings of an object such as a brand, we deduce only the evaluative beliefs of the brand, and that, too, only in terms of buyer's goal satisfaction as a consumer. This has two consequences. First, it is not necessary to have 55 or 60 scales as is usual in the semantic differential. A much smaller set of scales will suffice to extract information from the buyer, because salient criteria of evaluating brands are generally small in number. Second, since the relevant Motives, by definition, will differ from one product class to the other, the anchored descriptions are specific to a product class unlike the semantic differential. Thus for each product class, the researcher must obtain, by any of the ways suggested above, the relevant Motives and the attributes of a product that reflect those Motives.

2. A second derived difference is the fact that the *number* of scales may differ from one product class to another. In fact, we may safely state that because each scale reflects a particular anticipatory Motive, the more complex the purchase of a product class, the greater the number of relevant scales. The reader will note that the bipolar scales *define* the properties of the product class, and the relevant properties so defined are with respect to the satisfying potential of the various brands.

3. A third important distinction has to do with the anchorage points

of each scale, which provide the range of magnitude of brand potentials for each of the relevant Motives. The magnitudes of the range do not extend from plus infinity to minus infinity. For example, in the scales described earlier, taste has greater range (delicious—not delicious) but nutrition has somewhat less range (very—somewhat) because the latter could not be given the negative limit of not at all nutritions in view of the fact that the brands under investigation contained some amount of nutrition and the buyers perceived this. In other words, the descriptive adjectives or phrases do not encompass the complete range of bipolarity.

These deviations from the semantic differential are necessary because the scales define those properties of the brands that are relevant toward satisfaction of buyer's Motives. It is, for example, inconceivable, and even illegal, to have a convenience food product in the market that is nutritionally *harmful* to the buyer. On the other hand, we cannot scale the attitude simply in terms of the positive plane (4 to 7 or 0 to +3) because a given brand may not adequately satisfy a given criterion. To put it differently, what must be realized is that we define the properties of brands in terms of the degree of *satisfying* potential of a given relevant motive. And we ask the buyer to evaluate the brand only in terms of this defined property. It is similar to the degree of favorableness measure used in attitudes.

6.3.2.2 Evaluating Potential of a Brand

After a set of scales have been developed, the next step is to obtain buyers' evaluations of brands in their evoked sets. Not all buyers will have the same number or kind of brands in their evoked sets. It is, therefore, necessary to ask two questions which will qualify a brand as belonging to buyer's evoked set. (1) Is buyer aware of the brand? Awareness could be obtained by way of either aided or unaided recall. (2) Would he consider buying the brand? Since the content of the evoked set may change over time, a brand will be an element of buyer's evoked set if he would consider buying it and if the buyer were contemplating buying *at the time of the interview*. There are a large number of brands that the buyer, though he is aware of their existence, would not consider buying either because they are beyond his reach or because they are not perceived as adequate for his Motives.* On the other hand, any brand may become an alternative in the future either because buyer's Motives change or because many of the inhibiting factors dis-

---

* However, for long-range implications, a company may include brands that are not in buyer's evoked sets. The buyer must, however, be sufficiently knowledgeable on these brands to evaluate them appropriately.

appear over time. In short, a brand would be an element of buyer's evoked set if he would consider it as an alternative if purchase decision were made now. In an empirical study, this means that we may discard some respondents for whom a set of brands, in which the researcher is interested, do not become elements of their evoked sets.

On a sample of buyers, we can obtain, for each brand in the product class, a set of k_{ji} values that can be put in a matrix K. The K matrix contains n rows ($j = 1, 2, 3, n$) for each of the scales and N columns ($i = 1, 2, 3, N$) for each of the buyers. Thus each column contains the brand's profile as perceived by consumer i. The cell k_{ji} then reflects buyer i's evaluation of the brand in terms of the jth scale, which represents some relevant motive. Table 6.2 shows five buyers evaluating a convenience food item in terms of the four scales on the left side.

Table 6.2   A Hypothetical Example of Attitude' Data Matrix

			Buyers i				
			1	2	3	4	5
	Nutrition	1	6	5	5	6	3
Scales j	Calories	2	6	5	6	7	2
	Convenience	3	4	5	5	6	4
	Value	4	2	4	5	6	1

The first buyer has a highly favorable opinion of the brand's nutritional aspects, but considers it to be neither economical nor very convenient. A dietary product like Metrecal can easily obtain such profile from a buyer. The fifth buyer evaluates the brand negatively in general, and it is mostly directed toward "value" and "calories" scales. In contrast, the fourth buyer generally considers the brand as possessing substantial potential.

As mentioned earlier, the K matrix will contain as many row variables (scales) as there are salient purchase criteria in that product class. The number of columns (buyers) will depend on the sample size and sampling procedures. Furthermore, there will be as many K matrices as there are brands in buyers' evoked sets.

6.3.3 Deriving the Dimensionality of Choice Criteria

The data matrix K does not provide the structure of relevant Motives. As we have already seen, several attributes of a product class may all be interrelated because they satisfy the same underlying motive. Furthermore, the buyer does not keep these motives isolated but orders them or structures them in terms of their importance. It is in Choice Criteria that we see the goal structure related to a product class. Therefore, once matrix K is obtained, we must obtain the Choice Criteria. However, it must be pointed out that Choice Criteria like Motives are general to the product class and not limited to a brand. If, therefore, from each brand matrix K we obtain quite distinct sets of Choice Criteria, there exists sufficient evidence in the analysis to warrant the conclusion that various brands are not really elements of the same product class from the buyers' point of view although they are treated as such by the industry or the researcher.

Mathematically, we can obtain the Choice Criteria by utilizing certain theorems in matrix algebra which also underlie the techniques of factor analysis. Before we describe the mathematics, it is better to establish some correspondence between our hypothetical constructs and standard terminology in factor analysis. First, Choice Criteria are the factors that underlie the variables. Specific motives as reflected in purchase criteria are indicated by the scales, each of which is a variable. Second, what is known as "factor loadings" is the interrelationship of various relevant Motives, hence gives content to the Choice Criteria or factors. Third, what is known as "factor scores" become Attitude' scores in our analysis. Such factor (Attitude') scores can be unidimensional or multidimensional. In other words, evaluation of a brand may be in terms of either unidimensional or multidimensional Choice Criteria. Finally, there are several differences between the mathematical model presented here and standard factor analysis. (a) We preserve the information related to the mean and variance which would otherwise be lost in standard factor analysis based on a table of correlations among variables. (b) The analysis is more fundamental and therefore avoids many controversial issues related to factor analysis such as communality, rotations, and metric versus nonmetric data input. (c) The resultant derived statistics are not an end in themselves but rather starting positions for further analysis that the theory of buyer behavior demands.

A matrix K consisting of n rows ($j = 1, 2, 3, \ldots, n$) and N columns ($i = 1, 2, 3, \ldots, N$) and possessing an element k_{ji} (k_{ji} = buyer i's evaluation of the brand K in terms of an attribute j, the latter reflecting some relevant motive), can be approximated by a matrix K_r of rank r ($r < n$ or N) in the least-squares sense by using the procedures of Eckart and Young (1936) and Young and Householder (1938). According to them, any complete, filled (that is, all cell entries possessing values, including zero values) rectangular matrix K ($n < N$) can be resolved as follows:

$$K = U\Gamma W \qquad (6.1)$$

where $K =$ any rectangular matrix, in our case a data matrix containing i buyers' evaluations of a brand in terms of j scales

$U = n \times n$ orthogonal matrix of vectors called left principal vectors; $UU' = I$ and $U' = U^{-1}$

$\Gamma = n \times n$ diagonal matrix of roots containing positive values at first and zeros elsewhere

$W = n \times N$ orthogonal matrix of vectors called right principal vectors; $WW' = I$ and $W' = W^{-1}$

The resolution of the attitude data matrix K into the product of three matrices enables us to create the K_r matrix by taking the first r largest roots and the corresponding left and right vectors. Thus

$$\hat{K}_r = U_r \Gamma_r W_r \qquad (6.2)$$

is a matrix whose rank is $r(r < n$ or $N)$. The U_r is $n \times r$ section of U matrix, Γ_r is $r \times r$ section of Γ, and W_r is $r \times N$ section of W.

Mathematically, the elements in U_r represent the projections of points corresponding to the row variables (scales reflecting relevant Motives) on the unit-length principal vectors of K. Similarly, elements in W_r represent projections of points corresponding to column variables (buyers' evaluations of the brand) on the same unit-length principal vectors of K. These principal vectors of K determine its rank, complexity, and dimensionality. They are called factors in the standard terminology of factor analysis, and become Choice Criteria in our theory. Since the role of the Choice Criteria is to represent some structure among a set of relevant Motives, their content (factor loadings in standard terminology) enables us to see the interrelationships of various scales and Motives that underlie them. Now, the structuring of Motives is due to the learning process, which is an over-time phenomenon. We should, therefore, expect the Choice Criteria to emerge, over time, as well-defined factors after several buying experiences with a brand.

If we redefine terms in equation 6.2 so that

$$U_r \Gamma_r = A \qquad \text{and} \qquad W_r = S \qquad \text{then} \qquad K_r = AS \qquad (6.3)$$

Matrix A represents the Choice Criteria. The complexity of the product-specific motives can be inferred from the number of columns that A possesses: the more columns, the greater is the complexity. The *elements* of A matrix (its content) tell us the structure of the Motives.

The S matrix contains the Attitude' scores for all the buyers in the sample of analysis. The greater the number of rows of S, the more complex is the Attitude structure toward the brand K. Each column provides buyer i's Attitude' score.

In order to resolve the rectangular data matrix K into the product of three matrices U, Γ, and W, we convert it into a square symmetric matrix and then obtain characteristic roots and vectors of the latter. If we postmultiply K with its transpose K', we obtain a cross-products matrix P:

$$P = KK' = (U\Gamma W)(W'\Gamma U')$$
$$= U\Gamma^2 U' \tag{6.4}$$

The U contains the characteristic vectors and Γ^2 contains the characteristic roots of the cross-products matrix $KK' = P$. We thus obtain two of the three terms on the right side of equation 6.1. The third term W can be easily obtained by

$$W = \Gamma^{-1}U'K \tag{6.5}$$

Once the three matrices are obtained, it is easy to create the approximate matrix K_r. It should be pointed out that each root in Γ is so ordered that $\lambda_1 > \lambda_2 > \lambda_r \ldots \lambda_n$. Furthermore, the square of each root gives the percentage of total variance in the data explained by the principal vector, axis, or dimension. We may then judgmentally decide to take first r roots which, when combined, explain a certain satisfactory level of total variance, say 85 or 90 per cent. Moreover, if we plot the roots consecutively, there is likely to be a sudden discontinuity (kink) which is also a good criterion for choosing r roots. For further procedures, see Sheth (1966).

The matrix W_r is scaled so that $WW' = I$. Since W_r is a matrix of order $r \times N$, the resulting scaled coefficients are a function of the number of individuals (N) in the sample. Thus even if two studies differed only in sample size, the resulting numbers would not be comparable (Tucker, 1959; Weitzman, 1963; Tucker and Messick, 1963).

It is desirable, therefore, to rescale $W_r = S$ into a matrix V so that the coefficients in V are independent of sample size, that is,

$$\frac{1}{N} VV' = I \tag{6.6}$$

Now, V itself is a matrix—the result of multiplying W_r with a matrix K—which removes the sample bias:

$$V = KW_r \tag{6.7}$$

Both K and $1/N$ are scalar matrices with diagonal elements K and $1/N$ respectively. Substituting equation 6.7 into equation 6.6, we obtain

$$K = N^{1/2}$$

Thus $\qquad\qquad\qquad V = N^{1/2}W_r$

To maintain the basic relation, we must also rescale the U_r matrix so that

$$T = U_r N^{-\frac{1}{2}}$$

Then $Y = T\Gamma, V = U_r N^{-\frac{1}{2}}\Gamma_r N^{\frac{1}{2}}W_r = U_r\Gamma_r W_r$

The matrix T now contains scaled projections of the scales on principal vectors, and the matrix V contains scaled buyer projections on the same vectors. The rescaling procedure is necessary in all instances where sample size differs from one brand to the other. However, in our discussion we assume that sample size remains the same.

6.3.4   Measurement of Attitude' Scores

The matrix $S = W_r$ summarizes the relevant information for measurement of a buyer's Attitude' toward a brand. If our interest is in clustering buyers who have the same or similar Attitude' scores, we may plot each of the buyers as points in space whose dimensions are the Choice Criteria (factors or axes). We may find, for example, some distinct clusterings around each Choice Criterion. Psychologically, location of the buyer in terms of his evaluation of a brand in such space shows both the intensity of underlying Motives (by the length of n-dimensional vector) and the buyer's learning of the brand preference (by the direction or angle of the n-dimensional vector).

We may, however, focus on one buyer and see how various brands in his evoked set are evaluated by him. Then based on the common Choice Criteria across brands in the same product class, we can project as points each of the brands for a single buyer. Their clustering will enable us to state which brands are more similar and, therefore, about equally preferred.

Finally, it is also possible to look at the Attitude' scores over a period of time. Any learning of evaluative elements of the brand will result in change in the scores over time. This could also be represented graphically, which will usually communicate interbrand changes in their positions over time.

Based on Attitude' scores for several brands, we can obtain the relationships among them, thus learning which brands are perceived as similar in terms of their potential to satisfy a set of Motives. If verbal response as opposed to overt purchase behavior is considered a valid measure in microeconomic theory, then it is also possible to infer market structures in monopolistic competition which so far have had but a limited empirical content.

We can illustrate the procedure to obtain similarities among brands based on their Attitude' scores. Suppose that there are four brands A, B, C, and D of a convenience food item and that the buyer gives us his evaluation of each of the brands separately on the four scales discussed above. Furthermore, suppose that the analysis suggested in the preceding section shows that there are two Choice Criteria, namely nutrition and economic value, in that order of importance. Table 6.3

Table 6.3 Attitude' Scores of a Buyer for Four Brands

	Choice Criteria (Factors)	
	I (Nutrition)	II (Value)
Brand A	6	3
Brand B	3	4
Brand C	2	7
Brand D	9	8

gives some hypothetical Attitude' scores of a buyer for each of the four brands. As is easily seen, Attitude' scores are two-dimensional. Furthermore, brand D is rated highest on both dimensions, whereas brand B is rated lowest on both dimensions. Brand A is moderately high on nutrition only, and brand C is moderately high on value only. Figure 6.1 gives a graphical representation. The preference space is two-dimensional, and the four brands are located as points in this space.

Since each of the Choice Criteria is orthogonal to others, we can infer similarity of two brands by calculating the distance between them with the use of the Pythagorean theorem. The distance between brands k and l is then given by

$$d_{(kl)i} = \sqrt{\sum_{m=1}^{r} (s_{(mk)i} - s_{(ml)i})^2} \tag{6.8}$$

where $d_{(kl)i}$ = distance between brands k and l as perceived by buyer i

$s_{(mk)i}$ = Attitude' score of buyer i for brand k on the mth Choice Criterion

$s_{(ml)i}$ = Attitude' score of buyer i for brand l on the mth Choice Criterion

Then we can set up the distance matrix shown in Table 6.4, since the Attitude' scores for each of the four brands are known.

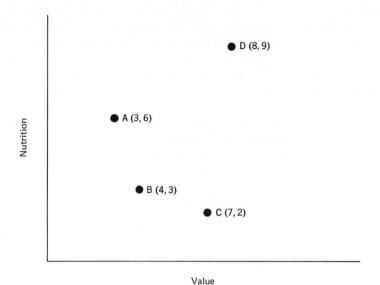

Figure 6.1 Preference space of a buyer.

The smaller the distance between two brands, the more similar they are. Hence the distance between the brand and itself is zero, as can be seen from the zero values in the diagonals. The more similar the brands, the more equally attractive they are. This results in greater substitution of one for the other and, therefore, greater brand switching. Moreover, brand D has uniformly greater distances from other brands, suggesting that possibly it is a "distinctive" brand in the market. Looking at the Attitude' scores in Table 6.3, we see that this brand is superior to other brands on both the dimensions of nutrition and of value. In addition, brands A and C have a very high distance between them because they are in reciprocal relation: brand A satisfies nutrition to a good extent but is economically not valuable, whereas brand C is

Table 6.4 Matrix of Interbrand Similarities for a Buyer

	A	B	C	D
A	0	3.2	5.6	5.8
B	3.2	0	3.2	7.2
C	5.6	3.2	0	7.1
D	5.8	7.2	7.1	0

very economical but does not possess a satisfactory level of nutrition. Finally, brand B is the least satisfying and is the "worst" brand: it is perhaps below par on both dimensions of Choice Criteria. It is, therefore, in reciprocal relation to brand D.

Another interesting feature of the distance matrix in Table 6.4 is that we can focus on any one particular brand as a standard and compare the similarities (distances) of pairs of other brands from that standard. For example, we can suppose that brand D is closest to being an ideal brand, and utilize it as a standard of comparison for similarities among other brands. This can be done by converting the distances $d_{(kl)i}$ into the distances $b_{(kl)i}$ from the origin of brand D. The following equation is suitable for such conversion:

$$b_{(kl)i} = \frac{1}{2}[d^2_{(ml)i} + d^2_{(km)i} - d^2_{(kl)i}] \tag{6.9}$$

In the above example, the similarities of other brands from the point of view of brand D's potential as perceived by buyer i are:

$$b_{(AB)i} = 38.0$$

$$b_{(AC)i} = 26.0$$

$$b_{(BC)i} = 46.0$$

The distance values are obviously meaningful in light of the raw data in Table 6.3.

The distance matrix D in Table 6.4, which provides us with similarities of n brands, contains values in $n(n-1)$ cells because distance between a brand K and itself is zero. Furthermore, the distance matrix is symmetrical, that is, $d_{(kl)i} = d_{(lk)i}$. It is then possible to rearrange the distance matrix of buyer i so that it becomes a column vector. Then we may stack up several column vectors, each representing a buyer's perception of similarities between the brands in the analysis. Thus we may create a data matrix X which contains $d_{(kl)i}$ as elements and has $n(n-1)/2$ rows of brand pairs and N columns of buyers (Tucker and Messick, 1963). In our previous example we had four brands, out of which six brand pairs can be formed, namely AB, AC, AD, BC, BD, and CD. The brand-pair distances for the buyer i can be obtained from Table 6.4, which would be written as a column vector. Each of the brand pairs then becomes a row in the data matrix X, and the number of columns is equal to the number of buyers in the sample. If we are dealing with a market that has many brands, the number of rows in matrix X may become quite large because the number of brand pairs is related to the square of the number of brands. For example, if we have 10 brands in the analysis, the number of brand pairs will be 45.

It is possible to obtain a definite picture of monopolistic competition from the data matrix X. As is well realized, there exist no procedures that enable us to define market structure in monopolistic competition. We believe that the Eckart-Young theorem of rank reduction processes, as described earlier, will enable us to obtain the market structure from the data matrix X. When X is factor-analyzed, scaled, and rotated, each of the resulting factors represents a separate market consisting of a few of the many brands included in the analysis. If there is only one factor, then apparently all the brands belong to the same market.

Since a market is what is perceived by the consumers as a set of substitute brands, our analysis gives a more realistic representation of the market structure. It tells us which brands compete and, therefore, constitute a market. The factor loadings, which are projections of brand pairs on the principal axes or factors, then give us the *structure* of the market by showing which pairs are clustered together. This, in turn, will enable us to say what brands, out of the total number in the study, form the evoked set.

6.4   DYNAMICS OF ATTITUDE CHANGE

What we are primarily concerned with is, of course, the Attitude change that occurs over a period of time because of learning on the part of the buyer. This learning, to repeat, may result from repeated purchase experiences or from information, the latter being either significative or symbolic. Over time, experience would probably be a major source. The theory of buyer behavior provides several feedback mechanisms which change the hypothetical constructs of Choice Criteria and Brand Comprehension. These changes in the hypothetical constructs must alter the structure of Attitude toward various brands over a period of time. In general, if the purchase experience has proved to be satisfactory, the perceived potential of that brand will be enhanced, which will increase the buyer's Attitude toward that brand. This, in turn, should result in greater Attitude' scores. Thus if we measure Attitude' of the buyer toward brand A before he makes a purchase and soon after he makes a purchase, given that the purchase is satisfactory, we should obtain higher scores at the second time period. This is tantamount to the feedback from Purchase onto Attitude' in the Response Sequence, and a variety of theoretical conceptions support this view, including cognitive dissonance theory.

On the other hand, if we want to use Attitude' as a predictor of

Purchase, the experimental design must be such that attitude measures on a set of alternative brands are obtained *before* the buyer makes any purchase. Then based on the Attitude' scores we may establish a preference map that will enable us to predict which brand will be purchased. The predicted behavior then can be matched against the actual behavior, taking into account the presence of any inhibitory factors (Intention).

It is appropriate here to digress and discuss Festinger's contention that despite the assumed relation of attitude· as a cause and behavior as an effect, no experimental evidence really exists in the literature (Festinger, 1964). Festinger suggests, based on cognitive dissonance theory, that probably the reverse is true, namely behavior is the cause and attitude is the effect. Earlier, we have suggested that over time, because of continuous feedback from behavior, what actually exists is an implicit functional relation between attitude and behavior. Thus each one is a cause and an effect at a certain point in time. Now, it is easy to obtain, in an experimental situation, the effect of behavior on attitude as a postdecision dissonance reduction mechanism, since no *inhibitory factors interfere* in the process of this effect. However, when Attitude' attempts to affect Purchase, a variety of inhibitory factors come into play and distort the smooth interaction. No one seems to have emphasized the role of such inhibitory factors as time pressure, lack of availability, financial constraint, or momentary price change in making it difficult to really measure the assumed attitude-behavior relation. For some preliminary attempts, however, see Lipstein (1965) and D. Campbell (1950). For a conceptual model that intervenes between attitude and behavior, see Nicosia (1966).

Coming back to the present discussion of measuring Attitude change, there are a number of possibilities related to attitude-behavior link. Here we discuss a few of them.

1. First, Attitude' can be a predictor of subsequent Purchase. If the Attitude' scores of buyers are unidimensional, a simple analysis would be to classify individuals as possessing high and low Attitude' scores. Prediction would be that a greater proportion of high Attitude' score buyers would in fact purchase the brand within some predefined time period subsequent to Attitude' measurement than would by chance. Similarly, a lesser proportion of low Attitude' score buyers would purchase it than by chance. If we also obtain the purchase information subsequent to Attitude' measurement, a simple chi-square analysis is sufficient.

If Attitude' scores are multidimensional, we may classify a sample of buyers based on their subsequent purchase behavior into two groups: those who bought the brand and those who did not. Then Attitude′ scores on various dimensions could be considered as predictor variables in performing discriminant analysis between the purchaser and the non-purchaser groups. Discriminant analysis would convert the multidimensional scores into single-valued discriminant scores (Sheth, 1966, 1968b). In addition, it would tell us whether Attitude′ scores have any predictive power in correctly classifying purchasers and nonpurchasers.

2. Second, rather than predicting subsequent behavior, we may desire to measure change in Attitude′ over time due to learning. Broadly, there are two sources of learning: information and experience. It is then possible to isolate sources of learning by experimental designs in field situations. Suppose that we measure Attitude′ at time t when the company has just introduced a brand of instant breakfast. The company then begins an extensive campaign primarily emphasizing the nutritional potential of the new brand compared to existing substitutes. Suppose that the campaign lasts for three months, during which time the same consumers are asked to evaluate the brand at the end of each month. Figure 6.2 shows aggregate Attitude′ scores of consumers. It will be noted that Attitude′ is two-dimensional, and these dimensions are labeled as nutrition and value. Over the three-month period, Attitude′ scores at the aggregate level have increased. However, the greatest increase on value

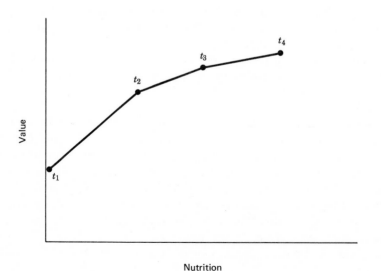

Figure 6.2   Dynamics of Attitude′ scores.

dimension has occurred within the first month, and there are only slight increases in subsequent two months. On the other hand, Attitude' scores on nutrition have increased throughout the three-month period. However, the increments are highest in the earlier months.

In a similar manner, we can isolate learning effects from word-of-mouth communication or sampling a new brand. In all cases, it is, of course, necessary to obtain from the buyer directly the *source* of learning rather than simply rely on the knowledge that a marketing strategy was implemented because of interaction among ways of learning.

3. Third, we may wish to measure Attitude' change that may result from Purchase. The design would be to obtain Attitude' scores both before and after the purchase and compare the change in Attitude' with another sample of buyers who did not purchase. If the Attitude' scores are unidimensional, it is relatively simple to see the effect of Purchase behavior on subsequent Attitude'. We obtain the difference in Attitude' scores between the two purchase events from two groups of buyers: those who bought during that time and those who did not. Then we test the change in the scores in the two groups for any significant differences. The hypothesis is that Attitude' scores would be considerably changed in favor of the brand among consumers who bought the brand as compared to those who did not buy.

If the Attitude' scores are multidimensional, it is necessary at first to convert them into single values. This can be done by performing a discriminant analysis between purchasers and nonpurchasers in which the predictor variables will have as values the *difference* between two Attitude' measures on various dimensions. Once the discriminant scores are obtained, they can be tested for significant differences between the purchasers and nonpurchasers.

4. Finally, in a situation where several consecutive Attitude' scores are obtained within a time period and we would like to estimate the *parameters* of growth, the following procedure is feasible. The first step is to "stack up" a series of Attitude' score matrices (W_r) to obtain a supermatrix. To illustrate, suppose that there are 4 buyers from whom Attitude' scores toward brand A over 4 occasions are obtained. The Attitude' scores have been with respect to, say, two dimensions of nutrition and value. In Table 6.5 we can create the supermatrix by defining columns as the buyers and rows as Attitude' scores on successive occasions. Thus we have 8 rows and 4 columns, the first referring to Attitude' score on nutrition dimension on first occasion, the second referring to Attitude' score on value dimension on the first occasion, third row showing Attitude' score on nutrition dimension on occasion 2, and so forth.

TABLE 6.5 Raw Data Matrix for Dynamics of Attitude Change

| | Buyers | | | |
	1	2	3	4
Occasion 1				
Nutrition	4	2	3	6
Value	3	5	6	6
Occasion 2				
Nutrition	5	3	4	6
Value	4	5	5	6
Occasion 3				
Nutrition	5	4	4	6
Value	5	6	5	7
Occasion 4				
Nutrition	5	4	4	6
Value	6	6	5	7

We thus have a data matrix that contains Attitude' scores over a number of occasions. It will be noticed that since the Attitude' scores (elements of S) are scores of individual buyers on common factors, the error elements for each occasion have been eliminated, thus resulting in more stable measures. Hence the Attitude' scores are more or less "true" measures, and any change between two occasions can be considered as "true" gain in Attitude toward the brand (Rao, 1958; Tucker and Messick, 1963; Torgerson, 1958; Lord, 1956).

We may define a matrix A as

$A = (n \times k)$ by N matrix consisting of

$a_{(jp)i}$ = Attitude' score of buyer i on dimension j at occasion p

$$j = 1, 2, 3, \ldots, n$$

$$p = 1, 2, 3, \ldots, k$$

$$i = 1, 2, 3, \ldots, N$$

Following the usual Eckart-Young procedures, we may resolve the data matrix A into its roots and vectors, as discussed earlier, to obtain an approximate matrix A, which has its rank b $[b < (n \times k)$ or $N]$. This can be accomplished by postmultiplying A with its transpose A' and obtaining the characteristic roots and vectors:

$$AA' = (U\Gamma W)(W'\Gamma U')$$

$$= U\Gamma^2 U'$$

Matrix U contains the characteristic vectors, and Γ^2 contains the characteristic roots. We then take the first b largest roots and corresponding vectors to create the approximate matrix A. Thus

$$A_b = U_b \Gamma_b W_b$$

The rank of matrix A is, in this particular instance, theoretically determined before the analysis. It will be noted that for each occasion, we have n dimensions that are orthogonal by definition. The same n dimensions exist throughout the analysis on which any change in Attitude' scores should result. Hence the rank of the approximate matrix A must also be n. In other words, $b = n$.

Now we may define the matrix of factor loadings as $B = U_b \Gamma_b$ and the matrix of factor scores as $C = W_b$. Thus

$$A = BC$$

Matrix B can be interpreted somewhat differently in this situation where the variables are consecutive occasions (Rao, 1958; Tucker, 1959; Sheth, 1966). This aspect will be more fully explained in the next chapter when we discuss brand loyalty measures. However, here we should point out that matrix B contains aggregate change over time with respect to each of the two dimensions. Since there are two Choice Criteria, it is predicted that we shall obtain two meaningful dimensions following the Eckart-Young procedure. Each factor or dimension has a series of loadings on various occasions, which can be plotted as a curve. The form and shape of the curve will reveal the manner of Attitude change over time with respect to that dimension.

Similarly, the C matrix of factor scores or cumulative Attitude' scores could be interpreted as parameters of individual buyers. Using these parameters as weights, we can obtain a least-squares fit to the raw Attitude' scores for each of the dimensions. The parameters then summarize for us the rate and form of attitude change for each buyer over a specific period of time.

The parameters or cumulative Attitude' scores over time are useful statistics for further analysis. For example, a company may begin a campaign in January and collect information from a sample of buyers until the end of June. Suppose that information collected includes, among other things, a monthly Attitude' measurement along the lines suggested in this chapter. In a real-world situation, we know that effects of communication are spread over time: some buyers internalize messages today, others a little later. Some buyers incorporate the learned information in their Attitude earlier than others. A cumulative Attitude' score over six occasions will not only capture the learning of information and subsequent Attitude change, but will also weigh the early as opposed to late learners. A true measure of campaign effectiveness will then come through in the cumulative Attitude' score.

6.5 SUMMARY AND CONCLUSIONS

In this chapter, we have pointed out the need for separating Attitude, the hypothetical construct, and Attitude', the intervening variable. Based on several comparisons, we suggested that Attitude' be defined as evaluative beliefs of the buyer toward a brand on a set of salient Choice Criteria. The rest of the chapter was devoted to the description of measurement of Attitude'.

The procedures outlined in this chapter to measure the buyer's Attitude' both toward a brand at a point in time and its changes over time seem very promising, although sufficient testing is not yet completed. Let us, however, compare them with a rigorous and mathematically complex technique currently used in marketing, namely nonmetric scaling (Coombs 1964, Kruskal 1964, Shepard 1962, Lingoes and Guttman 1967, Green, Carmone and Robinson 1967). This may put our procedures in proper perspective because there is considerable similarity between them.

Nonmetric scaling creates perception or preference space of multidimensions out of essentially what is a nonmetric information. We concentrate here on the preference map, inasmuch as our focus is on Attitude' and the underlying *evaluative* beliefs. Perceptual mapping, on the other hand, is related to the descriptive beliefs about the brands and product classes, hence is more relevant to Brand Comprehension' and Product Class Comprehension'. The starting point in nonmetric scaling is the simple rank preference of one brand over each of the others. This ordinally scaled information is transformed so as to create a multidimensional space in which brands are located as points. Similarity between pairs of brands is found by the proximity of their locations in the space. It is then possible to cluster the brands into types, to get insights into vacuum spots in the space for introducing new brands, and to interpret the relative substitutability of brands for market demand calculations. Inversely, buyers can be located on the space instead of the brands, and we can make similar inferences about the market segments. Among the four limitations of multidimensional scaling described earlier, the two limitations of additive constant problem and aggregate analysis are not present in nonmetric scaling. Hence it seems to be a useful approach. However, it also suffers from the other two problems of lack of conceptual foundations of buyer behavior and lack of incorporated multiattribute attitudes.

The first problem is not that of the technique but its use in marketing. Nonmetric scaling is essentially an empirical method, hence only inductive inference is more common with it. The data collection for the inputs to the technique is not unique to any theory. Indeed, the proximity measures based on ranked preferences are simple and general, similar to the affect scale (like-dislike) used in attitude measurement. The inductive inference limits the extent of generalization beyond the study.

The second problem is also anchored to the simple measure used to collect the data. What is obtained in the nonmetric analysis are the dimensions of only one attribute, namely preference. Furthermore, since there is no theory dictating the scales, the dimensions have to be labeled and interpreted by some outside information, for example, considerable knowledge about the market and the attributes of brands in that market. However, such dimensionality may not be obvious, and to that extent, it is a very useful description of buyer's preference. It is even possible to enhance prediction of purchase behavior considerably by using these dimensions as qualifying variables and segmenting the total market. However, explanation and use in marketing strategy may be lacking just as they are lacking in the simple affect scale. The company must not only know to what extent the buyers like its brand, it must also know on what grounds. The dimensions obtained in nonmetric scaling can provide the latter information only by external information at the disposal of the researcher.

The procedures outlined in this chapter to measure Attitude' are similar to nonmetric scaling, except that the theory explicitly asks for metric information instead of nonmetric information. Furthermore, the Eckart-Young theorem of rank reduction is common to both metric and nonmetric scaling. The main advantage of the procedures lies in the fact that they are derived from a theory in terms of *both* data collection and analysis. This avoids the problem of ignoring the buyer's point of view in labeling dimensions once they are obtained, because the dimensions are based on a set of evaluative beliefs. On the other hand, data collection in our system is more time-consuming and costly. We believe, however, that the extra effort and cost are almost mandatory for the long-term profitability of the company or for the development of a mature science in buyer behavior.

Another interesting aspect of the measurement of Attitude' is anchored to the hypothetical construct of Attitude. The theory of Attitude and its changes over time can be summarized as the law of expectancy: the buyer has a set of evaluative beliefs with the resultant affect toward a brand because of his expectations about it as a goal-object. Law of expectancy has been found to include (*a*) Miller's conflict theory with approach and avoidance gradients, (b) Hull's rg-sg and its refinement by Osgood as rm-sm, and (c) Lewin's vector theory. The procedures outlined in this chapter, therefore, seem potentially useful to quantitatively measure each of these theories in psychology. In fact, the valence-instrumentality paradigm of the Michigan researchers, which is very complementary to our system at the data collection stage, we find, is a step toward testing those theories of attitudes and their change which are based on Lewinian principles.

A complex measurement procedure is a must today. We have the necessary tools in advanced multivariate techniques and computer facilities. It would otherwise seem inappropriate to match the complexity of reality with that of research design and procedures.

CHAPTER 7

Purchase Behavior and Brand Loyalty

Attitude' as a response intervening variable was described in the preceding chapter. From the company's point of view, it is the purchase of the brand by the buyer that is important. Purchase is the factor by which the marketing staff is often evaluated and which is directly related (at least accountingwise) to the profitability of the company. However, there has been a drastic change since World War II in the emphasis of types of purchases by the consumers. The traditional emphasis on sales is today giving way to an emphasis on *repeat purchase* by the buyer. The newer emphasis is more compatible with the goal of *long-term* profits of the company (Sheth 1969h). It has also brought two realizations: first, psychology of the buyer must be carefully researched and understood, and, second, next purchase is a function of both the marketing activity and the buyer's attitude toward the brand as developed from prior experiences with the brand. Consequently, in this chapter we not only describe Purchase behavior but also deal extensively with the measurement of brand loyalty. In fact, greater attention is given to brand loyalty measures than to description of what constitutes a purchase.

Section 7.1 defines Purchase. An explanation is provided why it is treated as an intervening variable (hence a first-order abstraction) rather than some observed phenomenon per se. We also emphasize the distinction between the terminal act which results in purchase and the prior sequential mental and motor steps which lead to that terminal act.

In Section 7.2 we review the existing approaches to understanding brand loyalty and brand switching. Several methodological problems are brought to the attention of the reader. This is followed, in Section 7.3, by a discussion of factor-analytic methods of obtaining brand loyalty which eliminate some of the problems in present methods. Finally, Section 7.4 summarizes the chapter.

7.1 PURCHASE AS AN INTERVENING VARIABLE

As an intervening variable, Purchase is directly anchored to reality by way of rules of correspondence. These entail, as mentioned before, definition and measurement.

We treat Purchase as an intervening variable for several reasons. (1) It is a variable that must be measured specifically and perhaps uniquely for each product class where the theory of buyer behavior is put to work. For example, measurement of Purchase in consumer durables may not be the same as in nondurables because of the used goods market in durables and the differences in time interval of purchases. The variable itself transcends the unique properties of definition and measurement relevant to a product class and to that extent is abstract. (2) The abstraction, however, is first-order only; a number of observable properties of the buyer's behavior could be considered as separate indicants of Purchase behavior. To that extent, Purchase itself is a factor that is derived from one or more of these indicants (Lazarsfeld, 1959; Koch, 1954). (3) We use Purchase as a starting point to understand buyer's brand loyalty. Brand loyalty itself is an index or abstraction which is likely to be a function of the number and pattern of repeated purchases of a brand. (4) Our definition of Purchase and our methods for its measurement are general, so that they could be used for many product classes. It becomes necessary, possibly as an empirical case, to redefine Purchase of a particular brand belonging to a particular product class. This generality necessitates that Purchase be considered an intervening variable.*

* We are, to some extent, altering the meaning of intervening variables as given by MacCorquodale and Meehl (1948). We are here following Marganau (1950), Torgerson (1958), and Royce (1963), according to whom any scaling or rescaling of observable phenomena would qualify the resultant measure as intervening variable. Examples are social class as index of income, occupation, education, and so forth, and probability measures as rescaling of nominally observed data. MacCorquodale and Meehl would consider these (social class and probability) as data rather than constructs. However, we think that with our emphasis on brand loyalty as part of Purchase variable, we should treat it as an intervening variable.

7.1.1 Definition of Purchase

Purchase is defined as any visible, overt, objectively discernible act that entails exchange of goods or services for some consideration and can be taken to reliably indicate a financial commitment to a certain *brand* in a specified unit amount. It need not necessarily be an irrevocable commitment but some act that by custom and usage is accepted as a commitment. It refers to either a particular act or a series of acts in the total process of buying.

Purchase as defined above has some standardized objective definitions and measures in grocery products, due to the prevalence of commercial panels. A panel member, usually the housewife, records information about purchase of a brand such as brand name, quantity bought, date and place of purchase, price per predefined unit, and any premiums or deals obtained on that purchase. From this, Purchase is defined in several ways, depending on who uses the information. For example, for the accounting and managerial-control purposes, quantity, price, and quantity times price may be important definitions. For marketing purposes, the place of Purchase may be additionally useful, and so on.

However, the actual purchase of a brand could have resulted from a variety of paths that buyers may take. It would add to our descriptive and explanatory power if we knew the sequential steps that the buyer has gone through. In fact, if the sequential steps are observed by the researcher, he may obtain greater explanation than that supplied by Attitude' because the former are unique to a given purchase situation or decision. Furthermore, to the extent that attitude scales are standardized across individuals and brands, small individual differences ignored there could be brought to the forefront in observation of sequential buying process.

We wish, therefore, to emphasize the need to measure sequential purchase behavior. Interesting empirical research on methods of obtaining motor and mental steps involved in buying is given by Cyert, March, and Moore (1962), J. Howard and Moore (1963), Reitman (1965), and J. Howard and Morgenroth (1968). In Chapter 4, we described in some detail the measurement aspect of sequential steps involved in buying in the section on Intention.

Coming back to the definition of Purchase, we must state that despite the commonly accepted meaning of purchase as implied in the definition, the problem of defining Purchase in a product class is not simple. Admittedly, some cases are unambiguous, such as the purchase of a car. Here the timing of Purchase, the quantity of purchase, and so on, are standardized and objective. But consider the case of the industrial buyer who stocks all requisition slips for a week and then orders various quantities of bolts and nuts from three or four suppliers. What is the unit of purchase? Should we say that it is each bolt and nut, bolt alone, bolts as measured in standard weights or by dollar amount? Similar problems exist in regard to grocery items. For example, a housewife buys a can of soup two times in one day. Should we consider this as two separate purchases or only one? Would our definition in this specific situation include purchase of a can two days consecutively? The answers to these questions are not provided by the theory itself. Empirical knowledge, in addition to judgment, will enter into the picture when the theory is tested in a specific product class.

7.1.2 Measurement of Purchase

Measurement is, of course, closely related to definition. Hence measurement is also not unique across all product classes. It would, however, appear that there are some standard indicants which are measurable and which have been used in marketing research to understand brand loyalty and brand switching. We briefly describe them here (Herniter and R. Howard 1964; Farley and Kuehn, 1965).

Probably the most common way to measure Purchase is to obtain the incidence of buying. Each time a consumer goes through the terminal act of monetary sacrifice or commitment, incidence of Purchase is considered to occur and is counted accordingly. The purchase incidence is usually called a trial. It is then possible to obtain the relative frequency of purchase of a *brand* in a buyer's total purchases. This is presumed to give the measurement of his probability of buying.

Obviously, the measure ignores several other characteristics inherent in any purchase. One is the quantity that the buyer buys at each purchase incidence. The quantity of purchase is considered an important indicant in view of the fact that a very large percentage of total volume of sales of a brand is concentrated in a smaller percentage of total buyers in both consumer and industrial goods (Twedt, 1964; Brown, Hulswit, and Kettelle, 1956). Furthermore, Kuehn (1958), J. Howard (1963), and Sheth (1966) have generalized the amplitude measure of learning theory to buying behavior in terms of quantity of Purchase at a time. They suggest that the greater the brand loyalty, the greater the amplitude of buying. Some support of this comes from diffusion of new products in which it is found that the consumer buys the new product at first in small quantity to try it out and then increases the quantity if he likes the new product. To some extent, companies distribute free samples of new products to facilitate such trial purchases in the beginning.

Finally, a third major indicant of brand loyalty is the time interval between purchases. Based on the latency of response measure in learning theory, Kuehn (1958) and J. Howard (1963) have suggested that time interval between purchases may be a useful indicant. For some refinement of the notion, see Morrison (1966).

7.2 STOCHASTIC APPROACHES TO BRAND LOYALTY

With the availability of data from commercial panels, notably those of the Market Research Corporation of America and the *Chicago Tribune*, there has been considerable empirical investigation of brand loyalty in many grocery and personal care items.

Interest in repeat brand purchase and brand switching began during and since World War II. Churchill (1942), Womer (1944), Barton (1946), and Patterson and McAnally (1947), utilizing purchase records of fixed panels, suggested that the focus of interest and concern for the company should be the measure of brand loyalty rather than a single purchase. However, the recent entry of quantitative techniques to measure brand loyalty was strongly influenced by a series of articles written by G. Brown (1952a, b, c, d, e, f, 1953) and followed up by R. Cunningham (1955, 1956, 1959).

7.2.1 First-Order Markov Process

The phenomenon of development of brand loyalty over a period of time led to the application of stochastic methods in consumer behavior. The bulk of the research has been in terms of Markov chains. Specifically, actual research has been carried out with the assumption that buyer behavior is a first-order stationary Markov process (Draper and Nolin, 1964; Dukta and Frankel, 1962; Fourt, 1960; Harary and Lipstein, 1962; Herniter and Magee, 1961; Lipstein, 1959; Maffei, 1960, 1961; Robinson and Luck, 1964; Styan and H. Smith, 1964; Woodlock, 1964; Herniter and R. Howard, 1964; Morrison, 1965).

The first-order Markov process is the simplest conceptualization within the Markov processes. (1) It assumes that the effect on a given state i at time t is coming from the probability distribution of all states in the system at only time $t - 1$, and the transitional (conditional) probabilities of moving from those states to state i during the time interval $t - 1$ to t. The probability distribution of the states at time periods earlier than $t - 1$ is irrelevant and unnecessary. Hence the knowledge of probability distribution of the states of the last time period is sufficient to predict the probability distribution of states at the present time period. (2) The transition probabilities from state i to j, called p_{ij}, are assumed to be constant throughout the n transitions in the system. (3) There is a tendency toward equilibrium or stabilization after n transitions where the system converges to a probability distribution, which then is independent of past period probabilities (Kemeny and Snell, 1957).

Let us illustrate this with a hypothetical example. Suppose that there are only two brands in the market. Let us say that we are dealing with the canned-soup industry and that the two brands are Campbell's and Heinz. If we know the probability of purchase of one brand, we can determine the probability of the other easily because Markov process assumes that states (brands) are mutually exclusive and exhaustive. Furthermore, if we know the conditional probabilities of buying brand i, given that brand j was purchased last time, we can easily predict the probability of buying a brand during the next time period. Let us assume that at time t, the probability of buying Campbell is .5 and, therefore, that of Heinz is $1 - .5 = .5$. This can be written as a vector:

$$\begin{matrix} \text{C} & \text{H} \\ [.5 & .5] = A_t \end{matrix} \qquad (7.1)$$

If the transitional probabilities are

$$\text{time } t+1$$

$$\begin{matrix} & \text{C} & \text{H} \\ \text{time } t & \begin{matrix} \text{C} \\ \text{H} \end{matrix} & \begin{bmatrix} .7 & .3 \\ .4 & .6 \end{bmatrix} = T \end{matrix} \qquad (7.2)$$

then, based on principles of conditional probabilities, we can derive the probability distribution of Campbell's and Heinz at time $t+1$ by multiplying A_t and T.

$$A_t T = A_{t+1} = [.55 \quad .45] \qquad (7.3)$$

Similarly, since the transition matrix is stationary (same over time) and since we now have probability distribution at $t+1$, we can easily obtain the probability distribution at $t+2$ as follows:

$$A_{t+1} T = A_{t+2} = [.565 \quad .435] \qquad (7.4)$$

The same result can be obtained by redefining $A_{t+1} = A_t T$, which allows us to say that

$$A_t T(T) = A_{t+2} \qquad (7.5)$$

If we continue the process by moving forward as in a first-order Markov

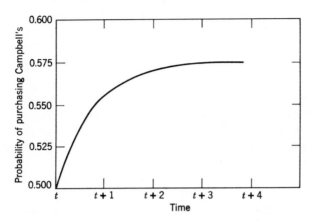

Figure 7.1   Probability of buying Campbell's soup.

process with stationary transitions, we calculate the probability distributions for time periods $t + 3, t + 4 \cdots t + n$.
  The probability distribution at $t + 3$, for example, is

$$A_{t+2}T = A_{t+1}T^2 = A_tT^3 = A_{t+3} = [.569 \quad .431] \qquad (7.6)$$

and that at $t + 4$ is

$$A_{t+3}T = A_{t+2}T^2 = A_{t+1}T^3 = A_tT^4 = A_{t+4} = [.57 \quad .43] \quad (7.7)$$

It will be noted that the changes in the *absolute* probabilities over
time are smaller and smaller. If we concentrate on Campbell's, the increments are at a decreasing rate. This gives us a negatively accelerated
curve similar to the learning curve proposed by Hull (1943, 1952) and
Bush and Mosteller (1955). Figure 7.1 gives the plots for Campbell's.
  At the fourth time period, the probability distribution stabilizes at
.57 for Campbell's and .43 for Heinz and thereafter remains unchanged.
The reader may check this out. Then, in the long run, the probability
of buyers buying Campbell's is .57. If we obtained a buyer's purchase
sequence *after* the equilibrium, we would obtain 57 per cent of his
purchases as being those of Campbell's. This is considered to be his
strength of brand loyalty toward Campbell's.
  There are two vital concepts behind the first-order Markov process.
First, only two types of information are really essential to carry forward
the analysis. They are (*a*) initial probability distribution and (*b*) the
transition matrix. We can derive the probability distribution at $t + 4$
by multiplying the initial probability matrix A_t with the fourth power
of the transition matrix, namely T^4. In general, to obtain the probability

distribution at $t + n$ time period, we use the following formula:

$$A_t T^n = A_{t+n} \qquad (7.8)$$

This has a decided advantage in calculating the equilibrium or stable state because it obviates the calculation of intermediate probability distributions.

Second, and more crucial from the point of view of empirical research in brand loyalty, is the fact that at the equilibrium state, or very near to it, the past purchase has very little influence. In other words, the system is independent of last (and, therefore, initial) probability distribution. In our example above, the equilibrium is at time periods $t + n$ $(t + n > t + 4)$ and is *independent* of earlier probability distributions. Technically, the process becomes a stationary Bernoulli process. It must be emphasized that the Bernoulli process at the equilibrium state, as measured by proportion of purchases in a sequence, is not a random process ("random" meaning chance behavior) but could have resulted from past systematization. In fact, if the probabilities were the same as in the example, we could say that the equilibrium state is the asymptote of traditional learning curve and shows the *extent of learning* rather than randomness of purchase behavior.

As for criticism of current applications of Markov chains, Ronald Howard (1963) has raised three major problems related to the extensive application of first-order Markov process in consumer behavior. They are (1) aggregation, (2) interpurchase times, and (3) estimation of transition probabilities from sample statistics.

The problem of aggregation arises because the researchers in consumer behavior have tended to use proportions of customers purchasing brand i as the probability of *each individual customer* buying that brand. In other words, the probability (in relative frequency terms) of purchasing a brand in the aggregate sample is used to infer the probability of purchase of that brand by each customer. "The Markov chain analysis is not being used as it was originally intended, but rather as some kind of flow model" (R. Howard, 1963, p. 36). On the other hand, if we assume a first-order Markov process for each customer, how do we combine the individuals to obtain a model for the market? Howard suggests that a "vector Markov process" may be appropriate. This involves convoluting N different binomial distributions, each of which has number of trials equal to the number of buyers originally in each state and a probability of "success" given by n-step transition probability for the underlying Markov process. Several problems exist with this formulation, however. First is the assumption that each customer acts independently, which is not tenable in light of the vast literature in diffusion of innovations (Rogers, 1962), opinion leadership (E. Katz and Lazarsfeld, 1955; E. Katz, 1957; Bourne, 1963), and risk taking (Bauer, 1960, 1963a) which suggest an active buyer seeking information and influence from other buyers. The theory of buyer behavior discussed in Part II also raises the question of the independence of buyers' decisions. However, in a national probability sample it is possible that buyers do not interact and therefore behave independently. But generalization from such a sample to the population then should be questioned on the grounds of sampling; the sample does not represent the population with regard to interaction processes. Second, this formulation assumes a homogeneous population of buyers having the same transition probability. Frank (1962), Kuehn (1962), Morrison (1965), and Sheth (1966) have found contrary empirical evidence. Finally, it involves an a priori hypothesis as to the transition matrix of a customer, which then can be accepted or rejected at a certain level of significance. It does not attempt to empirically derive the transition matrix which is really the important statistic in empirical data.

Another problem in applying Markov chains to brand purchase data is interpurchase time. It arises because of the diversity of the individual purchase cycles in a group of buyers and the inevitable discrepancy between the average purchase cycle and the time period chosen for Markov analysis. When the analysis is from one time period to another, the usual arbitrary procedure is to create a dummy state called "no purchase" and put in it those families that did not buy during a given time period. Conceptually, a purchase–no purchase decision is quite different from that of purchase a specific brand. R. Howard suggests that time be incorporated as a random variable, with the result that we have semi-Markov processes which are time-dependent. For other recent procedures to incorporate the difference of interpurchase times, see Kuehn and Rohloff (1965) and Morrison (1966).

Finally, the third problem is the generalization of the preliminary estimates obtained from a sample of consumers to the national population. In other words, the estimate of the transition probabilities derived from the sample has to be projected to the population. R. Howard (1963) and Herniter and R. Howard (1964) have suggested that some type of Bayesian approach may be relevant, in terms of change in an a priori probability by the additional information obtained from sample.

7.2.2 Alternative Approaches to First-Order Markov Process

Many researchers have found that the two assumptions of Markov chains, namely the *first order* and *stationarity* of transition matrix, are too restrictive for a complex behavior such as buying behavior. Kuehn, for example, has found that the probability of repurchase after four consecutive purchases of the same brand is much higher than the probability of repurchase after only one consecutive purchase of the same brand. This negates the assumption of a first-order chain. Recently, Sheth (1966) has found similar results.

7.2.2.1 Linear Learning Model

Kuehn has developed a linear learning model based on principles of statistical learning theory (Bush and Mosteller, 1955) that allows for effects other than the last purchase. The model assumes that the coefficient of effect parameter remains constant over time. Furthermore, the model, although identical to the exponential learning curve on a cumulative basis, differs from it in two ways. (1) It actually graphs the dependency on the last purchase, which itself is dependent on the purchase before, and thus cumulatively brings forward the *total* effect up to the last period. (2) It incorporates *separately* the effects of purchasing a given brand or purchasing some other brand. Incidentally, the model does not handle "no purchase" situations and therefore is more suitable for trial-by-trial analysis rather than an analysis by time periods.

Figure 7.2 is a graphic illustration of Kuehn's model. The model assumes that there is a lower bound and an upper bound within which the probability of purchase of a brand will change. If only brand A is purchased successively, it will eventually reach the upper bound,

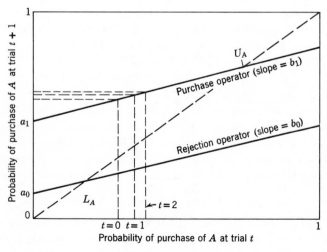

Figure 7.2   Kuehn's model.

the speed of reaching the upper limit (U_A) determined by the values of coefficients a_1 and b_1. Similarly, if successively other brands are bought, the probability of purchasing A will reach the lower limit (L_A), the speed of reaching it determined by the value of coefficients a_0 and b_0.

Given the probability of buying brand A at trial $t = 0$, we may calculate the change in probability by knowing the values of the two intercepts a_1 and a_0 and the slopes b_1 and b_0. Assuming that at trial $t = 0$ the brand A was purchased, we may calculate its probability of purchase at trial $t = 1$ by drawing a line from $t = 0$ up to the purchase operator and perpendicularly obtaining the corresponding value on the Y axis. If the brand A is purchased again, the probability of purchase at $t = 1$ is reflected onto the purchase operator, and again the corresponding value on the Y axis is obtained. *It will be noticed that the increment in purchase probability by the last purchase at $t = 1$ is less than the increase in probability by the purchase at $t = 0$.* This is consistent with the learning theory. Hence if we plot on a graph, which has the consecutive purchase of brand A on the X axis and the probability of purchase on the Y axis, we obtain a negatively accelerating exponential curve, same in shape as the curve in Figure 7.1. The difference, of course, lies in the fact that whereas Figure 7.1 is an aggregate market phenomenon, the linear learning model is for each individual buyer.

However, the buyer may intermix purchases of other brands. In those cases, the rejection operator is also working in the change in probability of purchase of A. We look up the rejection operator, obtain the corresponding Y-axis value, and find the new purchase probability of A. The effect of purchasing brand A at $t = 0$ on the probability of purchasing A at $t = 1$ is positive, whereas the effect of purchasing some other brand is negative. In order to keep the system linear, Kuehn assumes that the two effects are the same in magnitude, that is, $b_1 = b_0 = b$. He then makes a derivation which has created some impact on other researchers: *The purchases of brand A in the previous trials are geometrically weighted such that the most recent purchase of brand A has the greatest effect when the comparative base is probability of brand A given that other brands are purchased.* This distinction is important from the comparative base of some initial unconditional probability because, as we saw in the figure, each successive purchase adds a smaller fraction resulting in negative acceleration; in other words, the contribution of the last purchase in a sequence is the least in the cumulative probability of purchase.

In our opinion, it is not appropriate to say that the most recent purchase has the greatest independent effect (Sheth 1969f). Let us illustrate this with an example. Suppose that the following are the parameter values under Kuehn's model:

$$A_1 = .5 \qquad b = .4 \qquad P_t = .5$$
$$A_0 = .3$$

Suppose the brand S was purchased at t. The probability at $t + 1$ will be

$$P_{t+1}^S = a_1 + bP_t \qquad (7.9)$$
$$= .5 + .4(.5) = .7$$

The increment in probability is $.7 - .5 = .2$. Suppose that at $t + 1$ brand S was again purchased. Then

$$P_{t+2}^{SS} = a_1 + bP_{t+1} = a_1 + a_1b + b^2P_t \qquad (7.10)$$
$$= .5 + .4(.7) = .78$$

The increment in probability by the most recent trial independently is only $.78 - .7 = .08$. *It does not have greater effect than the previous trial.*

Let us intermix purchase of other brands. Suppose that at $t + 1$ the buyer buys some other brand. Then

$$P_{t+2}^{SO} = a_0 + bP_{t+1} = a_0 + a_1b + b^2P_t \qquad (7.11)$$
$$= .3 + .4(.7) = .58$$

Now suppose that at $t = 2$ the buyer buys brand S. Then

$$P_{t+3}^{SOS} = a_1 + bP_{t+2} = a_1 + a_0b + a_1b^2 + b^3P_t \qquad (7.12)$$
$$= .5 + .4(.58) = .732$$

The increment by the second purchase is $.732 - .58 = .182$, which is *less* than the increment of .20 provided by the first purchase of S. The graphical presentation of the model also suggested the same thing earlier: the most recent purchase adds the least to the total magnitude of learning. In fact, it is inevitable if the coefficient b is to have a value less than unity. The only way we may say that the more recent trial has greater effect is to provide a value of coefficient b that is greater than unity. But in that case, the model will provide probability of purchase of S at t greater than unity, which is inconsistent with the probability system.

It must be remembered, however, that if the comparison base is the probability of buying S *after the effects of purchases of other brands in some consecutive sequence are allowed for,* it is correct to state that the most recent trial will have greatest effect. For example, in the prior example

$$P^{000}_{t+3} = .5$$

$$P^{00S}_{t+3} = .7$$

and $$P^{0S0}_{t+3} = .58$$

When compared to the P^{000}_{t+3} (which states that the probability of purchase of S at trial 4 *given* the purchase sequence of three prior purchases of other brands), the effect of P^{00S}_{t+3} is greater than the effect of P^{0S0}_{t+3}.

But this comparison can only be made after finding the conditional probability of buying S given some sequences of purchases of other brands. Since the model has no estimation procedures, this is not directly possible. Even if this were possible, conceptually the statement seems to contradict the principles of learning, whereas the model is based on them. It is much better to state that if there is less learning (probability of purchase is less) prior to the purchase at t, the probability is likely to increase more by the purchase at t. Thus the increments in probability due to purchase of the brand will be inversely related to the strength or probability before purchase.

Using the parameters assumed in the previous example, if we work only with the gain operator by supposing that the buyer consecutively purchases the same brand, we obtain the usual exponential curve. Figure 7.3 provides the cumulative learning curve. The probability values are

$$P^{s}_{t+1} = .7 \qquad P^{ss}_{t+2} = .78 \qquad P^{sss}_{t+3} = .812$$

$$P^{ssss}_{t+4} = .8248 \qquad P^{sssss}_{t+5} = .8299 \qquad P^{ssssss}_{t+6} = .832 \text{ etc.}$$

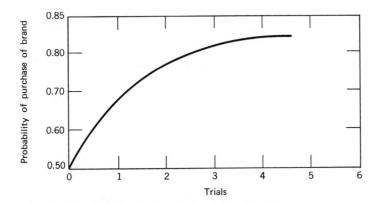

Figure 7.3   Kuehn's linear learning model: cumulative curve.

Bush and Mosteller (1955) combine the gain and loss parameters into a common coefficient and show the equivalence of the model to the first-order Markov process.

It must be pointed out that Kuehn's model has not yet attained the procedures for estimating the parameters. Recently, Carman (1965a) has attempted to obtain the two intercepts and the common slopes by three normal equations at the *aggregate* level. In fact, the model is at the *individual* level, but empirical validation has been at the aggregate level through a factorial design. We shall later present methods to measure individual brand loyalty.

7.2.2.2 Frank's Spurious Contagion

Frank (1962) has proposed another alternative to first-order Markov process. He suggests that probably the brand-loyalty phenomenon is *independent* of any past purchases—it is a Bernoulli process. He analyzed coffee data and found that what looked like a learning curve at the *aggregate* level, following the procedures similar to Kuehn's, was in fact "spurious contagion" rather than a genuine effect.

The spurious effect, according to Frank, arises because of the aggregation of consumers who have heterogeneous constant probabilities of Purchase as estimated by relative frequency measures. Several conceptual and methodological problems remain unsolved with regard to the "spurious contagion" which are elaborated by Sheth (1966) elsewhere.

The important point here is the alternative model to Markov chains, namely the Bernoulli process. The Bernoulli process assumes independence of path. Graphically, this can be represented as in Figure 7.4.

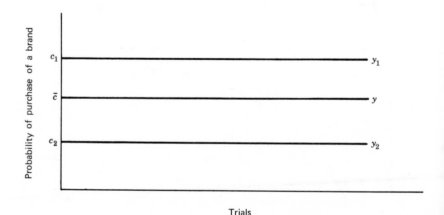

Figure 7.4   Bernoulli function relation.

The independence of trials results in a *constant* probability of purchase over time, which is represented functionally as $y = c$. The average curve is $\bar{y} = c$, and individual buyers 1 and 2 have $y_1 = c_1$, $y_2 = c_2$, respectively. The reader will note that this differs from the learning curve presented in Figures 7.1 and 7.3 and the Markov process shown in Figure 7.2. Later we shall have something to say on these functional relations, since they all relate to the methods described in this chapter.

7.2.2.3 Criticism of the Stationarity Assumption

Another area of criticism of the first-order Markov process centers on the assumption of *stationary* transition probabilities. Ehrenberg (1965) has recently strongly criticized this assumption on several grounds. First, there is no theoretical reasoning for the assumption to be valid. In fact, from the conceptual point of view, it would appear that the assumption should not be incorporated. The stationarity assumption, like the *ceteris paribus* assumption, is included for practical expediency only. Second, the Markov process, when worked backward rather than forward, blows up (gives negative values) if the stationarity assumption is kept in the model. Similarly, as a forward process but calculating *past* (as opposed to future) probability distribution, the model gives negative values when the stationarity assumption is kept. See also Massy and Morrison (1968), who point out the technical problems in Ehrenberg's attack.

Ehrenberg (1959) has elsewhere proposed a negative binomial approach to obtaining measures of brand loyalty. This approach seems promising at the aggregate level.

Farley (1964) has utilized the economic concept of ability to pay and its relation to effort directed toward search. High-income people will be willing to pay more and, therefore, search less, which results in strong brand preferences. Similarly heavy users may be expected to do more searching and thus either pay less or be less brand-loyal. The analysis has been again at the aggregate level.

7.2.3 Problems with Existing Research

In the various attempts to formulate quantitative models of brand loyalty, three problems seem to have remained unresolved.

7.2.3.1 Problem of Prior Trial Dependencies

The first one deals with the independence-of-path assumption: Is the consumer's purchase of a brand at time $t + 1$ independent of past purchases or is it dependent on them; and if it is dependent on more purchases than the last purchase, how many prior purchases are independently affecting the purchase behavior at time $t + 1$? Furthermore, is the effect the same from all such purchases? In more formal terms, the question inquires whether the buying process is a Bernoulli, first-order Markov, or a non-Markov process (Little, 1964). Frank (1962) has suggested that at the individual buyer level, probably the Bernoulli process as reflected in constant probability of purchase from trial to trial is operative; and at the aggregate level, the effect, which may look like non-Bernoulli process, is due to "spurious contagion" arising from aggregating a population of buyers who have heterogeneous constant probabilities. On the other hand, several researchers have argued that the dynamics of brand loyalty can be understood by applying the first-order Markov chains, as we saw earlier. They have, therefore, felt that the purchase at time $t + 1$ is dependent only on the immediate past purchase, say at time t, and earlier purchases have no influence. Finally, Kuehn (1962) and recently Sheth (1966) have found empirical evidence suggesting that the first-order Markov process is not adequate, since purchase at time $t + 1$ is found to be dependent on earlier trials than the most recent purchase. Although no research is available that will tell *how many* prior trials are likely to have effect, Kuehn has found that at least the last four trials are effective.

7.2.3.2 Problem of Aggregation

The second problem is that of aggregation. Almost all researchers have supported the view that the focus of attention and understanding should be the individual buyer or household. However, research has been almost exclusively concentrated at the aggregate level. The only exception so far has been Morrison's work (1965), which has assumed that the individual buyers are distributed as a beta distribution function within an aggregate Markov process. However, individual parameter estimates are lacking.

Two distinct sets of unresolved problems exist with respect to aggregation. The first one has to do with the physical process and legitimacy of aggregating individuals or brands. For example, suppose that we assume that the individual household behaves as a first-order Markov process; how can we aggregate a sample of households, each one having a first-order Markov process? As we saw earlier, the existing research has only considered conditional proportions of sampled households as the measure of transitional probabilities of moving from one state to others during the time interval between two purchases.

Similarly, researchers have aggregated several brands into a common state of "all other brands," concentrating on one or two brands in a product category when doing first-order Markov analysis. Rosenblatt

(1960) shows that a function of a Markov chain (such as would result when several states are collapsed into one state or when multistates are collapsed into binary states) is itself a Markov chain only under certain conditions and is not automatically guaranteed by the process. Thus such aggregation of brand states may result in some stochastic process other than the Markov process.

The second aspect of aggregation has to do with statistical inference: how and what to infer about the individual buyer when one has obtained group analysis. Much of the quantitative work has treated the time periods or trials as the independent variable and the purchase probability as the dependent variable. The question of inference from group data is then with respect to two elements. First, is the *form* of the aggregate functional relation the same as the form of the individual functional relationships? Second, is the *shape* of the individual function the same as the aggregate function? The shape is determined by the parameter estimates of the individual buyers' functions. The question, therefore, is one of the inference of individual parameters from aggregate parameters. This question of statistical inference will be elaborated later. It is sufficient here to note that it has received very little attention in marketing.

Before we discuss the third problem, it is important to see what the two issues discussed above imply. Not surprisingly, the implications relate to the necessity of a nomological net of hypothetical constructs or a theory. The two issues are unresolved because no one has provided a well-defined theoretical reasoning as to the use of a particular model, be it Bernoulli, Markov, or any other process. In other words, none of the formulations given so far has theoretical or rational functions. What has happened is that confronted with a set of empirical data such as those of the M.R.C.A. or the *Chicago Tribune* panel, researchers have attempted to fit them to a particular model, very often not realizing that the model may be irrelevant, from a theoretical point of view, to that set of data (Sheth, 1968a). A case in point seems to be Frank's explicit rejection of relevance of psychological learning theory to buying behavior (1962). He fitted with partial success the Bernoulli model to a set of data which suggest that, if anything, the majority of consumers may have *already learned the brand preferences*. In other words, for a well-established product like coffee, the majority of buyers may very well be at the asymptotic level of learning. At the level of completed learning, there should not be any further effect from past history, and, therefore, the analysis of the data from that time onward should show a Bernoulli process without rejecting effects of prior learning.

Another example comes from Styan and Smith's test of *stationary* transition matrices over time. As Ehrenberg (1965) points out, in order for the transition matrix of the first-order Markov chain to remain stationary over time, the absolute levels in various states must change except when the system is resting at the equilibrium state which is trivial for marketing purposes. Styan and Smith did test the assumption of stationarity (very few researchers have explicitly tested this) using techniques provided by Anderson and Goodman (1957), but since the absolute levels did not change appreciably, it must be concluded that analysis of the data was done for a time period when the system was resting at the equilibrium level.

Finally, Kuehn's utilization of learning theory to explain brand loyalty for frozen concentrated orange juice also suffers *to some extent* from the same limitations. The data analyzed were for a time period when the new product had been in the market for four years—a sufficiently long time for consumers to establish brand preferences for a frequently purchased item. The product in question, however, was a radical innovation, which many consumers may not have tried yet, as attested to by the low market penetration of the product. Kuehn's sample, then, may contain a large number of consumers trying the product for the first time, *but also* a segment of buyers who are already brand-loyal. Even a strict behavioristic learning theory requires that to measure learning from experience, there should be no prior experience with the brand. Moreover, as we saw in Part II, an individual buyer may learn the potential of a new brand in a number of ways, experience being only one of them; he can learn by generalization, by information seeking, or by imitative behavior. To measure a strict experience effect, then, one must use data obtained under conditions where the other avenues of learning are either absent or statistically controlled (Sheth, 1968a).

"In summary, for a finite amount of data, there exists no isomorphism between models of behavior and data describing behavior" (Morrison, 1965, p. 4). It is for precisely this reason that intervening variables are utilized—to establish rules of correspondence between a network of hypothetical constructs and the observable data, or between the C plane and the P plane depicted in Figure 3.1. Such rules of correspondence will then force the researcher to seek only the relevant data that the theory deductively demands, thus leading to proper construct validation (Cronbach and Meehl, 1955).

7.2.3.3 Problem of Parameter Estimation

The third unresolved problem in quantitative formulations has to do with parameter estimation. There exist no estimation procedures for the individual buyer's parameters. Whatever research has been done, has been at the aggregate level. Even at the aggregate level, the actual estimation procedures have been lacking. The only exception has been the maximum likelihood and the least-square estimations of transition, matrices for first-order stationary Markov chain and nonstationary Bernoulli process.

7.3 FACTOR-ANALYTIC METHODS OF MEASURING BRAND LOYALTY

To measure brand loyalty for each buyer, existing methods are inappropriate. In search for adequate techniques, we have found factor-analytic procedures to be very relevant (Sheth, 1966, 1968b). Interesting is the fact that factor analysis is here used for estimating parameters of functional relationships, based on suggestions of Rao (1958) and Tucker (1958, 1959, 1966).

In Section 7.3.1 we show how purchase data on a sample of buyers could be applied to functional relationships and then how the basic linear postulate underlying factor analysis can be used to estimate parameters of these functional relationships. Section 7.3.2 details a set of technical procedures related to the derivation of parameters, and Section 7.3.3 summarizes the sequential steps necessary to measure brand loyalty. Finally, Sections 7.3.4, 7.3.5, and 7.3.6 provide some examples based on empirical research on brand loyalty.

7.3.1 Using Factor Analysis to Estimate Parameters

Suppose that we wish to estimate the brand loyalty of five buyers from their purchase patterns that include their buying decisions on six occasions. Every time a buyer bought the brand under investigation, say brand A, is coded as 1, whereas his purchase of some other brand is coded as 0. The total data can be arranged to form a data matrix Y, which is shown in Table 7.1.

Table 7.1 A Hypothetical Data Matrix Representing Purchases

		Buyers				
		1	2	3	4	5
	1	1	0	1	0	0
	2	1	0	1	0	0
Trials	3	1	1	1	0	0
	4	1	1	1	1	0
	5	1	1	0	1	0
	6	1	1	0	1	0

It will be noted that the first buyer has consistently bought brand A and the fifth buyer has never bought it during the six occasions. The second buyer has begun to buy from the third trial, whereas the fourth buyer has begun to buy from the fourth trial. Finally, the third buyer has switched to some other brand after consecutively buying brand A for the first four trials.

Each buyer's purchase pattern is represented as a column vector in which the rows are consecutive purchase trials. It is possible to state that the purchase pattern of buyer i is a function of consecutive trials. In other words,

$$y_i = f(a_i, b_i, c_i, \ldots, x) \tag{7.13}$$

The exact form and shape of this functional relationship can be either theoretically stipulated or empirically derived from a finite set of data. From this, a specific event $y_{ji} = 1$ or 0 can be stated as

$$y_{ji} = f(a_i, b_i, c_i, \ldots, x_j) \tag{7.14}$$

By the process of linear transformation, Equation 7.14 can be written as

$$y_{ji} = \sum_{m=1}^{n} f_m(x_j) F_m(a_i, b_i, c_i, \ldots) \tag{7.15}$$

in which $f_m(x_j)$ are a finite number of functions of the independent variable x_j, and $F_m(a_i, b_i, c_i, \ldots)$ are corresponding number of functions of the constants of buyer i. It is this linear combination that permits us to state that factor-analytic procedures are useful for parameter estimation (Tucker, 1958). For when we define

$$f_m(x_j) \equiv a_{jm} \quad \text{and} \quad F_m(a_i, b_i, c_i, \ldots) \equiv s_{mi}$$

we obtain

$$y_{ji} = \sum_{m=1}^{n} a_{jm} s_{mi} \tag{7.16}$$

Those familiar with factor analysis will note that Equation 7.16 is the basic linear postulate underlying factor analysis. In the standard terminology, a_{jm} is a factor loading of variable j on factor m, and s_{mi} is a factor score of individual i on factor m.

A consecutive set of factor loadings on a factor $(a_{jm}s)$ can be plotted as a curve because the j variables in our case are consecutive trials. Such plotting of each factor is called a *reference curve*. A data matrix Y will have as many factors as there are dimensions of a functional relationship. The more complex a function, the larger the number of factors. Since each factor is a reference curve, the more complex a function, the larger the number of reference curves. In general, one is likely to obtain only two or three reference curves, however (Sheth, 1966).

Perhaps a simpler way to describe the transformation is to focus on factor scores. Later on, we suggest that the factor scores (s_{mi}) of a buyer are tantamount to his brand-loyalty scores. A factor score is a linear combination of the complete set of values on finite variables. In our case, the finite set of variables are consecutive trials. Then we can state that

$$s_i = a_1 y_{1i} + a_2 y_{2i} + a_3 y_{3i} + \cdots + a_n y_{ni} \qquad (7.17)$$

The linear combinations may generate more than one score for an individual, so that

$$s_{mi} = a_{m1} y_{1i} + a_{m2} y_{2i} + a_{m3} y_{3i} + \cdots + a_{mn} y_{ni} \qquad (7.18)$$

Thus a factor score is a linear combination of the observed purchase behavior on a series of trials. Since it is a function of purchase pattern, it can be considered a brand-loyalty score. This is what we do also when we obtain the relative frequency of a brand in total purchases and call it a probability of purchase for a buyer (Sheth, 1969h). Later we shall show that the method suggested here provides individual brand-loyalty scores that are based on *both* the frequency of purchase of a brand and the pattern of these purchases. In a time-dependent situation, the latter would be significantly influential in determining the strength of brand loyalty, as it was in Kuehn's linear learning model.

7.3.2 Technical Steps in Obtaining Brand-Loyalty Scores

To obtain the dimensionality of a data matrix with the resultant set of reference curves and factor scores, we may follow the Eckart-Young (1936) and Young and Householder (1938) theorem in matrix algebra. This was explained in Chapter 6, hence is not repeated here. However, it is worth noting that in order to resolve a data matrix Y into the product of three matrices U, Γ, and W, the first step is to postmultiply Y with its transpose Y'. The resultant matrix is a cross-products matrix whose cell values contain sum of squares and sum of cross products in the diagonals and off-diagonals respectively.

Now, when the data are *dichotomies,* as in Table 7.1, the cross-products matrix turns out to be a contigency table whose cells provide absolute joint frequencies of purchases between trials. If we postmultiply matrix Y in Table 7.1 with its transpose Y', we obtain the cross-products matrix shown in Table 7.2.

Table 7.2   Cross Products of Purchase Data

Trials

		1	2	3	4	5	6
Trials	1	2	2	2	2	1	1
	2		2	2	2	1	1
	3			3	3	2	2
	4				4	3	3
	5					3	3
	6						3

We have omitted the values below the diagonal because the matrix is symmetric. The diagonals give the absolute frequencies of purchases of brand A at each of the six trials. For example, at the first trial 2 out of 5 buyers bought the brand, whereas in the fourth trial 4 out of 5 buyers bought it. The off-diagonal values give the absolute joint frequencies of purchases of brand A at any two trials. For example, between trial 1 and trial 5, only one buyer bought brand A at both trials. Looking back at Table 7.1, we see that it is the first buyer. Similarly, between trials 4 and 5, as many as 3 buyers bought the brand at both trials. These are the first, second, and fourth buyers.

As mentioned in Chapter 6, the factor scores are scaled so that $WW' = I$. This means that factor scores are partly determined by the sample size. We cannot compare the results from two investigations if they differ in their sample sizes. We described a procedure of standardization in Chapter 6, which would remove the sample-size bias *after* the analysis had been done. In the present case, however, it is easy and even more meaningful to standardize the data before doing the analysis.

In the case of dichotomies, this simply means that we convert the absolute frequencies in Table 7.2 into *relative* frequencies. However, the resultant values, though similar to probabilities, are not treated as probabilities of buying brand A at various trials or as joint probabilities across two trials because of sampling problems inherent in small sample size of five consumers. Table 7.3 gives the relative frequencies by standardizing the cross-products matrix.

There are certain situations in which it is desirable to further divide the relative joint frequencies (p_{jk}) by the standard deviation $\sqrt{N_j N_k / N}$, where N_j is the absolute frequency at trial j, N_k is that at trial k, and N is the sample size. This is especially good when we wish to analyze simultaneously a set of mutually exclusive brands available to and bought by buyers at each trial (Burt, 1950). This will be elaborated

Table 7.3 Standardized Cross-Products Matrix

Trials	1	2	3	4	5	6
1	.40	.40	.40	.40	.20	.20
2		.40	.40	.40	.20	.20
3			.60	.60	.40	.40
4				.80	.60	.60
5					.60	.60
6						.60

later. Here, however, this further weighting results in a set of proportionate values, which may be designated as

$$y'_{jk} = p_{jk}/\sqrt{p_j p_k} = N_{jk}/\sqrt{N_j N_k} \tag{7.19}$$

Interestingly, this is equivalent to pre- and postmultiplying the cross-product matrix by a diagonal matrix $D^{-1/2}$ whose elements are $1/\sqrt{N_j}$. We may then write

$$R = D^{-1/2} Y Y' D^{-1/2} \tag{7.20}$$

where R is the standardized cross-products matrix. Moreover, this further standardization automatically places the unity values in the diagonals. Placing unity in the diagonals and values that range between zero and one elsewhere, makes the R matrix suitable for principal components analysis. This has the benefits of applying several analytical tests of significance to the derived factors and of easier interpretation of the analysis.

It must be pointed out, however, that the additional standardization by dividing relative joint frequencies with standard deviations is not mandatory in removing the sample bias.

The standardized cross-products matrix will be resolved into its characteristic roots and vectors. Thus $R = U\Gamma^2 U'$. There will be as many roots and vectors as the size of the matrix. However, we wish to choose a much smaller number of roots and corresponding vectors, which will be significant in explaining the variance in the data.

A number of tests are available for finding the significant number of characteristic roots (Γ^2) and corresponding vectors (U) in a situation such as ours. First, by inspection of the sizes of the roots, we can judgmentally select the first r set of roots and corresponding vectors which jointly explain a certain satisfactory level of variance. These roots are ordered in general, so that picking the first set of roots will be easier. Second, we can plot the roots successively. In general, there will be a discontinuity in the curve where the roots suddenly become very small. The point of discontinuity can be treated as a cutoff point. Third, if we expect a particular functional relationship in a set of data based on some theory, the number of roots will be dictated by the theory (Sheth, 1969c). Fourth, each factor with its loadings constitutes a reference curve, as mentioned before. The first reference curve, by the process of aggregating buyers in a sample, approximates the mean curve of those data. All the reference curves (factors) are mutually orthogonal, so that the remaining reference curves will fluctuate about the zero line. Any significant trend in this fluctuation can be detected by the runs test (Swed and Eisenhart, 1943; Siegel, 1956). By grouping the positive and negative loadings, we can test the null hypothesis that such grouping could have arisen by chance. If the hypothesis is rejected, the reference curve is accepted as systematic, meaningful, and one that explains a good deal of variance in the data.

Finally, the data are consecutive trials or time periods here. The series of coefficients in a reference curve $(a_{jm}s)$ show the rate of change. A quantitative statement of the smoothness of the curve can, therefore, be obtained by taking the first differences between consecutive coefficients (e.g., $a_{km} - a_{lm}$) and summing the squares of these differences. These sums of squares of first differences (Σd^2) help also in determining the significant number of vectors. Small values will be associated with a smooth curve, whereas large values will be associated with erratic or random curves. For a detailed description of these methods drawn from several sources the reader is referred to Sheth (1966, 1968b).

Once a small number of roots and vectors have been determined as significant and meaningful, we can obtain an approximate matrix $Y_r = U_r \Gamma_r W_r$, in which we already know U_r and Γ_r, by resolving the cross-products matrix into its characteristic roots and vectors. The W_r can be obtained as $W_r = \Gamma_r^{-1} U_r Y$.

If we define $U_r \Gamma_r = A$ which has a_{jm} as its elements and $W_r = S$ which has s_{mi} as its elements, then

$$Y = AS \quad \text{and} \quad y_{ji} = \sum_{m=1}^{r} a_{jm} s_{mi}.$$

It will be thus noted that the S matrix contains the brand-loyalty scores. Generally, the brand-loyalty scores will be unidimensional, but there are situations where they can be multidimensional. The dimensionality will be essentially a function of the complexity of the relationship of purchase with time.

The A matrix contains a set of reference curves. The first reference curve approximates the average curve of the data. Other reference curves are deviations from this average curve. The form and shape of these curves tell us the functional form of the individual buyers' curves. It is possible, in the same sample, to have a first reference curve that is a constant and a second reference curve that is monotonically increasing with trials. Any buyer who has brand-loyalty scores primarily concentrated on the first factor will then have a constant brand-loyalty pattern. Any buyer who has brand-loyalty scores primarily concentrated on the second factor will have a monotonically increasing brand-loyalty function of trials. This will become more meaningful later when we bring into the description some empirical evidence.

7.3.3 Summary of Steps Involved in the Measurement of Brand Loyalty

1. We begin by a score matrix Y that has n rows for trials or time periods and N columns for buyers. The first step is to postmultiply the data matrix by its transpose Y' to obtain the cross-products matrix YY'. If the data are dichotomous items as, for example, when the purchase of a specific brand is coded as 1 and purchase of all other brands is coded as 0, we may standardize the cross-products matrix to remove the bias from sample size. This is done by converting the absolute frequencies into relative frequencies. Also, in some cases, we may further divide the relative frequencies by standard deviations. The result is to pre- and postmultiply Y' with a diagonal matrix $D^{-\frac{1}{2}}$ whose elements are $1/\sqrt{N_j}$. The outcome is a standardized square symmetric matrix containing cell values between zero and one. Several standard computer programs are available to factor-analyze the matrix, since it looks like a correlation matrix.

2. However, if the cross-products matrix is not standardized, the procedure is to derive another matrix of lower rank by using the Eckart-Young theorem. The intent is to resolve the data matrix Y into the product of three matrices, containing a series of roots and vectors that are ordered. In other words,

$$Y = U\Gamma W$$

This is accomplished by obtaining the characteristic roots and vectors of the cross-products matrix YY'. Several computer programs are available to do the analysis. Thus

$$YY' = (U\Gamma W)(W'\Gamma U') = U\Gamma^2 U'$$

where U contains the characteristic vectors and Γ^2 contains the characteristic roots. They provide us with values of the U and Γ matrices needed for the Eckart-Young resolution. The orthogonal matrix W can then be obtained by

$$W = \Gamma^{-1}U'Y$$

Thus a complete set of left vectors (U), right vectors (W), and roots (Γ) are obtained. However, our interest is to approximate the original data matrix by a matrix with lower rank; the latter is either theoretically determined or empirically derived. This can be done by taking the first set of r significant principal roots and vectors and forming an approximate matrix

$$Y_r = U_r\Gamma_rW_r$$

3. To determine the number of significant reference curves, several procedures are available. We can apply the runs test on the reference curves contained in matrix $A = U\Gamma$. Also, we can test the mean-square ratios of the characteristic roots and judgmentally determine a cutoff point where the value suddenly becomes very low. A similar inspection of the characteristic roots itself can be done. Finally, we can take the square of the first differences of the consecutive coefficients of each reference curve and sum them. The value so provided, called Σd^2, may indicate the smoothness of the curve. If the data are prestandardized, and since the matrix resembles a correlation matrix, Bartlett's test of significance may be applied. A general criterion provided by the test is that the roots with values greater than one are significant.

4. We may also resort to a shortcut by first determining the significant roots and vectors, obtaining the matrix of reference curves $A = U_r\Gamma_r$, and then obtaining the approximate matrix Y_r by solving for

$$W_r = \Gamma_r^{-1}U_r'Y$$

Thus instead of multiplying with all the roots and vectors, we multiply the data matrix with only the significant roots and vectors. The approximate matrix Y_r is obtained easily as

$$Y_r = U_r\Gamma_rW_r = AS$$

The approximate matrix is the best approximation to the original data matrix in the least-squares sense.

5. If the data are not standardized before the analysis, it is necessary (for generalizations) to rescale the data so as to remove the bias due to sample size. This is done by obtaining matrices P and V:

$$P = (U_r\Gamma_r)N^{-\frac{1}{2}} = AN^{-\frac{1}{2}}$$

and

$$V = N^{\frac{1}{2}}W_r = N^{\frac{1}{2}}S$$

The approximate matrix now is

$$Y_r = PV = (U_r\Gamma_r)N^{-\frac{1}{2}} \cdot N^{\frac{1}{2}}W_r = U_r\Gamma_rW_r$$

and the basic Eckart-Young theorem is still maintained.

6. The number and the shapes of the reference curves will determine the complexity of the basic function that may be theoretically hypothesized or empirically derived. If only one significant reference curve is obtained or if there are two reference curves one of which is a constant, then we may say that the aggregate curve is of the same shape as the individual curves. In all other instances, it can be safely stated that the shapes of the individual curves will differ from the mean curve.

If we start out with an empirical analysis of the same data, and obtain a large number of reference curves, we may safely assume that the underlying basic function cannot be incorporated into the linear combination model without the use of infinite series. However, the knowledge that it is a complex function may enable us to transform the observations into logarithmic values which, in many instances, will suit the linear combination model. Similarly, if we a priori hypothesize based on some theory that the function is complex, we may begin with the transformed data. The reader will have noted the analogy of the procedure to the least-squares fit for linear and nonlinear curves. The advantage in all instances as compared to the least-squares curve fitting is that the model explicitly provides estimates of *individual* parameters. Also, it incorporates a variety of functional relations under a smaller set of reference curves.

7.3.4 Empirical Examples of Measuring Brand Loyalty

The empirical data to exemplify the factor-analytic method of brand loyalty come from Sheth (1966). A panel of foreign students was established on their arrival in the United States. The rationale for forming such a panel was to avoid the difficulty encountered with the existing panels of fixed households—they are not adequate to validate learning of brand loyalty because, for most nondurable goods such as grocery and personal care items, they may already be brand-loyal. Among the several sets of data gathered by Sheth, the one that is of interest here is the analysis of rice purchases by the panel of foreign students.

Two sets of data are analyzed for rice: a sequence of 6 purchase trials with 17 panel members as the sample size and a sequence of 7 purchase trials with 14 panel members as the sample size are used for measuring rice brand loyalty.

The first step in the analysis is to form the data matrix Y with y_{ji} elements representing the purchase behavior of the ith individual at the

Table 7.4   Standardized   Cross-Products   Matrix   for   Rice: Larger Sample

$(N = 17; n = 6)$

Trials

Trials		1	2	3	4	5	6
	1	1	.754	.660	.632	.586	.542
	2	.754	1	.961	.790	.847	.804
Trials	3	.660	.961	1	.801	.951	.907
	4	.632	.790	.801	1	.848	.804
	5	.586	.847	.951	.848	1	.951
	6	.542	.804	.907	.804	.951	1

SOURCE: Sheth, 1966, p. 144.

*j*th trial. The cells take the dichotomous values of 1 or 0, depending on whether the purchase at trial *j* for individual *i* was of the brand toward which he was developing some loyalty in general, rather than loyalty to a specific brand. Therefore, the brand that had the maximum total frequency was considered the preferred or loyal brand of that panel member. The data matrix Y is then postmultiplied with its transpose Y' to obtain the square symmetric matrix of cross products, namely YY'. The data matrix was standardized by pre- and postmultiplying the cross-products matrix YY' with the diagonal matrix $D^{-\frac{1}{2}}$ containing elements $1/\sqrt{N_j}$, N_j being the frequency of preferred brand on trial *j*. Thus

$$R = D^{-\frac{1}{2}}YY'D^{-\frac{1}{2}}$$

The standardized square-symmetric matrices for the two sets of rice data are given in Tables 7.4 and 7.5. The standardization results in placing values of 1 in the diagonals and proportionate values in the off-diagonal elements.

Table 7.5   Standardized   Cross-Products   Matrix   for   Rice: Smaller Sample

$(N = 14; n = 7)$

Trials

Trials		1	2	3	4	5	6	7
	1	1	.707	.650	.707	.554	.500	.597
	2	.707	1	.940	.877	.877	.823	.886
	3	.650	.940	1	.940	.940	.886	.944
Trials	4	.707	.877	.940	1	.877	.877	.886
	5	.554	.877	.940	.877	1	.940	.886
	6	.500	.823	.886	.877	.940	1	.944
	7	.597	.886	.944	.886	.886	.944	1

SOURCE: Sheth, 1966, p. 145.

Table 7.6 gives the first three reference curves for the rice data having 6 trials. The first reference curve explains about 83 *per cent of the total variance* and seems to be the only dominant curve. The run test is performed on all three curves, which also suggests that only the first reference curve is significant. The characteristic (latent) roots also show a sudden drop after the first root, and the Σd^2 calculations, too, suggest that probably the first curve is significant. It is, therefore, decided that

Table 7.6   Reference Curves and Brand-Loyalty Scores of Panel Members for Rice: Larger Sample

$$(n = 6; N = 17)$$

Trial	Reference Curve I	Reference Curve II	Reference Curve III	Run Test
1	.75020	−.64244	.02828	Reference curve I: $n = 6$, $m = 0$,
2	.94603	−.13152	−.18456	$u = 1$, significant
3	.97320	.08226	−.19472	Reference curve II: $n = 2$, $m = 4$,
4	.89436	.04899	.42613	$u = 2$, $p(u \leq u') = .133$
5	.95684	.22994	−.01200	Reference curve III: $n = 2$, $m = 4$,
6	.92521	.28370	−.02892	$u = 4$, $p(u \leq u') = .80$
Percentage variance explained	82.9	9.6	4.2	
Latent root	4.98	.57	.26	
Σd^2	.0549	.3432	.6232	

Brand-Loyalty Scores

Panel Member	Score	Panel Member	Score
1	.29168	10	.20009
2	.04648	11	.24405
3	.19313	12	.29168
4	.29168	13	.24405
5	.24405	14	.19591
6	.29168	15	.24354
7	.29168	16	.29168
8	.29168	17	.19313
9	.29168		

SOURCE: Sheth, 1966, p. 50.

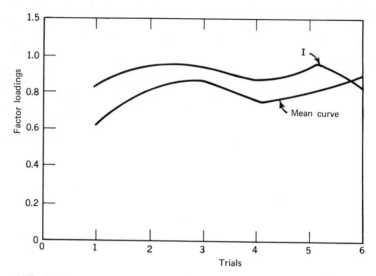

Figure 7.5   Reference curve for rice with 6 trials. (From Sheth, 1966, p. 148.)

only one reference curve underlies the data. The first reference curve is plotted in Figure 7.5; it is exponential in shape and seems to reach the asymptote very quickly, thus suggesting fast learning: not only is there strong brand preference, but it is established very quickly. The proportion of preferred brands at each trial is calculated and plotted in Figure 7.5 as the mean curve. The first reference curve and the mean curve (relative frequencies on each trial) have the same shape; however, they are not identical because the reference curve is obtained from the standardized matrix $D^{-\frac{1}{2}}Y$ and not the raw data matrix Y. In addition, the shape of the reference curve deviates slightly from that of the mean curve because the former is only a good approximation to the latter; the two will be identical only if differences in shape and form of the individual learning curves do not exist. Although the runs test and the latent root did suggest that the second reference curve was not significant, it will be seen from Table 7.6 that the $p(u \leq u')$ under the run test is .134, close to significance at .10 level. Also, the Σd^2 calculations show that the second curve may be quite smooth. It also explains about 10 per cent of the variance. All these factors suggest that the second curve may be acting as the one correction term to explain the deviation of the first reference curve from the mean curve. However, it does not explain enough variance to qualify as another dimension of the function.

Utilizing the first reference curve as the only significant curve, the brand-loyalty (factor) scores of the panel members are calculated. The scores range in value from .04648 to .29168. It will be recalled that the brand-loyalty scores act as weights to the reference curves. Accordingly, a buyer can be categorized as belonging to a given reference curve based on his brand loyalty scores. In this case, since there is only one reference curve, *the form of the individual curves remains the same. The shape of the individual curves will also be the same: the curves will be the same except for a multiplication factor.*

The brand-loyalty scores immediately show the n-trial dependency. In fact, they provide for all the 64 possible sequences of two-state (one-zero) system for 6 trials. For example, consider the following sequences and their corresponding brand loyalty scores:

$$
\begin{aligned}
&(1)\quad 1\ \ 1\ \ 1\ \ 1\ \ 1\ \ 1 = .29168 \text{ (panel member 1)} \\
&(2)\quad 0\ \ 1\ \ 1\ \ 1\ \ 1\ \ 1 = .24405 \text{ (panel member 5)} \\
&(3)\quad 0\ \ 0\ \ 1\ \ 1\ \ 1\ \ 1 = .19313 \text{ (panel member 3)} \\
&(4)\quad 1\ \ 1\ \ 1\ \ 1\ \ 0\ \ 0 = .20009 \text{ (panel member 10)} \\
&(5)\quad 0\ \ 1\ \ 1\ \ 0\ \ 1\ \ 1 = .19591 \text{ (panel member 14)}
\end{aligned}
$$

It will be noted that in sequences (3), (4), and (5), the frequency of purchase of the favorite brand is the same: it is four. However, the scores differ because of the arrangement of the purchases of the favorite brand. In fact, the method will provide brand-loyalty scores for each terminating branch of a tree diagram individually. All buyers belonging to a given branch (purchase sequence) will have the same brand-loyalty score (Table 7.6). It will also be noted that between sequences 001111 and 111100, the latter has greater brand-loyalty score. This is in line with the exponential learning curve where the additional consecutive trial adds a fraction of learning still not completed, and, therefore, each additional consecutive purchase of a favorite brand will add a smaller value. It contradicts the derivation that Kuehn makes from the linear learning model described earlier. However, we pointed out the inconsistency of that derivation with learning theory.

Table 7.7 provides the first three reference curves for rice data having 7 trials and 14 panel members. The first reference curve explains a little more than 85 per cent of total variance and seems to be the only dominant curve. The runs test performed on all the three reference curves shows that only the first curve is significant. The corresponding latent roots also support the fact that the first root is very large (5.97) and the second and third roots are much smaller in comparison (.62 and .15 respectively). Finally, the Σd^2 calculations also sugggest that the first curve is very smooth.

Table 7.7   *Reference Curves of Panel Members for Rice*
$(n = 7; N = 14)$

Trial	Reference Curve I	Reference Curve II	Reference Curve III	Run Test
1	.71356	.68768	−.10013	Reference curve I: $n = 7$, $m = 0$,
2	.94803	.08364	.27699	$u = 1$, significant
3	.98079	−.04790	.11731	Reference curve II: $n = 3$, $m = 4$,
4	.95665	.05332	−.09808	$u' = 4$, $p(u \le u') = .542$
5	.94803	−.19430	.02306	Reference curve III: $n = 3$, $m = 4$,
6	.93329	−.27832	−.19046	$u' = 5$, $p(u \le u') = .80$
7	.95750	−.13585	−.05899	
Percentage variance explained	85.3	8.8	2.2	
Latent root	5.97	.62	.15	
Σd^2	.0563	.4804	.2918	

SOURCE: Sheth, 1966, p. 151.

The first reference curve is plotted in Figure 7.6. Again, it has the same shape as the mean curve, the absolute difference in level being due to standardization of data. If we compare Figure 7.5 (rice with 6 trials) and Figure 7.6 (rice with 7 trials), we see that the slight deviations in the shape at each trial are much less in Figure 7.6. This can be explained by the fact that the second reference curve which acts as a correction term to the mean curve (reference curve I) is more random than the second reference curve for the earlier rice data having 6 trials. In other words, the first reference curve or the mean-constant curve is very similar to the mean curve in the case of rice data having 7 trials. This is because we have removed three panel members from the analysis here who tended to deviate from the aggregate tendency.

Taking the first reference curve as the only significant reference curve, the brand-loyalty scores of panel members are calculated in Table 7.8. The values range from .08623 to .31225. Again they act as weights to the reference curve and determine the type of buyer the panel member is likely to be. In this instance, since there is only one reference curve, all panel members belong to one type only with differential or heterogeneous loyalties. The brand-loyalty scores again exhaust all the logical possibilities of n-trial dependencies for 7 trials, which total 128. Each

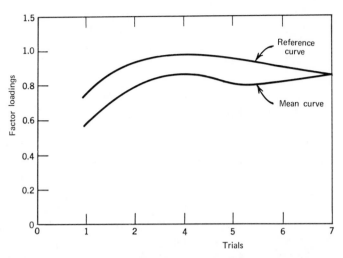

Figure 7.6   Reference curve for rice with 7 trials. (From Sheth, 1966, p. 152.)

possible arrangement has a differential effect on the brand-loyalty scores and thus there are as many possible values of brand-loyalty scores. For example, the following are some of the sequences and their brand-loyalty scores:

(1) 1 1 1 1 1 1 1 = .31225 (panel member 1)
(2) 0 1 1 1 1 1 1 = .26998 (panel member 5)
(3) 0 0 1 1 1 1 1 = .22407 (panel member 3)
(4) 1 1 1 1 0 0 1 = .22394 (panel member 10)
(5) 0 1 1 0 1 1 1 = .22366 (panel member 14)
(6) 0 0 0 0 0 1 1 = .08623 (panel member 2)

Table 7.8   Brand Loyalty Scores of Panel Members

Panel Member	Score	Panel Member	Score
1	.31225	8	.31225
2	.08623	9	.31225
3	.22407	10	.22395
4	.31225	11	.26998
5	.26998	12	.31225
6	.31225	13	.26998
7	.31225	14	.22366

SOURCE: Sheth, 1966, p. 151.

Again we see that the *frequency* of purchases of favorite brand does not determine the brand-loyalty scores; rather, it is the *arrangement of the frequency* in one of the possible combinations. Sequences (3), (4), and (5) have all 5 purchases of the preferred brand, but the scores are different.

Now let us compare the brand-loyalty scores for rice having 6 and 7 trial sequences. It will be remembered that when increasing the purchase sequence to 7 trials we have lost the last three panel members, 15, 16, and 17, but the preceding 14 members are the same. Also, since the data are standardized to remove sample bias, we can make a direct comparison of the members in the two sequences. Earlier, we mentioned that learning seems to be operating because of the exponential nature of the reference curve. Under the Hull-Spence learning formulation, the exponential shape results because the magnitude of learning performed at a given trial is considered a fraction of the learning that remains to be achieved. The latter is, of course, the asymptote of learning less the learning already completed prior to a given trial. If we have the probability measure of learning, then this can be expressed as $P_t = \alpha(U - P_{t-1})$. Now, at each trial some learning may occur, which will reduce the size of learning to be completed in succeeding trials. The same fraction coefficient α will now have a smaller value to be multiplied with. As a result the *increment* in learning at each successive trial will be smaller, as discussed earlier. This will manifest in an increase in learning at a decreasing rate, and we shall obtain exponential curves for the individuals, and aggregatively for the sample, if function is not modified by averaging. To see whether this is operating in our data, it is necessary only to compare the increments in different sequences for which the increments are calculated.

$$
\begin{aligned}
(1) &= 111111 - 1 = .31225 - .29168 = .02057 \text{ (panel member 1)} \\
(2) &= 011111 - 1 = .26998 - .24405 = .02593 \text{ (panel member 5)} \\
(3) &= 001111 - 1 = .22407 - .19313 = .03094 \text{ (panel member 3)} \\
(4) &= 111100 - 1 = .22394 - .20009 = .02385 \text{ (panel member 10)} \\
(5) &= 011011 - 1 = .22366 - .19591 = .02775 \text{ (panel member 14)} \\
(6) &= 000001 - 1 = .08623 - .04648 = .04175 \text{ (panel member 2)}
\end{aligned}
$$

Except for panel member 5, it will be seen that the magnitude of increments are inversely related to the magnitude of learning prior to trial 7: the less the learning prior to trial 7, the greater is the increment.

7.3.5 *Extensions to Multistate System*

An important result for the current marketing research on brand loyalty and brand switching comes from the fact that the contingency

Table 7.9   A Hypothetical Example of Raw Data of Multistate Brand Purchases

Trials \ Buyers		1	2	3	4	5	6	7	8	9	10
Trial 1	A	1	1	1	0	0	0	0	0	0	0
	B	0	0	0	1	1	1	0	0	0	1
	C	0	0	0	0	0	0	1	1	1	0
Trial 2	A	1	0	0	0	0	1	0	1	1	0
	B	0	1	0	1	1	0	0	0	0	1
	C	0	0	1	0	0	0	1	0	0	0

table that results from the cross-products matrix can be extended to "manifold" classifications reflecting the "states" of brands simultaneously over a number of trials. The raw data matrix then will have as many rows as the number of trials *times* each trial having a number of states. In other words, each trial itself will be multidimensional. The columns will be the buyers as usual. For example, if there are 2 trials, 3 brands, and 10 buyers, the data matrix would look like Table 7.9.

In the table, the "states" (brands) are assumed to be mutually exclusive; a buyer can buy only one brand at a given trial. When this data matrix Y is postmultiplied by its transpose Y', the resultant YY' will be square-symmetric supermatrix of a manifold contingency table. It will look like Table 7.10.

The cross-products matrix is really a supermatrix whose diagonal matrices have values only in the diagonals. This is because of the restriction that the states be mutually exclusive. The off-diagonal matrices provide the joint frequencies of purchases of the same or other brands.

Table 7.10   Cross-Products Matrix of a Multistate Data Matrix

		Trial 1			Trial 2		
		A	B	C	A	B	C
Trial 1	A	3	0	0	1	1	1
	B	0	4	0	1	3	0
	C	0	0	3	2	0	1
Trial 2	A	1	1	2	4	0	0
	B	1	3	0	0	4	0
	C	1	0	1	0	0	2

If we relax the assumption of mutual exclusiveness of the states as probably may be true in the purchase of dry cereals, for example, then the diagonal matrices will have values in the off-diagonal cells also. The analysis, however, will remain the same. Furthermore, if we analyze a set of data not on the trial criterion, but on the time-period criterion, then the assumption of mutually exclusive states does not really hold in the real world. In such instances, we may obtain a score for each family at each time period for each of the states based on the frequency of purchase of that brand state. The analysis will show the market shares of the brands over time, buyers who are loyal to a given brand, and extent of brand switching. This procedure has two advantages over Rohloff's gain-loss analysis (1963). First, there is no need to compute percentage scores of the family for brand-switching behavior, then obtain the volume-consumed measure for each family, and finally aggregate family scores; second, Rohloff's analysis is restricted to two time period interactions. Under the present system, such interaction may be extended to as many time periods as the researcher desires. Probably, the greatest benefit will come from the derivation of *individual* differences under the present system.

In instances where manifold states are incorporated into the analysis, but the states are mutually exclusive, one can standardize the data before the analysis and obtain a supermatrix that will have values between zero and one. In fact, the diagonal cells of the diagonal matrices of this standardized square-symmetric supermatrix will have ones as their values. However, if the states are not mutually exclusive and/or time periods are used, probably standardization by rescaling the results after the analysis would be better.

To illustrate the multistate factor-analytic procedure of obtaining brand loyalty measures, we utilize the rice buying behavior of the panel members in Sheth's study. Based on the frequency of purchases of a given brand, a three-state system was formulated consisting of River (R), Sultana (S), and all other brands (O). Only the first four purchases of rice by the panel members are included in the analysis. Based on a sample size of 21 panel members, the manifold contingency table shown in Table 7.11 is derived. The table can also be viewed as the joint absolute frequencies of purchases of the three brands over four trials. It is, in fact, the unstandardized product sum matrix YY' of the raw data matrix Y containing the i individual's purchase behavior with respect to the three states at the jth trial.

To remove the bias of sample size, the matrix is standardized by pre- and postmultiplying the cross-products matrix YY' with diagonal matrix $D^{-\frac{1}{2}}$. Table 7.12 gives the standardized matrix. It will be noted

Table 7.11 *Unstandardized Cross-Products Matrix for Rice Brand Switching*

Trials

		(1) S	(1) R	(1) O	(2) S	(2) R	(2) O	(3) S	(3) R	(3) O	(4) S	(4) R	(4) O	N_j
(1)	S	6			6			5		1	5		1	6
	R		9		1	7	1	1	7	1	1	5	3	9
	O			6			6		1	5		1	5	6
(2)	S	6	1		7			6		1	6		1	7
	R		7			7			7			5	2	7
	O		1	6			7		1	6		1	6	7
(3)	S	5	1		6			6			6			6
	R		7	1		7	1		8			6	2	8
	O	1	1	5	1		6			7			7	7
(4)	S	5	1		6			6			6			6
	R	1	5	1		5	1		6			6		6
	O	1	3	5	1	2	6		2	7			9	6

(Trials — left row grouping)

SOURCE: Sheth, 1966, p. 179.

Table 7.12 *Standardized Cross-Products Matrix for Rice Brand Switching*

Trials

		(1) S	(1) R	(1) O	(2) S	(2) R	(2) O	(3) S	(3) R	(3) O	(4) S	(4) R	(4) O
(1)	S	1			.926			.833		.125	.833		.136
	R		1		.125	.882	.125	.136	.824	.126	.136	.680	.333
	O			1			.926		.144	.771		.166	.680
(2)	S				1			.926		.128	.926		.126
	R					1			.936			.771	.252
	O						1		.134	.857		.154	.756
(3)	S							1			1.00		
	R								1			.865	.235
	O									1			.882
(4)	S										1		
	R											1	
	O												1

(Trials — left row grouping)

SOURCE: Sheth 1966, p. 181.

that the matrix contains values between zero and one, and the diagonals have values of one. The diagonal matrices contain values of one, which are placed in the diagonals. The off-diagonal empty cells wholly contain zero cell values, although they are not shown, and the matrix is completely filled.

Table 7.13 provides the first three reference curves that are considered to be significant. Together they explain almost 90 per cent of total variance. The run test cannot be performed in this instance because of the manifold classifications. Similarly, calculations of Σd^2 will not be meaningful. It is, however, possible to apply both criteria if each state is focused exclusively for n trial sequence. Based on the characteristic values (eigen values) and the amount of variance explained, only the first three curves seem to be the significant curves. This is also in ac-

Table 7.13   Reference Curves for Rice Brand Switching Matrix

	Unrotated			Rotated		
Trials	Reference Curve I	Reference Curve II	Reference Curve III	Reference Curve I	Reference Curve II	Reference Curve III
1—S	.53383	−.76077	−.01566	.01594	.92766	.05644
1—R	.65032	.33656	.55205	.90637	.09848	.09873
1—O	.53724	.35288	−.64437	.02761	−.02421	.90940
2—S	.57911	−.79189	.01300	.01738	.97965	.05118
2—R	.57234	.42066	.65811	.96825	−.01042	.00536
2—O	.58017	.37610	−.65916	.05281	−.02056	.95359
3—S	.53864	−.80983	.06971	.02454	.97458	−.02023
3—R	.57621	.43297	.65129	.97109	−.01883	.01694
3—O	.60754	.30856	−.66477	.03662	.05062	.94991
4—S	.53864	−.80983	.06971	.02454	.97458	−.02023
4—R	.57052	.42437	.52434	.87722	−.01975	.10303
4—O	.61840	.30830	−.56903	.10846	.06057	.88647
Percentage of variance explained	33.2	30.3	25.6			
Eigen values	3.99	3.63	3.06			

SOURCE: Sheth, 1966, p. 182.

cordance with the thinking that if there is strong brand loyalty toward each of the brands by segments of total sample, each state may stand in isolation from other states across n trial sequences. The number of significant reference curves then will be equal to the number of states in the system. We know from prior analysis that strong brand loyalty seemed present for rice. Since we have three states, we should expect only three reference curves.

The reference curves become more meaningful after a Varimax orthogonal rotation which attempts to put as many coefficients near zero or unity as possible. In the process, the particular state that is dominant for a given reference curve stands out more clearly. The rotated coefficients of the three reference curves are also shown in Table 7.13. They are plotted in Figures 7.7, 7.8, and 7.9. The first reference curve belongs to brand R. The curve slightly rises for the first three trials providing the effect of learning. However, at the fourth trial several members have switched to other brands. This is shown by a decrease in brand R_I and an increase in O_I. Looking back at the unstandardized cross-products matrix, we see that out of eight panel members buying brand R at trial 3, two (25 per cent) have switched to some other brand at trial 4. The reference curve for brand S is shown as slightly

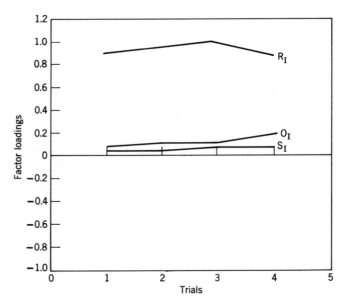

Figure 7.7 Brand-switching analysis of rice; first reference curve. (From Sheth, 1966, p. 184.)

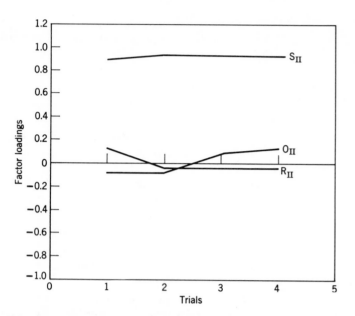

Figure 7.8 Brand-switching analysis of rice; second reference curve. (From Sheth, 1966, p. 185.)

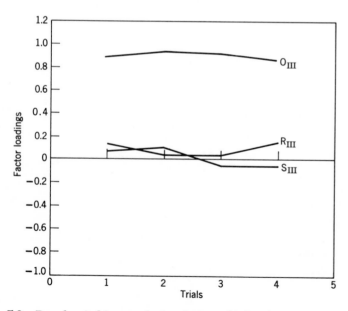

Figure 7.9 Brand-switching analysis of rice; third reference curve. (From Sheth, 1966, p. 186.)

increasing, but the increase is not sufficiently large to warrant investigation; it is caused by one panel member switching from R to S at trial 2, and continuing to buy S.

The second reference curve in Figure 7.7 is dominated by brand S. The brand slightly increases in the beginning and then stabilizes. The increase is associated with the switching of one panel member from brand R to S at trial 2. This results in a decrease in coefficient for R in Figure 7.8. From trial 2 to trial 3, one panel member switched from brand R to O, which is reflected in a very slight decrease in R and a substantial increase in O on the second reference curve. In this phenomenon we see the relevance of learning. The stronger learning created by the first two trials is reduced to a very slight extent by switching. It is also interesting to compare the values of O_{II} at trials 3 and 4; it has slightly increased without any corresponding decrease either in S or R. This can be attributed to the learning of preference of brand O by the panel member who switched from S to O at trial 3 *and continued* at trial 4.

Finally, Figure 7.9 clearly shows that the third reference curve is dominated by "other brands" state. The curve O_{III} is rising from trial 1 to 2, and correspondingly the curve R_{III} is decreasing. This is due to switching of a panel member from R to O. Then the curve O_{III} is very slightly diminishing and curve R_{III} is lightly increasing because a panel member switched from O to R from trial 2 to trial 3. We find that curve S_{III} is decreasing substantially, which is due to the switching of one panel member to O from S at trial 3. This particular change in the dominant state for the third reference curve, that is, O_{III}, is rather important. It will be noticed that between trials 2 and 3 the *number* of panel members buying other brands remains the same (see Table 7.7). Yet there is a slight *decrease*. If there were no brand switching at all, there would be an *increase* because of the learning effect. But there is brand switching: one panel member joins the state from S, and one leaves the state to R. If the pattern of past purchases of the two panel members were the same at least with respect to the state, there would be no change by the exchange occurring at trial 3. However, what has happened is that the state O has gained a *more transient* buyer so far as state O is concerned, but has lost a *more loyal buyer* for that state. The two panel members have sequences SSO and OOR.

It will also be seen from Figure 7.9 that there is a substantial decline in O_{III} and substantial increase in R_{III}. This is because the panel members who were lost at trial 3 have continued to buy brand R. The decline in O_{III} is more at trial 4 than it was at trial 3 because the latter was affected by an increase from gaining a transient panel member.

It will be noted that the gain of brand R is greater than the decline of brand O at trial 4. This is due to the panel member's continuation of buying brand R from trial 3 to 4. Now, if we look at Figure 7.7 we see that this increase has not helped brand R by any substantial amount. The coefficient of R on its reference curve declines from .97109 to .87722. This can be attributed to the fact that it lost two panel members at trial 4. And both of the members lost had a sequence RRO.

A final point of interest in our brand-switching analysis is that although the Sultana brand is only the second dominant brand, it has *more loyal customers* than the River brand. This can be seen from the greater interaction between states R and O than between states S and O. It is better to compare the interaction with the state O because it includes several brands to which the buyer may switch. Also, there is no real interaction between Sultana and River: for a given panel member *both* do not seem to be part of this evoked set. They are, therefore, not substitute brands and may not be competing with each other but with several other brands in the market. It is important to realize this, because economic theory does not provide an operational framework for considering two products as being substitutes, complementary, or independent. This is very likely to depend on the characteristics of the population to which several brands cater. For example, in Colombia (Latin America), people do not substitute tea for coffee, but they substitute, if at all, chocolate for coffee. In the United States, both may be equally substituted, probably tea being more frequently substituted than chocolate. In Great Britain, probably coffee would be decidedly more often substituted for tea than chocolate. Furthermore, within a given country or culture there may be subcultures with different evoked sets of alternatives.

7.3.6 *Implications of the Factor-Analytic Method of Measuring Brand Loyalty*

The factor-analytic model of brand loyalty presented here seems to provide a useful summary in terms of a limited number of reference curves, as well as parameter estimates for a variety of individual functional relations. The model appears to be compatible with Kuehn's aggregate approach. However, the model can provide parameter estimates for *n* sequences of purchase trials. It can also handle Bernoulli, non-Bernoulli, and nonlinear situations. This was not explicitly shown by analysis here. But Sheth has elsewhere analyzed data from existing panels for coffee and detergents and in those situations, *for the time period chosen for analysis,* the Bernoulli process seems operative: the reference curves have constant parameter coefficients for n purchase sequences. This is understandable in view of the fact that the buyer would manifest a stable purchase pattern for these frequently purchased products *after* buying them for a number of years.

One important implication of the factor-analytic model of brand loyalty lies in its use for further investigation of brand-loyalty scores. The model provides a single number for each buyer, which summarizes his pattern of purchase behavior over time. This is a much more desirable measure of the dependent variable than some measure of average tendency, such as the proportion of purchases of a brand in the total purchases of the buyer. Utilizing the brand-loyalty scores, we can discriminate between two or more groups having some explanatory or controlling variables. For example, if we do experimentation in a market in which some marketing activity is deliberately varied and wish to obtain the measure of the effect of the activity on brand-loyalty over time, then the sample of individuals in the experimental market can be compared based on their brand-loyalty scores with a matched sample of individuals from the control market. First, if the number of reference curves is only one and we wish to meaure the effect of a single marketing activity like advertising, we may use the Mann-Whitney U test. If there are more than one reference curve, we can first obtain a single "discriminant function" axis on which the individual brand loyalty-scores can be projected and then apply the Mann-Whitney U test to such discriminant axis projections.

When we have several experimentations each dealing with one particular marketing activity, there are more than two groups, and we may compare these groups simultaneously. If the reference curve found is only one, the Kruskal-Wallis technique of one-way analysis of variance by ranks may be performed to see if there are significant group differences. If there are several reference curves and several groups are to be discriminated, a discriminant axis that maximally separates each group from all other groups may be determined. The discriminant axis scores of the several groups can then be compared for any differences.

An important aspect of the brand-loyalty scores as the dependent variables is that they will handle time-lag effects of several promotional activities. In place of the distributed-lag models, we can utilize the factor-analytic model.

A second major implication of the factor-analytic model is in treating the brand-loyalty score as the dependent variable in a multiple discriminant analysis. If there is only one reference curve, we can look at the distribution of the scores and judgmentally establish cutoff levels to form two or more groups of a sample of panel households whose brand-loyalty scores are obtained. If there are several reference curves, we can obtain the discriminant axis score first, as described above, and then form two or more groups. The groups so formed can then be discriminated on some other independent variables. Two sets of such analysis may be pointed out here.

First, the buyers in a sample may differ in their learning because several environmental variables may be impinging on the hypothetical constructs of Motives, Choice Criteria, Attitude, Confidence and Brand Comprehension. In Chapter 3, we suggested that social class, reference groups, organization, and components of perceived risk may affect the hypothetical constructs. We may, therefore, do a multiple discriminant analysis with these environmental variables as the independent variables explaining the differences in the brand-loyalty scores or learning process. A concrete example of this comes from the adoption of innovations. It is generally considered that there are environmental (social and product) differences among the buyers who adopt innovations very early (innovators) and the buyers who adopt innovations much later. If we obtain measures of brand-loyalty scores for the new product within a given time, we can identify the characteristics of the buyers who adopt early by classifying the sample into groups and performing a multiple discriminant analysis based on several environmental variables as the independent variables. Very often the technique of multiple discriminant analysis has failed in marketing research because too much attention has been focused on the choice of independent variables and too little thought has been given to the dependent classificatory variable (Sheth, 1968e). In the studies of diffusion of innovations, this has been particularly true; a measure like the brand-loyalty score which summarizes the process taking place over time has invariably been lacking. Instead, groups have been formed based mostly on one-time purchase criteria.

Second, since the brand-loyalty score takes into account time-lag effects and since most firms have more than one marketing strategy to manipulate in nonexperimental markets, a multiple discriminant analysis having several marketing strategies as the independent variables and the brand-loyalty scores as the dependent, classifactory variable may enable us to understand the complexity of the real-world situation. We may discover how the response curves of the buyers change because of different marketing mixes.

7.4   SUMMARY AND CONCLUSIONS

In this chapter, we have presented a detailed description of brand-loyalty measurements for the individual buyers. Brand-loyalty measures of a buyer are mandatory because the theory of buyer behavior is a dynamic concept with implications of changes in probabilities of purchasing a brand because of learning.

We have discussed Purchase itself only briefly in this chapter for two reasons. First, the more intriguing and relevant is the measurement of sequential purchase behavior, which was described in another chapter. Its repetition here would serve no additional function. Second, there exists some objectivity and homogeneity of opinions as to what constitutes purchase in a product class. The same is not true with respect to the brand-loyalty concept. It is the lack of more robust measures of individual loyalty scores that has motivated us to describe in detail the brand-loyalty concept.

Some interesting implications relate to the Attitude'-Purchase link when we obtain brand-loyalty scores. The scores are derived from a finite set of purchase incidents. In the linear combination of these purchase incidents to obtain brand-loyalty scores, we tend to obtain more stable measures because the random errors at each trial are removed by the least-squares principle. In the preceding chapter, we showed how Attitude' scores over several occasions can be linearly combined to obtain a cumulative Attitude' score for each brand. Although so far we have not done any study, one would presume that correlation between brand-loyalty score and cumulative Attitude' score would be more stable and perhaps more "true," since in both measures random fluctuations specific to each occasion are removed.

The Theory and Its Application

CHAPTER 8

Product Innovation

In Part IV, the theory of buyer behavior is put to work to explain two important phenomena that confront both companies and public policy makers: product innovation and advertising. Also, in these chapters we move somewhat in the direction of suggesting courses of action to bring about change in goods and services that the buyer perceives as enabling him to reach his goals more efficiently.

We define product innovation as anything that is new to the buyer, irrespective of whether it is new to the seller. This definition excludes the company's view of what is new, but incorporates the case of a buyer moving into a new market or stumbling onto a new product that has been on the market for some time.

Product innovation has become increasingly significant. World War II triggered a massive flow of industrial research, which has transformed the nature of the marketing problem from both the company and the public policy points of view. In the food industry, for example, Buzzell and Nourse report that almost two-thirds of the sales in 1964 were made up of products that were introduced since 1954 (1967, p. 164). Two factors tend to obscure the pervasiveness of the effects of the research and development revolution of the last twenty years. First, although a very large proportion of this research—90 per cent—is devoted to new product development, the results are seldom quickly available and associated with the expenditure. Casual observation make it abundantly clear that many new products that appear to spring from nowhere, in fact, owe their existence to this organized research and development effort somewhere else in the economy. Second, because the company's ability to predict the success of an innovation is so inadequate, many products are initiated in vain hope: they fail to gain the consumer's acceptance. The practice is to try them out and see if they are adopted. Consequently, many more products fail and disappear from the market before we see them. Estimates of the proportion of failures vary. Buzzell and Nourse conclude that about "40% should be classed as failures" (1967, p. 170). Graf and Mueller (1968) report that of the new food items offered in 1966 only 23 per cent were accepted by the retailers. On the other hand, the profit margin on the new items was on the average 23.2 per cent, whereas it was only 19.4 per cent on the established items, according to Graf and Mueller.

The buyer's purchase of a new product, especially in the initial trial stage, but less in the adoption stage, is primarily a problem in the buyer's search for information. Search effort raises essentially five questions. (1) To what extent does the buyer search? (2) What are the psychological mechanisms that give rise to search? (3) Where does he search? (4) What are the influence processes that operate in the search effort? (5) What are the consequences of these psychological search mechanisms and influence processes in terms of their effects on the intervening variables? Predictions about the influence on intervening variables is obviously terribly important to an understanding of the nature of the buying process, because from the intervening variables we can inductively infer what is happening to the hypothetical constructs and so test the theory.

In examining innovation, we find that four new elements enter the picture. The most important of these is the concept of product class, which best illuminates the nature of the product-acceptance process. Its formation, nature, and consequences thus become central issues. Other key elements in the innovation process are the buyer's attention, the sources of the information, and interpersonal differences among buyers.

8.1 PRODUCT CLASS

So far, except for one instance in Chapter 5, we have proceeded on the simplifying assumption that the buyer has a repertoire of product class concepts firmly fixed in his mind, so that whenever he encounters any brand, he always has "a place to put it." We have assumed that the buyer has a set of words for describing that product class and criteria for valuing the brands that make it up, which we called Choice Criteria.

In practice, however, a buyer in an advanced economy often encounters a new brand of some product about whose identity he is not certain because he does not have a well-defined product class concept to accommodate it.

The need for knowing whether the buyer has an adequate product class concept has become far greater in recent years as the number of both new products coming onto the market and all products available at any point in time has increased, so that the "psychological distance" between product classes has become smaller and discrimination a correspondingly greater problem for the buyer. Like all class concepts, product class has both denotative and connotative attributes. The denotative characteristics are especially important. Contrary to the case of the brand, companies here deliberately try to set their brand apart from those of their competitors. Thus whether a unit of something is in a product class is much less clear than whether it is "in a brand." Furthermore, the elements (brands) that make up a product class constitute the most meaningful definition of industry which is the central concept of partial equilibrium theory from economics. Empirical researchers such as in the field of industrial organization now try to approximate the concept by using the Standard Industrial Classification code which is generally agreed to be inadequate. The connotative characteristics are captured in part by Choice Criteria, but another aspect not captured is the value the buyer places on this product class in relation to competing product classes. This is the product level counterpart of brand Attitude, which is essential if one wishes to apply the buyer behavior theory to the next higher level of abstraction to explain choice among product classes. We are not concerned in this chapter, however, with the problem of choice among product classes.

To deal with product innovation, some new conceptual tools are needed, in addition to those discussed in Chapters 3, 4, and 5. The first of these tools is Product Class Comprehension—a cognitive state of the buyer that incorporates both his ways of describing the common denotative characteristics of the set of brands constituting the product class and his ways of evaluating those brands. Thus it includes the hypothetical construct of Choice Criteria.

The second tool is the operational counterpart of the hypothetical construct, the intervening variable Product Class Comprehension'. It is defined as the buyer's verbal description of the denotative and connotative characteristics of the product class, where "product class" is defined as the set of brands that the buyer views as closely substitutable in meeting his needs.

With these two additions we can now formulate a more dynamic structure that enables us to apply the methods discussed in Chapters 3, 4, and 5 to a much broader range of problems, those associated with major product innovation.

The third new tool is a classification of new products: the classification of product innovations according to the information requirements of the buyer in purchasing the products, since the focus of the theory of buyer behavior is on information. Accordingly, we classify innovations as major, normal, and minor. Major innovation is the case where the new brand represents a new product class. Major innovations place much the heaviest burden on the buyer's information-processing capacities. With major innovations, the buyer has no place "to put them," he has no well-defined product class concept. One implication of this is that he must learn a set of words to identify, describe, and think about the brand. Words for talking about the brand become especially important because of the influence that other people may exert on the buyer, provided, of course, that he talks to them about it. Another implication follows from the first. As a result of talking and thinking about it, the buyer comes to develop criteria (Choice Criteria) by which he can value the brand and thus develop an Attitude. Behavior manifested here, both search and overt, would be Extensive Problem Solving.

A normal innovation is one that the buyer knows, in the sense of being able to place it in a product class, but about which he first needs information to learn that it exists, to learn to identify it (Brand Comprehension), and then to learn to judge it in terms of his existing Choice Criteria and in this way develop Attitude. We call this type "normal" because we believe that most people when they speak of innovation have in mind a new brand in an existing product class.

In the case of a minor innovation the buyer requires no information except to learn that it exists. He forms his judgment of it by generalization, both physical and semantic, and by calling upon the past experience recorded in his memory instead of utilizing information. Behavior manifested in the case of both normal and minor innovations would be Limited Problem Solving.

To add both meaning and relevance to these concepts, we now turn to the coffee market as a concrete example. The historical sales curve for the instant coffee product class is shown in Figure 8.1. It should not be confused with the product life cycle concept used to portray the acceptance of a particular brand. The life cycle idea has received a lot of attention and is often expressed as a logistic growth curve. Attempts have been made to predict from it, but even the most extensive efforts that we have seen are quite disappointing (Polli and Cook, 1967).

The instant coffee market, which began to develop about 1940

(Figure 8.1), was, as usual, initiated by a single brand, Nescafe. It was a major innovation. In time other brands entered the market, and the market continued to expand, partially as a result of the marketing effort of additional competitive brands. Also, costs of production tended to decline as companies learned to produce the product and to utilize their plants more fully. Thus profits were adequate to attract new entrants and for them to fulfill their profit expectations.

The additional new brands more and more tended to be normal innovations for the mass population as buyers came to be familiar with instant coffee and to form Choice Criteria for judging it. By the late fifties the growth rate of the instant coffee market had leveled off, as shown in Figure 8.1, and the production processes had become more similar across companies as each took advantage of the latest improved techniques. As a consequence, interbrand functional differences became smaller, which caused a greater emphasis on price and advertising as tools of competition. The emphasis on price added to an already existent tendency for profit margins to be pinched. This competitive situation was further intensified in the early sixties when the absolute peak in sales occurred, but thereafter began to decline, as shown in Figure 8.1.

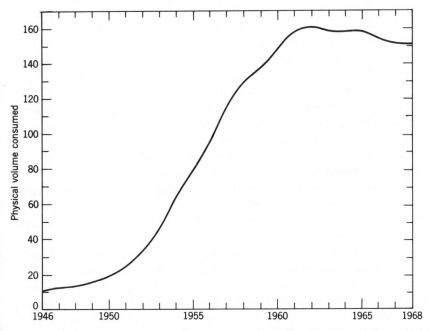

Figure 8.1   Product-class development: instant coffee (millions of pounds).

In some industries, such as in the cigarette industry, it is possible, even after functional differences among brands have disappeared, for a company to build into its brands *expressive or symbolic meaning* (R. Brown, 1965). The differences thus produced provide a means for the buyer to express himself in ways that have nothing to do with the usual function of the product: the association implied between the pleasure in smoking a cigarette and a handsome, virile young man pursuing a lovely young lady in the bucolic setting of a lush green pasture. This did not occur in the instant coffee market perhaps because here motivation is not so intense nor the social implications so prevalent as in cigarettes; however, little is known about the psychology of expressive meaning. This difference in the way in which buyers view product classes—their expressiveness role—is captured in the self-image concept implied in the exogenous variable of Social and Organizational Setting.

Faced in the early sixties with a leveling off in demand and declining profits, some of the coffee companies turned to the laboratory as a source of new products to supplement their instant and regular sales. The result was freeze-dried coffee. It is a product that is similar to instant coffee in convenience, but is more like regular coffee in flavor. The question is, "Where does the buyer put this new thing?" Is it merely a new element in the instant coffee class, the regular coffee class or a new product class? Is it a normal innovation or a major innovation? To examine this issue more carefully, we introduce the fourth new tool: a buyer's *conceptual structure* of goods and services.

A product class is a grouping of brands, but it is part of a broader structure that the buyer has in mind in satisfying his needs. It is part of a conceptual structure, a hierarchy of decreasing generality, from the most general categories of products and services to the specific brands. This hierarchy is made up of brand concepts, product class concepts, and still higher-order concepts. In this way, as in Figure 8.2, instant coffee may be seen as related to the other product classes in a small segment of the buyer's conceptual structure.

The figure illustrates the broader substitution possibilities for brands in usage. By showing the different levels at which products may be conceptualized in terms of their substitution possibilities, we see how it is possible to apply the theory of buyer behavior to any level of abstraction that we wish. We could, for example, go so far as to examine choice among alternative styles of life. It also graphically points up one obvious but often neglected fact in market research—it is essential that the researcher clearly identify the level at which he is operating when he asks the buyer questions about his attitudes and consumption habits. Otherwise, the buyer's responses are much less meaningful.

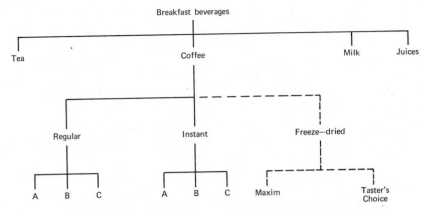

Figure 8.2   Conceptual structure for instant coffee.

The line to "Freeze-dried" is shown dashed because it is not clear at the moment whether freeze-dried coffee will become a separate product class, merge with either regular or instant, or merge with both into a single product class. Conceptual structure highlights one of the most difficult problems confronted by the initiator of a radical innovation: Where to attempt to place the innovation by his marketing activity? Where to position it? General Foods faced this very difficult *market-positioning* question when introducing Maxim, because the company was not at all certain how the consumer would conceptualize it and that it would not "cannibalize" the company's other three instant brands—Instant Maxwell House, Sanka, and Yuban—or even its regular brands.

Before going ahead, let us apply the idea of conceptual structure to industrial products. Figure 8.3 illustrates a possible conceptual struc-

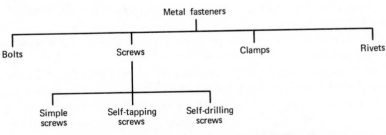

Figure 8.3   Conceptual structure for self-drilling screws.

ture for self-drilling screws. Simple screws require three operations: drilling the hole, tapping the thread, and inserting the screw. The self-tapping screw eliminates the second operation. The self-drilling screw, which has appeared recently, eliminates the first two operations.

This schema of conceptual structure and its relation to the product class concept (Product Class Comprehension) yields perspective, because the stage of development into which a new brand—an innovation—is introduced, we expect, makes a lot of difference in terms of the nature of the buyer's response to it, since the various stages require different amounts of information. Practitioners have long used the concept of "newness" without articulating quite what they mean.

At the risk of seeming repetitious, we discuss still further the three types of innovation. The brand representing the major innovation—the first brand in the product class—has a very heavy communication burden merely because it is first, and the risks for the initiator are high even though it may ultimately be successful. Home use of video tape recorder is an example. A brand entering late in the process has a simpler task, provided, of course, that it is superior to the existing brands. Let us examine this difference in more detail.

When confronted with the initiating brand in the product class, the major innovation, the buyer is not likely to pay much attention to it: his current needs are probably being met, hence he does not see the new brand as relevant, unless he is so familiar with the existing product that he has reached the "boredom stage," an idea presented in Chapter 5. Furthermore, it is difficult to demonstrate to the buyer that the new brand is better than the brands now making up the product class, because he has no well-defined set of criteria by which to judge the new brand, for example, zipper fastener and Xerox home reproduction unit. Also, the criteria that he does apply in judging the innovation may lead to goal conflicts which shape the nature of his stimuli-as-coded and his behavior and thus hamper the acceptance of new ideas. Finally, he does not have a familiar (highly codable) set of words for discussing the new brand with friends, for thinking about it, and for remembering it. Thus the communication burden is heavy, and the more complex the product, the heavier it becomes.

With normal innovation, the product class has already been developed. The buyer now has well-established Choice Criteria. Both the incomparability of the brands—the tendency to judge them by different criteria—and the goal conflicts have been reconciled. When a new brand of instant coffee appears, the label "instant coffee" is enough to permit the buyer to generalize it to the product *class* concept. Based on the principle that the abnormally ambiguous is less likely to get attention, we predict that the buyer will probably show greater attention to any advertising about it than he would to that about a radical innovation, but he still will be less than completely attentive unless he has reached the boredom stage. His vocabulary for this purpose may be somewhat limited, and effort will be required to cause him to perceive it as having certain values on the criteria by which he judges it. The communication burden is much less, however, than in the case of the major innovation.

Finally, still less distinctive are the minor innovations that probably began to occur in the instant coffee market during the mid-fifties, such as changes in the texture and size of the granules, in the package, and in the advertising. By definition, no new information is required for the decision. The product class concept is well formed in the buyer's mind, so that Choice Criteria are well-defined and the buyer has a highly codable language that serves as the vocabulary for thinking about and remembering the brand. Hence the buyer can more easily call up the available information from his memory and think—manipulate symbols—which helps him to come to a judgment about the merits of the new brand. Here generalization—a well-studied psychological process discussed in Chapter 4, both physical and semantic—will alone suffice to try the new product. The buyer has enough information stored in his memory to be able to make the choice. If the product is of low importance, the buyer's solution is typically a simple one: try it and let the experience be the chief source of guidance in future purchases. If the product is more important, the buyer will think about it and arrive at a decision.

A minor innovation is probably illustrated in an experiment in which sixty male beer-drinking Stanford students were offered three new brands of beer, all of which actually contained the same beer (McConnell, 1968). Even though the brands were identical in product content, firm preferences were soon developed, which were tested by varying the price. The only reported "search" effort was the amount of brand switching among the three brands. It was concluded that the students developed their preferences by using the price as a cue for quality. We guess that it was a minor innovation. First, we doubt that beer quality is much discussed. Second, there was no advertising reported. Third, clearly if the students were regular drinkers, they would have already developed Choice Criteria.

Broadly, it is necessary to explain in more detail the nature of the buyer's trial and acceptance processes because explanation is the foundation of prediction and control. Since the information requirements of a buyer vary sharply among different kinds of innovations, we shall dwell mainly on those instances where he does require information.

First, when he does use information, it is essential to know how he goes about getting it in order to understand the nature of the information and its consequences for his behavior. This is the problem of *buyer search*. Second, what he finds and how he goes about searching, too, depend on the nature of his informational environment. Thus his *sources of information* must be examined. Third, in previous chapters we have shown that there are *individual differences* among buyers and that they are important for both research and practice.

8.2   SEARCH BEHAVIOR

Let us turn to the search process and the psychological mechanisms that underlie it. Search, as the reader will recall from Chapter 5, is all of the activity associated with the buyer's acquisition of information, extending from his almost passive role of merely varying the intake of his sensory receptors to a very active role in which he talks with friends, seeks out different advertisements, investigates several retail stores, and even goes to the library to look up information. Specific and epistemic exploratory behavior will not be distinguished here; to simplify, both will be incorporated into "search." Anyone interested in research will want to make the distinction, however, and for this he can consult Chapter 5.

A central question is "What is the motivational basis for search effort?" How does it come about? The mechanisms that underlie search effort were set forth in Chapter 5, and here we put the principles to work. Another central question is, once that search is motivated, "Why does it take the path—Attention or Overt Search—that it does?" In answering the first, some light is thrown on the second, but let us try to treat them separately. We begin with Attention and then discuss Overt Search. Also, the reader should bear in mind that we are dealing with pretrial instead of posttrial search unless otherwise indicated. Dissonance theory has, of course, dealt with posttrial search.

8.2.1   Attention

The motivational basis of search effort can best be discussed in terms of Attention. The key mechanism in regulating attention is the Stimulus Ambiguity-arousal relation presented in Chapter 5. In bringing the mechanism to bear on the problem of innovation, it is helpful to distinguish between the shape of the relation and its level.

8.2.1.1   Shape of the Stimulus Ambiguity-Arousal Relation

The reader will recall from Figure 5.1 that the ambiguity-arousal curve first declines, from left to right, to the point of the buyer's desired level of stimulation. This decline occurs because, in response to any stimulus that is less ambiguous than this desired level, the buyer will be looking for a more stimulating environment, hence will be less likely to perceive the stimulus of lesser ambiguity. The consequences of this motivation show up in many ways. For example, we see a Volkswagen advertisement displaying a handsome new "bug," except that it has a flat tire. This incongruity catches our attention immediately. It is incongruous because we have leared from childhood to "put our best foot forward" and we know that advertisers are particularly prone to do this instead of publicizing such a potential disadvantage as a flat tire.

The basic mechanism underlying the Stimulus Ambiguity-arousal relation is conflict: the instantaneous instigation of incompatible responses. Stimulus Ambiguity, because it tends to elicit more than one response, causes an increase in arousal (Berlyne, 1963). The stimulus can be ambiguous in either of two ways. The sensory aspects of the stimulus such as smudged printing or "snow" in the television set can cause the message to be ambiguous. But the semantic or meaning aspects of the stimulus can also be unclear and so elicit incompatible responses.

Let us now examine the implications of the Stimulus Ambiguity-arousal relation. The buyer pays attention to some event, such as the appearance of an advertisement.

First, he pays attention because he believes that the information is useful in solving some of his buying problems, and the motivation is the conflict arising from ambiguous stimuli. This is the X_1X_2 stage of the Stimulus Ambiguity-arousal relation in Figure 5.1.

Second, if the buyer is bored, if his general state of stimulation is less than his desired state, he will likely perceive any new stimulus that comes within the purview of his receptors, and he even may deliberately seek "interesting" stimuli. This is the OX_1 stage of Figure 5.1. It is illustrated by a patient who glances idly through the magazines as he waits for the dentist or doctor. The function of the information is to relieve boredom. The buyer, in the process of seeking this additional stimulation, is especially likely to perceive information about new products; the symbols representing an unfamiliar concept (the brand) are particularly apt to become stimuli, to attract his Attention.

Third, if the Stimulus Display is too ambiguous, the buyer will reinterpret it or close it out. This is the X_2 to X_3 range of Figure 5.1.

8.2.1.2 Level of the Stimulus Ambiguity-Arousal Relation

Given the ambiguity of the stimulus, attention is also affected by other factors that influence the search effort, and these can be conceptualized as determining the level of the Stimulus Ambiguity-arousal relation. There is probably some interaction between the shape and the level of the relation, for example, if the brand is unambiguous, we would expect the symbols representing it to be less ambiguous.

At least four influences set the level of the relation: Confidence, Attitude, ambiguity of Intention, incomparability of brands, and goal conflict.

Just as ambiguity of Stimulus Display causes conflict, which in turn increases arousal, so does ambiguity of the brand concept—the inverse of Confidence—as reflected in Attitude and Intention. To the extent the buyer does not have enough information to place the brand on well-defined product class criteria, arousal will be high. This is the message that we receive about Attitude from consistency theory: seeking information is one way of resolving possible inconsistencies among cognitions. Here the buyer needs information in order to know whether the cognitions are consistent. The higher the Brand Comprehension, the less ambiguous will be the brand denotatively which should reduce the ambiguity of the brands connotative characteristics, and the higher will be the buyer's confidence in judging the brand. Similarly, to the extent that the buyer is uncertain about the *future* state of his inhibitors, he will have low Confidence.

Correspondingly, the brand can become too familiar and boring, which causes the increase in arousal at the low end of an ambiguity-arousal relation where brand ambiguity instead of stimulus ambiguity is on the horizontal axis of Figure 5.1. In fact, we expect that this effect operates through the level of aspiration mechanism. An increase in the level of aspiration brings about a decrease in Satisfaction and it in turn lowers Attitude. This explains why people often seem to be seeking mere "newness" in a purchase. In toothpaste and soap, for example, 15 per cent of the respondents gave "newness" as the reason for trying the new products (Haines, 1966, p. 691). Studies in India indicate that as many as 58 per cent of the consumers there buy a new product because it is new. One way in which to describe this situation is to say that the buyer has an empty position in his evoked set which he is attempting to fill because one brand has become unacceptable, as contrasted with the case where a new brand must dislodge an existing brand. We predict that it is much easier to get a product tried in the first case than in the second.

Second, the extremity of the Attitude will also affect the Stimulus Ambiguity-arousal relation. We postulate that, irrespective of whether Attitude is positive or negative, an extreme value will cause the level to be higher. An explanation is that it is more efficient for a buyer to get information on the brands that he likes and dislikes the most than to search all brands. He wishes to buy the preferred brand and to avoid the disliked brand. As an empirical fact, however, we believe that a buyer seldom dislikes a brand.

Third, until a product class concept is well formed the buyer may try to judge two brands by different criteria. For him the brands are incomparable. This attempt will increase arousal analogous to the effects of goal conflict.

The fourth factor affecting the level of the Stimulus Ambiguity-arousal relation is incompatible goals. In the case of major innovations, we expect goal conflict to be a very common phenomenon, especially if the innovations have high social or economic significance. The process of product class concept formation, we believe, reconciles both incomparability of brands and goal conflict.

The best-articulated mechanism for explaining goal conflict is Miller's conflict "model," which is especially relevant here because it postulates a description of and provides a rationale for the *intensity* of search in relation to *time* of purchase. To simplify, we deal only with the approach-avoidance situation, for example, the housewife who likes the *convenience* of instant breakfast and so is inclined to "approach" it, but *fears its unfavorable effect on her role in the home* and so is inclined to "avoid" it. This approach-avoidance situation in choosing a new product can be pictured as in Figure 8.4, where there are two curves relating the remoteness of the buyer from the decision in a temporal sense (time on the horizontal axis) and the strength of his desire to "approach" or "avoid" the purchase (on the vertical axis). For "the strength of his desire," it may help to think of probability of response. The solid line is the approach gradient, and the dotted line, the avoidance gradient.

The first guiding principle in analyzing this situation is that as the buyer comes closer to buying the brand—the "distance" either in time or space is decreased—the response tendency increases. Typically, when the housewife is first motivated to contemplate the purchase of the new instant breakfast product, for example, when she first becomes aware of it and that it might serve some of her urgent needs, she "moves" toward it; she "approaches" it. As she "moves" from X to O in Figure 8.4 where O is the point of purchase, the new brand's convenience appeal causes the OY value to become greater as shown by the solid line. The approach gradient increases: her desire to buy it becomes greater.

A second psychological principle also operates, however. As the housewife comes closer to buying, the negative or undesirable gradient, such as her fear that the new breakfast may decrease the family's need for her, the avoidance is *steeper* than is the positive (approach) gradient,

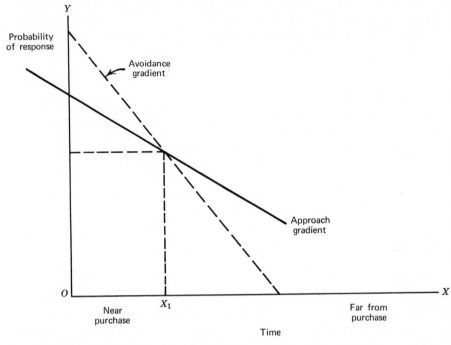

Figure 8.4   Approach-avoidance conflict in the purchase of a new brand.

which represents the convenience of instant breakfast. The negative aspect of the new brand—the expected effect on her role in the home—*increases even more* than does the approach effect. The conflict occurs at the point of intersection of the two lines, which is shown by X_1 on the horizontal axis; hence as she "approaches" the decision and reaches the point of intersection, she will vacillate around this "dead center" position.

However, the housewife can "get off dead center" by accepting or deliberately seeking additional information to clarify her goals and in this way resolving the goal incompatibility. The effect of information could be, for example, to shift the positions of the avoidance function to the left of that in Figure 8.4, to the point where the intersection is at O or to the left of it. As a consequence, the approach gradient will be greater at Purchase than will the avoidance gradient, and so she will buy without excessive conflict. On the other hand, if the goals are firmly inconsistent and not amenable to adjustment, additional information may merely make the conflict stronger. She might then reinterpret the information, that is, Perceptual Bias could operate. In addition to the hypothesis that vacillation will occur as the buyer approaches the decision, a number of other very useful predictions have been deduced from this well-articulated theory (N. Miller, 1959). These can be shown by imagining the various ways in which the functions might shift and their consequences. Also, the theory has been applied to the case of stimulus discrimination as well as to goal conflict.

8.2.2   Overt Search

With an understanding of how search behavior is motivated, let us turn to the search behavior itself. Why does the buyer seek out one source of information instead of another?

In general, we would expect reinforcement (Satisfaction) to play a major role—the buyer will search where his search has been rewarded in the past. For an adult, experienced buyer, however, generalization from previous experience is undoubtedly common. A relatively small portion of buyers use *Consumer Reports* as a source of information, but they use them repeatedly and thus can be said to be generalizing from their past experience.

Search in the form of shopping can be viewed as a metaplan which triggers and guides a part of the plan that underlies a consumer's Intention to buy a particular brand. Consider, for example, how heavily a housewife's search for cookies is conditioned by her grocery shopping habits. Shopping for consumer durables is obviously a much more extensive process. The successful elements of the search plan are retained and the less successful ones are dropped. Thus through generalization and by trial and error a buyer develops search behavior.

8.2.3   Some Implications of Search

The consequence of search effort is to change the values of Motives, Product Class Comprehension, Brand Comprehension, Attitude, Confidence, and Intention. These effects are reflected in their counterpart, intervening variables.

If Attention is high, the buyer acquires a vocabulary to identify the brand and to describe it so that he can discuss it with others and think about it; thus in the case of a major innovation the buyer is on his way to increasing Product Class Comprehension, to forming a product class concept which includes Choice Criteria. Technically, he must develop a linguistic and nonlinguistic equivalence, an equivalence between (1) the label that he attaches to the product class and (2) the attributes and behaviors that he assigns to it. In other words, he must establish an isomorphism between the naming behavior and the other culturally patterned behavior of purchasing and consuming the brand.

Unfortunately, not much is known about the formation of a class concept. Most of the research in psychology has been directed toward *utilization* of existing concepts instead of how they are formed (Osgood, 1963b, pp. 288–290). Brand is a lower-order class concept, and Attitude is the connotative part of it. Roughly Attitude and Brand Comprehension together make up the brand concept. We say "roughly" because Brand Comprehension also includes the idea of evoked set, which is in addition to what is normally thought of as the denotative aspect of a class concept. Attitude research on brand buying is not very relevant, however, because the manufacturer does everything he can to facilitate the learning of his brand concept, the conceptualizing of his brand. He often attaches a well-established brand name and advertises it widely in simple language. Also, he keeps the within-brand variability to an absolute minimum by effective quality-control procedures. On the other hand, no one provides such information for the product class concept and the within-class variability is considerable because manufacturers deliberately build it in to differentiate their brand from those of competitors.

It is true, however, that in introducing a major innovation, manufacturers in their advertising will often emphasize its product class as well as its brand. This along with other sources of information would support deductive learning of the concept. Experience with the brand and information about the particular brand would support inductive learning of it. Some propositions about concept formation are the following (Carroll, 1964, pp. 86–87). (1) Concept attainment becomes more difficult as the number of relevant attributes increases, the number of values of attributes increases, and the salience of the attributes decreases. (2) Also, it becomes more difficult as the information load that must be handled by the subject to solve the concept increases, and the information is increasingly carried by negative instead of positive instances. (3) Various strategies for handling the information load are possible, and some are in the long run more successful than others.

The effect of the information on Attitude, given that the information is credible and favorable, depends on the current level of Attitude. The higher it already is, the less will any given piece of information increase it. Put more precisely, the amount of change is inversely proportional to the original position (R. Brown, 1965, p. 561). This is the so-called polarity principle.

An implication of this is that information about new brands will be less effective in getting Attention and changing preferences in product classes in which brand loyalty is high. In addition to posing this cognitive barrier, the change in brand may require learning some new overt acts in connnection with the purchase or consumption of it, and this inertia

information—whether it affects the intensity of Motives—makes a differ-
too provides a barrier to change. If so, the particular content of the
ence. As noted in Chapter 4, too little or too much motivation is less
favorable to learning than a medium level of motivation. Once a series
of acts are well learned, however, the higher the motivation, the better
the *performance* of this series of acts. Incidentally, insofar as these acts
are prepurchase and are anticipated, they are contained in Intention.

In the face of these barriers to trying a new brand, manufacturers
have turned increasingly to sampling and couponing. Sampling is the
practice of making available free samples of the new brand. The most
obvious effect of this is to eliminate the price barrier of Intention (inhibitor) of the new brand and the effort of purchasing it. Colgate-Palmolive
is reported to have distributed free to 80 per cent of American households 40 million units of a regular package of Ultrabrite toothpaste
at a total cost of about $50 million. Couponing is a similar practice;
for example, to introduce Folger's coffee into the Chicago market in
1959, 1.5 million coupons, each good for a free pound of coffee, were
distributed (Frank and Massy, 1963, p. 97). A closer look at the psychological mechanisms involved would probably provide a better
rationale than we now have for choosing between these two methods
or not using either of them.

The process by which Intention is formed is less well studied than
that which develops Attitude. We presume that the experienced adult,
when buying most of the conventional products that a family buys on
a frequent purchase cycle, most commonly generalizes a plan (see Chapter 4) from other purchasing experience. In less familiar situations,
there are heuristics—rules of thumb—operating that are not well understood. Newell and Simon have done some of the most interesting work
in developing an understanding of them. For some products, however,
the plan that underlies Intention is probably so simple—includes so few
inhibitors—that learning Intention is a simple matter except in those
cases where social restrictions may constitute some of the inhibitors.

8.2.4 Intervening Variables

In Chapter 3 we questioned the validity of the sequential order postulated in the "hierarchy of effects" (Lavidge and Steiner, 1961), doubting
that a change in each variable is even a necessary condition for change
in the next, much less a necessary and sufficient condition. It is probably
in the innovation process that this rigid sequential view is most nearly
justified. Some Attention is a necessary condition to changing the values
of the other variables. Brand Comprehension, we suspect, does largely
precede the development of Attitude, although Robertson (1968) in his

test of the hierarchy did not find this to be so and others have had similar experiences. Our guess is that we have not devised an adequate measure. McGuire (1968b, p. 306) found a biserial correlation of +.53 between recall of content and immediate opinion change, but others have been less successful in demonstrating any sizable change. We know from Pelleman's work (1969) that attitude formation precedes the formation of Intention, as Robertson found, and we predict that Intention formation precedes Purchase. Hence we shall discuss the innovation process as though this sequential structure were a roughly valid description of the relations among the output intervening variables. We would not, however, at all take this position in analyzing the purchasing behavior of established brands. Our view on this is set forth in Chapter 9.

8.3 SOURCES OF INFORMATION

Having discussed the nature of search effort, including the psychological mechanisms that underlie it, we now turn to the nature of the buyer's informational environment and the influence processes that operate: who says what to whom, how and with what effects. We will deal here with the *who* and *what* and some of the *how*. The *whom* is obviously the buyer, and some of the *effects* of Lasswell's famous paradigm will also be included. We often speak at a very general level of the richness or the barrenness of an organism's environment, the amount of search effort required, the cost of information. The richness or lack of it is determined by the sources and content of the information that is available.

Availability of the information is important because it determines *how much* search effort is necessary to utilize it. To the extent that it is difficult to utilize, the buyer will be deterred. Contrast the effort required of the buyer in perceiving a television advertisement appearing during an attractive show with the energy necessary to obtain facts by reading a copy of *Consumer Reports*, which if the buyer is not a subscriber must usually be secured from the public library. This "minimum effort" principle, we suspect, partially explains how the buyer selects from among given sources of information and why television is an effective medium.

The nature of the buyer's information—its content and sources—is quite varied. He obviously receives his facts from a great number of sources: newspaper, billboard, television, radio, his relatives, his friends, members of his family, accidental conversations with strangers, sales clerks; he may go so far as to read *Consumer Reports* in his search for information. The sources can be categorized in numerous ways. We have found the following classification to be especially fruitful for identifying relationships in buying behavior: buyer sources, commercial sources, and neutral sources (Cox, 1967). This classification, more than others that exist, focuses attention on factors that the innovating company can influence. This framework also enables us to integrate into the theory the pioneering work in perceived risk of Bauer, Cox, Cunningham, Arndt (Cox, 1967; see also Sheth, 1968 and Sheth and Venkatesan, 1968). We thus provide both a substantial underpinning for and an elaboration of this concept.

The perceived risk concept postulates that a buyer in contemplating purchase experiences varying degrees of subjective risk. First, this risk is the product of two variables: value and certainty. Second, perceived risk motivates the search for information. Third, the buyer selects information in part according to the extent to which it would reduce his risk. Unfortunately, the empirical work has tended to be at the product class level instead of the brand level. Value, for example, is inferred by asking consumers to compare product classes in terms of the danger of making a mistake, and confidence is inferred by asking them to compare these product classes in terms of how certain they are that a new brand in the product class will work as well as the one they are now using. (S. Cunningham, 1967b). The theory of buyer behavior incorporates the findings in a more systematic way.

Let us proceed to explore the three sources: buyer, commercial, and neutral.

8.3.1 Buyer Sources

"Buyer sources" refers to interpersonal sources, such as word-of-mouth, which are not under the control of the seller. Buyer sources are known to play a central role in new product acceptance and to be much more important than in the case of established products (Arndt 1967c, pp. 236ff). Because of their complexity, we devote considerable space to elaborating on them, including a brief discussion of the theory of social structure.

8.3.1.1 Social Structure: Interaction

Buying behavior in most cases is merely a part of the interrelated total ongoing behavioral pattern, and not a unique kind of behavior independent of other daily activities. Research in sociology and psychology has revealed the great importance of interaction—face-to-face relations—with other people in influencing our behavior, especially of the effect of our reference groups. Analogous processes are being found in buying. Even in the critical decision of choosing doctors, family, friends, neighbors, and co-workers are found to be more important sources than are professional advice and independent judgment (Sidney Feldman, 1966, p. 763). This influence is transmitted from person to person by word-of-mouth information, and it matters not only *what* the other person says but *who* he is, as well as to *whom* it is said. This influence is the heart of the theory of social structure. Here we deal only with the basic unit of social analysis, the single dyad—the relation between the buyer and his immediate influencer—but later, in discussing advertising, we shall incorporate the full view of social structure and shall deal also with the case where the other person in the dyad is a salesman.

A clarifying comment is in order. The reader will recall that in the theory of buyer behavior social structure operates in two ways. First, it affects the nature of the buyer's current information input. Second, it is reflected in the exogenous variable of Social and Organizational Setting which captures the past social effects of this nature. We expect both effects to operate, but our emphasis here will be on the information input.

What influence processes operating in the social dyad determine the effect of the "other person" on the buyer? The Kelman (1961) typology of three distinct types of social influence—compliance, identification, and internalization—is helpful as a framework or setting within which to discuss the influence processes that operate. It is especially useful for innovation because it emphasizes the nature of the source of information, and in innovation different sources operate at different times.

Compliance occurs when the buyer accepts the influence of the communicator—the other person in the dyad—because he hopes to induce a favorable reaction from him. By complying, he does what the source, the other person, wants him to do because he sees this as a way of achieving a desired response from the other person. He accepts the communication not because he believes in its content, but because it will be instrumental in producing a satisfying social effect. Thus the *social effect* of his behavior is the thing that is crucially relevant.

Identification occurs when the buyer is influenced by the communication, because there is a role relationship with the other person that forms a part of the buyer's self-image. By this we mean that the communicator is a part of the buyer's immediate social structure, that the two form a regularly interacting dyad, which implies common interest and activity. Identification is then a way of establishing or maintaining a desired relation with the other, and self-definition—the buyer's own self-image—is anchored in this relation. Thus the *social anchorage* of his behavior is crucial. This will be elaborated later.

Internalization occurs when the buyer accepts the influence because the induced behavior is congruent with his value system. The content of the communication is, or implies a course of action that is, intrinsically rewarding to him. The buyer adopts the suggested point of view for a number of reasons, all of which are essentially the same: because he finds it useful in the solution of a problem, because it is congenial to his own orientation, or because his own values demand it. *Value congruence*—the congruence between his values and those of the other person—is the crucial distinction here. The most obvious examples of internalization are those that involve evaluation and acceptance of induced behavior on rational or goal-directed grounds. Several hypothetical constructs related to information come into play here. If the message is congruous with his own value system (Motives reflected in *Choice Criteria*), the buyer will be more sensitive to information and perceptual bias will be minimal. When the information from the other person is ambiguous, the buyer will search for clarification and thus further internalize the message. However, internalization need not be equated to rationality as defined by some objective standard. Internalization would also occur in the adoption of the message because of its congruence with a value system that conflicts with socially imposed values.

There is a difference between the three types of influence in terms of their consequences for changes in certain of the intervening variables. If the other person's influence occurs because he has *power* derived from either actual or potential control over specific rewards and punishments that shape the buyer's social position (status, authority, or prestige), the resultant behavior by the buyer would be *compliance*. Presumably Intention will be affected directly. If the other person's influence is due to *attractiveness* in terms of the *role* the buyer wishes to play or *a role reciprocal* to the one he desires, his resultant behavior would be *identification*. Here the functional role of Attitude mentioned in Chapter 4 is being emphasized, specifically the ego-defensive function: a buyer changes his Attitude toward a brand, not because he comes to believe that the new brand will better meet his needs (Motives), but because to change his Attitude to favor the brand will further his role relationship with someone, a relationship in which he finds and maintains his self-image. This self-image provides him with identity (one is somebody only in relation to others) and so protects his ego from the shocks encountered if one has no identity.

This enables us to bring together four interrelated and important ideas: expressive behavior, self-concept, role relationship, and attitude change. Expressive behavior—behavior which indicates the kind of a person we are—we believe, is quite common at least in some consumer buying and is probably the area toward which the most social criticism against marketing, especially advertising, is directed.

Self-image, which is a constellation of attitudes, is a device for linking the individual buyer to an identifiable reference group (Sherif, 1968, p. 156), provided that the particular reference group is *self-identifying*, that is, forms a part of the buyer's self-image (Kelman, 1961, p. 63). The desire to maintain this role relationship will cause the buyer to change or stabilize his Attitude, although the change will not be so great as it would have been if internalization were operating (Kelman, 1961, p. 74). The effect may be more to change Confidence than Attitude. In an economy where the standard of living is above the subsistence level, the buyer exhibits expressive behavior (R. Brown, 1965, p. 567): to some extent he purchases products because they *express* to others how he would like to appear, not because the products are intrinsically rewarding. He uses the product to act out his self-image, and this self-image reflects his self-identifying role relationship. Thus we have an explanation for the frequently observed phenomenon of seemingly "irrational" buying which is roundly condemned by social critics. The explanation suggests that the behavior is really quite meaningful. As Roger Brown has cogently put it, ". . . we should not expect a symbol-using animal to be interested in nothing but food and drink" (1965, p. 568).

Finally, in regard to the third type of influence, if the other person exerts influence because his information is credible, the resultant behavior would spring from *internalization*. The emphasis here is on information processing: the buyer changes his Attitude because the information that he receives from his partner in the dyad convinces him that the new brand will serve his needs (motive) better than does the old brand. We postulate that Confidence is also affected.

This analysis can be elaborated still more by viewing the compliance and identification processes as essentially a psychosocial game and internalization as a problem-solving game, respectively (Bauer, 1965b). The characteristics of the source that lead to the first two—compliance and identification—have to do with the buyer's motivation to ingratiate himself or to defend his ego, his pride. He seeks in his buying to emulate other people. In the case of the third process, the buyer is motivated to engage in social interaction by the desire to solve a problem, a buying problem. Wilding and Bauer (1968) conclude that housewives differ in their relative emphasis on these goals and that those who favor problem-solving goals are more likely to respond to the competence of the source and those who emphasize social goals respond more to the social attractiveness of the source.

This evidence suggests that buying motives are complex and also that the distinction between Attitude and Intention is essential in utilizing an attitude measure. In the problem-solving approach a change in Attitude will precede the change in purchase behavior, whereas in the second approach, where there is an emphasis on social goals, we would expect no change in Attitude even though behavior changed. The second would not be internalized, but would instead be reflected in social inhibitors (Intention).

The source attributes, the consequent types of influence, and the nature of the buyer's motivation (the "game" he plays) in each, are summarized in Table 8.1.

Table 8.1   Social Influence Processes

Attribute of Source	Influence Process	Game Being Played
Power	Compliance	Psychosocial
Attractiveness	Identification	
Credibility	Internalization	Problem solving

The psychosocial aspects of social interaction have been emphasized by psychologists, and that they are relevant for buying behavior is indicated by Arndt. He found, for example, that each person needing information tended to steer the conversation in such a way as to make the act of getting the information less obvious, presumably for fear of losing status (1966). Where Importance of Purchase is high, we would expect the problem-solving aspects of the buying-decision process to swamp the game-playing aspects. With this brief survey of social structure, we now proceed to examine the specific implications of social structure by discussing the significance of word-of-mouth information. The social structure idea will also be used, however, in discussing company sources.

8.3.1.2   *Buyer Sources and Type of Innovation*

In thinking about commercial innovation as influenced by social interaction, we begin with the dyad—our buyer and some other person—the other person being the influencer. True, a prior question is, "How did the *other* person learn about the innovation?" but let us ignore it until we discuss commercial sources, specifically the indirect effects of advertising.

We now turn to a generalized discussion of buyer sources in terms of the theory of buyer behavior. One of the essential distinctions is according to the kind of innovation: whether the product is radically new (major innovation) or is merely a change in an existing product (normal innovation). We leave it to the reader to extend the analysis to minor innovations. The reader might wish to compare our approach to the economic view of new product introduction and should then see Weinberg (1960).

The kind of innovation determines the ambiguity that the brand holds for the buyer and when the brand is ambiguous, the stimulus representing it is also more likely to be ambiguous. One determinant of the amount of affect of that brand ambiguity on the buyer is how involved the buyer is in the product class (Importance of Purchase). Other determinants are Attitude and goal conflict, which especially affect the amount of his search behavior. Next is the characteristic of the buyer's source of information and the consequent influence process. Does it operate mainly through power, attractiveness, or credibility? Also, we wish to know which of the output intervening variables are affected because these effects must be specified to test the truth of the theory. Finally, is there a difference between first trial of the innovation and acceptance?

We begin with the major innovation. One of the key issues with a radically new product is to obtain the buyer's Attention enough so that he will accept information that at first may not have appeared relevant, although we suspect that there are great differences among people on this issue. Without this relevance, the buyer has a low probability of perceiving information about it except if he is below his desired level of stimulation, hence is seeking stimulation. What appears to be a clever advertising device for getting attention was illustrated in a recent television advertisement that showed a beautifully gowned and coiffeured young matron listening to a magnificent symphony concert—the lady, the epitome of stateliness, suddenly turns to the audience and in a cultured voice complains, "My girdle is killing me!" The incongruity of the entire scene with her comment was startlingly attention-getting for the girdle advertisement. Had the girdle been a major innovation, our guess is that the advertisement would have been quite effective.

The psychosocial game, especially compliance, would seem to be particularly effective in calling the buyer's attention to the innovation. A dyadic partner who has high status in our buyer's peer group—the president of the local League of Women Voters—could possibly serve effectively this attention-getting function for our housewife with social aspirations. The discussion that ensued between them could provide the buyer with many, if not all, of the words she needs to identify the new object, to think about it, and to discuss it and thus her Brand Comprehension and Product Class Comprehension would rise. From this linguistic view, the discussion is the beginning of the process by which a linguistic equivalence is established among brands, which is then matched by some sort of nonlinguistic equivalence, some sort of judgment equivalence in terms of the brands' ability to satisfy the buyer's needs. There develops an isomorphism between naming behavior and the other culturally patterned behavior of purchasing and consuming the brand.

Let us turn to the psychological processes by which these linguistic consequences develop. In this process the housewife's Intention to buy would have been affected, not her Attitude, because with compliance social pressure is an inhibitor. From the experience with the brand (Satisfaction), however, she might build the values of Attitude and so would continue to buy it even though she suddenly lost her social aspirations, which, let us assume, would render the other ladies in the league of Women Voters impotent as an influence.

If the type of influence were identification instead, we would predict that Attitude would be affected. Attitude toward the old product would decline, and Attitude toward the new brand would increase but probably not sufficiently to cause Purchase. More likely, the decision process would require more time and more information. Our guess, however, is that identification will not operate in product classes of high importance because then the effect of the role relationship will be swamped by the internalization process. When it does operate, the effect on Attitude is considerably less, we expect, than if internalization operates, but it also shows up in Confidence. As evidence for the effect on Confidence, Kelman (1961) has suggested that people have greater doubts about their attitudes when identification operates than when internalization is the type of process.

On the other hand, Attention may not be a problem. The buyer may already be experiencing a felt need, such as when a family moves to a new community and must find a family doctor. We consider this decision a major innovation as Sidney Feldman has shown (1966) because for most people it is made so infrequently that each decision requires anew the development of a product class concept. The choice of a doctor is an important decision because of its health implications, and it is also hoped to be a long-term decision, not subject to change until the buyer moves to another community. There are no standardized criteria for evaluating doctors at least before first trial. This extreme ambiguity discourages extensive information seeking. Such ambiguity could result in the buyer closing out the information because of ego defense. Also, the high intensity of Motives could discourage learning and cause a stereotyped response; this possibility was supported by Feldman who reported that the subjects of his study searched little. The information appears to be kept at some vague level, as such "Is he a good doctor?" with an expected yes or no answer. Also, even though the buyer had well-formulated criteria such as would arise with a person who had had experience with a number of doctors, information in such specific terms is probably not available. Unfortunately, the study was done in the simple sociological tradition of who-talks-to-whom, with apparently no attention paid to the content of what was said.

That compliance operates in the purchase of doctor's services is suggested by the number of people who consulted persons of higher social status. Yet, that identification operates to a still larger extent was indicated by the fact that a much larger proporaion sought information from people like themselves, members of their peer group. Identification would be difficult to disentangle empirically here from internalization. A buyer obtains problem-solving information in the easiest possible way, and friends may be the easiest source available. To complicate matters further, not much problem-solving information was used here because of the complexity in evaluating a doctor.

Let us turn now from the purchase of doctor's services to that of products in general. As Choice Criteria begin to take shape, the questions of goal conflict and brand incomparability arise; for example, an instant breakfast may have contradictory consequences for the houseife. Except for the extreme case where the buyer shuts out or reinterprets the information because of its very great ambiguity or his motive intensity, the goal conflict will enhance Attention. Brand incomparability, we postulate, has similar effects.

For the sake of clarity, we continue the discussion as though product class and brand concepts were formed separately. The attractiveness characteristic of the source now becomes important, because the buyer finds it necessary to identify which of the goals possibly served by the product class are socially acceptable. Also, in terms of the buyer's total interpersonal contacts, the chances are much higher that an attractive person will be a source—the buyer's exposure in ordinary life is higher to persons whom he finds attractive because he seeks out such people. Consequently, he will learn from them not only about the social acceptibility of the goals, but also about the technical effectiveness of the criteria of choice that he intends to use. These conversations will, at first, be handicapped by the lack of an efficient vocabulary, a need that properly designed advertising can help to satisfy. Both Product Class Comprehension and Brand Comprehension would, of course, rise as a result of such conversations. The speed and ease with which comprehension develops depends on the complexity of the class. Doctor's services, for example, are a complex product class. Moreover, most people need to make the decision to purchase doctor's services infrequently, so that because of forgetting each choice requires almost a new formation of a product class concept.

Once the product class concept is formed and Choice Criteria exist, we have a full-fledged *problem-solving game*, especially if Importance of Purchase is high and the buyer faces an informationally rich environment that encourages search, as contrasted with the case of doctor's services. How well the person is socially integrated will affect information availability. The credibility of the source begins to operate. If the buyer believes that the other person is *competent* and *trustworthy*, he will consider the information received as having both high predictive value—it is a good measure of probable performance—and high confidence value: he feels very confident in utilizing the measure. Attitude begins to form through internalization as the buyer discovers from his partner where this brand should be placed on the Choice Criteria (Product Class Comprehension) that he has developed from the identification process. If the information is favorable to the innovation, the rising Attitude will cause the buyer to pay still greater attention to his environment in order to obtain relevant information. If the information is unfavorable, the incipient Attitude will have a low value, which will cause the buyer to close off information, cease his search, and switch his conversations to other topics.

Assuming that the information is favorable, Intention will build as inhibitors become clear unless, of course, they are unfavorable. One of the serious inhibiting effects could be Financial Status reflected in the price of the innovation. Unless the buyer's income is expanding, the purchase of the innovation must draw purchasing power from some other current expenditure. Intention will form more rapidly to the extent that the buyer has a metaplan, such as an overall shopping plan in the case of a housewife, from which she can generalize to the particular situation and so develop a specific plan to underly Intention.

If Importance of Purchase is high, the buyer's environment is informationally rich, and there is goal conflict, the effort of this search process may be considerable. And as the buyer approaches the decision with consequent intensified search effort, as predicted by the Miller model, the attractiveness aspect of the source of information can remove the uncertainty through internalization, so that the strength of Attitude, Confidence and Intention are further increased. Thus trial, the first stage of the adoption process, occurs: he buys. Temporarily, motivational equilibrium has been achieved, because the need that gave rise to disequilibrium has been met.

We have emphasized pretrial behavior. One of the most important determinants of repeat purchase behavior, however, can be the actual acts of purchase and of consumption, and with the increasing complexity of products in use that is obvious to anyone, the postpurchase aspect of innovation has also become increasingly important. For example, after a new jello product had been placed on the market, it was found that in the soft-water areas of the United States, the new jello passed through the high-consistency stage into a liquid again after being beaten for 30 seconds. When hard water was used, only 10 seconds of beating was necessary. Hence in these areas new patterns of consumption behavior had to be developed. To the extent that new behavior in consumption is required by the new brand, the initiating company has a more difficult task of communicating the additional information that is required in consuming its brand.

In fact, we believe that the most significant determinant of repeat purchase and adoption is the feedback from purchase and consumption that is contained in Satisfaction, as shown in the linear model of Satisfaction in Chapter 4. How much satisfaction a buyer receives from purchase and consumption depends on the relation between expected (ex ante) satisfaction (Attitude) and actual (ex post) Satisfaction, the ambiguity of Satisfaction, the latency of Satisfaction, and the periodicity of Satisfaction, as we learned in Chapter 4.

Even after the first purchase, however, the buyer's continued interaction with other people as well as information from other sources will help to ensure adoption, because he can use additional information in anticipation of the next purchase and perhaps to rationalize his past purchase. This postdecision sensitivity to information has been stressed by the dissonance researchers on the grounds that the buyer needs support for his past decision. In terms of general consistency theory, which includes dissonance as we saw in Chapter 4, the buyer has accumulated tension as a consequence of choosing from somewhat equally attractive alternatives. This tension motivates the search. Ehrlich et al. (1957), for example, provide evidence of a greater tendency to see information about the brand just purchased. One wonders, however, how much of this effort is in anticipation of future purchase, rather than to justify past behavior. Also, the person may be hoping to learn from the information how to make better use of the brand.

As the buyer repeatedly purchases the brand, firm Choice Criteria, Attitude, Confidence, and Intention develop. As a result, his information requirements decline. He has achieved a brand equilibrium, which implies loyalty in his brand purchase and no information seeking. Except for two events, one external to the buyer and the other internal, this equilibrium state would continue indefinitely. One event that will create disequilibrium is the shock that the buyer receives from his environment in the form of a superior, well-publicized new brand in the product class. Second, if the product class is not high in Importance of Purchase, the effects of the loyalty-disloyalty cycle, through either a feeling of boredom or a rise in his aspiration level, produce a new disequilibrium, and the buyer begins to look for information about a new brand. Thus the stage is set for those aspects in our buyer's purchasing behavior that are associated with normal innovation.

Let us now examine the normal innovation. Here information sources need operate to a considerably less extent. The buyer has worked out all goal conflicts and so has firm, clear criteria by which to judge the new brand. Also, he is likely to have a highly codable vocabulary to use in discussing the brand, thinking about it, and remembering facts and making judgments about it, because typically mere new brands do not require a major change in vocabulary. A new central issue arises here, however, that does not exist with major innovation: is he highly loyal to his current brand or is his choice almost random among the brands in his evoked set? To simplify, let us consider the two extremes— very loyal and random choice.

Normal innovation where high loyalty exists can be illustrated by an experiment involving a new regular coffee labeled "Perky" introduced into the commissary store of a university-operated housing complex for married students (Arndt, 1966). Coupons that had to be redeemed within 16 days were distributed to each of the 495 students' wives living in the complex. At the end of the 16-day period, 30-minute interviews were completed with 449 of the wives, in which their information-giving and information-receiving activities during the period were elicited, and all reports were cross-checked with the alleged recipient or source, respectively. Arndt reports that 90 per cent of the comments were confirmed. Forty-four per cent of the 449 received at least one comment from a neighbor. Forty-two per cent bought at least one can of Perky. Although not everyone is loyal in his coffee purchasing, a large proportion of the people are.

When high loyalty exists, getting the buyer to pay attention to a new brand will still be something of a problem because his Confidence toward the loyal brand is high, though perhaps less difficult than in the case of the radically new product, the major innovation. He will be less likely to perceive information about a new brand than he will about his current brand. In the Folger study brand-loyal persons were less innovative (Frank, Massy, and Morrison, 1964, p. 320), but it is not known whether it was because they were less inclined to admit information or were more difficult to persuade, that is, whether it was a matter of the perceptual subsystem or the learning subsystem.

Compliance could make a great difference in the speed of adoption because it could create Attention. And if Satisfaction is strong enough after trial purchase, the feedback from Satisfaction can probably be the greatest of all influences on adoption.

The attractiveness characteristic of the other person will probably suffice to create Attention to the new brand.

The credibility characteristic of the source will be useful here because the buyer does not know that he has a problem, that there is possibly a better brand than his current one, and the task is to get enough information into his nervous system to raise doubts about the superiority of his current brand. Both the trust and competence characteristics of the dyadic partner would matter. Another important consideration here would be the reason for loyalty: is the buyer really convinced that his current brand is better or is it mainly that Importance of Purchase is very high and loyalty is a way of reducing the risk? The first case would seem to pose a more difficult attention-getting problem.

Once enough attention has been created so that the information (assuming it to be all favorable) can give the buyer a significant level of Brand Comprehension, a sufficient intensity of Attitude can be produced toward the new brand to cause him to be aware that he has a problem. Perhaps, he thinks, there is something better. This interest combined with the low Confidence toward the new brand will cause increased attention to information about it and even Overt Search into impersonal sources as well. That Confidence and Importance of Purchase stimulate search effort is suggested by the Arndt study, in which people with high perceived risk were significantly more likely to obtain word-of-mouth information than were people that exhibited low perceived risk. We cannot be sure of this evidence, however, because the analysis was not sharply pointed toward the brand.

Credibility of the source now becomes paramount, especially if it is both competent and trustworthy, because the problem-solving or internalization process is under way. This will help provide the buyer with the Attitude and Confidence essential to first purchase. That word-of-mouth does make a difference in the purchase of a normal innovation is supported by the Arndt study in which 54 per cent of those who had been exposed to favorable word-of-mouth information bought the coffee, whereas only 42 per cent of those not exposed did so.

If inhibitors are few, Intention will form rapidly because Attitude and Confidence effects are left as the major components of Intention. If inhibitors are complex and different from those of the old brand, more information and time will be required for Intention to form. Another factor, however, is whether this product is bought as a part of a regular shopping trip, which will serve as a metaplan to provide a specific-plan from which the buyer can generalize to form a plan to underlie Intention for the purchase of the new brand.

With repeated purchase Attitude, Confidence and Intention, become strong, and brand equilibrium is achieved which continues until there is a shock from the environment or the loyalty-disloyalty cycle becomes operative. This shift from loyalty to nonloyalty status because Attitude for the existing brand has declined, however, merely leads us, in terms of the nature of the problem, to the second case: random choice within the buyer's evoked set.

Random choice within the evoked set can occur when the product class is not serving important needs and there are no differences among the brands, functional or expressive. If it occurs because the product class is important and there are no differences among brands or, as indicated above, because the buyer is seeking stimulation, attention will raise no problems. His Attention will be high. Other than for the important issue of Attention, trial and adoption should proceed, if the new brand is superior, much like the loyal case except that the new brand will be accepted more easily because Attitude toward the new brand will develop more easily since the buyer has less to unlearn than in the loyal case.

The state of the new brand's inhibitors, for example, price, will obviously make a difference, however. Social interaction will be a major source of essential information, so that the influence processes will operate largely in terms of the credibility characteristic of the source of information. Internalization will operate to achieve first purchase. If the new brand is not functionally superior, the satisfaction of expressive needs might be a possible appeal. Otherwise, there will probably be trial without adoption.

It is our belief as implied in the foregoing discussion that normal innovations will in general be more easily accepted than a major innovation: certain conditions, however, could render this belief untrue. It could be, for example, that the major innovation is not too ambiguous but instead at something of an optimal level for attention getting. Also, advertising perhaps will tend to be less competitive, and so in this situation the buyer may "let down his guard" and be more receptive than if the advertising is competitive. Finally, the buyer may not have to "unlearn" as much as if he is loyal to a given brand which is being replaced by another brand in the same product class.

A number of complications have been sidestepped in this discussion of buyer sources and type of innovation. First, nothing has been said so far about the influence of the content of the information transmitted in the dyadic relation. Not much is known, but again we are fortunate in having Arndt's study. As the reader will recall, only 18 per cent of those who received unfavorable information but 54 per cent of those who received favorable word-of-mouth information bought the new brand of coffee.

Second, there is the question of the role of individual differences. Are there fairly permanent differences among people that could be called Personality Traits (exogenous variable), that influence their information seeking and their perception of risk and therefore must be considered in understanding innovation? Cunningham reports a linear relationship between level of "general self-confidence," which is probably related to self-esteem, and word-of-mouth information seeking. Arndt reports that his findings tended to support Cunningham but not at a statistically significantly level (but see Shuchman and Perry, 1969). When we turn to the effect of word-of-mouth information, however, the curvilinear relation found earlier between general self-confidence and acceptance is reported by Arndt to hold: the medium self-confidence housewives were more likely to accept than was either extreme. Our belief is that these self-esteem effects operate on the perceptual subsystem instead of the learning subsystem: high-esteem people close out the information because they think they have the best answer, and low-esteem people also close it out but because they are fearful of the unfamiliar.

Another interesting point also emerged from Arndt's study. People with low self-confidence were even more likely to buy if they received unfavorable information than if they received favorable information.

Third, are there differences among products in the role of word-of-mouth in influencing adoption? A seminar at the Bureau of Applied Social Research (Bourne, 1963) examined a number of products and came to some conclusions; in our discussion here the products about which there was more than speculative evidence are indicated by an asterisk, but the evidence is not given. A distinction was made as to whether social influence was important for product class or brand. Unfortunately, the criteria that underlay the analysis were not made explicit.

For clothing, furniture, magazines, refrigerators (type), and toilet soap, it was concluded that the brand purchase was influenced but not the choice of product class. But for cars, cigarettes, beer (premium versus regular), and drugs, it was felt that social influence was important for both types of choice. For soap, canned peaches, laundry soap, refrigerator (brand), and radios, it was felt to be relevant for neither. Finally, personal influence was thought to be important for the product purchase but not for brand in the case of air-conditioners*, instant coffee, and television (black and white). One can only speculate about why these alleged differences exist if they do. Arndt clearly indicates that in regular coffee, brand choice is affected by social influence.

Our theory suggests that word-of-mouth will be used in any situation where this source is readily available (the person is well integrated into the social structure), Importance of Purchase is high, and Confidence is low.

Finally, the question might be raised whether personal influence is becoming more or less dominant in shaping our behavior; for example, is social influence more dominant as a society becomes more industrialized? Our usual inclination is to assume that it is; yet anthropologists have found evidence of actual starvation in primitive societies because the available food, though edible and nutritious, is inconsistent with tribal traditions. The answer to the question of whether personal influence is becoming more significant seems to be found, in part at least, in the concept of the dominance or means-end hierarchy of motives that we discussed in Chapter 4.

As standards of living rise, it becomes possible to satisfy motives that are lower and lower in the dominance hierarchy of Motives. As we are able to satisfy these lesser basic needs, we become more and more discriminating in identifying the many alternative ways to satisfy them. Hence we as a society seek a greater variety of product classes by which to meet them, and so we are descending in the means-end hierarchy as well.

Our peers are probably more influential at the lower levels in the hierarchy, where there is a greater variety of product classes that will satisfy our needs, because the lower-level needs tend to be learned motives. Above all, there is operative here the self-image–dyad–role-expressive behavior complex used earlier to explain attitude change.

Riesman's (1950) distinction between tradition-directed, inner-directed, and other-directed personalities sets a broader, more historical framework within which these social forces can be seen to operate. We do seem to be more other-directed, and Arndt (1966, p. 94) found that other-directed people were more likely to adopt a new product. Riesman's distinctions may be especially helpful when marketing goods and services across cultures; for example, one might postulate, as we did above, that more advanced economies are subject to greater personal influence.

8.3.2 Commercial Sources

Commercial sources represent the information disseminated by the innovating company in consumer goods, for example, by such means as advertising, salesmen, merchandising effort, pricing, packaging, distribution channels, and display, retail and otherwise. They are under the control of the seller. To understand their consequences, we must look at them from the buyer's point of view—how the buyer uses them as sources of information. This view can be summarized, "How much does the source reduce my risk and how much does it cost me in money, effort or time to use it?" Cost is an inhibitory factor on search to be used when explaining Overt Search, just as price is an inhibitor used in explaining overt purchase behavior.

The initiating company has two broad avenues for disseminating information: advertising and personal selling.

8.3.2.1 Advertising

Advertising is, of course, intimately related to mass communication, which is systematically dealt with in Chapter 9. Our purpose in this chapter is to set forth the communication framework of product innovation. Chapter 9 spells out the details of certain aspects of this framework and, in addition, takes a broader view of buying behavior, not being confined to innovation.

As emphasized in discussing buyer sources, if the social structure—the buyer's neighbors, his friends, and other sources of face-to-face interaction—has absorbed information about the innovation, it will make a difference in whether a buyer tries an innovation. Hence advertising can be used indirectly by merely making the brand known on a broadcast basis throughout the social structure, so that the "other person" in the dyad is familiar with the innovation. Without doubt, advertising serves much more this purpose than do salesmen. On the other hand, advertisers usually view the buyer as though they were approaching him directly. We shall call the first approach "indirect advertising," and the second, "direct advertising."

1. *Indirect advertising.* In indirect advertising, a commercial source (advertising) is used to influence buyer sources. In fact, advertising appears to be the most common way by which a person learns about a new brand. Arndt (1967c, pp. 194–195) summarizes a considerable body of evidence, but it does not permit making a careful distinction

between "learning about it" and the evaluative effects (Attitude change). At least we can safely conclude that advertising does make the product known; it serves the attention-getting function in the social structure. Furthermore, the whole social network—not just the portion represented by the buyer–other person dyad—makes a difference. One dyad tells another dyad, and so on ad infinitum, as suggested by casual observation. For example, Arndt (1966) found that those buyers who were integrated into the community were more likely to receive word-of-mouth information and quicker to adopt Perky than were isolated residents.

But what is the nature of the social links—the social *network*, the *process* of transmission, and the *content* transmitted—by which influence is passed to the "other person" in the dyadic relation and through him to the buyer? Is this person merely a link in the transmission activity with no interest in the product class, and if so, how is he rewarded? We can assume that if this transmission behavior was not being rewarded, it would not be carried on for long.

To ask the last question is to get at the heart of the social structure concept as applied to buying, which has been lurking under all of our interaction discussion so far: are there roles in society the fulfillers of which we label "opinion leaders"? If so, these people are rewarded for carrying out this information-giving activity by being granted positions of status within the group where this role is being fulfilled as one of the set of roles associated with that position in the social system (Merton, 1957, pp. 368–386). Thus the role concept becomes the basic unit in analyzing social structure.

We must be careful in our definition, however. "Role" is typically used in the sociological literature to refer to positionally prescribed sets of behaviors or "expectations" about what that position should be. This definition provides a name or a label for a phenomenon, but not a useful tool for its analysis. In it there is no place for the buyer's *rational calculation* in performing role behavior; his behavior is completely determined by the social structure. Yet something like the role concept is needed to distinguish between the objective and subjective environments of choice. A solution is to use *decision premise* as the unit of role description in place of *behavior*. A role is a social prescription of *some*, but not *all*, of the premises that enter into an individual's choices of behaviors.

One of the simplest explanations of the function of social structure in innovation is the "two-step flow" which, stated in its most extreme form, holds that there are people in every social group who act as gatekeepers of information flowing into the group. As might be expected when stated in this extreme form, the proposition is not true. The leader also seeks information from other leaders, for example. It has been well documented that opinion leaders are more exposed to mass media than are nonleaders (Arndt, 1967c, pp. 217–220), but a large proportion of the receivers initiate the conversation with the leader.

Myers (1966) provides support for the role of the opinion leader in buying. He carried out an interesting experiment with the introduction of a new food (Armour's Starlight Chicken and Rice dinner). Fifteen groups of women in which the members of each group interacted regularly with others in their respective group were identified. Then opinion leaders were identified within each group. In nine of the groups, a sample of the product was given to the opinion leader. She was asked first to serve it to her family and then within two days to give samples to her friends and ask them to serve it to their families. In the remaining six groups, a nonleader was asked to do the same. When the opinion leader was the introducer, most of the people's attitudes changed in the same direction as that of the introducer. The results were quite different, however, when the nonleader was the introducer. Not only did the people's attitudes change less in a favorable direction, thus proving the existence of opinion leaders; they appeared to change in the opposite direction.

The second finding is quite important. It had been reported earlier in studies of the introduction of new agricultural practices. If generally true, it would complicate the utilization of the opinion leader principle in the sale of mass consumer products by the usual marketing procedures, such as mass advertising. In using the standard marketing procedures, it would be necessary to identify the motivation of the opinion leader in order to reach the buyer with advertising, for example, with advertising that is likely to appeal to the leader but *not* to the nonleader. Sheth (1968) contends that opinion leadership is in part a function of the characteristics of the innovation, for example, a low risk–high advantage product is less subject to word-of-mouth.

Are opinion leaders merely other innovators? If so, they should be treated as just another buyer in terms of the motives used to appeal to them, and the regular direct advertising should suffice. Robertson and Rossiter (undated) conclude, however, that the innovator and the opinion leader are different people, but even here, it could be that opinion leaders are merely *later* adopters. More broadly, however, Katz and Lazarsfeld (1955, pp. 321ff) concluded that there are generalized opinion leaders, people who transmit information across more than one field of interest, specifically across marketing, fashion, and public affairs. They did encounter a contradiction. They found that though a leader in one area is five times more likely than by chance to be a leader in three areas, he was no more likely to be a leader in two areas. Marcus and Bauer (1964, pp. 628–632) reconciled this contradiction in a re-examination of Katz and Lazarsfeld's data by finding that the conclusion does hold in the case of two areas as well. Thus since there are gen-eralized opinion leaders, we can infer that the chances are very high that some of the links in the communication network are not buyers and *should be appealed to on some basis other than their buying motives.*

There are a number of possible motives for a person to be an opinion leader. Arndt (1967c, pp. 222–228) reviews the evidence, but finds that it is varied and, worse yet, developed from a variety of theoretical orien-tations. The main conclusion is that high ego involvement (Importance of Purchase) makes a difference, which is to say that whatever the leader's motivation, if it is intense, he is more likely to participate. It is possible, however, that motivation could be too intense and cause stereotyped instead of adaptive behavior. This does not carry us far toward an explanation.

We can go one step further by proceeding on an a priori basis by asking, "Does society offer a reward for serving solely as a transmitter, a reward from which we might infer motivation?" Our guess is that there is some reward in the form of additional status, but that it is typically not enough to justify great effort. In other words, they must be appealed to primarily as buyers, and all of the analysis used in connection with direct advertising is appropriate. These issues are par-ticularly interesting because the massive increase in new products must be having some effect on increasing this transmission role in highly industrialized societies. New social behaviors pertinent to this need must be developed and institutionalized. Perhaps the lack of such sources currently is the reason for the consumer discontent that is implied in "consumerism."

Moving from the idea of generalized opinion leaders, what can we say about the nature of the people in the buyer–other person dyad? How about social status? Are the two members from the same or from different social classes? There is some contradictory evidence on this issue across different contexts such as shopping and voting, but in gen-eral they are of the same status (King, 1967, p. 241). Also, they tend to be of the same age. In addition, the sheer physical proximity of the two members of the dyad is a factor, as might be expected. People who are physically close to each other, such as living in the same dwell-ing, are more likely to interact. The family unit is an important source of interaction. Finally, whether the person is one whose advice is per-ceived as being more competent is not clear.

In choosing doctors we can infer, however, that the buyer depends on his dyadic counterpart's competence. Parents (people with experience with children) were more inclined to consult other parents and even parents with children of the same age. Because of our normal interaction patterns—the tendency for people to associate with others like ourselves—this could occur, but it would seem unlikely to be as high as 61 per cent of the people with children under six years of age who sought the advice of parents with children of the same age (Sidney Feldman, 1966, p. 772).

The tendency to utilize competence would suggest that an internalization influence process (problem solving) is operating. Other than this, the tendency to seek out people like ourselves implies an identification process. Appeal to others of higher social status suggests a compliance type of process.

It would be very helpful if we knew more about the nature of the information *content* that is transmitted in a dyadic situation. Knowing this would clarify the function being served by the dyadic relation such as whether it is psychosocial or problem-solving. In other words, we now know that the dyadic relation makes a difference but not in which way it does so. We know, however, from Arndt's coffee study that unfavorable information has a negative effect. Only 18 per cent of the persons receiving negative information bought the product, whereas 42 per cent of those receiving no word-of-mouth information and 54 per cent of those receiving positive word-of-mouth information bought (Arndt, 1966).

In a study of the diffusion of women's fashions, it appeared that word-of-mouth was most important in supplying personalized fashion information, such as what will look good on the respondent, what friends are wearing, and styles for particular occasions. It was less significant as the source of general fashion trends, and still less for fashion shopping information such as availability and price in local retail stores (King, and Summers, 1967, Table 8.5, p. 255). It is important to note, however, that fashion is a type of product where socially sanctioned criteria are particularly significant, and even here such mundane information as availability and price was important in the word-of-mouth process. There is some relevant literature on what information is transmitted in social networks—much of it drawn from outside the interaction area per se, especially mass communications research—but it is not easily summarized (McGuire, 1968b). Some of it will be brought to bear upon mass communication in Chapter 9.

What can we conclude about the role of indirect advertising? We can say with limited evidence that indirect advertising does make a difference in product innovation, and that, there are intermediate human links between the person reading the advertising and the buyer. The reader transmits the advertisement information to the "other person" in the buyer's dyad. The line can be still more complex. Second, this diffusion process causes the effects of advertising to be slower than they would be if these links did not exist. Third, it is desirable for marketing activity (1) to encourage the "other person" in the dyad to transmit information and (2) to attempt to ensure that the information be favorable to the new product instead of unfavorable. Fourth, it is desirable that opinion leaders initiate the use of products. Fifth, especially with radically new products (major innovations), the initiating seller should communicate in words that will provide the social intermediary with an adequate vocabulary to make him effective in transmitting the information. Sixth, if we know the type of influence process that is operating in the ultimate dyad that includes the buyer—compliance, identification, or internalization—we can better predict which of the intervening variables will be affected.

We have now linked the social structure to the dyad. We have shown how the dyadic process itself shapes this flow between the broader structure and the buyer in the dyad; for example, it makes a difference whether the other person in the dyad is an opinion leader. There remains the question of whether the broader structure itself actually influences the nature of the process in the dyad other than serving as merely an information input and thereby shaping the nature of that input. This is a much broader sociological issue, too broad to be dealt with here, but from our analysis a number of inferences can be made; for example, the values represented in the structure will influence what is perceived (and therefore passed on) and how the information is modified (distorted). Anyone wishing to pursue this topic further will find Nicosia (1964) exceedingly helpful.

2. *Direct advertising.* Most conventional advertising—advertising aimed directly at the buyer—has difficulty in getting attention, as we saw in Chapter 3 from the large number of persons who tend to "tune out" television advertising. Let us take the case of a major innovation first.

Only if the new product class satisfies an obvious or urgent (Importance of Purchase) unmet need, the buyer has moved into the disloyalty stage of the loyalty-disloyalty cycle, or the buyer has learned to look systematically for new products in general, as a purchasing agent might, is a message from the mass media, likely to receive strong attention. If it does receive the buyer's attention, its credibility is probably not high and it is perhaps viewed as being more competent than trustworthy

On the other hand, the appearance of a product in national advertising does seem to endow it with some credibility, especially if the company itself (the source) has a favorable image. Companies are more and more concerned about their public image, largely, we suspect, because of management's growing belief that the image significantly affects the acceptance of the company's new products. Limited objective evidence on the effects of company image is offered by Kerby's work (1966). Above all, advertising is convenient and its cost to the buyer is low if it appears on his television screen or in his regular magazine.

Direct advertising, however, is seriously handicapped in providing buyers with Choice Criteria, especially if the motives have social implications. It can tell the buyer little if anything about the criteria that are socially acceptable. The social network is probably much superior. Similarly, if the product itself or its consumption is complex, advertising is handicapped.

On the other hand, except for these handicaps, advertising may have a relatively easier time with a major innovation than with a minor one because there is less to be unlearned.

In the case of a normal innovation, direct advertising can be quite effective, we think, if current choice is random within the buyer's evoked set and especially if it meets his needs better than does his current brand. Getting attention will not be difficult, and advertising is easily accessible. Its credibility, however, is probably somewhat suspect.

When buyers are loyal to their existing brands, the effectiveness of advertising would seem to be severely limited both in first getting attention and then in creating change in Attitude, Confidence, or Intention because of its questionable credibility. If loyalty is based more on Importance of Purchase than on a belief in the current brand's quality, Attention is more likely.

We would expect considerable distortion of the information under normal innovation. We expect it because (1) advertising tends to be ambiguous and (2) the buyer has already developed many associations with the product class, even (3) strong associations with a particular brand if he is a loyal buyer. Also, it is important to discuss the distortion of information because we expect that much of the interpersonal differences in purchasing come about because of it. This distortion of information after it has entered the nervous system via the buyer's receptors (Attention) undoubtedly occurs with all sources, but some are probably more subject to it than others. We have implied its existence in earlier discussions in this chapter, but now we examine it systematically.

The reader will recall that Perceptual Bias was the hypothetical construct postulated in Chapter 4 to incorporate these distortion effects.

Also, he will recall from Chapter 5 that Perceptual Bias was identified as a *process* construct instead of a state description, since the complexity of the concept forced us for the sake of exposition to treat it as a process. Here, however, we break it down to some extent into its component mechanisms (see Chapter 5) in applying it to innovation.

First, the familiar words and sentences are more likely to be "seen" than the unfamiliar. This is the principle of stimulus integration first discussed in Chapter 4 within the three levels of psychological analysis developed in Chapter 5. Learning of this type (stimulus integration) takes place without reinforcement.

Second, a concept—a product class—that has been associated with a stimulus through reinforcement in the past is more likely to be called up by that stimulus, that is, a familiar idea is more likely to be stimulated by it than an unfamiliar idea. The buyer is more likely to think of his familiar product class than of the new product class when he sees an advertisement. The same argument applies to a particular brand within that class; a company's advertising of the new brand will call up its competitor's advertisement of the buyer's established brand, hence will promote the competitor's sales, a phenomenon often revealed in sales analysis. A cereal company is reported to have used an advertisement that, its management believed, served to double its competitor's sales.

Which concept is "called up"—which product class is brought to mind by the stimulus—is also influenced by the contextual cues surrounding Stimulus Display. A sports equipment advertisement appearing on a sports page will have a higher readership than it would if it had appeared elsewhere in the newspaper.

Third, which motive is operative at the moment will affect which class is called up. A person who has a headache is more likely to "see" an analgesic advertisement.

Fourth, the ambiguity of the information (Stimulus Ambiguity) makes a difference, and advertising under the casual conditions in which it is usually seen is ambiguous. The greater the ambiguity, the more alternative interpretations the buyer can make of it and correspondingly the greater the number of product class and brand alternatives that can be "called up." Our guess is that advertising is on the whole much more ambiguous than word-of-mouth information, although no systematic evidence is available.

Fifth, once a product class is called up, it will feed back to sensory integration and cause the buyer to "see" information pertinent to that product class and not "see" information for another product class. In this way information is distorted. The same argument applies to the desired brand within the product class, the brand that most satisfies the buyer's motives that are met by this product class. A more conversational way of describing the effects of the feedback is to say that the buyer *reinterprets* the information in light of his needs. The specific mechanism by which this reinterpretation occurs, it will be recalled from Chapter 5, can be either selective or energizing.

Finally, considerable differences among buyers (Importance of Purchase and Personality Traits) would be expected in these perceptual effects.

All of these perceptual factors taken together suggest the great variability in advertising effects that shape the stimuli-as-coded. It is not worthwhile to pursue them here; they constitute major research programs.

8.3.2.2 *Salesmen*

Now we turn to the case where the other person in the dyad is a salesman. There is not much good literature on the selling relation, and the major task of integrating it with the research on interaction to bring it to bear on the sales function still remains.

Offhand, it would seem that the analysis of social interaction ought to be particularly appropriate for salesmen because of the nature of the salesman-client relation. On the other hand, casual observation tells us that this case can differ considerably from that discussed earlier where the "other person" who supplies buyer information is a friend or neighbor. Sometimes the salesman is of a "lower status" than the buyer, although not when he is a person of high technical competence or during periods when a seller's market exists, as during wartime rationing. Finally, the salesman is a member of a formal organization, a fact that strongly influences his behavior. In industrial markets, both members of the dyad represent formal organizations.

Even in the case of a radically new product, the salesman can usually get some attention at least, especially if he is backed by a company that practices trade relations (reciprocity). Also, that the salesman's personality, his aggressiveness, for example, makes a difference in his role is suggested by casual observation. Getting attention is about as far as the compliance process will usually take a salesman. Perhaps at its best, compliance can only secure trial, although some trade relations arrangements may be effective enough to secure adoption.

If the salesman and client have developed the mutually satisfying role relation so often found in industrial purchasing, we predict that identification may often go far in providing Product Class Comprehension, Brand Comprehension, Attitude, Confidence, and Intention. We must bear in mind, however, that if the salesmen are of a lower status, the role relationship will probably be less effective in changing behavior. The problem-solving influence process, to a considerable extent, is operative because of the two-way conversation that is possible. Credibility, although the salesman is perhaps typically low on the trust component, will contribute to internalization because of his expertise. This seems to occur in mechanical products where the salesman, usually being an engineer, has the technical know-how that the buyer does not have (Howard and Moore, 1963). Casual observation suggests that some salesmen achieve so good a working relation with their clients that their credibility is exceedingly high as a result of the combination of trust and competence dimensions. The salesman is often in a position to help the buyer; for example, an unexpected fast delivery can very much help the industrial buyer to give the impression to his superiors and peers that he is effectively doing his job.

Bauer (1961) concludes from a study of the drug industry that doctors are influenced in their preference for drugs by the identity of the company that sells the drug. He also concludes that, with the riskier drugs, doctors are more likely to be swayed by their preference for a certain company than by that for the salesman (detail man). The conclusions confirm the importance of company image as an influence in the trial and adoption stages of a new product. Finally, Bauer implies that the influence of the internalization process (problem solving) is operative with salesmen because doctors state that their preference for a salesman is largely determined by their confidence in him. He does not indicate, however, whether it is the competence or the trust components that matter most.

The buyer's search effort when utilizing salesmen is not costless. His time is required in talking with salesmen. True enough, he can be selective, but only if he works for a firm that salesmen visit regularly, which is sometimes true only of larger companies.

Most of the salesman-client relations involve organizational instead of consumer buyers, and therefore the formal organization instead of the looser social structure is involved. With radically new products this fact is especially important, because the "buyer" is usually several people and almost always at least two, the buyer and the product designer.

There appear considerable differences between large and small firms in their effort to obtain information. Large firms are specialized enough to have made institutional arrangements for search especially the search for new alternatives, such as having special purchasing *research* departments. The buyer in the small firm, because of lack of specialization, probably thinks of a new product only when he is approached by a salesman, when he observes a competitor making use of it, or, of course, when he accidentally encounters it. Also, he is in a barren environment because he is so tied down with the details of his position that he can seldom "look outward" and expose himself to new sources of information, as he would when participating in professional and trade association activities.

In normal innovation, when a new product is merely a change from an existing brand, the salesman plays quite a different role. Here the buyer has his own criteria by which to judge the new product, but even if he is highly loyal, getting his attention is a problem with which the salesman can probably deal. Some salesmen are perhaps much more adept in getting attention than are others. The salesman with high credibility—both competence and trust—would seem to have a great advantage because, in addition to getting attention, by indirection he can reduce the buyer's loyalty to his current brand and at the same time increase his loyalty to the new brand by the process of identification. How important the product is will make a difference.

When the buyer is not loyal—makes random choices from within his evoked set—the salesman would seem to be truly effective, particularly if the salesman is credible.

8.3.2.3 New Media Needed

New ways of reaching potential buyers to inform them about the availability and qualities of new products would seem to be needed because of the vastly increased flow of new products. In a sense, conventional marketing channels of communication are overloaded.

In one recently developed scheme, the national advertiser inserts into his advertising a telephone number that the consumer can call collect from anywhere in the United States to learn more about the new product. Other such devices will undoubtedly be developed in the future. In the meantime, government agencies such as FDA have been experimenting with new consumer communication devices. Some major technological developments involving the computer will have important consequences for industrial buying.

8.3.3 Neutral Sources

Having discussed buyer and commercial sources of information, we turn to neutral sources, which, by definition, are more objective in the information they transmit.

Also, by definition, neutral sources are limited in their capacity to transmit goal information. Choice Criteria that imply certain goals are conveyed, for example, by Consumer Reports, which give information on technical performance and price. They imply that the buyer ought to at least use technical criteria and price. The buyer will not learn about radically new products from such a source because some time elapses before these are reported upon, although he may learn about aspects of conventionally new products. Also, the use of these sources requires time, effort, and skill. Skill is implied by the fact that people who utilize them tend to be above average in education and in income. Much of the population simply lacks the reading and comprehension skill and the interest to use such sources in their present form. If the product is important enough and the buyer has the skill, the sources play a large role in the buyer's search effort, but they appear to be confined largely to consumer durables.

Women's fashion magazines, on the other hand, do provide not only information about what is recently available, but also nontechnical criteria of choice.

One of the most common neutral sources is news stories, which probably play a large role in regard to radically new products, the radically new usually being more newsworthy. A recent news story on the home electronic range now in test market in Chicago, for example, gave a great amount of useful information, including peoples' attitudes, from which the buyer could infer something about socially acceptable criteria in judging it. The credibility of these reports is probably quite high in trust, and if they are taken from a scientific report, as many of them are, the competence would be viewed as high. If the intellectual integrity of the editorial policy is questionable, these news stories degenerate into advertising and perceptive readers come to recognize them as such. Advertising agencies and their clients devote considerable resources to public relations activities that utilize the news story approach.

8.4 EXOGENOUS VARIABLES

The third major set of factors influencing trial and adoption are the exogenous variables. These provide for individual differences among buyers, but they may also change over a fairly long period of time, hence explain intertemporal differences for a given buyer. Ideally, from an action point of view, these differences would be such as to guide market segmentation. Even considerably short of market segmentation, however, knowledge of the differences can be helpful in data analysis, in inferring the "why" of trial and adoption.

This step of incorporating the exogenous variables, which are causally related to the output intervening variables via the hypothetical constructs, is particularly essential for fundamental research, because in research on acceptance the role of the central processes—perceptual and learning—has seldom been articulated. Instead, these underlying processes have usually been bypassed and left implicit, with attention being focused on the relation between such things as we have called exogenous variables and actual purchase and occasionally between information and actual purchase. By making the linking process equally explicit, we may be able to extend earlier research.

Because of their practical importance in market segmentation, a great amount of effort is now being directed toward identifying the buyer's stable characteristics. There is growing skepticism of the use of demographic characteristics in predicting trial or adoption (Frank, Green, and Sieber, 1967; Frank, 1967a, 1967b; but see Carman, 1968). Psychological variables, especially personality variables, are receiving more attention, but little heed is being given to new products. These should be studied, however, in connection with the current information inputs to the buyer—advertising, word-of-mouth, and so on—in order to identify the nature of the underlying process, which will reveal the interactions that are now being hidden. As an example, our guess is that current operating research is missing the key role of the internally generated motivation to look for new products implied in the Stimulus Ambiguity-arousal relation.

8.4.1 Importance of Purchase

Increased Importance of Purchase will increase Attention for all brands in the product class, that is, the level of the Stimulus Ambiguity-arousal curve will be higher and the buyer will be more receptive to new products. The Folger study found this to be so and concluded:

It may be that for products where very little risk is involved in purchase and consumption, the more important the product is in relation to total consumption the more analysis and experimentation are undertaken with respect to new alternatives—thus contributing to a higher rate of adoption. [Frank, Massy, and Morrison, 1964, p. 320].

Also, Arndt (undated) found that innovators were significantly higher on perceived risk, which has Importance of Purchase as one component than were noninnovators. As we saw earlier, not only does Importance of Purchase make a difference in the amount of search, but it also encourages problem solving as an influence process instead of compliance or identification.

Not only does Importance of Purchase cause differences in search effort; it also makes a difference directly in purchasing behavior. A person who considers a product class to be important is more likely to be brand-loyal than one who does not.

Also, Importance of Purchase not only explains differences in purchase behavior among people, but also in individual purchase behavior across product classes. Casual observance and some systematic evidence suggest great differences in Importance of Purchase across products.

8.4.2   Personality Traits

It is sometimes alleged that the early adopters and late adopters are people with different personality traits. By "trait" is meant an enduring or persisting characteristic of a person that distinguishes him from another person and is predictive of his behavior.

Lowery suggested several years ago that early adopters prefer "newness," as though it were a personality characteristic. "Observers have noted that venturesomeness is almost an obsession with innovators" (Rogers, 1962, p. 169). Rogers (1962, pp. 172–178) also states that early adopters are younger, have higher social status, and higher financial position, but at the same time (pp. 189–190) he points out that individuals shift among categories, which would negate the conclusion that these are personality differences. Robertson and Rossiter (undated, p. 15) found that innovators were highly venturesome, although the mechanism underlying it is not suggested. Perhaps a part of the explanation lies in the position that an individual occupies on the Stimulus Ambiguity-arousal continuum; that is, late adopters tend to become aware of the innovation as quickly as do early adopters, but late adopters find the situation more ambiguous and require more time to resolve the ambiguity.

This comment on ambiguity leads us to general self-confidence as it has been used in the perceived risk research, or the presumably related concept of "self-esteem" as it is labeled in the psychological literature. Self-esteem has been one of the most widely researched personality characteristics. McGuire hpothesizes that low-esteem people avoid being influenced by closing out the information (low Attention), whereas high-esteem persons take in the information (high Attention) but evaluate it, hence may not be influenced. Consequently, the output intervening variables would respond differently between the two personality types.

Bauer hypothesizes that buyers differ with respect to whether psychosocial goals or problem-solving goals are dominant, and assembles evidence that their consequent behavior, such as reactions to a communications source, is different (Wilding and Bauer, 1968). As a further consideration, however, he concludes that to the extent that there is high ego involvement in the purchase (high Importance of Purchase), problem-solving goals will dominate (Bauer, 1961).

In using the concept of personality traits, the student of buying behavior probably needs to go beyond the individual buyer and apply it to others in the social network. First, the nature of the opinion leader can perhaps profitably be explored by means of the concept. It has been reported, for example, that opinion leaders are less venturesome than innovators (Robertson and Rossiter, undated, p. 15). Such conclusions can possibly be useful in designing messages to stimulate the opinion leader to exert his role in behalf of an innovation. Second, it has long been believed, though on limited evidence, that the personality traits of the other person in the dyad when that person is a salesman make a lot of difference. Our guess is that research will bear out the truth of this belief.

8.4.3 Social Class

In Chapter 3 evidence was presented indicating that Social Class influenced the rate of acceptance of three innovations. For other evidence, see Carman (1965b). In examining the purchasing patterns of buyers of Crest toothpaste during the first twelve months after it received the ADA endorsement in 1960, Shuchman reports finding a linear relation between social class (income, education, and occupation) and probability of acceptance. Homans (1961, p. 357) alleges that middle-class people are the least susceptible to innovation, but his prediction is not borne out by the evidence.

Rich and Jain (1968) conclude that social-class distinctions in terms of effects on purchasing behavior have become obscured by rising incomes and educational levels. From their own data, however, we find that relatively large differences still exist between social class in their purchasing behavior.

It must be recognized that the relationship between social class and innovation can be negative as well. Graham found this to be so in television, except in the case of the lowest class. Graham was investigating the degree to which the innovation is consistent with the values of each social class. Diffusion researchers often discuss "compatibility"— meaning compatibility with the motives and behaviors of an individual—as a criterion of whether an innovation will be adopted.

One question is, "How much information seeking is there across social-class lines?" In general, there is less than within the class.

8.4.4 Culture

The values and behaviors of buyers vary across cultures; in fact, these differences are largely what we mean by "culture." We would expect them to have both perceptual and information-processing implications. Consequently, it would be surprising if there were not considerable intercultural differences in rate of acceptance of many new products. Some evidence by Tax (1958) was presented in Chapter 3.

8.4.5 Time Pressure

Buyers under time pressure are less apt to adopt a new brand. They are probably less likely to learn about it (low Attention) and less likely to change their behavior even if they do learn about it. In a study of the introduction of Folger's coffee in the Chicago market, Frank, Massy, and Morrison (1964) as well as Myers (1967) found that one of the most important differences among innovators and noninnovators was the wife's employment status. Working wives were less inclined to adopt the new brand and we infer that Time Pressure is the explanation. Income, education, and occupation were relatively unimportant.

A recent international study of time allocations in which the Survey Research Center, University of Michigan, is participating may provide a way of measuring this variable directly by the normal time allocations now used by people engaged in a great variety of activities.

8.4.6 Social and Organizational Setting

Largely through historical accident we have come to see the consumer and the organizational buyer as acting in very different environments; the consequence has been a marked separation of the two in both teaching and research. Here we think of the consumer as in a Social Setting and of the distributive, industrial, and institutional buyers as in an Organizational Setting, the difference being only the degree of structure or formality of the social setting. The relevance is, of course, that to the extent that we can treat the buyer as being independent of his social setting in terms of its past conditioning effect, we must only "map his head," whereas to the extent that he is not independent of it, we must, in addition, "map the structure of that setting" in order to explain his behavior.

What a buyer is exposed to and from whom, is strongly influenced by the buyer's Social and Organizational Setting, so that the incorporation of this exogenous variable reduces the range of variance in the output intervening variables. In the buyer's *past* he has become a part of the social or organizational structure: in carrying out his daily activities including his job, he associates with (forms dyads with) some people and not others. These people tend to be his peers and are physically proximate. They tend to have similar values, and since they have similar values, associate together, and thus are subject to the same stimuli over a fairly long period, they tend to behave in the same way.

Furthemore, when the buyer is confronted with an innovation, (1) he not only begins from the same behavioral base as the others in his group, especially those with whom he has regularly interacted in the past, but (2) much of his current information about this particular innovation, its use, and evaluation will also have been filtered through this structure of similar values and behaviors. We have seen (1) how one's values influence what he pays attention to and (2) how this admitted information is distorted by perceptual processes. Consequently, we have substantial reason to believe that Mrs. Jones's product innovation behavior *could* differ sharply from that of Mrs. Smith who comes from quite a different social setting. However, would we necessarily expect differences in their responses to all new products? Not unless the new products served values that were different between the two structures or unless the behavior required in their purchase and consumption conflicted with some other part of the buyer's behavior that was socially significant.

By concentrating for the moment on the looser social structure that we associate with the consumer, we can bring together a number of ideas that may have appeared to be unrelated. First, as was said in defining the concept of social class, people are valued in a society and are viewed as having differential statuses. Thus we can look at social structure as pins (people) in a large "social" map at the bottom which is the lowest status and the top, the highest. Second, across this map from left to right run large belts of areas which we call "social classes." "Style of life" is perhaps a better term, because it does not imply the sharply demarcated boundaries of these belts that "social class" does. Third, because of the routine of daily activity, their job locations in relation to their homes, and many other factors, these people tend to be related in reference groups, which can influence the buyer's behavior. Fourth, a buyer acquires a status in each reference group of which he is a member. Fifth, within each group, members tend to interact, and this interaction relation is called a dyad—A in face-to-face relation with B. Sixth, in the interaction process (and in other ways too), a buyer develops impressions about the nature of the other person. These impressions are grouped into traits, constructs by which the buyer identifies other people and attempts to predict their behavior. Seventh, the buyer's conception of his own self and his conception of the traits of others are highly interdependent entities. Specifically, the buyer develops a self-image. He forms impressions about himself and ascribes certain traits to himself, just as he does to the other person in the dyad. He comes to think of himself as "warm" or "cold," "mature" or "immature," "intelligent" or "unintelligent," and so forth. Is there a relation between the traits he ascribes to himself, those he ascribes to others who use his preferred brand, and those he ascribes to others who use a competing brand? Specifically, does he view himself as similar to others who like the same brand and as different from others who use a competing brand? In other words, does he use the brands to express himself or for their functional utility? Grubb and Hupp (1968) report from a study of car owners that some people do buy to express themselves. Dolich (1967) has performed a more detailed analysis with somewhat similar results.

There is the further question whether the buyer's ideal self-image may be more predictive of brand purchase than his real self-image (Hall and Lindzey, 1957, p. 404), the ideal being how the person would like to appear and the real image is how he thinks he actually appears to others. Dolich's evidence (1967, p. 86) was not clear on this issue.

Now let us explore the interdependency between self and others, which leads us to the dynamics of the interaction situation. The buyer interacts with Jones partially because he finds him attractive, since Jones has traits he admires (identification). When Jones tells him about a new brand C, then he must like C or not like Jones so much. If he does, in fact, like C, there is no problem. But if, in fact, he does not like the taste of it, what does he do? One solution is to lower his opinion of himself as a judge and say, in effect, that he must learn to like it. Alternatively, of course, he can maintain his own self-conception and conclude that Jones is not a good judge, that he has, for example, uncultured tastes; such a conclusion, however, if important enough, will hamper his future relations with Jones in the dyad. Thus we see how the buyer's self-concept depends in part on his views of others; we see also something of the dynamics of the interaction situation in purchasing. Presumably, the more Important the Purchase including its implications for social relations, the more significant will be the role of social structure. Since the formal organization is merely a tighter social structure, the same conclusions apply to industrial purchasing.

Furthermore, differences among formal organizations in acceptance rates would be expected for other reasons than the dynamics of the interaction situation. Some organizations have more effective arrangements for learning about innovations than others, such as the larger and therefore more specialized companies. Also, there are obviously great technological differences among companies. Leading practitioners—industrial buying executives—believe that degree of company decentralization is one of the most important influences on industrial buying practices. In the case of radical new industrial products and often of ordinary new ones, the trial decision is made by a group representing product design, production, and sales, as well as purchasing.

8.4.7   *Financial Status*

Financial Status would seem to be an important limitation on major innovation because, with an income constraint, the major innovation will force the buyer to forgo the purchase of something he has been regularly buying. On the other hand an economy with increasing income would be conducive to major innovation.

Normal and minor innovation would not seem to be affected by Financial Status unless the new alternative is of a higher price than the one it will replace.

8.5   SUMMARY

The kind of innovation—major, normal, or minor—was postulated as a central determinant of the buyer's search effort, which in turn influences whether and how the innovation is accepted. In the normal innovation case the buyer has a well-defined product class concept and a set of terms that enable him to talk about the innovation, to think about it, and to remember it. In technical terms, the words are highly codable. Also, the buyer has well-formulated criteria by which to judge the new product. Furthermore, if he is doubtful about the applicability of these criteria to the new brand, he can quickly discuss the problem with his friends because he has an efficient vocabulary for doing so. In this conversation he will discuss both the appropriateness of the usual criteria implied in the product class concept and how well this new brand measures up on these criteria. In this way he develops an isomorphism between the naming behavior and the other culturally conditioned behavior of purchase and consumption.

In the major innovation case, he does not have an appropriate well-defined product class concept and he must learn the things that would otherwise be supplied by the concept. Also, goal conflicts must be reconciled. Hence the buyer is faced with great uncertainty and a major learning task. There is the possibility, however, that product class concept learning is less difficult than we might think, because the seller's advertising, for example, is less competitive. It can then identify more effectively with the buyer's interest than when it is competitive. As R. Brown (1958) has pointed out, we learn from childhood to be skilled analysts of persuasion and thus quickly detect the persuasive elements of a competitive advertisement. With advertisements advocating new class concepts perhaps "our guard is down," so that we are receptive.

Another central determinant of whether an innovation is tried is the buyer's state of attention. Unless the information is accepted into his receptors, there is no possibility of trial, irrespective of the persuasive power of the message. Attention is but a special aspect of the problem of search; a number of mechanisms underlying search effort were set forth in this chapter.

Still another central determinant of trial is the richness or barrenness of the buyer's informational environment. The three sources of information—other people (except for salesmen), commercial, and neutral—their respective influence processes, and their consequent effect on the output intervening variables were discussed. The salesman was dealt with as a special case.

The equilibrium concept is a useful way to think about the innovating process. First, some event creates a need, motivational disequilibrium occurs, a brand is purchased, and equilibrium is restored. Second, this temporary motivational equilibrating process takes place within a more comprehensive process. Let us assume the new brand is a major innovation and so the buyer is in Extensive Problem Solving in which with open receptors he searches for information about such things as the quality of the brand and the motives that are socially appropriate. As he receives information and tries the brand, Product Class Comprehension, Brand Comprehension, Attitude, Confidence, and Intention form. He tries the brand. Provided that it is found to meet his needs, he repeats the purchase, becomes loyal, and closes out further information: the psychology of simplification is operative.

With time a second new brand enters the industry, and his attention is accidentally called to it or, the psychology of complication, the loyalty-disloyalty cycle growing out of boredom or rising aspiration level is the source of change. Now he is in Limited Problem Solving. He searches for information on the quality of the brand, and perhaps tries it. If he finds it to be superior, he will repeat the purchase and so move toward Routinized Response Behavior, a state that will continue until a change in his environment obtrudes on him or the loyalty-disloyalty cycle triggers change. It will continue because he closes out information. He is in information-purchase equilibrium.

Also, interpersonal differences exist among the buyers and shape their individual behaviors according to differences in the exogenous or market-segmenting variables.

Finally, all of the description of the process by which innovation is accepted into a population has been at the verbal level in this chapter. Obviously, a more rigorous way of describing this diffusion process is highly desirable. Not a lot has been done in developing the techniques appropriate to our kinds of problems. Nearly all of the models of social diffusion assume a completely intermixed population, by which is meant the case where one person is just as likely to interact with any other person in the population. In our situations, a buyer is much more likely to interact with someone like himself than with someone who is different, such as with respect to social class. Even for this case, there are some promising directions of development, however (Coleman, 1964). A number of models have been developed specifically for the prediction of product innovation; for example, see Bass (1969).

CHAPTER 9

Symbolic Communication

In this chapter, we continue to put the theory of buyer behavior to work. Here the task is to describe and explain existing empirical research and to generate new hypotheses for future investigation in the area of mass communication—more generally, in the area of symbolic communication.

Our aim in this chapter is manifold: (1) Show the role that symbolic communication (mass media and word-of-mouth) plays in enabling the buyer to make brand choice decisions. (2) Explain a large body of empirical research with the help of some of the hypothetical constructs of the theory. (3) Provide implications for both public policy and company practice and research in the area of mass communication, that is, serve the generative function of the theory. (4) Systematically integrate independent empirical research in several disciplines and present several insights. The latter include (*a*) putting communications research in an S-O-R paradigm, (*b*) integrating functional approach to attitude with Kelman's classification of source characteristics, (*c*) explicitly bringing in advertising research in mass communication literature, and (*d*) a more systematic use of Osgood's representational mediation process and other learning principles.

In a sense Chapter 9 is further elaboration of ideas presented in Chapter 8. However, it exclusively focuses attention on Symbolic Communication and carries it to much greater detail. At the same time, this chapter does not retain the elaborate typology of innovations developed in Chapter 8 but simplifies by treating all types of innovations together.

The chapter begins by contrasting significative and symbolic communication. Section 9.2 presents a paradigm that puts together mass communication research and advertising. Then both are brought closer to buying behavior by taking the introspective perspective of the buyer. Essentially, we state that activation or change in any of the variables in Response Sequence depends on (1) buyer's internal state (classified into the Attention, Attitude, and Intention constructs) and (2) a series of factors of mass communication such as source, channel, and massage.

Section 9.3 discusses the influence of source of communication on buying behavior, including the relative importance of the power, attractiveness, and credibility of a source in symbolic communication.

Channel characteristics, such as the capacity for one-way or two-way communication, and many of the mass media attributes, such as layout, color, illustration, and audio and video facilities, are described in terms of their effect on buying behavior in Section 9.4.

In Section 9.5, we discuss the message factor in terms of two broad classifications: content and structure. Content includes discussion of rational versus emotional appeals, fear-arousing appeals, and presentation of the brand as a goal-object. Under structure we discuss the relative merits of one-sided versus two-sided messages, climax versus anticlimax presentation, and similar topics.

Section 9.6 concludes the chapter with a summary diagram of all the variables that we think are useful in understanding the effect of symbolic communication on buying behavior. In addition, the ways in which the hypothetical constructs can be useful in measuring advertising effectiveness are enumerated for further research.

9.1 SIGNIFICATIVE VERSUS SYMBOLIC COMMUNICATION

A buyer is informed of the existence, availability, or usefulness of a brand either by the physical product itself or in symbolic ways such as advertising, personal selling, and promotion. There are, however, several important differences between these two major channels, which become relevant in their comparative effectiveness of communication.

First, Symbolic Communication only approximates the physical brand in representing reality to the buyer. It underrepresents attributes of the brand to the extent that it can communicate via only two sensory channels—hearing and vision.* In product categories where the buyer relies on touch, smell, or taste, Symbolic Communication is limited in its capacity to represent the brand. For instance, direct observation and tactile manipulation seems so important in buying meats, fruits, and fresh vegetables that these industries even abstain from adopting many packaging innovations so as not to interfere with such observations or manipulation. In industrial buying, vision and touch are extremely important. The buyer wants to physically see the product, observe its operating and functional characteristics, and more often than not manipulate the product before making a purchase decision, especially when buying major capital expenditure items. This compels the seller in an industry such as machine tools to render complete service, including the erection and installation of, for example, a complicated lathe or drilling machine, as well as teaching the machinists to operate it. In short, the limitations of Symbolic Communication are anchored to the representational mediation process discussed in Chapter 4 in which signs elicit only fraction (R_X) of total behavior (R_T).

Symbolic Communication, however, can also overrepresent the physical brand. This arises when advertisements make exaggerated claims, using words, phrases, and pictorial representations that imply qualities superior to those that the brand actually possesses. Such overrepresentation produces disparity, at times quite large, between the buyer's expectation and reality, which probably results in dissatisfaction, frustration, and disillusionment with the brand.

Second, Significative Communication, to a large extent, provides comparative evaluation to the buyer. The retail outlet contiguously stocks several brands of a product class from which the buyer can choose. Symbolic Communication is lacking in such contiguity, particularly in radio and television media. This means that an additional burden is placed on the buyer to mentally store, classify, and retrieve information in order to compare the various brands.

Finally, Symbolic Communication inherits the problems of semantics. Language is an integral part of mass communication and word-of-mouth. However, owing to the multiordinality of meanings of words and phrases (language is itself an abstraction process, one of labeling), greater ambiguity and individual differences among receivers persist in Symbolic

* To a very limited extent, it is possible to utilize one or more of the other senses even in mass communication. Examples are perfumed advertisements in newspapers, the advertisement space giving out discriminable scent, and, recently, the attachment of a Handi-Wipe paper towel to the newspaper, so that the buyer can get a free sample and use it. However, for a majority of cases, symbolic communication involves only two senses, and often only one.

Communication. Consequently, the encoding on the part of the communicators and the decoding on the part of the buyers are not always matched: communication misfires, so to speak. The problem is severe enough to warrant pretesting procedures in advertising (Lucas and Britt, 1950, 1963; Reeves, 1961; Schwerin, 1955).

In short, we see that symbolic communication is more complex and ambiguous than significative communication, hence also more difficult to understand (describe and explain). In the remainder of this chapter, therefore, we attempt to simplify and comprehend the many complicated influences that Symbolic Communication exerts on buying behavior.

9.2 A PARADIGM OF SYMBOLIC COMMUNICATION

Empirical research in mass communication is extensive enough for us to attempt to combine it in a paradigm. The pioneering research by Hovland (1954, 1957, 1959), Hovland, Lumsdaine, and Sheffield (1949), Hovland, Janis, and Kelly (1953), Hovland and Rosenberg (1960), Lasswell (1948), Lasswell and Kaplan (1950), Lazarsfeld and Kendall (1948), Lazarsfeld (1954), E. Katz and Lazarsfeld (1955), and Lewin (1951, 1958) has diffused sufficiently so that today a vast literature exists on mass communication. However, any attempt to pull together diverse findings and viewpoints is beset with problems of reconciling methodological and substantive issues. When we wish to integrate them in order to show implications for buyer behavior, and bring in the research on advertising, this task becomes particularly difficult.

Methodologically, mass communication research followed two distinct patterns: experimental and survey (Hovland, 1959). The general agreements reached by these two methods differ somewhat. The experimental approach of Hovland has led to the conclusion that mass communication produces significant attitude change, whereas the results of the survey method admit only limited effect. Hovland (1959) attempted to reconcile the findings by arguing that individual differences (subject is a student, hence more receptive and involved in the experiments, and the experimenter is either his teacher or his confederate, which motivates attention to and reception of messages) and situational differences (greater trust in experiment, forced reception of messages, more salient and ego-involved issues in experimental approach, etc.) are responsible for the discrepancies in the conclusions.

Another problem is the almost exclusive attention to attitude change as the dependent variable. In buying behavior, what ultimately is important to the marketing manager is sales, even though he feels that other intermediate effects such as comprehension of the brand, its positive evaluation, and behavioral intentions toward it may all be relevant effects of mass communication. This is because they do contribute toward buying at some later stage. In short, in buying behavior as well as in research on advertising effectiveness, we are concerned with the complete sequence of responses (Attention' → Brand Comprehension' → Attitude' → Intention' → Purchase), not just attitude change.

A related problem is the fact that mass communication research in general has not studied the effects of such variables as size, shape, color, and illustration of the message. On the other hand, these are important considerations in advertising and buying behavior. In Chapter 3, it was pointed out that the best way to handle a complex phenomenon such as buyer behavior is to conceptualize a complex and adequate theory. Treating several influences as random errors, instead of incorporating them in the research design, has proved to be of limited usefulness in the past. A clear example of this occurs in the area of market segmentation where focus has been narrowly put on the socioeconomic or personality variables. Hence here we include several additional response variables, other than attitude formation and change, as well as additional dimensions of Stimulus Display.

9.2.1 Description of the Paradigm

Despite problems in integrating mass communication research and advertising research in terms of buyer behavior, it would appear that we can develop a simplified integrative framework using the S-O-R paradigm common to psychology.* For example, R is considered to be a response vector consisting of a number of buyer's responses as described above. The S is a stimulus vector consisting of a number of factors integral to Symbolic Communication. Finally, O is an organism vector consisting of a number of constructs that classify the buyer's internal state at the time of receiving a communication. Indeed, we feel that by borrowing the S-O-R paradigm, we are able to emphasize the neglect of explicit hypothetical constructs in mass communication research.

Lasswell (1948) has presented an interrogative formulation which has wide currency: *who* says *what*, to *whom, how*, with *what effect?*

---

* Strictly speaking, there are some R-R relationships that are implied in further discussion in the chapter. For example, we talk about feedback from Attitude' to Attention' in the Response Sequence. Since these feedbacks are manifestations of more fundamental feedbacks among the hypothetical constructs (Attitude and Attention), they can be looked upon as certain O-O relationships. However, the major thrust of the chapter is to explain the effects of stimuli from Symbolic Communication, hence there is more concern with S-O-R relationships.

These, according to Lasswell, are the five factors important in understanding symbolic communication.

1. *Who* refers to the *source* of communication. Many characteristics of the source have been extensively studied as having a differential effect on the attitude change of the recipient of a communication. The reader will recall from Part II that there may be perceptual distortions of the information because of the source of communication. Generally, sources to which greater *credibility* is ascribed because of their competence and trustworthiness, have been found to be more effective for an identical message of communication than those with lower credibility in terms of opinion change, at least in the short run. Similarly, other attributes of the source such as *power* and *likability* have been studied. In buying behavior, source becomes important in personal selling as well as in understanding the importance of brand and corporate imagery.

2. *What* refers to the *message* of the communication. Variables studied as a part of this factor have been broadly classified into (*a*) content variables, such as types of appeals (e.g., rational versus emotional appeals), inclusion or omission of a material, and amount of attitude change advocated, and (*b*) structural variables, such as amount of material and order of presentation. Empirical research has been directed to answer such questions as which appeals—emotional or rational—are more effective in attitude change and whether drawing a conclusion in the message is better than leaving the message open-ended. Messages become relevant in buying behavior to the extent that information contained in them creates or changes comprehension as well as evaluation of the brands.

3. *How* takes into account the *channels* or *media* through which the communicator sends the message. A channel can be personal or impersonal; it can also be commercial or noncommercial. Commercial impersonal channels are various forms of mass media such as newspapers, magazines, radio, television, billboards, and direct mail. Commercial personal channels are salesmen, product demonstrators, sales clerks, detailmen, and so on. Noncommercial personal sources include friends, family, and other reference groups of the buyer. They also include some neutral sources such as experts. Finally, noncommercial impersonal sources are a number of neutral sources such as *Consumer Reports, Consumer Magazine, Good Housekeeping,* and *Parents Magazine.* Several government agencies also act as noncommercial impersonal sources. Each channel has certain advantages in terms of the buyer's receptivity of information. We shall elaborate these later.

These three factors—source, channel, and message—generate stimuli (S) in the S-O-R paradigm.

4. *To whom* refers to the *recipient* of the communication, in our case, the buyer. Most of the endogenous variables of the buyer behavior theory are relevant here. In particular, the hypothetical constructs of Attention, Perceptual Bias, and Stimulus Ambiguity become critical in the discussion of symbolic communication as a source of learning. As mentioned earlier, communications research has generally neglected this factor. The only variables recently studied are personality variables such as self-esteem and self-confidence (Janis, 1954, 1955, 1958; Janis and Field 1959). In Chapter 3, we included these personality variables in the category of exogenous variables because we do not explain changes in them. Later in this section, we isolate some of the constructs of the theory of buyer behavior and use them to define the state of organism (O) to the extent that they seem relevant in understanding symbolic communication.

5. *With what effect* refers to the destination or the dependent factor. What did the communication attempt and how well did it suceed? Destination is the dependent factor, and the previous four factors are the independent factors.* We here replace the attitude change as the dependent factor with the buyer's Response Sequence (Attention' → Brand Comprehension' → Attitude' → Intention' → Purchase).

Figure 9.1 puts Lasswell's interrogative formulation in the S-O-R framework. Later we elaborate on each of the three independent factors constituting S and, in addition, bring into focus O and R.

Strictly speaking, the three independent stimulus factors are not simultaneous. At least, it would appear that *how* (channel) is sequential to *who* and *what*. However, we treat all three as simultaneous combinations that represent various factors underlying a communication.

---

* We have consistently labeled the five components of communication as factors because each component has a number of specific variables. For example, source has at least the three broad variables of credibility, power, and attractiveness, each of which could have still further more specific variables.

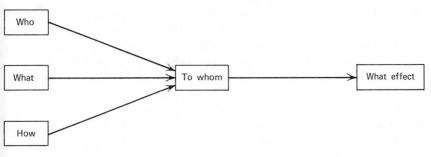

Figure 9.1 An S-O-R paradigm of communication.

9.2.2   Hypothetical Constructs

We now wish to define the buyer's internal state using some of the hypothetical constructs of the theory that we consider to be important in symbolic communication. Strictly speaking, most of the hypothetical constructs seem relevant in understanding symbolic communication and its effect on buying behavior. However, we believe that the rule of parsimony can be applied here and thus limit ourselves to using only the most important constructs. Such constructs are Attention, Attitude, and Intention. The reader can, however, relate other hypothetical constructs to the process of Symbolic Communication for specific investigations or for further developing the theory.

Attention refers to the buyer's sensitivity to incoming information. To the extent that we are looking at the effect that a *given* communication has on the buyer's responses, what seems more important are the perceptual processes by which he selectively takes in information rather than his active seeking of information. This does not mean that Overt Search is not important in buying behavior. Attention includes a number of aspects. (1) The ambiguity-arousal relation is important, which leads us to state that the buyer will be sensitive to information (pay attention) only when the communication is at the moderate level of ambiguity; too great an ambiguity will result in ignoring the communication, just as will too little ambiguity. (2) The feedback from Attitude, either favorable or unfavorable, must also be included. The buyer will pay attention to a commercial message if it comes from a reputable firm but will ignore it if it comes from an untrustworthy firm or individual. (3) As one aspect of Overt Search, the buyer may be generally "tuned up" to receive any information, hence to pay attention. For example, the buyer may be looking for a used automobile. He will then be generally sensitive to classified advertisements in all newspapers that he reads because he needs the product and believes from his experience that he is very likely to encounter used-car advertisements.

Attention determines the buyer's selective exposure and paying attention to Symbolic Communication. A number of source, channels, and message characteristics are capable of discriminately raising or lowering buyer's sensitivity to information because each of them arouses a certain amount of motivation force. This is important to isolate, because paying attention is a necessary condition to some response on the part of the buyer.

Attitude is another important construct. It refers to the affect associated with the brand and other objects based on the buyer's evaluative beliefs, which is one of the antecedents to acquiring the brand.

Attitude serves the following functions in determining the effectiveness of Symbolic Communication. (1) Attitude is a major explanatory construct for purchase. Whether or not a Symbolic Communication will become a stimulus to precipitate buying will to a large extent depend on the level of buyer's Attitude. For example, impulse buying arises because the buyer is favorably predisposed to buy an item in the store when he either hears on the intercom or reads in a display that it is a "good buy." (2) Attitude is created and changed (as opposed to aroused in the example above) by Symbolic Communication as a process of learning. According to learning principles, change in Attitude may be high in the early stages when its strength is low (much has to be learned), but as more and more is learned (Attitude is well established), Symbolic Communication may be less effective in bringing further change. These relations have implications in measurement of Attitude' change over time, as was explained in Chapter 6. (3) Attitude governs both selective attention and retention of information. We take into account sensitivity to information (paying attention) because of favorable Attitude in the previous construct (Attention), but qualitative distortion in the meaning of information once received (Perceptual Bias) is taken into account here. In other words, Attitude will determine perceptual distortion of Symbolic Communication, hence its effect on buying behavior.

Finally, we add a third construct—Intention. It refers to the behavioral intention of the buyer to purchase a particular brand in the near future. Intention brings together many of the contingencies that the buyer takes into account in buying decisions. In particular, we feel that inclusion of many of the inhibitory barriers increases our explanation of buying behavior.

Intention is important in symbolic communication in several ways. (1) A large amount of substantive research on advertising effectiveness has shown that advertising may bring about attitude change, but that to expect sales to result from this change is much too big a jump (Palda, 1966; Sheth, 1969b). We believe, therefore, that there is much greater inertia between attitude and buying, which could be explained by Intention. (2) Mass communication is intended to create positive affect toward a brand, but there are a number of latent aspects in a communication that potently become inhibitors from the buyer's point of view. For example, inclusion of price in an advertisement may result in inhibitory tendency in a buyer who cannot afford the brand at that price. Similarly, past exaggerations in advertisements have created enough mistrust to result in inhibitions for future purchases. (3) The opposite is equally possible. Mass communication attempts, sometimes, to remove some of the inhibitions that barricade favorable Attitude from manifesting itself in purchase. This is particularly true of availability, temporary financial problems, and similar factors.

In summary, we have taken the three hypothetical constructs that seem relevant to the understanding of the effectiveness of mass communication. We believe that, as a rule of parsimony, this is a better approach for proper communication to the reader.

9.2.3 Response Sequence*

Response Sequence (Attention' → Brand Comprehension' → Attitude' → Intention' → Purchase) becomes more important in symbolic communication, particularly in measuring advertising effectiveness. In the past, several attempts have been made to get at the multiple effects of advertising (Lavidge and Steiner, 1961; Palda, 1966; Sheth, 1969b). Even the marketing practitioners firmly believe that advertising effectiveness should be measured on multiple dimensions such as awareness, recall, recognition, attitude, and purchase (Adler, Greenberg, and Lucas, 1965).

In comparing Response Sequence with most of the common multiple measures of advertising effectiveness, a number of distinctions should be emphasized. First, Attention' is almost unique to our Response Sequence. Others have used awareness as a measure, which we think is really a part of Brand Comprehension', along with other measures of knowledge such as recall and recognition. Second, we have Intentions' as an added intermediate step between Attitude' and Purchase. The poor relation empirically shown between attitude and behavior in advertising effectiveness (Palda, 1966) is most probably due to ignoring the inhibitory influences that intervene between favorable opinion and overt behavior. By measuring them through Intention', we probably are linking attitude and behavior on a firmer ground. Third, most of the variables in Response Sequence are uniquely defined to some extent, although there is overlap with similar definitions given by other researchers. These definitions were given in Chapter 3 and are not repeated here.

In symbolic communication, Response Sequence also becomes useful because some factors of mass communication have unique effects on only some of the variables in the hierarchy. For example, most of the

---

* The feedback effects explicitly drawn among variables in Response Sequence are, in fact, simply manifestations of more fundamental and appropriate feedbacks among the hypothetical constructs. The latter were elaborated in Chapter 3, and the underlying theory was presented in Chapters 4 and 5. In this chapter, we show these feedbacks in Response Sequence because much of advertising research is concerned with measurement of effectiveness, and similar paradigms are given, as discussed further in this subsection.

variables related to channel capacity (layout, illustrations, etc.) are primarily relevant for arousing or changing Attention' or Brand Comprehension'. We elaborate on these unique effects later in the chapter when discussing each of the stimulus factors (source, channel, and message).

9.3   SOURCE OF COMMUNICATION

Empirically, the role that the communicator plays in determining the effectiveness of a communication has been extensively studied (McGuire, 1968b). However, in the process of identifying those characteristics of the communicator that seem to have differential effectiveness, research has been inconclusive at best. Researchers have, in general, isolated such aspects as credibility, power, prestige, likability, and dynamism of the communicator (Bauer, 1965a).

9.3.1   Kelman's Classification of Source Attributes

Perhaps the best analysis of source effect is that of Kelman (1958, 1961; Kelman and Eagly 1965). As we saw in Chapter 8, Kelman classifies three separate types of influences that the source exerts: compliance, identification, and internalization on the buyer's part if source possesses the power, attractiveness, and credibility characteristics, respectively. In Symbolic Communication, we are primarily concerned with mass media effects although, it also includes both personal selling and word-of-mouth communication. Most of Kelman's analysis, although restricted to personal communication (and that too only experimentally), seems to be relevant for all symbolic communications including advertising. The relevance can be seen by hypothesizing the effects of each of the source's attributes on the Response Sequence via the hypothetical constructs.

Compliance occurs when the buyer accepts the influence of the communicator because he hopes to induce a favorable reaction from the communicator. By complying, he does what the source wants him to do because he sees this as a way of achieving a desired response from the source. He does not necessarily believe in the message, however. Kelman suggests that compliance will occur in all situations where the buyer perceives potential power in the source in controlling rewards and punishments.

It is easy to envision such powers vested in salesmen, because of the reciprocity relationship agreed upon by the buying and the selling firms (J. Howard and Moore, 1963; Strauss, 1962). Similarly, the housewife, because of the authority role, obtains compliance from children and young adults (Coulson, 1966). Although it is unlikely that a company possesses such power over its buyers, there are numerous situations in buying of services (plumber, doctor, barber, etc.) in which the buyer seems to comply because of powerful role that the seller possesses.

It would appear that, in general, where the buyer has high perceived risk (Bauer, 1960; Cox, 1967) because he lacks competence to evaluate alternatives or is ignorant, he is likely to comply on the ground that he finds the seller in a powerful position. As a derivative, we can then state that in a seller's economy (most of the developing countries), power is likely to be an important source attribute vested in the selling company.

Obviously, power is influential in producing overt Purchase because by imposing external criteria in the buying situation, power will create behavioral intention that may be contrary to buyer's Attitude. Finally, it is necessary that the buyer pay attention to the message in order for him to react. However, he need not acquire any knowledge related to the buying situation (Brand or Product Class Comprehension), nor is it necessary that he change his Attitude or even arouse favorable Attitude prior to manifesting Purchase. In summary, through compliance, power will evoke buyer's Attention, Intention, and Purchase. This will be accordingly manifested in the Response Sequence, on Attention', Intention', and Purchase. It is possible, however, that in a repetitive compliance situation, the buyer may adjust his Attitude via the feedback effect. In other words, in the long run, persistence of compliance and the resultant behavior may also produce change in buyer's Attitude.

The behavioral effects of power through compliance measured in Attention', Intention', and Purchase can be analyzed using the hypothetical constructs of Attention and Intention. In any symbolic communication, as soon as the buyer perceives the power position of the seller, his motivation will be aroused because of his attitude toward the *source* learned from past experiences. The buyer may also generalize his compliance behavior from the source to any representation of the source such as the salesman, the direct mail, or the advertisement. Arousal of motivation produces Attention. Furthermore, motivation is strong enough to alleviate any perceptual distortions of the message itself. Because the motivation aroused is not necessarily relevant to making the best choice among the alternatives, the message will not affect Attitude toward a brand. Furthermore, motivation to comply is strong enough to result in Intention, which then manifests in Purchase.

Of course, what we have described is likely to occur only when power in the source is high. At lesser degrees of power, compliance may arouse some behavior in the Response Sequence and not others. For example, in the industrial buying situation, the reciprocity principle may be only loosely followed by the selling company. Then the purchasing agent may allow the salesman to pay him visits and may listen attentively to his sales pitch, but may not manifest either Intention' or Purchase.

Identification occurs when the buyer accepts the communication because there is a role relationship with the source that forms a part of the buyer's self-image. Identification is then a way of establishing or maintaining a desired relationship with the source, and self-definition is anchored in this relation. Kelman suggests that *attractiveness* of the source to the buyer in terms of the role the buyer wishes to play or a role reciprocal to the one he desires will be responsible for manifestation of identification-type responses.

It is easy to envision situations in buying behavior where attractiveness of the source creates identification. For example, identification is common in most conspicuous consumption when Symbolic Communication comes from a number of buyer's reference groups (Bourne, 1963; E. Katz and Lazarsfeld, 1955; E. Katz, 1957). In fact, Purchase is manifested as an identification-type response not only in terms of buying or not buying a product class, but also in terms of which brand or type of product to buy. In industrial buying, identification with the salesman is not uncommon (J. Howard and Moore, 1963). Finally, conspicuous consumption (expressive behavior) seems to have enabled companies to differentiate brands and inject them with actual or perceived quality differences so that there are a number of brands that have become status symbols or stereotypes with which to identify and which serve the expressive function. Examples are too numerous to describe here. In advertising, identification is common in instances where the person communicating is a well-known personality such as a baseball or football player or a show business entity.

Identification as a process is important in understanding source influence on Response Sequence. First, it will create behavioral intention in the buyer (Intention'). Second, the buyer will pay attention to the message (Attention'). In addition, the buyer may force himself to learn Brand Comprehension'. He is likely to manifest strong evaluative judgments toward the brand (Attitude') that he finds attractive because it is identified with some person. In short, it would appear that identification will produce all of the behaviors in Response Sequence.

However, there are two exceptions. First, Brand Comprehension' and Attitude', although strongly positive, are not likely to be so durable.

They could be changed easily by any change in the attractiveness of the source either because the source has deteriorated or because a new source is found to be even more attractive. Second, the buyer may show Intention' but not manifest it in Purchase. Purchase would require a monetary commitment on the part of the buyer, which may be too great a sacrifice. This is not likely to be revealed in buyer's Intention because he may not admit it. Admittance may suggest that he is aspiring to a group that is beyond his reach: he is daydreaming. In fact, we believe that in all cases of identification-produced buyer responses, marketing research may break down in obtaining a true picture (as opposed to exaggerated picture) unless some indirect methods such as projective techniques (Anderson and Anderson, 1951; Ferber and Wales, 1958) are used. This would be true for both positive identification with some products and brands and avoidance of others, both arising because of attractiveness of the source.

It is easy to hypothesize how attractiveness as an attribute in the source of communication produces some of the buyer responses by analyzing the changes it brings in the hypothetical constructs. When attractiveness is anchored more to the communicator (salesman, friend, show business personality, etc.) than to the brand per se, motivation that is aroused is again irrelevant to buying decision. However, it is strong and powerful enough for the buyer to open his receptors, hence to pay Attention. This is brought about by the feedback from positive attitude toward the source. The same positive attitude also causes Perceptual Bias to enhance whatever message the source is communicating. To that extent, there is a positive bias (from the company's point of view) in the manipulation of information. Brand Comprehension is learned to a considerable extent. Furthermore, the buyer is likely to adopt many of the evaluative judgments proposed by the source partly because he perceives the brand as an object of expressive behavior, which will result in positive Attitude.

In the event that attractiveness is anchored to the brand or the company itself (Mercedes-Benz is an ideal car, Proctor and Gamble is a progressive company, etc.), the motivation aroused is likely to be specific to the product class. In such cases, Attitude will be even more durable than when source's attractiveness does not emanate from the brand or the company.

When compared to influence of power characteristic, attractiveness produces more durable changes, particularly when attractiveness is derived from the brand or the company.

Internalization occurs when the buyer accepts the influencing message because it is congruent with his value system. The buyer adopts the suggested point of view because he finds it useful in the solution of a problem, because it is congenial to his own orientation, or because his own values demand it. Kelman suggests that if the source possesses credibility as an attribute, it is likely to start the internalization process. Credibility, in general, refers to two components, namely trust and competence (Hovland, Janis, and Kelley, 1953; Kelman, 1958; Hovland and Weiss, 1951; Kelman and Hovland, 1953; McGuire, 1968b). Trust relates to the source's motivation in communicating about the issue, that is, to his objectivity. It is this aspect of source that is mostly responsible for the low influence of mass media when compared to personal sources in many survey studies on mass communication and diffusion of innovations. Competence refers to the expertise, knowledge, ability, or technical understanding of an issue by the source. Using the cognition-affect-conation paradigm, it is possible to state that credibility consists of two elements—a cognitive element that reflects the source's competence and prestige and an affect element that reflects its trust and likability (Rarick, 1963).

Unlike power and attractiveness, credibility of the source is likely to be topic-bound; for example, a source may be credible only on some issue or object, not on all. The housewife may be perceived as a credible source in matters related to purchase of groceries, but not to purchase of an automobile, if our research on male-dominated buying of the latter product is at all valid (Wolgast, 1958). Differential credibility of the same individual for different occasions is definitely a function of his competence rather than trust.

In Symbolic Communication, credibility perhaps is the most important attribute of source. In fact, it is the lack of credibility (particularly trust) in advertising that has raised numerous problems for advertising agencies, which have to exert much effort to even catch the attention of the viewers, readers, or listeners. The buyer ignores advertisements because he feels that the advertiser has an ax to grind and that whatever he says is not truthful. In a recent survey by Media/Scope, for example, it was estimated that out of the 15,000 messages to which a housewife is exposed in a day of television watching, she is not even aware of more than 75 per cent of them being at all broadcast. The problem is further aggravated by the large number of advertisements. On the other hand, it is credibility (particularly trustworthiness) that seems extremely important in the powerful word-of-mouth communication (Arndt, 1967a). The buyer thinks that communication about a brand coming from friends or even neutral sources is likely to be not biased against his own value system or his welfare. He thinks that commercial sources (advertising, salesmen, display, etc.) have their own motives which are generally opposite to those in his value system or contributing to his welfare. In fact, it is this questionable objective of the companies that can explain the ambivalent feelings of the buyer toward advertising in general: he needs it as a source of information, but he also complains about it as being untruthful, exaggerated, too frequent, and an imposition on his leisure time.

Credibility of the source is likely to affect several variables in the buyer's Response Sequence. It will arouse the buyer's Attention', will enhance his Brand Comprehension', and will change his Attitude'. It will, however, have limited influence on Intention' and Purchase because a number of inhibitory forces may not allow the buyer to manifest Intention' or Purchase. Even in the case of Intention', it is not likely to be so high as that created by either power or attractiveness. On the other hand, because the buyer internalizes the message, both Brand Comprehension' and Attitude' changes are likely to be more durable than in the case of either power or attractiveness.

Credibility of the source is hypothesized to have the influences just discussed on the Response Sequence because of its effects on the hypothetical constructs of the theory of buyer behavior. The buyer is likely to pay more attention to the message because of the feedback from positive attitude toward the source. Furthermore, the information will not be perceptually distorted because the buyer *relies* on credible sources for information (Bauer, 1960; Cox, 1963, 1967). Indeed, we suspect that in the case of personal informal sources such as friends and family, the buyer relegates the perceptual processes to the source of information, and he himself takes the information at face value. Information coming from a credible source will then change Brand Comprehension as well as Attitude in a positive manner. It is also very likely that information will influence buyer's Choice Criteria as well, inasmuch as it is related to a product class and it is better served to a particular brand.

However, unlike the power and attractiveness attributes which supersede buyer's own Attitude toward a brand, credibility tends, by the process of internalization, to bring about change in existing Brand Comprehension and Attitude. Hence it is likely that the behavioral manifestation will be determined by the *interaction* between source credibility and buyer's existing Brand Comprehension as well as Attitude at the time of communication. Then given a combination of buyer's own Attitude toward the brand, the source's extent of credibility and the particular position that message advocates, numerous combinations exist, each determining a set of slightly different responses on the part of the buyer.

To simplify, we present, in Table 9.1, a classificatory interaction of the three variables. The buyer is assumed to have favorable, neutral, or unfavorable Attitude toward a brand prior to receiving a message, the source is credible, neutral, or not credible, and the message contains elements either favoring the brand or condemning the brand. It is highly unlikely that a company will condemn its own brand in any advertisement. To this extent the unfavorable (con) position of the message is less relevant in mass commercial communication. However, this is quite likely to occur in other symbolic communications such as through friends and relatives (credible sources) or even strangers (neutral source) and publications like *Consumers Reports* (either credible or neutral source). Furthermore, it is becoming more and more popular to advertise the weak points of the brand along with the strong points in what amounts to two-sided message, or, more popularly, negative advertising. Finally, a number of competing products attempt to bring out weaker aspects of competition in the message. In short, there are several situations where unfavorable position is likely to be advocated in Symbolic Communication.

A total of 18 combinations are presented in Table 9.1. Each cell hypothesizes three separate reactions on the part of the buyer: (1) change in Brand Comprehension, (2) change in Attitude, and (3) change in source's credibility. A change in source's credibility is important to understand because, over a period of time, it may make the source more or less credible. This is what seems to have happened in advertising where the buyer generally discounts some of the claims and at times, even, ignores an advertisement.

Most of the cells are self-explanatory. Rather than discuss them, it is better to describe a good experiment about the influence of source credibility on opinion change, which provides some data on 8 of the 18 cells. Hovland and Weiss (1951), in a classic experiment, took four topics (antihistamines, atomic submarines, steel shortage, and future of movies) and created two kinds of communications, one presenting the "affirmative" and the other the "negative" position on the issue. Essentially the same material was used for both "pro" and "con" positions, and an equal number of facts were incorporated in them. Furthermore, two kinds of sources were given as the authors of the messages, one with high credibility (e.g., Robert Oppenheimer on the subject of atomic submarines) and the other with low credibility (e.g., *Pravda* on the subject of atomic submarines). Thus there were two types of credibility—high and low—and two types of positions—pro and con—in the experiment. Finally, there were two types of subjects—those who were initially in agreement with a message and those who were initially in

Table 9.1 Credibility of Source and the Resultant Change in Brand Comprehension and Attitude

Source Credibility	Message Content Is	Buyer's Attitude toward the Brand Prior to Receiving Message		
		Favorable	Neutral	Unfavorable
Credible	Favorable	Good comprehension. Strengthen attitude. Enhance source credibility.	Good comprehension Strengthen favorable attitude.	Low comprehension. Distort source credibility or change attitude
	Unfavorable	Low comprehension. Distort credibility or change attitude.	Good comprehension. Strengthen unfavorable attitude.	Good comprehension. Strengthen unfavorable attitude. Enhance source credibility.
Neutral	Favorable	Comprehension depends on message. Strengthen favorable attitude.	Comprehension depends on message. Strengthen favorable attitude.	Low comprehension. Distort source credibility strongly.
	Unfavorable	Low comprehension. Distort source credibility.	Comprehension depends on message. Strengthen unfavorable attitude.	Good comprehension. Enhance source credibility. Strengthen unfavorable attitude.
Not credible	Favorable	Low comprehension or will depend on message. Enhance source credibility.	Low comprehension or will depend on message. Remain neutral.	Low comprehension. Distort source further.
	Unfavorable	Low comprehension. Distort source credibility.	Low comprehension or will depend upon message. Remain neutral.	Low comprehension or will depend on message. Enhance source credibility.

disagreement with it. This provides 8 possible combinations in terms of Table 9.1.

On the average, high-credibility sources were considered to be more fair in their presentations and their conclusions to be more justified by the facts than the low-credibility sources. However, initial agreement or disagreement qualified this finding. Those in agreement in both the high- and low-credibility groups tended to evaluate sources as more "fair" and "justified" than those who disagreed.

Regarding comprehension of the topics, as measured by the number of items correct on the information quiz given subsequent to the communication, there were no significant differences between high- and low-credibility sources. This would contradict the hypotheses laid down in Table 9.1, although measurement of comprehension is not the same in our theory and their experiment. Also, it is unfortunate that data are not further broken down according to the initial positions of the respondents as in the previous finding, because the insignificant differences could be due to aggregation of opposing tendencies.

Finally, subjects changed their initial opinion in the direction advocated by the communicator in a significantly greater number of cases when the material was attributed to a high-credibility source than when attributed to a low-credibility source. For example, on the average, 23 per cent of the subjects in the high-credibility group, as compared to only 6.6 per cent in the low-credibility group, changed their opinion in the direction of the communication. This finding would also support the hypotheses in Table 9.1 about attitude or opinion change. It is again unfortunate that data are not further broken down by the initial position of the subjects, that is, according to whether they agreed or disagreed with the position advocated.

However, a curious phenomenon has been observed in empirical investigations. The enhancing effects of high-credibility sources and the depressing effects of low-credibility sources on opinion change are only short-lived and disappear with time. In other words, the credibility of the source is inversely related to *retention* of attitude change. This phenomenon has been called the "sleeper effect" (Hovland, Lumsdaine, and Sheffield, 1949; Hovland and Weiss, 1951) and is illustrated in Figure 9.2.

What seems to happen is that the person may not forget the source, but fails to associate it with the message after a lapse of time. Then, if the credibility of the source is *reinstated* after a period of time, the effect is to create a greater attitude change by a highly credible source and less change by the less credible source. Kelman and Hovland (1953) have found that *recall* of information as the measure of retention of

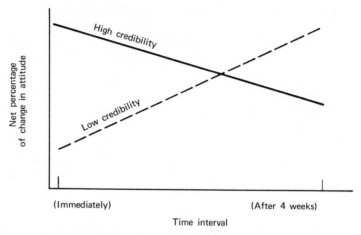

Figure 9.2   The sleeper effect.

attitude is significantly better when the communication comes from a *neutral* source than when it comes from either a positive or a negative source.

9.3.2 Source and the Functional Approach to Attitude Change

In Chapter 8, we also described Bauer's (1965a) classification of the buyer's mental processes into two types of game playing: (1) psychosocial game playing and (2) problem-solving game playing. It would appear that psychosocial game playing is manifested because those attitudes that serve the ego-defense (protecting against internal conflicts and external dangers) and the value-expression (enhancing self-image, maintaining self-identity, etc.) needs (D. Katz, 1960) are aroused. On the other hand, problem solving is manifested because the attitudes that serve the need for knowledge (understanding that makes possible a meaningful organization of information, etc.) and the need for adjustment (utility of the brand, maximizing rewards and minimizing punishment, etc.) are aroused.

If we follow the reasoning of Bauer, such source attributes as power and attractiveness are meaningful in that they allow the buyer to play the psychosocial game, hence serve the ego-defense and value-expression needs. Similarly, such attributes as credibility are meaningful to the buyer in playing the problem-solving game. In other words, any knowledge of the types of games that the buyer wants to play in order to

Table 9.2   Source, Game Playing, and Functional Attitudes

Source Characteristic	Process Manifested	Game Played	Needs Aroused
Power	Compliance	Psychosocial	Ego defense
Attractiveness	Identification	Psychosocial	Value expression
Credibility	Internalization	Problem solving	Knowledge and adjustment

serve some functions, will enable the marketer to manipulate symbolic communication, at least with respect to the dominance of source characteristic.

9.3.3 Summary and Implications

The influence of source attributes on buyer's Response Sequence is depicted in Figure 9.3. To summarize, power influences Attention', Intention', and Purchase through the hypothetical constructs of Attention and Intention. Attractiveness influences all the responses in the sequence, but with varying strengths. It will produce stronger effects on Attention' and Intention' than on Purchase. Furthermore, it will change also Brand

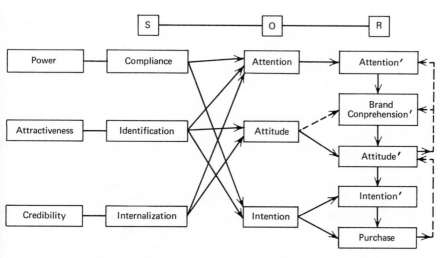

Figure 9.3   Source characteristics and their effectiveness.

Comprehension' and Attitude', but with less durability or permanency. Figure 9.3 shows that Attractiveness brings about these changes through all the hypothetical constructs. Finally, credibility will bring out Attention' and change buyer's Brand Comprehension' as well as Attitude'. This is shown by arrows from credibility on to the Attention and Attitude constructs. Earlier, we described the "sleeper effect" (enhancing the message or dampening it if the source has high or low credibility, respectively), which suggests that source credibility alone is only temporary but becomes permanent in conjunction with a message.

From our discussion of source we can draw a number of implications for competitive strategies. We list only a few of them below.

1. Power and attractiveness are largely social attributes, hence enter in Symbolic Communication primarily in personal selling or word-of-mouth advertising. However, they are capable of arousing ego-defense and value-expression needs of the buyer and thus allow him to play the psychosocial game. Finally, both of them, but particularly power, bring about immediate Attention' and Purchase, but these responses are likely to be unstable over time; they are manifested so long as source possesses those characteristics.

In personal selling, we are aware of the salesmen turnover problem. In addition, there is the problem of salesmen transfer and rotation in assignment to clients. A salesman may be able to generate sales because of power or attractiveness, but such sales may vanish as soon as the salesman stops interacting with the buyer. In the same manner, we believe that sales derived from word-of-mouth may be based, in some buying situations, more on informal personal source's power and attractiveness than on buyer's trust in him. It is important to separate these influences for any long-term commitments in marketing strategy.

2. We believe that the buyer manifests psychosocial game playing in buying behavior only when he is not problem-solving oriented. He is problem-solving-oriented in most of the situations dealing with innovations or, in short, in all situations where he is in the Extensive Problem Solving stage of decision making. Thus psychosocial game playing will be more common in Routinized Response Behavior and to some extent in Limited Problem Solving.

In industrial buying, it has been found that the psychosocial game is played by the buyer when it comes to deciding which supplier to choose from a list of preferred suppliers but not when a new supplier is to be added to a list of preferred suppliers (J. Howard and Moore, 1963).

It would be advantageous in the long run for a company not to introduce power and attractiveness attributes in its Symbolic Communication (mass media and personal selling) in all of those situations where the consumer is primarily problem-solving-oriented. But how to find out when the buyer is likely to be in Extensive Problem Solving situations? An interesting hypothesis is derived by combining the classification of goods, as defined by Bucklin (1963), into shopping, convenience, and specialty goods and the various stages of psychology of simplification, namely Extensive Problem Solving, Limited Problem Solving, and Routinized Response Behavior, respectively. Extensive problem solving resembles closely the definition of shopping goods, which suggests that in that case credibility may be more appropriate than either power or attractiveness.

3. There are several implications that are useful in symbolic communication of new products. First, it seems that underlying the difference between short-lived phenomena such as fads and fashions and the more durable diffusions of innovations based on the relative advantage, there exists the heavy influence of power and, more importantly, attractiveness in the former case. A subgroup or subculture adopts the fad or the fashion because the source (peers) demands from it either compliance or identification by reason of its power or attractiveness.

Second, importance of word-of-mouth communication in diffusion of innovations (Rogers, 1962) as discussed in Chapter 8 can be explained by the fact that informal personal sources are more trustworthy and also exercise compliance or identification influences on the buyer. The latter occur because the sources not only provide goals but also legitimize the buying decision.

Finally, there are important implications for the marketing mix strategy that will lead to successful diffusion of an innovation. The buyer is likely to be problem-solving-oriented in the case of new product introduction, which suggests that the essential guiding principle in marketing mix decision should be to facilitate internalization. This can be done by using the credibility of brand or of company image. However, it is unlikely that all companies possess such an attribute. Therefore, it may become inevitable to resort to sampling (giving away free samples). This means Significative as opposed to Symbolic Communication. In general, Symbolic Communication is less influential when (a) innovation is radical and thus much more information has to be transmitted, (b) buyer's inhibitions based on cultural mores interfere with symbolic communication, for example, in explaining the advantage of a new brand of tampons, and (c) the relative advantage of the new product is not visible, as, for example, fertilizer designed to kill weeds before they come up (pre-weed killers).

9.4 CHANNELS OF COMMUNICATION

The channel through which a message is communicated by the firm—the medium—contains several characteristics, which affect different levels of Response Sequence. It is important to separate channel effects from source effects, although it is often difficult to do so, particularly in word-of-mouth communication.

At a broad level, we classify all channels as being either personal or impersonal. This classification is useful, because personal channels have a vastly superior capacity to communicate, since they permit *two-way* communication. In addition, some important variables add to the power of personal sources, which we discuss later in the chapter.

From the channel capacity point of view, the process by which the buyer receives, perceives, and makes a communication meaningful becomes extremely important. All symbolic communication is received by the buyer through the two senses of vision and hearing. Then the three-stage mediation process involving projection, integration, and representation (Chapter 5) suggests certain mechanisms that modify the information. This has implications for various media, since each of them has some limitation.

Finally, because of past learning, various media acquire meanings other than the specific commercial communication. These evaluative meanings, in turn, affect the content of message, similar to the source attribute. Generally, this aspect is researched under the area of medium context and its influence on advertisement.

In Section 9.4.1 we present a summary description of channel effects, including the relevance of some of the hypothetical constructs as mediators between channel characteristics and the buyer's responses. In 9.4.2 we discuss various aspects of mass media in terms of their capacities to communicate. Much of this is a summary of standard chapters in advertising textbooks.* Section 9.4.3 examines the superiority of personal informal sources over mass media in terms of channel efficiency and buyer's greater trust in them.

---

* Section 9.4.2 is probably less relevant to a reader from disciplines other than marketing. Even within marketing, some readers may find it too simple or boring. We have included this (a) to complete the listing of all aspects of mass communication and (b) to provide theoretical underpinnings to many of the common advertising practices in the hope that such theory will enable the practitioner to generalize to new situations and encourage basic research.

9.4.1   Summary Description of Channel Effects

Selection of proper media to communicate to the buyer is an essential part of the marketing function. The basic decision, as explained in Chapter 1, is the marketing mix of significative and/or symbolic communications. The latter is further broken down into specific channels or media.

Complex mathematical models have been designed to obtain optimum combinations of media (Bass et al., 1961; Frank, Kuehn, and Massy, 1962), but they all assume that the relationship between media inputs and the dependent output (usually one of the stages in the Response Sequence ranging from exposure to sales) is known *and* that we know how to manipulate it. Obviously, this implies that we have a theory of advertising effectiveness. However, in fact, there exists complete lack of knowledge about the mediating hypothetical constructs between the advertising stimulus and the buyer responses, which has led to the confused and controversial state that exists in media research today (Sheth, 1969b). The theory of buyer behavior is primarily concerned with filling this gap. In this section, we point out how many of the channel effects can be explained using the three hypothetical constructs of Attention, Attitude, and Intention.

Each channel has some limitations in encoding the communications that a company would prefer to send to buyers. These limitations are clear and unambiguous. All media can transmit words (linguistic signs). All media except radio can transmit pictures (pictorial or symbolic pictorial signs). Radio and television can transmit sound. Television is the most powerful channel because it can transmit sound, pictures, and movements. Printed media have one advantage over auditory channels such as radio in that they provide *visual* stimuli. Most people can read faster than an announcer can speak, so that print is more efficient in transmitting a lot of words in a limited time. With printed media, the buyer can also reread a portion that he does not grasp on the first reading. Finally, printed media provide both pictorial and linguistic representations (Crane, 1965).

The differential capabilities of various media are relevant considerations because the buyer's perception of communication is a function of both the information he has stored *and* the degree of meaningful representation that the new communication possesses. Hence what is important is to distinguish those attributes of various media that affect perceptual variables such as Attention, Perceptual Bias, and Stimulus Ambiguity.

In Figure 9.4, we isolate major attributes of mass media and show how they influence buyer's responses through the hypothetical constructs

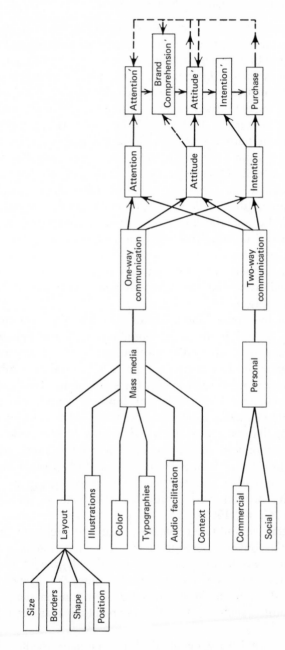

Figure 9.4 Attributes of the channel factor and their effect on Response Sequence.

of the theory of buyer behavior. In general, most of them become relevant in arousing buyer's Attention and facilitating his Brand Comprehension. For example, size, borders, and position in a printed layout arouse buyer's motivation either because they are ambiguous or novel or because they are very pleasing to him; hence positive attitude acts as a feedback. The result is that the buyer pays attention. Similarly, either an aesthetically pleasing or an incongruent picture may arouse the buyer's attention. Many of the same characteristics also facilitate the buyer's attempts to grasp the communication, to comprehend the message. The result is a change in his Brand Comprehension'.

However, to a limited extent, many of the characteristics also change the buyer's Attitude. For example, certain colors, textures, illustrations, types, sizes, and so on, are meaningful and positive (negative) to the buyer in their own right (G. Smith, 1954; Maccoby, Newcomb, and Hartley, 1958; Lynes, 1949; Lee, 1957; Bullock, 1961; McClelland, 1961; Martineau, 1957; Britt, 1966). These positive (negative) evaluations are transferred to the brand, altering the buyer's Attitude'. Similarly, such evaluations are capable of raising barriers that inhibit actual purchase despite any positive Attitude to influence Intention.

In the case of personal communication, in addition to the channel superiority caused by two-way communication, other attributes of the source create Attention, Attitude, or Intention. In later subsections, we fully describe these effects.

9.4.2 Attributes of Mass Media and Their Effect on Attention' and Brand Comprehension'

Several technical devices are available in mass media to achieve appropriate representation of the brand despite the fact that symbolic communication is limited to hearing and vision. Advertising practitioners have exploited these devices to encode a communication in such a manner that the buyer will not only comprehend the message properly, but also build exaggerated expectations about the potential of the brand. These technical mechanisms are effective in arousing the buyer's Attention and, through positive feedback from Attitude, to create perceptual distortions (Perceptual Bias), which ultimately change the learning constructs of Motives, Brand Comprehension, and Choice Criteria. It is unfortunate that, over time, the buyer has learned how expectations built up in mass media are not borne out in reality. Consequently, he has begun to mistrust advertisements in general. The discussion that follows is from the buyer's point of view only; it can serve as a guide to the marketing practitioner in how to use (rather than misuse) various facilitating devices. For a review of various effects, see Sheth (1969b).

9.4.2.1 Layout

Advertising layout has a number of elements, such as size, contrast, shape, and position. Layout is considered to be a means of attracting the buyer's attention in two ways: (1) by providing rewards, for example, by dramatizing some means of satisyfing his relevant Motives or offering some aesthetic satisfaction through entertainment, and (2) by requiring the least effort from the buyer (Stanley, 1954; Baker, 1959; Wales, Gentry, and Wales, 1958; Dunn, 1961). The latter—the principle of least effort—refers to reduction of ambiguity in the message, which, in the terminology of the ambiguity-arousal relationship described in Chapter 5, is beyond the X_1 level. Both elements apparently represent stimuli that are strong enough to become motivational and result in paying attention. However, the first is an instance of context, whereas the second is probably the influence of insufficient information.

Size is an attention-getting factor in print media. A full-page advertisement will almost always attract more readers than a half-page one. However, it is not likely to attract twice as many readers, as documented by extensive readership studies (Starch, 1956, 1957). One study has also shown the interaction of size with the receiver's past experience and attitude toward the brand. Larger advertisements attract a greater proportion of nonusers than do smaller ones (Hadley, 1950).

One explanation of this attention-producing reaction is provided by the effect of size on Stimulus Ambiguity. Since most advertisements are smaller than full-page, the normal anticipation is changed by a larger advertisement, which creates some incongruence and ambiguity. This arouses motivation, which facilitates further Attention. A reader who is not actively seeking information (is passive) will usually skip the smaller advertisement, but now he will find in the larger size incongruence or at least an unexpected phenomenon. He will, therefore, become sensitive to information. The result is greater Attention. The same phenomenon can explain the differences in attention between two full identical advertisements—one placed in a newspaper that seldom carries full-page advertisements and the other in a newspaper that usually does.

The additional space that is available in a large advertisement may be used in various ways. There is an opportunity to include more illustration and more text. Sometimes, the additional space is employed simply as "white space," which tends to attract attention because of novelty, stark simplicity, and startling appearance (Dunn, 1961). A good study (Bogart and Tolley, 1964) shows how attention is brought about by a blank space in a weekly newspaper. An earlier study by Twedt (1952) also found size to be the single most important variable for predicting advertising readership.

Contrast and *borders* also stimulate Attention, and particularly increase Brand and Product Class Comprehension. Contrast and borders facilitate "closure" resulting in evocative integration. Heavy dark masses against a light background or vividly contracting colors help attract attention to a layout (Helson and Rohles, 1959). Borders place the elements of an advertisement together in a unified whole and thus set it apart from its competitors. The reader will have noticed that it is the spatial contiguity that is important here. By becoming distinctive, by way of an unusual contrast or border, the stimulus may become strong enough to arouse the buyer's Attention. However, contrast and borders will be more useful in adequately communicating the attributes of the brand and will, therefore, result in greater Brand Comprehension.

Shape is another variable that makes an important difference in the efficiency of a channel; it also facilitates comprehension, in the same way as does border or contrast. The buyer is generally used to certain shapes in advertisements, such as a square or a rectangular. By providing variation in shape, the firm may inject sufficient novelty, complexity, or ambiguity to make the stimulus go beyond the OX_1 range in the stimulus-ambiguity relationship described in Chapter 5 and thus produce Attention.

Considerable study has been devoted to the *position* of an advertisement in a magazine or newspaper. It has been found that the content of a particular page has more effect on reader attention than the physical position of the page in the magazine or newspaper (Anastasi, 1964; Rudolph, 1947; Starch, 1961a; Starch and Staff, 1961). In other words, the context becomes relevant in that it creates vigilance. Placing an advertisement near a popular editorial or a columnist gives it an advantage. The only physical position that itself creates an advantage is the cover page. Cover-page advertisements have a readership advantage of as much as 30 to 64 per cent over those on inside pages (Lucas, 1937; Starch, 1961a; Starch and Staff, 1961). This can be explained by the fact that the context creates Attention because of the feedback from buyer's attitude (the reader likes the column or editorial), which encourages him to look at nearby material, including the advertisement, by reason of the cue effect of motivation, which was discussed in Part II.

9.4.2.2 Illustration

At the core of visual communication in advertising is the illustration. Illustrations are pictorial signs, and, like linguistic signs, they are symbolic in nature. Illustrations can be static, as in magazines and other print media, or changing, as on television. Furthermore, illustrations show the product or a situation. The latter are used as a context that, hopefully, will create attention and interest in the message. Illustrations are generally better encoding devices than words, because they provide a more realistic representation of the product or situation. However, this depends on the complexity of the brand and on the buyer's past familiarity with it.

Illustrations of both the brand and the situational context are likely to arouse Attention by bringing out appropriate meaning. They will also, by being better representations of the brand than is language, provide easier comprehension of the attributes of the brand. Finally, they may affect Attitude directly, because they have definite connotative meanings. We shall examine each of these effects in the following pages.

In choosing an illustration for a context that will attract maximum attention, art directors are often on the horns of a dilemma. They know that certain types of pictures are bound to attract high readership. On the other hand, such illustrations are not necessarily relevant to the brand and may actually draw attention away from it. Pictures of people and animals have the greatest attention value (Dunn, 1959). An anlysis conducted by Starch indicated that advertisements portraying people are more often read than those showing only the product (Starch, 1961b). Some sort of connection—direct or indirect—should be made between the product and the illustration, however. We have already referred (Chapter 5) to Scot Tissue advertisements in which the picture of mother and baby is connected to the brand through such health features as softness, cleanliness, and protection.

Studies of the relative attention value of *photographs* and *drawings* have revealed that the former have a slight advantage, probably because they tend to be less ambiguous (Starch, 1961c). In an experimental study in which photographs and hand-drawn versions of the same advertisements were compared, it was found that on each of the three measures—liking, believability, and recall—photographic versions had higher scores. The one clear-cut exception was an advertisement containing a semihumorous illustration that could be better expressed in cartoon form (Winick, 1959). The difference, however, is not very large. See also Ryan and Schwartz (1956).

As for *comprehension,* illustrations in general are much better ways to encode product stimuli than are words. The more novel the product, and, therefore, the less the buyer can generalize, the better it is to communicate by illustration. The advertiser may not be able to properly encode the novel features, and more importantly, the decoding on the part of the buyer may vary. Moreover, the more complex and technical the product, the better it is to use illustrations as symbolic communications. Since they are visual encodings, the fidelity of representation reduces ambiguity and distortion. Photographs are preferable when one is trying to create the impression of absolute accuracy. This is particularly necessary in industrial and trade publications where all the details of an industrial product can be shown accurately for technical scrutiny.

Comprehension of the brand is affected via buyer's Attitude toward that brand. Depending on his prior learning of brand preferences, he may resort to perceptual biases and still further distort the information from the illustration. For example, he may misread the copy of an advertisement. However, if the information is photographic as opposed to verbal, objective reality leads to less perceptual distortion.

Regarding *attitude* toward brand, many illustrations acquire some connotative meanings from past presentations. These connotative meanings arise more easily from an illustration than from any amount of linguistic encoding. A good example is "Uncle Sam." Indeed, many illustrative symbols (trademarks) associated with brands serve exactly this function. The attitudes associated with these symbols are suggested in illustrative communications and may directly help to change the buyer's future attitude toward the product. For example, the G.E. trademark symbol on a standard appliance drawing in ordinary newspaper advertising may create different meaning than would one without the symbol.

9.4.2.3 *Color*

Color is now employed in the majority of magazine and television advertisements and is rapidly becoming common in newspapers as well. Color provides another characteristic to visual encoding by permitting greater fidelity. In some instances, color becomes absolutely necessary in representing the product because its quality attributes are very closely related to color. For example, color is an important feature of many fruits and vegetables.

Color, like illustrations, is likely to affect Attention, Brand Comprehension, Attitude, and Intention. It may, therefore, have attention value, improve comprehension of the product, and even imply connotative meanings that create direct attitude change. We shall examine these aspects below. It must be emphasized that the connotative meanings of both illustrations and color often result in inhibitions which may affect the buyer's Intention' and Purchase. For example, a red or a white limousine for funeral parlors is not considered appropriate, since in our culture black color is associated with death.

Stanley (1954) lists the following advantages of color: (1) attracting attention; (2) representing objects with complete fidelity; (3) suggesting abstract qualities appropriate to the selling appeal; (4) emphasizing some special part of the message or product; (5) creating a pleasant first impression; (6) creating prestige for the product, service, or advertiser; (7) fastening visual impressions in the memory. The reader will notice that 1 and 5 are color's effect on Attention, 2 and 7 are its effects on Brand Comprehension, and 3, 4, and 6 are its effects on the buyer's Attitude, presumably via his preferences toward the colors.

The available evidence on the *attention* value of color is not clear-cut. Rudolph (1947) found that advertisements that used black and one color had only about 1 per cent higher readership than comparable black and white advertisements. Since the two-color ones cost an average of 17 per cent more, this use of color did not seem justified. However, four-color displays averaged a 54 per cent higher readership and increased cost by an average of only 44 per cent, which would suggest some superiority for color. But in other studies by Starch (1956) the color advantage is questioned.

The research problem in the studies may be the use of color as an *independently* attention-arousing device without consideration of other factors. What we have argued is to utilize color to *properly represent* the product. Then the hypothesis is that if the product is communicated in appropriate color configuration, it will have greater attention than if it is communicated in black and white. Similarly, if color is improperly used, it is likely that attention will diminish. The latter is important today because the imperfect technology of color television does create improper color configuration which repulses the viewer, for example, meat represented in blue color.

Studies are lacking which would explicitly show that color may add to the *comprehension* of the brand. In some products, as mentioned earlier, this is absolutely necessary, and to that extent if symbolic communication does not provide color, the buyer may not decide to buy the product without actually seeing the product.

As for *attitude*, colors have some connotative meanings like illustrations (Schiller, 1935). Many emotional reactions are associated with some specific colors by acculturation and past usage, (Poffenberger, 1928; Wexner, 1954; Murray and Deabler, 1957; Berry, 1961). For example, red color is associated with fire, heat, excitement, or danger; white with purity, cleanliness, chastity. The feedback effects from the meaningful mediators associated with colors can facilitate the comprehension of the advertisement, and the reception of the message may be increased. Similarly, color can summarize much of the information that the firm would like to communicate as representing the brand. To that extent, appropriate color may add to communication content and the resultant attitude change of the buyer. For example, in the ScotTissue advertisements referred to earlier, white or pink would be more relevant than either red or black. However, in the case of a sports car, red color may be very appropriate, and for a funeral limousine, black would be quite appropriate. Similarly, to show a red, ripe watermelon, a black and white combination is not effective. In most food products, color in a pictorial representation would seem to be a must for proper representation (r_m-s_m) to evoke a substantial proportion of the total behavior associated with the product itself. In other words, food pictorially represented with adequate colors may bring out impulse purchase by intensifying desire for it.

9.4.2.4 *Typefaces and Other Graphic Elements*

The legibility of printed material has been extensively studied in advertising (Burt, Cooper, and Martin, 1955; Tinker, 1958, 1963). The various sizes and shapes of types have definite relation to the Attention of the message and Brand Comprehension because legibility will, among other factors, influence the mental integrations that can occur (Paterson and Tinker, 1940). Furthermore, typefaces and styles are associated with mediators by acquiring connotative meanings, and feedbacks from these mediators may further increase Attention and Brand Comprehension.

Legibility is, therefore, primarily related to Attention and Brand Comprehension, and secondarily to Attitude and Intention. For example, poor legibility of a message is very likely to create frustration in the buyer. The buyer is motivated to read the message (by having interest in product, searching for information, etc.) which will be thwarted by illegibility. This may result in frustration which, as explained in Part II, may raise irrelevant motivation beyond the optimum level and result in perceptual defenses such as withdrawal or aggression.

Psychologists have done considerable research on the legibility of typefaces. Among the criteria employed to measure legibility are accuracy of perceiving letters or words in brief tachistoscopic exposures; reading speed and comprehension of long passages; distances at which letters, words, or sentences can be correctly read; indices of eye fatigue after continuous reading; and number and nature of eye movements during reading. Through these measures, it has been demonstrated that printing type varies significantly in legibility. Simple typefaces are read faster than old English or other typefaces with elaborations and curlicues. The relative legibility of different typefaces varies somewhat with other factors such as size, boldness, width of margins, and interlinear spacing. The use of colored inks and colored backgrounds also affects legibility chiefly by altering the degree of brightness and contrast. Fastest reading and fewest eye fixations have been found with black print on a white background. About equally good are such combinations as green on white, blue on white, and black on yellow (Anastasi, 1964).

Since legibility affects the proper integrations of words and sentences, the past frequency of such integrations, both predictive and evocative, with which the buyer is familiar should have some effect. This has been found to be true with respect to both type and arrangement. A passage or headline printed in lowercase letters, for example, is read at a faster rate than one set in capitals. Also, familiarity of layout facilitates legibility. We are used to sequences of sentences from left to right. If, however, in a message the sequence is from top to bottom or from right to left, legibility is impaired. Legibility thus affects Attention' and Brand Comprehension'.

Different typefaces acquire some connotative association by acculturation and usage, and these change over time. Typefaces popular a generation ago, look quaint and old-fashioned today. People tend to have evaluative feelings toward typefaces; they like some and dislike others (Davis and Smith, 1933; Poffenberger, 1928; Poffenberger and Barrows, 1924; Poffenberger and Franklin, 1923; Schiller, 1935). Such beliefs act as feedbacks on Attention and Perceptual Bias. Thus by proper type usage one may raise Attention' and Brand Comprehension'.

Finally, the connotative meanings associated with typefaces may be utilized to convey some quality attribute of a brand. For example, by printing in royal-looking types we may convey the feeling of high class. By italics we may convey friendliness and informality. A good deal of company research in packaging is in this area of investigation.

9.4.2.5 *Audio Facilitation Effects*

So far we have emphasized visual encoding and decoding processes, so as to point up the advantages that television and print media seem to have over radio. Radio has one advantage—it communicates fast and very inexpensively. Also, recently two-way communication has been made possible in radio by the telephone method. In those instances where sound is important in judging the product attribute, radio is likely to have an edge over print media. For example, one may wish to express the quietness of durable appliances like air-conditioners or the quietness in the cabin of a jet airplane. Similarly, one may wish to express the speed of a product as, for example, in electric shaving. An interesting study deals with the change in perception of quality of power lawn mowers due to change in its sound (Britt, 1966, pp. 163–164). Above and beyond auditory representations to connote product attributes, radio has a decided advantage in providing such vital attention-getting auditory devices as jingles, music, and rhymes. The best example of this can be seen in Schaeffer Beer commercials. The music is so good that the impression tends to last considerably longer. In fact, the tune cannot be separated from words.

Since television has both auditory and visual facilities, it becomes a powerful device; it provides decoding through both the sense of vision and the sense of hearing. Other media provide one or the other, but not both. Commercially, technology can do two things for improvement. (1) It can provide much better representation of the physical product by incorporating more characteristics in the existing two-sense system. Proper color fidelity in television is an area for improvement. Another possible future improvement is to provide a true three-dimensional representation of the product. Both of these are currently being researched and are within the realm of reality. Auditory advances have been already made to provide accurate representations. (2) Technology can also develop some other medium that will add one more sensory signal to the buyer. For example, besides audio and video representations, such medium may transmit appropriate smell.

9.4.2.6   Context

Each medium provides a certain context in which symbolic communication is represented. For example, newspapers are primarily for general information and education, and magazines for education, relaxation, and entertainment (Crane, 1965). The different contexts (sets) in which advertising is presented create differential motivational and directional effects as discussed in Part II (Chapter 5). The context modifies the absolute unconditional probability of Attention' and Brand Comprehension' by providing a condition for selection. If an advertisement appears in *Reader's Digest,* the buyer may be motivated to read the message about a brand that is high in perceived risk and may evaluate the brand positively because of his positive image of the magazine. Similarly, we may also hypothesize that if advertisement of a product is done in two different daily newspapers, for example, the *Daily News* and the *New York Times,* the effects on Attention' and Brand Comprehension' may differ. The reader will have noticed that the context provides in many ways *credibility of the medium* similar to the credibility of the source discussed earlier. Sheth (1969b) reviews several studies about the influence of medium credibility on the buyer's perception of the product or the company.

Another advantage of the medium's context is to segment the buyers into certain groups which are likely to have specific requirements, hence will find specific products more appealing. For example, women's fashion magazines carry mostly advertisements of the products related to women's wear. Magazines catering to males carry advertisements of products meant for male consumption. The numerous home magazines carry a tremendous amount of advertisements related to the food and shelter needs of the buyer. Similarly, the weekend daytime programs on television dominated by sports carry advertisements of products primarily used by adult male members of the family. The children's programs carry advertisements for products to be used by young people. Schwartz (1966) demonstrates the advantage of direct mail over newspapers and magazines for redemption of coupons. With the increased understanding of household decision making in recent years, however, such classification does not seem to be optimal. It has been found that joint decision making between husband and wife and between parents and children is more common (Foote, 1961; Kenkel and Hoffman, 1956; Kenkel, 1961; Alderson and Sessions, 1957; *Printers' Ink*, 1958b; Granbois, 1963; Coulson, 1966).

It is also found that advertisements of the products on the page on which editorials appear is advantageous (Anastasi, 1964). It is probably true that the buyers sharply separate the advertisements from the other contents of the medium and, therefore, the context may not be associated in the mind of the buyer. However, very often, by past experience and practice, the buyer begins to *expect* or *anticipate* certain advertisements in certain media and at certain times. Thus when he actively seeks information because he wants either to simplify the buying situation or to complicate his purchase behavior by seeking unfamiliar information to reduce boredom, monotony, or satiation, he may find the proper medium easily. For example, anyone interested in hi-fi is likely to learn that the advertisements of a variety of brands will be found in magazines catering to hi-fi enthusiasts. Finally, daily newspapers usually carry advertisements of grocery products on certain days, and housewives come to expect them on those days. When they are not available, for example, because of a newspaper strike, the buyer is found to actively seek information elsewhere (Simon and Marks, 1965).

9.4.3   Mass Media versus Personal Sources of Communication

In the preceding section, we examined the effects of several technical aspects related to mass media. We attempted to provide an understanding of the usefulness as well as limitations of the technical facilities that each medium seems to possess. We did not try to directly contrast the major media, because the variety in each medium is so great that it must be taken into account if comparisons are to be meaningful, and such variety cannot be considered in a single chapter. The basic purpose of this chapter is to provide a framework for understanding the mass media not from the point of view of the communicator but from that of the receiver.

9.4.3.1 Superiority of Personal Channels

There is substantial evidence that seems to support the argument that personal sources like salesmen and friends are more effective in attitude change than the mass media (Katona and Mueller, 1955; Alderson, 1952; Coleman, Katz and Menzel, 1959; Bauer, 1961, 1963a; Klapper, 1960; Arndt, 1967a).

Katona and Mueller (1955), for example, found that 50 per cent of the consumers questioned about durable-appliance purchases turned to their friends and relatives for information and influence; personal sources were the single most important source in affecting their decision. Katz and Lazarsfeld (1955) found that personal influence was almost seven times more effective than magazine or newspaper advertising in persuading women to switch brands of household products. They also found that most consumer brand-shifting influence was from outside the family except for such products as coffee for men and cereals for children. Beal and Rogers (1957) found interpersonal sources to be more influential in convincing housewives to purchase new fabrics such as Dacron and nylon. Atkin (1962) found that heavy exposure to advertising which advocated switching supermarkets actually switched fewer housewives than did strong interpersonal pressures. Finally, Bauer (1961) finds that detailmen in the pharmaceutical industry are very effective in influencing the doctors.

The relative effectiveness of mass media vis-à-vis the personal sources is best summarized by Klapper (1960). After reviewing the existing literature on communication and opinion change, Klapper finds that mass communications have been more successful as *reinforcers* to the existing opinions of the audience rather than as *changers* of its attitudes. Mass communications have proved least useful as converters but have shown some influence in minor attitude changes. Klapper also finds that mass media are quite efficient in *creating* opinions among people who are not previously inclined one way or another on an issue.

Katz and Lazarsfeld (1955) have hypothesized, with some weak evidence, that there exists a *two-step flow of communication* particularly in the introduction of new products and practices. The mass media transmit the information and influence a small group called the opinion leaders in a community. The opinion leaders in a community, in turn, influence the majority of the members of the community. Katz and

Lazarsfeld (1955) conclude that mass media only indirectly influence opinion change on a mass level. Sheth (1968d) shows empirical evidence that there is, in fact, a *sequence of opinion leaderships* which makes personal sources doubly influential. The reader is directed to Chapter 8 where the aspect was analyzed in greater detail.

We have briefly summarized the existing evidence on the superiority of personal sources. In the next subsection, we attempt to explain this superiority.

9.4.3.2   *Theoretical Explanations*

The explanation of the superiority of personal sources of communication over impersonal sources or mass media can be attributed to (*a*) source attributes and (*b*) channel efficiency in transmitting information.

Personal sources are likely to have the social attributes of both power and attractiveness, the latter being more relevant in buying behavior. In addition to power and attractiveness, personal sources are likely to be superior because the buyer ascribes to them *greater trust* and sometimes greater competence. Greater trust in personal informal sources arises because the buyer perceives the source as having no vested interest in communicating. He believes that source is actually doing him a favor in giving information and advice.

However, our analysis here is primarily in terms of the efficiency of the channel as a transmitting device, and, therefore, we assume the source effects to be constant between the personal sources and the mass media. The explanation then boils down to the superiority of two-way communication possible in personal sources over the one-way communication in mass media.

1. Mass media communicate the message with the least effort and cost to the buyer, and they are quick (Cox, 1963). But mass media have grown to have such great variety and are so numerous that the buyer has probably built selective perceptual mechanisms, with the result that ordinarily the messages do not even catch the buyers Attention. In fact, the buyer very often seems to *completely ignore them,* as shown by the Dollard studies for DuPont (Chapter 3). Thus extraordinary effort is now required to capture his Attention. This is vividly brought out when one compares the successful advertisements in underdeveloped economies with advertisements in our economy. Mass media and mass commercial communication are very recent in underdeveloped countries, hence still a novelty. The buyer, therefore, still is quite attentive to commercial messages that would be considered ordinary by a buyer

in an advanced economy. In a recent (April 1968) survey of three cities in India, where preliminary attempts were made to put commercials on one popular radio program, 89 per cent of the respondents favored having commercials on a national level. It is highly unlikely that so high a percentage of favorable comments would be obtained in the United States. Perceptual processes, such as those mentioned in Chapter 5, are more difficult to manifest in personal communications, particularly with friends and relatives, because there are likely to be more serious consequences flowing from their manifestation. This is not to say that such processes do not occur at all. Perceptual defenses may occur even in personal sources if the consequences are not punitive to the buyer. What is emphasized is the fact that because of social etiquette they are less likely to occur in personal communications.

However, in those instances where the buyer is actively seeking information and, therefore, is likely to be attentive anyhow, personal sources probably do not have a greater advantage over mass media in terms of perceptual defenses. This needs to be thoroughly researched.

2. Mass media cater to the mass, and they have a standard communication to be attended to and comprehended by many buyers. (*a*) The *individual* differences in decoding processes are held constant because they are difficult to incorporate. The message is designed for and communicated to the typical buyer. This may result in a variety of decoding processes depending on individual differences in past experiences of integrative associations and connotative meanings of the message. As we saw in Chapter 5, a number of variables, all internal to the buyer, are available to him to make the change from objective stimulus to stimulus-as-coded. (*b*) Furthermore, because it is a *one-way communication*, the buyer has no chance to clarify ambiguity. The consequence is likely to be distortion of the message. (*c*) Finally, the message from mass media may communicate on only some aspects of total buying behavior, and the buyer may actively seek information on some other aspects. Again, one-way communication acts as a limitation in mass media. All the three problems cited above are obviated in personal two-way communication. The message is individually tailored to the buyer, the buyer can clarify his ambiguity, and, more often than not, the communication is likely to be relevant. In fact, we may suggest that the difference between *commercial personal sources* and *buyer personal sources* in their effectiveness can be attributed to the first and the third issues. Commercial personal sources are likely to be less individually tailored and less relevant to individual buyer's specific points of clarification than are informal sources. However, commercial personal sources are likely to be much superior to mass media.

There are some interesting implications of this explanation in situations where the product class concept is not well defined (the situation is one that is perceived as major innovation). The buyer needs considerable amount of information to learn the denotative cognitive elements (Product Class Comprehension is low). He has probably little or no possibility of generalization from past experiences with similar situations. Furthermore, the information he receives is likely to be more ambiguous to him. It is likely that he will prefer a channel that transmits information individually tailored to his level of comprehension, with which he can exchange information, and of which he can ask questions so as to properly comprehend the product class and develop appropriate Choice Criteria, and that will also give him confidence as well as motivation to explore the new area. Personal informal sources have all these advantages. Personal *commercial* sources have the first two, but probably to a somewhat lesser extent. Mass media may not be adequate for any of these functions. However, they have wide reach and are inexpensive compared to personal sources. They may, therefore, be useful in informing the buyers of the existence of the radical innovation, but must leave it to personal selling and opinion leadership to enable the buyer to fully comprehend the product class. In many ways, the diffusion research supports this in terms of empirical evidence (Rogers, 1962).

9.5 MESSAGE AND ITS EFFECTS ON RESPONSE SEQUENCE

The substantive part of the communication is the message itself, which is often called an "appeal" in marketing literature (Anastasi, 1964). We do not discuss here the linguistic creativity of the copywriter, that is, how he should express his ideas, what words he should choose, and how sentences should be integrated. The reader can learn these from standard advertising books such as those of Kleppner (1966), Mandell (1968), Reeves (1961), and Ogilvy (1963). Much of that should be, in fact, a part of the channel factor, although we do not specifically deal with it in this book. This does not mean that an understanding of the encoding process is not crucial. In fact, we mentioned earlier that one of the major reasons for the limitations of the Symbolic Communication as opposed to Significate Communication is the discrepancy that invariably exists between the encoding and the decoding of messages in Symbolic Communication. We shall, however, concentrate on two aspects of the message in this section: (a) the content of the message itself as an appeal and its relation to the hypothetical constructs of Attention, Attitude, and Intention and (b) the structure of the content but from a nonlinguistic point of view.

Message is likely to affect all the components of the Response Sequence because it is likely to affect all the hypothetical constructs. It is difficult to classify the content of the message to suggest that certain attributes of the message will mediate via Attention because the motives called up are irrelevant, for example, boredom, and some other attribute will mediate via Attitude because the buyer is actively seeking information. However, based on the theory of buyer behavior, we suggest some broad generalizations in the following pages.

9.5.1. *Content of the Message*

The primary purpose of marketing effort is to establish linkage between the brand and the buyer's needs. The essence of message content, therefore, is the evaluative favorable beliefs about the brand that the buyer should learn. In addition, it becomes necessary, in some instances, to enable the buyer to learn descriptive beliefs about the brand and the product class as well as developing appropriate Choice Criteria. The latter two functions of message content are helpful in forming positive Attitude and Intention toward the brand, but more commonly they are treated as "image" advertisements.

Message content is likely to arouse and change all three hypothetical constructs, namely Attention, Attitude, and Intention, although its effect is largely on the last two constructs. However, the complexity with which message affects these constructs is great, and all we can do in one chapter is to provide some broad generalizations.

1. Message will alter the buyer's *comprehension of the product class as a whole and of the particular brands in his evoked set* about which the firm communicates. In Chapter 8, we extensively developed the notion of product class, based on principles of concept formation and related research. It is extremely important to properly communicate about the brand, especially an innovation, so that the buyer places it as an alternative in his evoked set. There are numerous examples from industry reports that have shown how a brand has been misperceived by the buyer. The reason for emphasizing comprehension of the brand is that any misperception may place a brand in a weaker position relative to other brands despite the fact that it possesses good attributes.

So far we have included only those learning effects of the message that are related to the buyer's denotative, judgmental meaning of the brand and the product class. The message will also affect his evaluative, connotative meaning of the brand. Since the evaluation of the brand is anchored to the buyer's Choice Criteria (and underlying motives), we separate the message's influence on the buyer's learning of the brand as a perceived instrument and its influence on the buyer's Motives themselves.

2. Content of the message may make a brand a *perceived instrument* of the buyer's goal satisfaction. It provides the buyer with enough evaluative characteristics of the brand to adequately order it as one of the several alternatives in the evoked set. It may communicate the attributes of the brand well enough to even place the brand at the top of the preference hierarchy of alternatives stored in the buyer's Attitude. More likely is the case where a brand already in the preference hierarchy is pushed up by appropriate and effective content of the message.

3. Another effect of the content is that it may change (a) the intensity of Choice Criteria by intensifying the underlying Motives or (b) the content of Choice Criteria by changing the number of relevant and product-specific Motives. Both influences will alter buyer's Choice Criteria and, in the terminology of Chapter 6 (Attitude'), will result in a new market space whose dimensions may not be the same as those of the old one. Since the brands are evaluated and anchored to Choice Criteria, the location of the brand in this market space will also be affected. Of course, the firm hopes to communicate in such a manner that the relocation of the brand will be more favorable to it.

Before we proceed to analyze each of these learning effects of the message, it is important to bring forth some related points. First, the last two effects (perceived instrumentality and altering Choice Criteria) closely resemble the process of attitude change via belief or the valence components of attitude put forward by Fishbein (1967). However, there are some differences. (a) We include only the evaluative, connotative meaning of the brand as part of perceived instrumentality, and not the total meaning of the brand, the latter also including the denotative, descriptive meaning. Fishbein implicitly does have this distinction, but any explicit statement is lacking. (b) The effect on the valence component is refined in several ways by, first, having Choice Criteria as an additional process that orders and brings the saliency of Motives to the forefront and, second, by separating the effect on intensity and the content of Motives. We think that these refinements will enable us to understand the process of communication more adequately.

Furthermore, the role of the message in teaching comprehension of the brand and the product class as well as in making it a perceived instrumentality (the first two effects) is more relevant when the buyer experiences the psychology of simplification. This is because the buyer's Motives are structured and well set, against which he evaluates various alternatives; he is a problem solver, with the problem defined for him. On the other hand, changing the intensity or the content of the Motives is likely to be more relevant when he experiences the psychology of complication. This is because at this age the buyer's Motives are in a state of transition, either due to satiation or unacceptability created by change in level of aspiration.

Content of the message may also affect the irrelevant motivation. This is likely to occur when the message appeals to the irrelevant Motives as discussed in Chapter 4. For example, the message may use one of the personality variables, exhibitionism or autonomy, to appeal to the buyer.

Finally, message content will influence Intention. This arises in two ways: (*a*) unwitting emphasis of an attribute may create inhibition in the buyer so that he decides not to buy it or (*b*) competing brands may create Intention discrepant to Attitude by pointing out the weaker aspects of this brand.

9.5.1.1 *Message and Product Class Comprehension'*

With the heavy emphasis on innovation as a marketing strategy, understanding the descriptive knowledge (Product Class Comprehension) of what a product class is and where a brand fits has become both complex and important. The complexity is greater on two dimensions. First, there are totally new product classes which did not exist even fifteen years ago, and this area is expanding rapidly with the constant technological breakthroughs. Second, there is enormous variety within the existing product classes. This can be gauged by the astronomical number of brands and package sizes in a product class. Much of product change (innovation) falls in this category. Along with the rise in complexity there has been the increase in mass communication. Despite skeptical views on advertising's effectiveness on sales, the annual expenditure in advertising at the aggregate level is constantly rising, probably because we have more things to sell.

There are two major aspects to the role of the message in buyer's proper comprehension of the product class and the brands. First, faced with the variety of new product introductions and the ways in which information about them is communicated to him, the buyer is likely to simplify his buying behavior by creating the perceptual mechanisms of ignoring, withdrawing, and disbelieving the commercial environment. That this is a widespread belief today can be seen from the trade journals. In terms of the theory if buyer behavior, these perceptual processes are summarized in Attention and Perceptual Bias. This means that either there must exist a facilitating context such as source credibility or channel credibility that will lower the perceptual barriers or the message itself must be good enough to keep the buyer interested or motivated. The latter is not a simple matter, particularly when several media constraints are operating. In fact, companies consider this perceptual problem sufficiently serious to resort to free sampling as a means of communications, which is a costly proposition at least initially.

Second, technical breakthroughs have created products that cannot be adequately encoded into symbolic communication. For example, it is very difficult to communicate the nature and meaning of freeze-dried coffee to the buyer without introducing some erroneous generalizations from either regular or instant coffee into his product comprehension. The problem is further compounded by the fact that generalization from one or the other becomes a critical issue for the profitability and, therefore, survival of the innovation. Similar examples are video-tape recorders and "checkless" society.

A problem related to the difficulty of encoding attributes of a radical innovation is the buyer's tendency to use a word, a phrase, or a symbol to store a denotative complex meaning of the object. This tendency is motivated by the ease with which he can communicate socially with others. Very often, he uses the brand name or trademark of the innovating firm as the symbol or sign with the consequence that later in the product life cycle, the brand name becomes a generic term. Examples of this are aspirin, mimeograph, and nylon.

The message's influence on Product Class and Brand Comprehension is anchored in the psychology of simplification. Hence it becomes imperative that the message simplify the attributes so that the buyer can comprehend. In other words, the message should try to reduce the ambiguity to the X_2 or lower level (but not as low as X_1) in the ambiguity-arousal relation discussed in Chapter 5.

9.5.1.2   Message and Perceived Instrumentality

Perceived instrumentality of a brand can be achieved by proper association of the brand with the Choice Criteria. For example, an over-weight man or a diet-conscious woman may have acquired a criterion, "Diet foods are good," from past learning. A given brand of soft drinks can be made a perceived instrument of satisfying dietary motives of the buyer by advertisements that emphasize its low calorie content. Of course, we assume that the brand has the necessary characteristic. If the brand does not possess the attribute that is considered important (e.g., Coca-Cola cannot emphasize low calorie content), it may be necessary to change the brand or introduce a new product (such as Tab). The decision would, of course, depend on the number of marginal buyers for whom the particular Choice Criteria are very relevant.

It is, however, not easy to make a brand a perceived instrument of gratification. (1) Although the message may include it in the buyer's definition of situation (he is aware of its existence), it may not become a part of his evoked set. It may also become a preferred brand because other brands in the evoked set may be higher in the preference hierarchy. (2) Choice Criteria themselves are not easily identified by the company, although the concept of market space discussed in Chapters 3 and 6 is intended to serve just that purpose. A good example of this can be found in a study in which the company selling a household product emphasized that it "works faster." However, a consumer survey revealed that 58 per cent of the housewives who used the brand said that they did so because "it is easy on the hands" while only 2 per cent mentioned that "it is quicker" (Hepner, 1956). Another example is from the advertising appeals for men's shoes which traditionally stressed style, price, and details about the construction of the shoe. A survey of 5000 men conducted for the Bostonian Shoe Company found that, when asked what they liked about the shoes they were wearing, 42 per cent referred to "fit and feel," 32 per cent to "wear and tear," 16 per cent to "style and looks," and 9 per cent to "price and value." On the basis of these results, advertising appeal (message) was changed, the shoes now being described in such terms as "walk-fitted" (Giles, 1939). In both examples, the change in appeals was believed to have resulted in greater sales of the products. For other examples, see Anastasi (1964).

However, in certain product classes the buyer may perceive himself as being compelled to suggest an attribute that he really does not prefer because of social and reference group influences. For example, General Foods has repeatedly found that instant coffee drinkers *like* instant coffee and would not substitute it with regular coffee. However, when asked to rank-order various types of coffee, they would express preference for regular coffee. The projective techniques utilized in motivation research may help in such instances to remove the inhibitory effects of social norms. Another approach may be to separate the buyers' notions of "ideal" product and the existing products. For in situations where social inhibitions are prevalent, the buyer is likely to play the psychosocial game (to defend his ego or for value expression, as explained earlier when discussing the source effects). From the marketing research point of view, these instances may suggest impersonal methods of data collection such as mailing.

The content of a message that attempts to communicate the perceived instrumentality of a brand will change the buyer's Attitude depending on the strength of his existing Attitude toward competing brands. If he is very strongly predisposed toward a competing brand, he may ignore or even debunk the message.

9.5.1.3 Message and Change in Choice Criteria

As mentioned earlier, message influences and changes Choice Criteria either by increasing the intensity of the Motives (both relevant and irrelevant) or by altering the content of the Motives. Below we describe each influence separately in more detail. However, we may also look at the message influences slightly differently. For example, when the buyer is problem-solving-oriented, the message actually enables the buyer to develop, to formulate his Choice Criteria. It is a source of learning by which he structures his motives. On the other hand, when the buyer is satiated with a buying situation and feels bored, the message will bring about change in existing Choice Criteria. The discussion here, although labeled as change in Choice Criteria, also includes the formulation and development of Choice Criteria in the initial phases of buying.

1. *Change in intensity of motives.* Content of a message may attempt to modify the buyer's Motives. We expect the modification basically involves changing the intensity of some part of the total motive structure. For example, let us assume that in eating cereals the buyer has the three Motives of *taste, substantiveness,* and *nutrition* in that order of importance. A particular brand of cereals (Special K, Total, or Product 19) may attempt, through the message content, to intensify the nutrition motive. This will result in raising the intensity of that motive. With sufficient change in intensity, nutrition, may outweigh substantiveness. The resultant reordering will then enhance nutrition, which will become second only to taste.

It will be noted that any significant change in the intensity of a motive will result in a reordering of the Motives. Consequently, the Choice Criteria will also change. In the process, the brand that brought about the restructuring may become the preferred brand if it, in fact, does possess attributes appropriate to the new structure. In other words, *perceived instrumentality may automatically follow, given a change in the structure of motives.* Carrying our example further, if nutrition becomes the second most important motive, the buyer may place Special K very high in his preference hierarchy. For other examples, see Kleppner (1966, Chapter 4).

Another approach to changing the intensity of Motives would be to simply lift the complete motive structure still further from the threshold level. The structure will not change, but some motive that was dormant before may now become active. In the cereal example, all the three motives may be intensified without any shift in the hierarchy of taste, substantiveness, and nutrition. Thus a company may communicate some medical finding suggesting that it is better to eat breakfast rather than skip it and may thereby raise the intensity of the total motive structure that indicates Choice Criteria. If nutrition was a dormant motive before, it may now become an active motive, and the buyer may reposition his brands on *three* dimensions of taste, substantiveness, and nutrition as opposed to only two dimensions of taste and substantiveness.

Another and probably more common approach to raising the intensity of the total motive structure is to arouse the irrelevant Motives. (See Chapter 4). We are quite familiar with *fear-arousing appeals*. Similarly, communication may arouse anxiety, conflict, or frustration. It may arouse, too, socially anchored Motives of power, prestige, or affiliation. Messages may also be directed to any of the variables discussed in personality theories such as exhibitionism, extroversion, or autonomy. Since the motivation aroused is not product-specific, it is likely to have the same type of relation to the communication as that between arousal and Attention. If the strength of total motivation is only moderate, the dominant response will be made even more probable. The buyer will consequently pay attention to the message (vigilance), will comprehend the arguments in the message, and will change his attitude in the direction of the position advocated in the message. However, it is crucial that intensity of motivation not exceed the optimum-moderate level. If it is greater, perceptual defense will set in, and consequently both Brand Comprehension and Attitude will not change. The nonmonotonic relation between intensity of motivation and opinion change has been suggested by several researchers, particularly with regard to motivation aroused by fear appeals (Janis and Feshbach, 1953; Janis, 1967; McGuire, 1961, 1963). At a general level, Osgood (1957b) presents considerable evidence to support the nonmonotonic relation between intensity of motivation and probability of a given response.

As mentioned earlier, fear-arousing appeals have been extensively researched in their effect on attitude or opinion change. The pioneering study that gave impetus to this area of communications research is the dental hygiene experimental study of Janis and Feshbach (1953). An illustrated lecture on dental hygiene was prepared in three different forms, representing three intensities of fear appeal: the strong appeal emphasized and graphically illustrated the threat of pain, disease, and body damage; the moderate appeal described the same dangers in a milder and more factual manner; the minimal appeal rarely referred to the unpleasant consequences of improper dental hygiene. Although differing in the amount of fear-arousing material presented, the three forms of the communication contained the same essential information and the same set of recommendations.

Equivalent groups of high school students were exposed to the three different forms of the communication as part of the school's hygiene program. In addition, the experiment included an equated control group, which was not exposed to the dental hygiene communication but was given a similar communication on an irrelevant topic. Altogether there were 200 students in the experiment, with 50 in each group. A questionnaire containing a series of items on dental hygiene beliefs, practices, and attitudes was administered to all four groups one week before the communications were presented. In order to observe the changes produced by the illustrated talk, postcommunication questionnaires were given immediately after exposure and again one week later.

The fear-arousing appeals were effective in that they did arouse the motivation of the groups. The strong-appeal group showed the greatest worry and the minimal group showed the least worry. However, information learned from the three types was about the same on 23 separate items. This seems to contradict our hypothesis that strong motivation would result in perceptual defense and inattention to the message. However, other incentives and factors may be operating here, such as the wish to ingratiate oneself with the teacher by cooperating with the experimenter and the fact that it is a "forced" communication to a "captive audience," which would not be present in natural situations. In addition, more students in the strong-appeal group had favorable comments about the communication than did those in the moderate- or the minimal-appeal group. However, more students in the strong-appeal group also expressed greater complaints about the communication. This suggests an ambivalent feeling toward the communication in the strong-appeal group.

More important and interesting is their finding that the net change in conformity to the recommendations was highest in the minimal-appeal group (36 per cent), second in the moderate-appeal group (22 per cent), and least in the strong-appeal group (8 per cent). This suggests a reciprocal relation between intensity of fear appeals and attitude change and would contradict the nonmonotonic hypothesis discussed above. We may summarize the study by saying that students' learning of information was about the same despite different levels of anxiety produced by communications, but their behavior change was inversely related to the strength of fear appeals. This contradictory relation can best be explained by the within-group variability on ambivalency toward communication, and perhaps variability in assimilation and contrast tendency to perceive similar cognitions as more similar and dissimilar cognitions as more dissimilar effects (Sherif and Hovland, 1961; Sherif, Sherif, and Nebergall, 1965). The latter is deduced from the varying percentages of students in each group who did not change one way or the other as a result of communication. Finally, we may speculate on several outside factors such as intra- and intergroup interaction in the one week following the communication, possible parental influence following comments at home on the study by the student, and differential exposure to other communications from natural settings.

A considerable number of studies, on the other hand, have found a positive relation between intensity of fear appeals and opinion or behavior change (Berkowitz and Cottingham, 1960; Leventhal, 1965; Leventhal and Niles, 1964, 1965; Leventhal, Singer, and Jones, 1965; Leventhal and Watts, 1966; Singer, 1965; Niles, 1964). This set of empirical evidence would negate both the nonmonotonic hypothesis as well as the findings of the Janis and Feshbach study. McGuire (1968b) suggests that possibly several situational and personality factors also add to the influence of intensity of fear appeals, with the result that no generalization is likely to emerge.

Another area of research that falls into the category of changing intensity of motives is the controversy about the superiority of emotional over rational appeals. Some studies have found that emotional appeals are more effective than rational appeals (Eldersveld, 1956). However, several other studies find no difference (Weiss, 1960). One of the major problems in this area is that of standard definitions of emotional and rational appeals (Bauer and Cox, 1963; Cox, 1962). Several researchers have suggested an orthogonal independent relation between the two types of appeals as opposed to bipolar extreme positions on a single continuum relation (Becker, 1963; Knepprath and Clevenger, 1965). Cox (1962) argues for the presence of both types of appeals in a single communication for maximum impact and effectiveness, although he does not take any position as to whether they are correlated or uncorrelated.

We believe that an emotional appeal should be defined as one in which the communication produces only the energizing or tuning-up effect by appealing to the irrelevant Motives described in Chapter 4. A rational appeal, on the other hand, is one that attempts to show perceived instrumentality of a brand for the buyer's goal satisfaction or changes intensity of relevant and product-specific Motives. A single communication may be classified as a rational or emotional appeal depending on how it affects (as described above) a majority of buyers. In other words, if an appeal only energizes motivation, it is an emotional appeal, but if it also directs behavior, it is a rational appeal.

2. *Change in content of motives.* Appeals can also modify the existing Motives. We believe that this is, from the company's point of view, the most difficult of the three processes. It implies that the buyer must be made to use a different set of Motives in his decision-making process.

This is likely to be difficult because, more often than not, it involves incompatibility with the goals provided by the social environment of the buyer. For example, in 1950 the motive of convenience at the expense of taste was not compatible with the social norms in the consumption of coffee. Instant coffee, therefore, had a very slow start (Haire, 1950; Westfall et al., 1957). We think that it would have died had it not been for the fact that social norms rapidly changed. Similarly, it is believed that at a time when the buyer's Motives were related to economy of the car, Ford introduced Edsel and communicated the car as providing luxury, comfort, and bigness. It failed because the buyer did not change his Motives (Brooks, 1964). Then Mustang became the fastest-selling car because the company, rather than attempting to change the Motives, took an early lead in identifying a new motive—the need for a personal passenger car with sports-car styling.

However, in a few situations, a company can provide different Motives and probably succeed. This is more likely in those product categories that are technical breakthroughs. Still, the Motives provided by the product should not be incompatible with the existing social norms, but should be such that the buyer can replace them with the new ones. A good example is the low-calorie foods and beverages. The buyer may be provided an additional motive of dietary control besides taste, nutrition, or substantiveness.

Another important way in which the company can change the motives of the buyer is to provide added uses of the product. For example, Alka-Seltzer attempts to show the product as an effective remedy not only for stomach upset but also for headaches and anxiety. Similarly, Carnation Instant Breakfast may be shown as not only good for breakfast but also as a snack or meal substitute. The suggestion of additional uses may add to the existing motives and make the product broader in its consumption (Kleppner, 1966, Chapter 4). We believe that this is what happened in the change of Spic and Span from "spring" cleaner to an "all-purpose" cleaner several years ago. Again, it should be remembered that if the change creates incompatibility, the buyer may not adopt the change.

9.5.1.4 Content and Its Relation to Inhibitors

The message may also create temporary barriers that inhibit the purchase of the product. It is very unlikely that a company would knowingly insert such inhibitory messsages in its symbolic communications. It is our belief that much of a copywriter's time is spent in reducing such inhibitions.

There are several ways in which the message can create inhibition.

First, it can bring to the buyer's attention those variables that are inhibitory to the purchase. In earlier chapters, we talked about four variables namely high price, lack of availability, Time Pressure, and Financial Status. If the price of a brand is higher than the industry price, it may be better not to bring price to the attention of the buyer in the communication. We know that generally price is mentioned in communication only to the extent that it is considered to be advantageous. However, there are at least two instances where price may be mentioned or emphasized in the message even for the more expensive brand. (a) For several product classes the buyer has price-quality association (Leavitt, 1954; Tull, Boring, and Gonsior, 1964). If the price-quality association is empirically verified, it may be advantageous to bring this association to the buyer's attention by emphasizing price. The effect then will be not to create inhibition, but rather a more favorable Attitude. (b) The brand may have certain characteristics that entail additional cost and make the product more expensive. Under such circumstances, high price may be emphasized to explain why it is high.

Second, the message can create inhibition by bringing Time Pressure to the forefront. This is likely to be more common in many communications, since the inhibitory variable is buyer-oriented and not brand-oriented. For example, the messsage may describe the preparation of the product in order to bring out good aspects of the brand. However, it may create inhibition in a buyer by being perceived as time-consuming.

Finally, when the message is about a radically new product, the attributes of the product may possess inhibitory factors in the mind of the buyer because of his social and cultural norms; for example, communication about a new tampon that fills any-size cavity and is being test-marketed by Playtex Corporation.

9.5.2 Structure of the Message

Extensive research has been done on the structure of communication content, that is, on how the various elements in the message are arranged. Structure refers to the manner of presentation and to some dimensions of the content of message presentation. For example, studies have explored the relative effectiveness of (1) a message that draws conclusions for the audience as opposed to one that leaves it to the audience to draw its own conclusions, (2) presenting two-sided arguments as opposed to a one-sided argument, and (3) presenting the message as a climax or anticlimax.

Most of these variables related to the structure of message have to do with proper Attention and Brand Comprehension, and to that extent they are similar in effect to the variables discussed under channel factor.

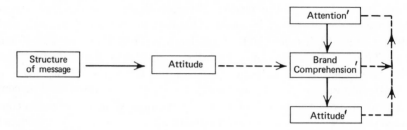

Figure 9.5   Effect of structure of message on Response Sequence.

The hypothetical construct that becomes important as the mediating vehicle is Attitude. Through Attitude via its feedback effects the variables are directly related to Brand Comprehension' and Attention'. We may show the relations schematically as in Figure 9.5.

In this section, we briefly examine major research findings about the structure of the message in the light of the theory.

9.5.2.1 Conclusion Drawing

The basic issue is whether it is better to simply give all the facts to the buyer and let him draw whatever conclusions he wishes or to draw conclusions from the facts and present them to the buyer in the message. The theoretical discussion coming out of group therapy suggests that implicit communication is likely to be more effective. However, much of the empirical research shows that conclusion drawing (explicit communication) is more effective in attitude or opinion change (Hovland and Mandell, 1952; Hovland, Lumsdaine, and Sheffield, 1949; Hadley, 1953; Maier and Maier, 1957). Furthermore, other variables such as education and intelligence seem to affect the relation (Hovland, Janis, and Kelley, 1953). McGuire (1968b) suggests that since implicit communication takes time to sink into the unorganized or unmotivated person, the conclusion drawing would be more effective immediately, but over time there are not likely to be any differences.

We shall attempt to understand what conclusion drawing does to the buyer, which may help in giving some leads.

Conclusion drawing has the same effect as border has in layout. Both integrate the various elements into a unified whole and make them distinct from other elements. Conclusion drawing may help comprehension by providing appropriate stimulus integration. It will also reduce ambiguity, but it may decrease it to so low a level that arousal is no longer created and the buyer does not pay attention to the message. *What is needed is providing a conclusion that will reduce ambiguity to some level but not the minimal level.* This suggests that if the elements in the message are too many or if the message is technically complex, it is advantageous to draw a conclusion. On the other hand, if the elements are few and the product is not too technically complex for the buyer to comprehend, it is advisable not to draw any conclusion. In those instances where the product is radically new, it may be advisable to draw conclusion so that the buyer properly comprehends the product class and the brand in that product class.

Conclusion drawing seems justified from another point of view. The message will create some anticipations on the part of the buyer; it will create expected satisfaction from the purchase of the brand. If the buyer has no prior familiarity with the brand and the conclusion is not drawn, he may create expectations that the product may not possess. Thus the buyer may have favorable Attitude toward the brand on certain attributes that, *he has concluded,* the brand possesses. Then when the actual purchase is made, and the resultant satisfaction is evaluated in terms of expectations, the buyer may feel unsatisfied. This will result in lessening of Attitude toward the brand. A secondary effect would be to reduce credibility of the source of communication for future messages. The result may be the permanent loss of a customer after the first purchase.

There is, however, a counterargument that would favor not drawing the conclusion. It may be argued that buyers have different evaluative meanings associated with a brand. In other words, a brand may satisfy different configurations of motives, which emerge as different segments in the market. For example, to a segment of the buyers, a foreign automobile may represent status, whereas to another it may represent economy and to still another it may seem to be unpatriotic or un-American. In other words, the buyers buy or reject a brand for a variety of motives. It is impossible to satisfy all segments by the same conclusions in a single advertisement; therefore, if conclusion drawing is left to the buyers, the same advertisement may successfully create favorable Attitude and overt action among all the segments. The most recent example of the variety of appeals that a product holds for different segments is the Mustang car (Reynolds, 1965). The car was designed for, and communicated to, the youth group, but it was found that many older people were also buying the car. Ford changed its advertising and stopped drawing any conclusions about the kind of buyer that a Mustang owner will be.

To summarize, in at least two instances, it may be better not to draw any conclusions: first, when the product is quite familiar to the buyer and the buyer is technically capable of comprehending it; and second, when the product is capable of serving a variety of uses and satisfying a variety of users.

9.5.2.2 One-Sided versus Two-Sided Messages

Some experimental research has been done on whether it is more effective to present both pros and cons or pros alone. The evidence suggests that only if some qualifying variables, such as education, are taken into account, is there any conclusive evidence one way or the other.

An important variable is the existing Attitude of the buyer toward the object or situation that the message communicates. If the buyer is favorably predisposed toward the brand, for example, if he is a loyal customer, one-sided message is found to be more effective. On the other hand, if the buyer is loyal to a competing brand, a two-sided message will be more effective. Several important implications are related to this finding. Thus in order to obtain a market share from existing brands for a newly introduced brand, a two-sided message will be more effective. The success of the Volkswagen advertisements can easily be attributed to such two-sided communication, in addition to the ingeneous unexpected element in the copy. Avis Rent-A-Car's suggestion as being only Number Two falls in the same category. It would appear to us that in those product categories whose market is mature and life cycle rather low as, for example, in detergent industry, two-sided messages may be more effective, contrary to the current practice. Finally, provided that we can segment buyers into loyal and nonloyal customers, it would be better, in sending out pamphlets requested through coupons or in the mail-order business, for example, to present two-sided arguments to the nonloyal segment and one-sided arguments to the loyal segment.

Education has been found to affect the relation of one-sided versus two-sided arguments and the Response Sequence. The greater the education, the more the Brand Comprehension' of both one-sided and two-sided arguments. However, Attitude' change is positively related to only two-sided arguments when there is increased education (Bauer and Buzzell, 1964; Hovland, Lumsdaine, and Sheffield, 1949). With the expected rise in education, it would appear that two-sided messages may become more relevant in the future.

More importantly, it has been found that two-sided arguments are better in terms of *retention* of attitude change. In other words, attitude change brought about by two-sided arguments is more durable than that produced by one-sided arguments. Several months before the Soviet Union set off its first atomic bomb, taped messages arguing that it would not be able to produce such bombs in quantity for at least five years more were played to high school students. One-sided messages changed the opinions of 64 per cent of the respondents, about the same as for two-sided messages. A week later, however, half the students heard new messages describing four plants in Russia that were supposed to be already producing bombs. Almost all of the change caused by the original one-sided message was wiped out; only 2 per cent of the students in this group held to the belief that Russia lagged five years behind the United States. In contrast, 61 per cent of the group that originally heard the two-sided message held to the belief that Russia lagged behind the United States. Even the actual explosion of the Soviet Union's first atomic bomb did not wipe out the effects of the two-sided message received months earlier (McGuire and Papageorgis, 1961). This phenomenon of resistance to change after being presented with the cons of the argument has been explained by the *inoculation hypothesis*. Just as in biology a mild dose of the germs of a disease inoculates a person against the disease, McGuire (1964) argues that exposure to the counterargument in a mild form creates a wall of resistance that later arguments cannot penetrate.

This finding is of some interest to the marketing practitioner, especially when introducing a new product, because counterarguments from competitors are invariably present. This is particularly true of very competitive industries such as drugs and cosmetics where a brand is very often directly attacked in a comparative manner. Listing the limitations of one's own brand, however, may alienate the buyer. Probably the best way would be to show the limitations in a comparative manner in which the advantages are, in the end, stressed. The best examples of two-sided messages can be found in the numerous advertisements of Volkswagen and Avis Rent-A-Car.

On the whole, it would appear that two-sided messages are likely to succeed better. Particularly, if the limitations are given in a tongue-in-cheek manner, the advertisements may prove to be very effective.

9.5.2.3   Climax versus Anticlimax

Some research also exists on the presentation of arguments in a climax or anticlimax form (Cromwell, 1950). Climax refers to a message in which the strongest arguments are presented at the end of the message. In anticlimax, the strongest arguments are presented in the beginning. The evidence is sparse and inconclusive.

It is found, however, that the presentation in a climax or anticlimax form depends on the content of the message and on the buyer's Attitude.

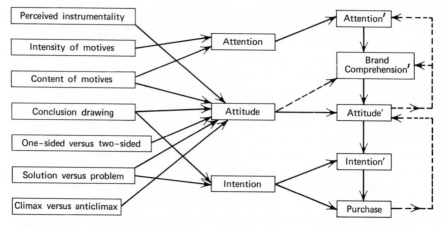

Figure 9.6   Attributes of message and their effect on Response Sequence.

When the buyer is familiar with the product and Importance of Purchase is high, a climax presentation is likely to be effective. Anticlimax is probably more effective when the product is unfamiliar to the buyer or the buyer has low interest. Logically, this can be explained by Attitude's beedback on both the perceptual processes of Perceptual Bias and Attention.

A related aspect has been studied in two-sided arguments. Is it better to present positive arguments first and negative arguments later? At least one study has found that it is more effective to present the positive aspects first (Janis and Feierabend, 1957).

9.5.3   Summary of Message Effects on the Response Sequence

Message is probably the one single factor of communication that heavily mediates via Attitude in its effects on the Response Sequence. The perceptual and evaluative processes, therefore, play a much greater role in terms of both facilitating the message and distorting it to make it congruent with the store of information that the buyer has. Message is likely to have more clear-cut effects than do source and channel factors: it will either succeed or fail more vividly.

Message also affects other links in the Response Sequence because it mediates via other hypothetical constructs. We saw that message may alter the intensity or content of nonspecific motives. It thus affects Attention. Finally, message affects Intention and subsequent Purchase behavior.

Figure 9.6 provides the summary relations.

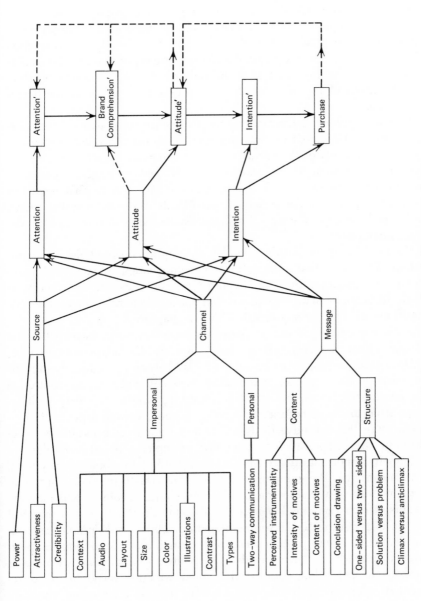

Figure 9.7 A summary of symbolic communication.

387

9.6   SUMMARY AND CONCLUSIONS

Symbolic communication is both complex and important to understand. Its complexity rests primarily in the multidimensionality of a single communication and in the fact that it is already an abstraction of the reality by being a pictorial and linguistic representation. Its importance lies in the fact that it is the only alternative to communicating via the physical product, which has limitations in terms of reach and cost efficiency.

In this chapter we have attempted to describe and explain considerable empirical research in mass communication using a number of hypothetical constructs of the theory of buyer behavior. Based on the S-O-R paradigm, we isolated the source, channel, and message attributes as representing various stimuli that could influence the buyer's responses (aggregately the Response Sequence). Finally, the influence was shown to be mediating via the three important constructs of Attention, Attitude, and Intention.

Figure 9.7 summarizes the complete description on symbolic communication. We think that putting mass communication in an S-O-R paradigm, and incorporating the hypothetical constructs of the theory, is likely to generate new hypotheses and speculations relevant to advertising. Some of these were pointed out in the chapter.

From Figure 9.7, several implications for advertising research become obvious. First, a direct relation between a specific advertising variable such as medium, copy, or size and sales is likely to be extremely difficult to measure; there are too many other variables that must be controlled to obtain such cause-and-effect relationship, which may very well be impossible to do in naturalistic setting. Second, certain aspects of communicating through advertising are more relevant for some of the reactions in the Response Sequence. For example, channel variables are extremely important in arousing and sustaining the buyer's Attention. This means that the company must seek answers to obtaining optimum combinations of variables included under source, channel, and message factors, which combined together will influence the buyer to manifest all the responses in the Response Sequence. Third, considerable research available on media selection seems only a small part of the total complexity. To properly understand advertising effectiveness, what we need is perhaps a major long-term study which would incorporate measurement of complex interrelationships among output intervening variables with the use of the theory of buyer behavior. Then only we would comprehend the complexity of the problem at hand (Sheth 1969b).

Summary and Implications

CHAPTER *10*
Theory: Structure, Function, and Need

10.1 INTRODUCTION

In this chapter, we summarize the description of the structure of the theory, then turn to the functions of the theory, and finally discuss the needs of the field. Also, we bring together the three strands of thought—structure, function, and need—to obtain a clearer view of one process of theory development. The company executive, or anyone who is interested in the immediate application of the theory to company needs, may wish to read only Section 10.3.2 on company policy needs. Similarly, the government executive may wish to read only Section 10.3.3 on public policy needs.

Having read the earlier chapters the reader is now in a position to judge for himself whether the structure of the theory conforms to the description of it contained in Chapter 1.

First, the theory was said to be at a moderate level of abstraction, because it deals only with buying behavior, but nevertheless to be abstract enough to encompass consumer buying, institutional buying, distributive buying, and industrial buying. We suspect that the theory, although we have not systematically attempted to extend it, can incorporate other types of decision making as well; for example, the executive pricing decision model that we used in Chapter 4 seemed to be completely consistent with the theory.

Second, the theory is fairly idealistic in the sense that no commitment is necessarily made that the structure it imposes on the empirical facts of buying behavior is really there. Some of the constructs do exist in physical or neurophysical fact, but we are not certain about all of them. If such a structure does exist and can be reconciled with underlying physiological structures, it is a real advantage, but it is not absolutely essential. We think it would be naïve and would impede research to lay this realistic requirement upon it. For almost two thousand years since Democritus the construct of an atom has been effective in furthering research, but only quite recently could we have any real hope of identifying it. Had a realistic requirement been laid upon those who speculated about physics in the past several hundred years, the field would probably have been much less productive.

Third, the theory is objective. In developing a body of knowledge, scientists and practitioners must agree on what they are talking about. To further this, the definitions of the constructs, both hypothetical and intervening, have been made explicit.

Fourth, the theory is very introspective, having its constructs developed more from the buyer's point of view than from that of the observer. According to Dulany:

Classical introspection was unproductive because it combined (a) a phenomenological observation language, (b) an attempt to inventory the ultimate constituents of a generalized human mind, by observers with variable histories, and (c) refined analysis of conscious contents that exceeded the observer's capacities for linguistic description, memory and veracity [Dulany, 1968, p. 379].

Taking Attitude' as an example, we have shown in Chapter 6 that neither of the three limitations need exist. A phenomenological language is avoided when observational rules are implied by the use of a scale and the way in which it is administered. Also, the scale prevents heavy demands being placed on the observer's capacities, and the observer bias referred to in (b) can be held to a minimum as well.

Finally, the theory is at a medium level of formality. It can easily be simulated (Perry, 1968), but the form of its equations, which are numerous, are not specified. The formality dimension will be further discussed below.

More important now than the question of structure, however, is, "How well does the structure fulfill the functions that a theory is supposed to fullfill?" Furthermore, "In fulfilling these desirable functions, how well does the theory meet the needs that it was designed to satisfy?" We summarize the extent to which the theory fulfills the functions and then proceed to describe in some detail the needs that the theory will meet.

10.2   FUNCTIONS OF THE THEORY

The functions that a theory may serve, as described in Chapter 1, are description, delimitation, integration, and generation. We now examine the extent to which each of these functions is fulfilled.

10.2.1   Descriptive Function

Does the theory succeed in describing the phenomenon of buying *behavior* in terms of the current needs of the field? We believe that the five output intervening variables that we postulate do describe most of the relevant aspects of the behavior of the buyer. Also, the hypothetical constructs that have no counterpart intervening variables suggest additional explanatory power that we have not fully utilized because we did not postulate the intervening variables. This remains a task for the future.

Explanation of the phenomenon—the "why" question—is encompassed by description. To explain behavior is to describe fully the conditions under which it varies, and explanation is specifically implied by the total consequences of the relations among the eleven hypothetical constructs that are postulated.

The comprehensiveness of this description of behavior is one of the dominant characteristics of the theory as contrasted with others that we know. We believe that the phenomenon with which we are dealing is very complex and that therefore the high degree of comprehensiveness is essential for effective work at the detailed level of analysis specified by our needs. If one has a pretzel he must have a pretzel-shaped hypothesis to understand it. Many marketing influences, for example, are small in an absolute sense, and we must have a theory that will bring to the surface and highlight these small effects. It becomes especially essential in designing studies to be carried out under naturalistic conditions. This is not to say that we expect all investigations to be field studies, most of them will be. Even in laboratory studies, the more fully the phenomenon is understood, the better the control that can be built into the experiments.

10.2.2   Delimiting Function

Description is what the theory says that it is talking about, and delimitation is what the theory says it is not talking about. Because the theory here is comprehensive, delimitation is especially essential. Unfamiliar boundaries have been established, and unless these are fully recognized, the user of the theory will either stop short of the boundaries and miss some of the power of the theory or exceed the boundaries by inserting his own unconscious extensions and thus perhaps place unjustified demands on the theory.

Does the theory adequately delimit the scope of inquiry? To answer more precisely, let us first spell out the meaning of "meaning," which is tied to the delimiting function, not to the descriptive function, of the theory. The hypothetical constructs impose meaning at the beginning, hence their nature determines the kind of meaning that the theory contains. The meaning of hypothetical constructs and propositions depends on their *relation* to other constructs and propositions. Meaning is, of course, not yet knowledge, just as explanation used in connection with description is not *knowledge*. Knowledge is both the *understanding* that a proposition about the relations among hypothetical constructs is true after it has been *tested* and why it is true. Knowledge takes in both theory and method of testing. *Prediction* and *control* used in the sense of how knowledge is created are, of course, related to this understanding. With these various epistemological concepts spelled out, let us turn to an evaluation of the theory of buyer behavior in terms of serving the delimiting function.

The meaning of the theory is delimited first by careful definition of the hypothetical constructs. Although the meaning of the hypothetical constructs is the source of the explanation of their counterpart intervening variables, the operational definition of the intervening variables does further delimit the meaning of the theory. The operationism implied in their definition serves to clarify communication among researchers in the field. Also, the exogenous variables have been defined and discussed in detail, and these strongly delimit the theory.

Finally, lurking below the surface of most of the discussion throughout the book has been the spirit of logical positivism: theory delimitation is aided by dealing only with that which is, in principle, verifiable. By "verifiable" is meant that the hypothesized relations can be tested by comparing them with the corresponding relation among empirical facts. Things that are not verifiable are not problems but pseudoproblems which can be discussed, but not systematically researched. Although we do not quite go to this extreme, our approach does fall into the tradition of logical positivism.

10.2.3   Integrative Function

We believe that in a variety of ways the theory serves the integrative function and that this integration is the source of much of its generative power, to be discussed next.

The theory accomplishes two important broad types of integration. First, perhaps partly as a result of the atomized state of psychology, but probably more because of the specialization of labor inherent in a large company, where until recently almost all of the buyer behavior research was done, advertising, pricing, selling, distribution, and similar activities have been studied *in vacuo* almost completely insulated from one another. The theory enables us to pull together these disparate *problem* areas and look at them as a unified whole. Second, psychology since Hull's integrating efforts has tended to be highly atomistic. Each of a number of areas such as perception, learning, personality, cognition, and motivation has been researched and theory developed independent of other psychological aspects of the same person. This was encouraged by the three separate traditions that have divided psychology: learning theory, cognitive theory, and personality theory. The theory of buyer behavior brings these disparate theory areas together in a systematic way.

Apparently, because of a misunderstanding of the nature of the theory, Kassarjian (1969) would have us forgo this attempt at theoretical integration, return to a Lewinian structure of more than thirty years ago, and worse yet, be quite dogmatic about it. Lewin contributed enormously to psychology by introducing concepts for dealing with problems that were ignored by the more behavioristic psychologists. As the perceptive reader will have noted, we have used a number of his ideas. Science typically progresses, however, by finding the flaws of past formulations and introducing improved formulations. Kassarjian advocates this backward step in spite of the progress that has been made. More than fifteen years ago Simon (1954, p. 389) wrote: "The social sciences-weakened by a half-century of schisms among economist, political scientists, sociologists, anthropologists and social psychologists are undergoing at present a very rapid process of reintegration." Almost a decade ago D. Campbell (1963) in various early drafts circulated privately was showing the high congruency between Hull and Lewin, a similarity that was subtly hidden by differences in problems, by methodologies, and above all, by terminologies. Also, see Atkinson (1964) for a splendid integration of views on motivation.

One particular theoretical integration is a central theme of the theory. The theme is conflict. Here instead of integrating a number of concepts, we have brought together a number of formulations of the same concept which we believe greatly increases the power of that concept to provide an understanding of behavior.

The reconciliation of these various views of conflict has not been completely worked out, but we have gone far enough to convince ourselves that there are no serious inconsistencies. Also, more productive developments in the theory of buyer behavior will be generated in the future, if the theory is made available in its current form, because this reconciliation is a long-run task and to a considerable extent will have to be done in the context of empirical studies.

Conflict arising from an ambiguous stimulus is one of the regulators of buyer attention and overt search behavior (Berlyne, 1966), as we saw in Chapter 5. Also, there we saw how it shapes the nature of how the buyer perceives whatever information he admits into his nervous system (Osgood, 1957b). Conflict in overt buying behavior—incompatible responses—also influences his attention and overt search behavior (N. Miller, 1959), as indicated in Chapter 8. Given that a buyer has well-formed Choice Criteria for a specified product class, the certainty (Confidence) with which he judges a brand in that class leads to a decrease in cognitive conflict. The cognitive conflict that occurs with low Confidence is manifested by search for information, for example, as postulated by one version of the consistency principle, namely dissonance theory (Brehm and Cohen, 1962). "Inconsistency" is also used to describe cognitive conflict when it is manifested in attitude change. Furthermore, expectancy as used by Lewin and others roughly to mean probability of payoff (Atkinson, 1964) implies conflict as a consequence of being unable to choose when certainty is low. "Inconsistency in the mind threatens to paralyze action" (R. Brown, 1965, p. 606). The behavioral manifestation of low "expectancy" (low Confidence) is vacillation (N. Miller, 1959). Thus by postulating the construct of Confidence we bring together (1) the processes by which the buyer obtains his *informational inputs,* (2) their *cognitive* consequences that will affect future purchases, and (3) their *behavioral* consequences for the current purchases. In using the concept of conflict to explain search effort we have developed a specific mechanism to explain what was postulated in an earlier version of the theory (J. Howard, 1963, p. 58), namely, that buyers further along on the learning curve with respect to a brand are less inclined to seek information.

A second type of theoretical integration involves conflict, information processing, and related ideas. Incongruency (conflict) between the value of an inhibitor that the buyer expects (ex ante) and the value that he perceives it actually has (ex post) is postulated by G. Miller et al. (1960) to be the driving force that, given his attitude, motivates him, step by step, to solve the problem posed by his inhibitors which underlie his intention to buy and in this way connect attitude to the ultimate purchase act. Each inhibitor involves an information-processing rule, as we saw in Chapter 4, which leads to a decision rule. Thus we are able to describe what we mean by information processing when the information is being used to decide how to act with respect to a concept, for example, in solving the problem of whether to buy a Ford car. Information must also be processed, however, in valuing a concept, for example, in deciding whether one likes or prefers a Chevrolet. The valuation process was discussed in Chapter 4 in connection with attitude formation and change. Finally, if the buyer does not have the concept of product class in the first place, he must process information in order to form the concept, for example, he must form the concept of car, the product class. Presumably, the process by which a brand concept is formed is no different from the formation of a product class concept. Thus we move the information processing idea to all levels of the conceptual structure discussed in Chapter 8.

Furthermore, by setting attitude formation and changes as well as research on information seeking into the framework of concept formation and information processing we believe that a number of phenomena that seemed unrelated now fit snugly together. Going further, we believe that this particular integration has still greater significance for the future as Patrick Suppes (1966, p. 27) has suggested: ". . . the theory of information processing and concept formation might even give quantum mechanics and molecular biology a run for their money for the title of most important scientific development of the twentieth century."

A third theoretical integration has largely been due to the integration of differing formulations of the concept of conflict with the information-processing idea. It has been possible to bring together a great amount of empirical research around the idea of *search* for information. Much of these ideas have been around for some time but left implicit. So far as we know we have set forth a more systematic description of the search process than has heretofore been available.

A fourth area of theoretical integration has to do with the equilibrium idea. We believe that the equilibrium concept—motivational and information—purchase—which this integration has made possible can strongly contribute to development in the buyer behavior area just as it has elsewhere in social science such as in economics.

A fifth type of integration enables us to view the buyer as forward-looking instead of backward-looking. We have gotten away from the "strict law of effect" that characterized classical learning theory. By taking instead the more cognitive position that it is "the expectancy of the goal"—a forward-looking view—that motivates the buyer and then by integrating this view with the analysis of the temporal pattern of reinforcement, it has been possible to develop a more systematic construct Satisfaction. This new construct opens up a number of new research opportunities with fascinating implications.

Sixth, and largely in an implicit manner, we have in a sense brought the Motivation Research point of view that was so popular in the fifties into juxtaposition with cognitive and behavioral theory. As a result we believe we see at least one reason why the Motivation Research view was not fruitful, why we find such poor relations between personality measures and purchase behavior as has been shown by Evans (1959), for example. Motives attacked at this higher level in the motive structure are too general to permit a close relationship. Motives at lower, more specific levels we expect will be more fruitful.

Seventh, one of the difficult problems faced by the researcher in buyer behavior has been to integrate two different levels of choice—choice among brands and buy or not buy—into a systematic framework. The concept of the "stop rule" discussed in connection with Intention in Chapter 4 provides this integration so that the two levels of choice fit snugly together. True enough, the "no-buy" case is often the decision to buy some other product class, but it can be handled more simply as "no-buy". This two-level integration is especially important for such products as life insurance where the "buy—not buy" problem is probably much greater than the brand choice problem and yet they must be dealt with together. Throughout the book for the sake of clarity we have emphasized the competitive level and left the "no-buy" case implicit.

Eighth, the various integrations have taken place within the outlines of systems theory and a number of the specific systems concepts were employed (Howard, 1968).

Finally, we believe that the stage is set for an integration of the marketing view of buyer behavior with the economist's view of consumer choice. This will be discussed more in connection with public policy.

Aside from integrating concepts, we have attempted to integrate the theory with some of the available data. We do not pretend to have been exhaustive by any means. We have done only enough to reassure ourselves and our readers that such integration is possible in a number of cases at least. Moreover, the data we used were chosen on the basis of expediency. True, they met a certain minimum level of quality, but beyond this, it was a matter of whether we were familiar with them. Many equally good studies have probably not been included. Systematic integrations will be separate research projects for the future.

10.2.4   Generative Function

The generative function—the generation of hypotheses—is very much the alpha and the omega of theory, toward which the other functions are ultimately directed. To achieve a greater generative effect, we have intended to be somewhat loose and vague at times, as contrasted with the extreme case, for example, of the axiomatized theory of consumer choice (Georgescu-Roegen, 1954). We believe that our approach is more productive of fruitful hunches, ideas, and new hypotheses. It leaves one free for imaginative theorizing. In this form, our approach will be more heuristically productive; it will stimulate further research. By using the hypothetical construct–intervening variable distinction we hope to have achieved the best of both possible worlds: flexibility and rigor. Also, in spite of the recently accelerated flow of research findings, our data are yet pitifully limited so that we think it unwise to "close in" the theory to a logical system that is too tight.

Especially to operations researchers who learned Newton's simple system as an ideal, this system may seem quite unexciting. True enough, Keynes made a great contribution to the social sciences with his income-consumption relationship which required only a four-equation system for explaining the level of economic activity. The reader should bear in mind, however, that those who are using the Keynesian system for policy purposes have had to develop systems of tens of equations.

Finally, too much emphasis on measurability in the design of the theory can be a loss. As an example we would cite the intention-to-buy hypothetical construct that we have formulated in contrast with the definition implied in the conventional method of measuring it. We believe that the former will in the long run be more productive in this important area than would the latter. More effective research is likely to be the result. Another example is the use of stochastic models of brand loyalty where the data did not match with the assumptions of the models (Sheth, 1966; 1968b).

Many of the propositions generated by the theory are simply carried over to a new field of application, namely to buyer behavior. Others are obviously implicit in previous formulations. Some, however, are new, for example, the loyalty-disloyalty cycle, and they show the power of a systematic, comprehensive, integrated system. The information-purchase equilibrium that occurs within this more dynamic system represented by the loyalty-disloyalty cycle is another example. Finally, the concept of motivational equilibrium within the framework of the purchase-information equilibrium and of the path to it is still another new idea. As other researchers work with the theory, we are confident that yet more hypotheses will be deduced.

To summarize, all of the specific propositions generated from the theory predict the kind of buying behavior that we seem to observe. It is a plausible picture. History will tell us whether it is an adequately true one for now.

10.3   NEED FOR THE THEORY

Given the degree to which the theory serves the usual functions of a theory, how well does it satisfy the current needs? The epistemological needs of a field of knowledge vary from time to time. For the understanding of buyer behavior here and now, these can be conveniently discussed under the three headings of basic research, company policy, and public policy that were set forth in Chapter 1 where the way we view the problem of buyer behavior was described and which goes far in defining the needs of the field as we see them. We present them in this order for reasons that will become apparent later.

10.3.1   Basic Research Needs

Within the past five years the flow of buyer behavior findings has accelerated. A review of issues of the *Journal of Marketing Research, Journal of Marketing* and the *Journal of Advertising Research,* for example, will quickly substantiate this contention. This flow is in part a reflection of the strengthened faculty research capabilities and doctoral programs developing out of the business school "revolution" of the late fifties. Professional market researchers, broadly defined to include advertising researchers are also contributing substantially to the flow. It is reported that academics are responsible for 70 per cent of this flow in the *Journal of Marketing Research,* and industry representatives, 30 per cent (Lotshaw, 1969).

Unless there is available a broad theoretical structure by which to integrate, interpret and evaluate the pieces that make up the flow, we shall be seriously handicapped in the further development of new knowledge. Without a guiding road map there is a danger in this situation that research will degenerate into dealing with small issues and be characterized by a considerable amount of nonproductive gamesmanship. We detect that some of this tendency is beginning to appear. Also, doctrine of any sort comes easy in the early stages of a field. In the face of great uncertainty the scientist, like the buyer, tends to be loyal.

We have attempted to meet this research need by providing a comprehensive structure, and all of the various integrations of theory were intended for this purpose. One particular area of integration we believe will be especially significant in furthering basic research. This is the integration of Berlyne's curiosity work, Osgood's analysis of perception, and the communication research concepts such as supportive exposure. From this the buyer is viewed as behaving in a more rational way than has been encouraged by dissonance research; for example, the buyer does not delude himself; he is merely equipped with limited information-processing capacities.

Another contribution that we have made is to maintain the terminology from the basic areas on which the theory has drawn and the relationship to the basic areas at each point of development has been shown. We somewhat immediately hope that thereby the theory will serve as a *two-way* path. First, it is a path by which the specialist in buying behavior can find his way to the basic areas with a minimum of effort. Anyone who has worked in the behavioral sciences will appreciate the need for this because the terrain of these highly atomized fields of knowledge is not conducive to easy approach by the nonprofessional. Going back to the basic science is essential in many cases for a sharper statement of the hypothesis. Also, the researcher can learn from the method used there how to design studies and also how much of the findings might be an artifact of the method.

Second, the same path should be useful to those hardy souls who have the courage to come forward from the basic disciplines to our problems. The formation of the Consumer Psychology Division of the American Psychological Association is encouraging in this respect. In some ways the study of buyer behavior has advantages over such things as political issues; for example, the attitude-object or goal-object is usually concrete except in the case of services.

In the research under field conditions, propositions from psychology and social psychology, we hope, will be validated and extended beyond the range of the laboratory that uses college sophomores as subjects, which has been the context of so much psychological and social psychological findings. Such extension will not only strengthen the basic sciences, but will add immensely to the intellectual strength of the applied area. At the same time crucial hypotheses will be developed that need the precision of the laboratory and that can be realistically approximated in the laboratory.

We hope also that the theory will encourage the statistically well-trained student to break away from static cross-sectional and highly aggregative studies. The theory suggests the limitations of these assumptions. It indicates that individual buyers can change rapidly over time, and Kuehn's pioneering work in developing a linear learning model is relevant here (Kuehn, 1962). Morrison (1966) has extended the aggregate Markov process to incorporate individual differences which, the theory also suggests, are a fact, especially insofar as the purchase behavior is influenced by the level of the buyer's search effort. Sheth (1968b, 1969) has extended the learning concept by a statistical method that provide individual measures of brand Loyalty. It is reported that

Kuehn's work is being extended further to incorporate social effects to explain differing rates of diffusion.

This attention to the more formal aspects is not at all meant to imply that we are more optimistic about their contribution. We hope that the theory will suggest new statistical approaches. We have included Chapters 6 and 7 to indicate other alternatives. These are approaches to studying the relations among the outputs, R-R relations in psychological terminology. There is, of course, the great potential for investigating the conventional S-R relations. Finally, we believe that there is also a splendid potential for studying the relations among the inputs, S-S relations in other words, such as those between advertising and word-of-mouth information.

In addition to these searches into a few relations, there is the global approach, which is possible in simulation of dealing with the whole system or at least much of it. The one simulation study that has been done (Perry, 1968) performed splendidly at the aggregate level when tested against test market data, but not much better than chance at the individual level. Its predictions were made, however, from information that was available before the new product was introduced into the market, which for practical purposes makes it a much more interesting example. Until the simulation is tested against a new set of data, however, we cannot be certain that its power did not derive from being tested against the data out of which it was developed although precautions were taken to avoid this possibility. More rigorous still than simulation is the multiple-equation model derived from the theory that John U. Farley and Winston L. Ring are now testing empirically. McGuire (1967) has urged the use of this more rigorous approach in social psychological research.

There are encouraging developments in the broader environment of our field. Social psychology has in recent years hooked its roots more firmly into general psychology, but at the same time it is becoming truly social, with the attitude-object being another person. Furthermore, it exhibits a growing interest in theory-oriented research in natural settings (McGuire, 1967, p. 125). This is not to say that buyer behavior studies will be done only in the field. In fact, some good laboratory work has already been done, particularly in advertising. We believe with others (Sherif and Koslin, 1960, p. 16), however, that laboratory work will be more productive when the ideas are very sharply expressed. We suspect that in general this will not be for some time yet in the field of buyer behavior.

Another development is the growing support for the social sciences by the federal government. "The overwhelming concern of Congress for R&D (Vietnam notwithstanding) is directed to the civilian sector of society; this focus has generated growing interest in the social sciences" (Kash, 1968, p. 1314). This is related to the new role that American universities are expected to play—participating in applied research—in addition to their traditional role as strongholds of basic research.

10.3.2 Company Policy Needs

Referring back to the discussion in Chapter 1 of the theory and buyer behavior, especially Figure 1.1 the company's interest in an understanding of the buyer comes about because the company can alter the buyer's environment so as to alter his behavior. The company can change the product quality, its price, and its availability; equally important, it can change the symbolic information content in the buyer's environment.

For the purposes of exposition it will be helpful to distinguish between the role of the theory as an aid (1) in interpreting the data that the executive is exposed to and (2) in deciding what data to collect in the first place. However, this distinction in a sense perpetuates a weakness that often plagues marketing, which is to clearly separate—and even isolate—data collection from data interpretation, decision making and marketing planning, a problem that may become worse as a result of introducing computerized marketing information systems. One of the serious limitations in modern market research activities is their separation from the actual decision-making and planning processes. Specialization of labor obviously demands some separation, but the coordination requirements are so subtle in market research and its utilization that the result is sometimes a breakdown of communication between the executive and the market researcher.

10.3.2.1 Interpretation and Utilization of Facts

Some people might argue that because the theory has not been thoroughly tested, it should not be offered to the executive as an aid, but instead should be evaluated only in terms of its contribution to basic research. Referring back to the discussion of the delimitation function of the theory, they would say that the understanding that the theory provides is primarily at the explanatory level and not the knowledge level required by the decision maker or planner, that the testing is inadequate for purposes of prediction and control.

Our answer to this is, first, that there is substantial empirical support for a number of the postulated relations among the hypothetical constructs. Second, the perceptive, experienced marketing executive has acquired a great number of subtle hunches and hypotheses, even if he is not aware of many of them. As one market research director has put it, ". . . this marketing model of man is only implicit in such an internalized manner that marketing people may never be conscious of it" (Kover, 1967, p. 129). The intense pressures of his position do not permit the marketing executive the luxury of making all his hunches explicit, but he is often able to do so when confronted with a statement of the theory. For example, if he is confronted with propositions from Chapters 8 and 9 and is given the opportunity to think about them, he is likely to remember past experiences that were consistent and others that were inconsistent with them.

The mere act of making the propositions explicit is a major practical contribution. It enables the marketing executive to (1) detect inconsistencies within his own set of hunches, (2) understand why another executive looking at the same set of facts—the same research report—comes to different conclusions, and (3) be of enormous help to the market research director in designing studies to collect the information that he, the executive, needs to solve his problems. It is impossible to overemphasize the third point.

With these hunches or beliefs articulated, communication across the company and up and down the hierarchy is vastly improved. The market research director has in large measure had to serve this function in the past, but it has often been a very difficult role, fraught with frustration for both him and the executive. Charges and countercharges sometime resulted. The executive was said not to know what he wanted, and the market research director was alleged to be unimaginative. We believe that the rational flavor of the theory connotes a certain plausibility which will contribute to its acceptance among executives. The consistency with commonsense notions should help, although what is common sense to one person is often quite uncommon sense to another.

Finally, the theory suggests that in interpreting facts about the buyer one should expect to find great change for any given buyer and variability among buyers. We believe that the desire to segment markets has caused us to take a static view of the buyer, to view him as an unchanging entity as implied in the use of personality criteria in attempted segmentation. The theory suggests that the contrary is true—that the buyer is strongly dynamic. Even in the Routinized Response Behavior stage, his purchasing is subject to the effects of changes in his environment that operate through the inhibitors underlying Intention. Furthermore, the loyalty-disloyalty cycle suggests that his stay in this stage may be short-lived.

The emerging knowledge will contribute a number of techniques useful to management. First we have in mind relationships among constructs that will give clues to the marketing executive. Data are often collected in a test market on both attitude and intention, for example, and it would appear possible to establish explanations of why the values of these two relate to each other in the way that they do and thus be able to infer much that is hidden below the surface. From these relationships techniques can be developed.

Second, by and large operations research techniques have not been successful in marketing, and this failure has been believed to be due to a lack of the appropriate input data. Buyer behavior research can begin to supply some of the input data. In some cases the exact data specified by the operations research model can be obtained. In other instances, the operations research model will have to be reformulated in order to use the new data.

Third, the trichotomy that classifies buyers according to their information needs—Routinized Response Behavior, Limited Problem Solving, and Extensive Problem Solving—may be helpful guides to action. These appear to coincide roughly with Copeland's very early classification of products as specialty convenience, and shopping which was designed to provide guidance to the development of marketing strategies by retailers (Bucklin, 1963). Bucklin has proceeded in an imaginative way to develop this traditional classification. We believe that our classification could make the Bucklin classification into an operational procedure.

10.3.2.2 Collection of Facts

That some hunches, hypotheses, and beliefs underlie the collection of any facts may seem so obvious as not to be worth mentioning. The inexperienced researcher usually has to discover this the hard way, however; he goes through the experience of collecting facts that throw no light on the question that prompted the data collection in the first place.

The theory not only offers new hypotheses but also provides a sharper statement of many hypotheses than the market researcher typically has in mind. In addition to supplying the hypotheses, it is a source of ideas for building control into a study; the exogenous variables were constructed specifically to ensure greater control. In field investigations, which market research studies typically are, this control is crucial.

A new development on the horizon holds many significant implications for data collection, the market research function, and the whole marketing decision-making and planning process. It is the concept of a computerized marketing-information system. Data are collected on a regular ongoing basis. This procedure implies a heavy investment in particular data; hence a careful analysis of why these data should be collected, instead of many others that might be collected, is essential. In a nutshell, the procedure requires particular attention to the constructs that underlie the data collection. As these systems are now being designed, probably not nearly enough attention is being paid to the executive's information-processing capacities (Simon, 1968; Howard and Morgenroth, 1968), that is, to his hunches and beliefs, which now tend to remain implicit but which crucially shape his thinking, the way he processes his facts. Unless the data conform to his thinking processes, it is doubtful in our opinion they will be used. We feel that retraining of senior executives will be difficult because of the subtle and deeply ingrained nature of these thinking processes.

These systems are now being thought of primarily in terms of their immediate contribution to planning and control (Cox and Good, 1967). Equally important, however, will be their stimulation of basic research *within the company*. By and large, company market research in terms of its contribution to decision making and planning has had a highly *ad hoc* flavor. The marketing information system, with its repeated measurements of the same constructs, will permit and encourage dynamic analysis that heretofore has been lacking. This will open a new era of interaction between theory and data and of consequent theory development. To the extent that security limitations will permit, it will make for fruitful cooperative arrangements between companies and universities.

The concern is often expressed especially by the marketing executive that he is being swamped with facts. Clearly, the flow of information will become greater instead of smaller. What we are suggesting here, however, and what Simon has suggested elsewhere, is that the executive will have to learn to compress and distill his facts by fitting them into a theory (Simon, 1968) in order to be able to handle the information flow.

There is one specific area of development that, because of its transcendent importance, we would like to discuss here. Traditionally, in company practice advertising research, sales research, and the rest of the company's market research have been quite separate from each other. A certain amount of separation may be essential, because of the creative nature of advertising and the role of the advertising agency, for example. We feel, however, that in spite of this the theory offers the opportunity to integrate the disparate areas of research, to strengthen them, and to relate them to the ongoing behavioral research stream. Krugman (1967) has implied the need for this in describing his thinking-looking-feeling paradigm for laboratory research on advertising, and we use his work here to illustrate what we have in mind. "Looking" describes the extent to which the buyer surveys the advertisement; it is measured mechanically by eye movements, not pupil dilation. "Feeling" is defined as the intensity of the buyer's emotional response to the advertisement which can be measured by pupil dilation. "Thinking", in Krugman's context, refers to thoughts that come spontaneously to the buyer's mind when he views an advertisement.

In terms of the theory of buyer behavior, "looking" is a part of Overt Search and is subject to the same principles as other manifestations of overt search behavior. Feeling is indicated by the level of arousal, which Hess (1965) and Krugman (1964) have used as a measure of the intensity of the general attitude toward a brand. "General" attitude is used here to contrast with the specific attitude dimensions emphasized in the theory. The reader will also recall that there is a feedback to Attention from Attitude via arousal, but that there are other feedbacks, too, especially from Confidence.

We would view Krugman's "thinking" as a measure of the associations that were triggered by the stimulus-as-coded hence it represents a description of the immediate consequences of the output of the buyer's perceptual subsystem, the s-a-c. Some developmental effort will be needed to construct a procedure for measuring what would become an intervening variable in the system and would connect the perceptual and learning subsystems.

The virtue of making use of a stimulus-as-coded hypothetical construct and intervening variable is that the conventional market research studies could then also obtain measurements of the stimulus-as-coded as an input to the learning subsystem and so relate it to such variables as Attitude, Intention, and Purchase. In this way, we believe that two separate research streams—advertising and conventional market research—can be brought together to the mutual profit of both.

10.3.2.3   Company Buying Policy

While both company and government are concerned with efficiency in buying, in the case of a company, the buyers are its own buyers—those specialists who spend all of their time procuring the products and services needed by the firm. From a descriptive standpoint the problem here is no different than what has been implied with respect to organizational buyers throughout the book. With the development of industrial purchasing departments, particularly since World War II, companies have placed increasing emphasis on how to buy more efficiently. At the same time there have been a number of developments in formal, normative decision models.

Value analysis—the attempt to be more explicit in the statement and application of criteria of choice—was the first major effort toward obtaining rationality in the industrial purchasing process. More recently, attempts have been made to incorporate formal decision-theoretic concepts into the procedures. Still more recently, a system consisting of a network of information flows between industrial sellers and buyers and centered in an elaborate, centralized, digital computer arrangement has been developed.

After having participated in some of this development work, we think that one of the most serious barriers to progress has been the lack of understanding of the buyer's capacity to process information, that is, how he seeks, identifies, selects, takes in, makes sense of, and acts on the basis of it. The constructs from the theory can provide some of the necessary understanding.

10.3.2.4   Top Management's Need for Theory

Company top management is becoming aware of a new need for theory. The rise of so-called "consumerism" and controls in advertising such as the British government's directive to Unilever and Procter and Gamble to cut their advertising budgets by 40 per cent, has awakened some industries to the crucial need for a better rationale for their marketing activity. The Congressional hearings on the Hart bill—the so-called "truth-in-packaging" legislation—has had a similar effect. A far better articulated understanding of the market is essential to building such a rationale.

Anyone who has participated in Congressional hearings on such issues is impressed by two things. First, on the whole the Congressmen are sincerely attempting to obtain answers to very complex problems and they enthusiastically welcome clarification and evidence. Second, management by and large does not do a very good job of articulating its case (Bauer and Greyser, 1967). This inadequacy is by no means willful; the opposite, in fact, is true. Top management simply does not have available the vocabulary for articulating its policies in terms of the public interest. Also, company market research departments do not seem to be playing nearly the role that they might in providing their top management with relevant evidence on public policy issues. Efforts are now being made to satisfy the need for a social rationale for marketing practices. Some corporate leaders are taking the position that they want better social evaluation of current marketing practices, and if found wanting the practices will be changed. The grocery manufacturing industry, for example, has established the Consumer Research Institute to grant major funds for the support of basic research on public policy issues in marketing.

The theory of buyer behavior can provide the needed vocabulary and guide the research.

Finally, to the extent that theory is available and is found effective in furthering the company's ends, top management will also be concerned with its implications for the organization, selection, training, supervision, and promotion of people within the company.

10.3.3 Public Policy Needs

We believe that we are beginning to witness a revival of the strong interest in public policy that characterized the academic marketing specialist of an earlier period. This revival was stimulated at least in part by E. T. Grether's recent thoughtful article linking some of the earlier views to current research in marketing (Grether, 1965).

In terms of Figure 1.1, government can affect the buyer-seller relationship by changing the environment of either the buyer or the seller, or both. Traditionally, public policy has been directed to the seller's environment, either his competitive environment, by imposing limitations on company size, for example, or his legal environment, hoping in this way to force the company to change the buyer's environment to a more favorable state. This has usually been discussed under the rubric of "antitrust."

Recently, however, because of "consumerism" and the growing concern for the poor and the underprivileged, government has greatly expanded its interest in the consumer buyer. In its new role, it is taking a much more direct view of the consumer and attempting to alter his environment directly. For example, the Food and Drug Administration experimented with making available a well-publicized telephone number that the consumer could call to obtain information about products and brands. It also contemplated the use of a public address system on a truck as another alternative device for providing information to the consumer.

Perhaps as a consequence of this expanded interest, the government appears to be shifting from its traditional concern with protecting the consumer against deception—the doctrine that anything that deceives the buyer must be prohibited—to one of shielding him from confusion in his purchasing activities (J. Howard, 1966).

It seems to us that, as a result, the government's needs have become, and will increasingly become, more like those of the company, and for that reason we discussed the company's needs first. The government traditionally has required information about the buyer only on an *ad hoc* basis, when a particular policy issue was at stake. Its broadened interests will require and economically justify data collection on more regular bases. The government, too, will need a "marketing information system." As evidence for this we would cite the interest that the Department of Health, Education, and Welfare has expressed in a government-sponsored and government-supported set of social indicators. Furthermore, the government in this endeavor can learn from company market research practices in developing and utilizing such a set of social indicators, and we believe that in Bauer's (1967) splendid discussion of them we detect the strong influence of his market research experience.

Obviously, the company and government criteria for evaluating good and bad behavior must be different. The company hopes that the buyer will purchase its product at a profitable price on a continuing basis. The government wishes the consumer to be efficient in his buying. The government's criteria for evaluating buyer behavior, we suspect, are largely still to be formulated.

As a source of such criteria, the traditional theory of consumer demand, with its assumption of perfect information and other restrictions is of little value. Recent work by Lancaster (1966a, 1966b) and also Quandt and Baumol (1966) however, is encouraging. Lancaster makes the careful distinction between a brand and its attributes, in contrast to the traditional view that ". . . . the only characteristic of an apple was appleness and the only source of appleness was an apple" (Lancaster, 1966a, p. 15). The similarity between Lancaster's view and that implied in the theory of buyer behavior is obvious, and we believe that the theory can be useful in empirically testing his theory. First, in the tradition of economics, he focuses on "bundles of goods" without specifying the alternatives, but implying that it is at the product class or higher level in the conceptual structure, not the brand level. Second, in Chapter 6 we have shown in detail the procedures for obtaining the relevant criteria that a buyer uses in making choices among brands. This intellectual apparatus—both the theory and the measurement techniques—can be transferred and applied to choices among product classes, or at any other level in the conceptual structure, for that matter. Third, especially if the Lancaster theory is applied in natural settings, the construct of Intention should be incorporated to connect Attitude to Purchase.

Implicit in the Lancaster theory is the concept of utility, and here again we believe that the theory of buyer behavior can make a contribution. Attitude is the psychological counterpart of the economic concept of utility. As Lancaster has recognized, it is more fruitful to work at the level of the attributes of the alternative instead of the total preference for the alternative. This is especially so when the aim of the researcher is to attempt to understand the effects of marketing effort. Lancaster has not recognized, however, that there is a need for an intermediate construct linking preference and purchase. We postulate the construct of Intention to serve this purpose.

Finally and implicit in all of our comments here, we believe with Simon (1963, p. 694) that to reexamine the utility concept in terms of conflict as suggested by the theory may be an even more fruitful approach than was the von Neuman-Morgenstern method of using uncertainty, which is also implicit in the normative decision theory that makes use of the standard gamble. Fortunately, the positive and normative views of decision are coming closer together. Because of Allais' paradox, for example, the logical implications of normative rules are being worked out (Morrison, 1967; Borch, 1968), which opens the possibility of subjecting the implications to empirical test.

In the process of applying the psychological notion of conflict to the concept of utility, we encounter the same problems that economists have had to face: the relative strengths of values. In Chapter 6 and elsewhere we have dealt with just this issue. Utility theory predicts that in any choice situation involving both negative and positive values—probably the typical case—there exists an exactly equivalent simple *net* value and that the buyer's response is the same between the two situations, the negative-positive and the simple positive. Most psychologists, being conflict-oriented, however, predict that a person behaves differently in the negative-positive situation than when confronted with a choice involving an equivalent positive value. As pointed out in Chapter 8 in connection with the conflict analysis, for example, he may seek information or, when the conflict is stronger, may simply vacillate around the interesection of the approach and avoidance gradients and thus manifest fixation, regression, aggression, and withdrawal.

We have not, however, dealt explicitly with the problem of transitivity that occurs in predicting behavior from Attitude. The social psychologists have been concerned with a slightly different version of consistency: Jones can like Smith only if Smith likes the things that Jones likes. There has been growing concern among some psychologists that man can be inconsistent in this respect and still do nothing to restore consistency to his cognitions, particularly when the issue is one in which he is not deeply involved (low Importance of Purchase). McGuire (1968e) has reservations about this requirement that the person must be involved, however. We believe that lack of transitivity may not be a serious problem in buying. If the concept of evoked set is used in empirical research, the problem of intransitivity, we think, will be much less. At the moment we have only limited evidence. B. Campbell (1969) found that for the brand's in the buyer's evoked set there was a wider range of probabilities of repeat purchase. This suggests to us that if we confine our empirical research to the brands that the buyer has in his evoked set at the time of choice, the transitivity will be much greater than if we force him to choose among alternatives not included in it.

Furthermore, from here it is but a step to incorporating, analyzing, and evaluating in social welfare terms such phenomena as expressive behavior: people buy a brand not for its intrinsic, functional utility, but because it confers social status, for example. We suspect that much of the severe condemnation of marketing practices is implicitly focused on expressive behavior. Yet, a recent social psychology text states that "It seems to us that he gets what he pays for, and we should not expect a symbol-using animal to be interested in nothing but food and drink" (R. Brown, 1965, p. 568).

We are not by any means suggesting that "the case of expressive behavior is closed," that we accept it as good; what we are questioning is the adequacy of the basis for the common conclusion that it is bad. The question is still open, and we use expressive behavior to merely illustrate a general tendency for intelligent, thoughtful, influential people to make firm evaluations of marketing practices with little or no analysis. There is a long tradition of such conclusions that should be systematically reexamined in light of the fundamental technological, social, and economic changes that have occurred. It seems to us that the housewife, confronted with the great flow of new products that exists today and being able to purchase many more products than in the past because of a higher standard of living, does carry a heavier burden in her shopping than previously. Hence new public policy may be needed, but the nature of that policy should be determined on a much more rational basis than it has been in most of the recent consumer legislation. True enough very little of the buyer behavior research has been directed toward the broader social issues. It is therefore especially encouraging to see the thoughtful and systematic analysis by Kassarjian (1969) on the Negro's role in advertisements.

Finally, we believe that we have sharpened the concept of an industry (Product Class Comprehension), presented a rationale for buyer response to a change in the concept, and made the concept operational. It is clear that much of the empirical research done from the viewpoint of partial equilibrium theory from economics now suffers from an inadequate definition of industry. The usual practice is to use the Standard Industrial Classification code and typically at the four-digit level. Its limitation as the empirical counterpart of the theoretical concept of industry is obvious to anyone who has worked with it.

10.4   SUMMARY OF RELATIONS AMONG STRUCTURE, FUNCTION, AND NEED

Since the earlier parts of the chapter dealt separately with each of the three elements—structure, function, and need—let us now try to be more explicit about how they are interrelated.

By constructing the theory at a medium degree of abstraction it has been possible to achieve the level of detail in the analysis which enables the user to capture essential distinctions required to integrate a variety of bodies of theory and research which in turn incorporate the distinctions required for dealing with problems at what we think of as the "marketing level." This is the level at which most company questions get asked, and for this reason it can be useful in contemplating new marketing strategies. Also, we believe that it is this level at which many antitrust questions should be asked, as well as many of the economic questions of the underprivileged. We could have, for example, treated buyer behavior at a more abstract level, primarily as a problem in learning as we did in an earlier attempt (J. Howard, 1963). To do this, however, would cause us to miss the opportunity to integrate with buying research on perception which incorporates essential distinctions for understanding advertising for both company and public policy purposes. We believe it can thus integrate the myriad of empirical findings in company files on advertising, sales activity, attitude research, and brand-switching studies. Equally significant, the empirical findings on consumer and industrial buyers can be related. On the other hand, had we been less abstract than we were, there would have been the danger of developing an unmanageable theory.

The structure tended toward idealism because to drop to a neurological level, for example, or even still more detailed, to a biochemical level of explanation, we believe, would involve us in a system that is much too complex to be manageable and therefore to serve many of the application needs of private and public policy. On the other hand had we been completely idealistic, we could not have nearly so well integrated several areas of psychological research and our empirical foundations would have suffered.

We strove for a high level of objectivity. First, unless the structure can be easily communicated, it cannot be used in applications to private and public policy issues. Second, we hope that one of its major contributions will be to stimulate others to do basic research. Clearly it could not serve this role unless it can be communicated. True enough, it could be that the disciplining effect of making it objective may well have hindered our own imagination in developing the theory.

Also, the objectivity of the structure combined with its formality encourages verification. These dimensions were supplemented with an introspective view in order to yield meaningful data. These three characteristics, we believe, will facilitate verification which is essential for the basic research to, in turn, meet the private and public policy needs.

The highly introspective nature of the structure does raise the problem of communication. Constructs and terminology that are more familiar to the policy maker would facilitate communication with him and perhaps with others. This would argue for a more extrospective structure. On the other hand, since we find it more useful to work at a psychological rather than a physiological level, we must often use constructs that in a sense must be communicated to the buyer to elicit the information as a part of the measurement process. It is obviously essential that the measurements be adequately accurate because if they are not, the theory will be of limited value for either basic research or application to private and public policy needs. Therefore, we forego the communication advantage that a more extrospective structure might provide.

As for the formality dimension, the lack of knowledge prevents us from presenting a more formal structure. The contribution of formality to verification has already been discussed, but it also facilitates communication. To set forth a very formal structure could, however, be misleading. As a separate research project a particular formal version has been developed, and testing of this particular version of the structure against empirical data is now going forward.

In closing, we should say explicitly that we have had two motives for writing this book. First and obvious, we wanted to develop a theory of buyer behavior. Second, however, we wanted to develop a point of view about developing theory, because we believe that in other areas of what we label "marketing" there is need for building theory. Hopefully, our experience will be of some help to those courageous people who attempt to work in the problem areas that are generally less well developed than that of buyer behavior.

Glossary of Terms:
Definitions of Central Concepts

I HYPOTHETICAL CONSTRUCTS

1. *Attention*—the degree of "openness" of the buyer's sensory receptors for a particular feature of a specific Stimulus Display and a consequent narrowing of the range of objects to which the buyer is responding. It is one of the three sources by which the buyer controls the nature of the flow of information into his nervous system. The other two sources are Overt Search and Perceptual Bias.

2. *Overt Search*—the *process* by which the buyer selects a particular element of the Stimulus Display in order to clarify the descriptive and evaluative cognitions related to a brand or the product class as well as to satisfy motives such as novelty or to clarify the saliency of motives in a given situation. It involves at the least the buyer shifting his head, for example, and extends at the other extreme to seeking out and talking with particular people in order to obtain the information he wants and to formal search efforts. Hence it extends to extensive thinking, to manipulating the symbols acquired in the process of exerting the physical movement. It is a central device the buyer has for regulating his information input.

3. *Perceptual Bias*—a complex process consisting of the perceptual and cognitive devices whereby the buyer distorts or changes the meaning of the information he has already taken into his nervous system through Attention. A number of subprocesses make it up such as sensory integrations, each consisting of a number of hypothetical constructs. The output of this total process is the stimulus-as-coded (s-a-c).

4. *Stimulus Ambiguity*—the lack of clarity of the Stimulus Display in communicating the descriptive and evaluative aspects of the brand and product class and the nature of motives. This lack of clarity is in itself satisfying

415

for such motives as the need for novelty. It is the tendency for Stimulus Display to be seen in two or more ways.

5. *Motives*—the biogenic or psychogenic needs, wants, or desires of the buyer in buying and consuming a product class. They include the consciously sought goals that are considered to determine behavior. Motives have two elements. First, there is an energizing or arousing effect which gives impetus to behavior. Second, there is a directional effect which drives the individual toward one particular brand instead of another. Some of the motives are related to the product class at hand and so are called relevant motives. If not related at all to the product class under investigation, they are irrelevant. Revelant motives can be specific or nonspecific, "specific" referring to those motives that are served only by the product class at hand.

6. *Choice Criteria*—a cognitive state of the buyer that reflects those attributes of the brands in the product class that are salient in the buyer's evaluation of a brand. These attributes are intimately related to the buyer's motives that are relevant to this product class in the sense that the product class has the potential for satisfying them.

7. *Brand Comprehension*—a cognitive state of the buyer that reflects the extent to which the buyer has sufficient knowledge to exhibit well-defined criteria for identifying and discussing brands in his evoked set but not for evaluating them. Evoked set is defined as those brands the buyer considers when he contemplates purchasing a unit of the product class. Evoked set is a central concept because it delimits the nature of the problem by setting the field of choice.

8. *Attitude*—a cognitive state that on a number of dimensions reflects the extent to which the buyer prefers in terms of Motives each brand in his evoked set in relation to all other brands in that set. It represents only a directive motivational effect, not an energizing or arousal effect.

9. *Intention*—a cognitive state that reflects the buyer's plan to purchase some specified number of units of a particular brand in some specified time period given his Attitude, his Confidence, and his perception of those constraints that inhibit the effects of Attitude in the direction of the choice. The inhibitors can be classified but not mutually exclusively as *ex ante*— those the buyer expects to encounter—and *ex post*—those looking backward in time from the purchase that he did encounter. Examples of these inhibitors are social influence, high price, lack of availability of the brand such as in the local retail store, and the time available for the purchase process. Intention is the uncompleted portion of that plan to purchase. Relevant and irrelevant motives affect Intention to buy a brand which results in a direct causal relation between Motives and Intention.

10. *Confidence*—the degree of certainty that a buyer subjectively experiences with respect to the expected value of his denotative abstractions (Brand Comprehension), his connotative abstractions (Attitude), his situational abstractions (Intention), and his abstractions about his postpurchase experience.

11. *Satisfaction*—satisfaction is a mental state of being adequately or inadequately rewarded in a buying situation for the sacrifice the buyer has undergone. The adequacy is the consequence of matching actual past purchase

experience with the reward that was expected from the brand in terms of its potential to satisfy the motives served by the particular product class. It includes not only the reward from consumption of the brand but any other reward received in the purchasing and consuming process.

12. *Product Class Comprehension*—a cognitive state of the buyer that incorporates his ways of describing the common denotative characteristics of the set of brands constituting the product class and of evaluating those brands. Thus it includes Choice Criteria.

II INTERVENING VARIABLES AS CONSTRUCTS

A. *Output Variables*

1. *Attention'*—some psychophysical measure that conveys the opening and closing of the buyer's various sensory receptors such as fixation of the eyes or pupil dilation, indicating concentration or the lack of it in a specified Stimulus Display.

2. *Brand Comprehension'*—the completeness of the buyer's verbal description of each brand of a product or service on a set of bipolar adjectival scales that serve to communicate about the denotative meaning of the brand to others. It does not include the buyer's evaluation of the brand. It includes all brands in the buyer's evoked set, that set of brands he considers when he contemplates the purchase of a product class. Although comprehension is often used by the layman to refer to a process, it is used here strictly as a state construct.

3. *Attitude'*—the buyer's evaluation of a brand or service as measured—either verbally or self-administered—on a *set* of bipolar scales reflecting salient purchase criteria common to the product class in which the brand is one element of the class.

4. *Intention'*—a verbal statement or combination of statements by the buyer in response to a question about the strength of his intention to buy a unit of the brand during some specific time period.

5. *Purchase*—any visible, overt, objectively discernible act that entails exchange of goods or services for some consideration and can be taken to reliably indicate a financial commitment to a certain *brand* in a specified unit amount. It need not necessarily be an irrevocable commitment but some act that by custom and usage is accepted as a commitment. It refers only to a particular act or series of acts in the total purchase process.

6. *Product Class Comprehension'*—the buyer's verbal description of the denotative and connotative characteristics of the product class where "product class" is defined as the set of brands that the buyer views as closely substitutable in meeting his needs. "Connotative" refers to those characteristics by which he judges this set of brands in terms of the respective set of needs: his Choice Criteria. "Denotative" applies to those attributes by which he identifies it and describes it to others.

Finally, there is a typology or set of classes of buyer decision processes in terms of the amount of search activity being carried out by the buyer, and these classes are analogous to the output intervening variables but necessarily represent large aggregates of behavior.

7. *Routinized Response Behavior*—the buyer is not only very familiar with the product class but with all brands in his evoked set so that the only information that he needs has to do with the values of the inhibitors that constitute his purchasing plan which underlies his Intention. The buyer has a definite preference for one brand over other brands in his evoked set.

8. *Limited Problem Solving*—the buyer has well-formed Choice Criteria, hence a well-defined product class concept. His Attitude, though positive toward brands in his evoked set, is not strongly favorable to any one brand because his information to judge one of them is inadequate.

9. *Extensive Problem Solving*—the buyer does not have well-formed Choice Criteria and does not have a product class concept. He needs information to provide the basis for forming his Choice Criteria, and correspondingly he has very limited preference (Attitude) for any one brand.

10. *Response Sequence*—the network of relations among the output intervening variables such as Attention', Brand Comprehension', Attitude', Intention' and Purchase although we do not exclude the intervening counterparts of the other hypothetical constructs. It is a process operating over time and summarizing the functional relations among these intervening variables. We think of it as being quantitatively described by a set of simultaneous equations that represent the network.

B. *Input Variables*

1. *Stimulus Display*—a physical event(s) to which the buyer is exposed and that stirs or prods the buyer, is external to the buyer and is associated with sensory processes. Stimulus Display is classified into three types: Significative, Symbolic, and Social. This is not an exhaustive classification because it omits such things as pages of *Consumer Reports*(symbolic, noncommercial) and the salesman's comments, (social, commercial) but it will suffice for most purposes.

This definition is in contrast to internal stimuli which are a part of a buyer's organized cognitions related to the product class and the specific brands. Internal stimuli are the internal effects that are created by the external physical event. Contextual cues are those outside Stimulus Display.

2. *Significative Stimuli*—those impersonal, external stimuli, unidimensional or multidimensional, produced by the *commercial* activity on the part of the company in displaying the physical brand as a total entity.

3. *Symbolic Stimuli*—impersonal, external stimuli, unidimensional or multidimensional, produced by commercial signs to stand for the significate (the brand), hence to transmit information about the brand to the buyer. These signs may be linguistic (the spoken word), orthographic (the printed word), or pictorial (a picture or cartoon).

4. *Social Stimuli*—those stimuli, unidimensional or multidimensional, that

emanate from other people, particularly the buyer's friends and relatives, and provide the buyer with information about the product class, the brand, or the acts of purchasing or consuming the brand. These may be linguistic or nonlinguistic such as the other person's grimaces or other physical movements that transmit information to other people.

5. *Stimulus-as-Coded*—an internal stimulus that results from the influence of such things as Motives, and Attitudes, on the original sensory input from the attributes of the objective stimulus. It is the result of a coding process in which the attributes of the objective external physical event are modified by the hypothetical constructs of Attention and Perceptual Bias to yield an internal event that is an input to the learning subsystem.

III EXOGENOUS VARIABLES

1. *Importance of Purchase*—a variable in the buyer's frame of reference that corresponds to intensity of Motives. It is product-class-specific only and does not distinguish among brands. It is the saliency of one product class with respect to another. It includes criteria on which the buyer can order various product classes on intensity of motives. It is variously labeled degree of involvement, importance of cognitions, importance of the task, and seriousness of the consequences.

2. *Personality Traits*—enduring dispositions or qualitites of a person that account for his relative consistency in emotional, temperamental, and social behavior. They are traits that account for differences among people. They contain motivational elements on which people differ but these are anchored to more basic motives.

3. *Financial Status*—the quantity of funds that a buyer expects to have available for expenditure on goods and services during some specified time period. It is a function of current income or saved past income (assets).

4. *Time Pressure*—the inverse of the amount of time the buyer has available to perform the behavior involving the purchase and consumption acts associated with a particular product class and the information seeking that precedes the purchase act. The time available at the disposal of the buyer as defined above is determined by the subjective evaluation of some units of appropriate time he should set aside to do the task properly. This concept incorporates momentary instead of long-term changes in the time available for the purchasing activity.

5. *Social and Organizational Setting*—this variable involves two separate but closely related ideas. First, the "social" aspect of the setting of the buyer's purchase and consumption acts refer to the loose social arrangement implied by the term *reference* group. By the latter we mean any group with which the buyer identifies and/or compares himself to such an extent that he tends to adopt its standards, attitudes, and behavior as his own. This group provides a *social anchoring* for the buyer whereby his brand judgments and purchase and consumption acts are influenced by this relationship as well as by other

facts that he perceives. Second, the "organizational" aspects of the purchase and consumption setting refers to the much more structured arrangement represented by such formal organizations as a company. It is the environment in which the industrial buyer, distributive buyer, and institutional (governmental, nonprofit, etc.) buyer carries out his purchasing activity. We also include family as an informal organization having an environment similar to that of the formal organization.

6. *Social Class*—a description of the condition that society is divided into classes, some of which are viewed by members of the society as being more important than others. In a society these classes can be ranked according to the views of its members as to the value of each class in term of its contribution to the society as a whole. As implied by the style-of-life concept, empirically, these classes are not clearly demarcated but instead represent arbitrary cuts across a continuum of status positions.

7. *Culture*—a selective man-made way of responding to experiences, consisting of patterns of behavior transmitted from person to person. In general, it reflects a sense of homogeneity among people bound together and separated from other sets of people by various physical boundaries. Its essential core consists of a tradition and especially its attached values, a system of subcultures, and a set of universals.

Bibliography

Abelson, Robert P. (1968), "Computers, Polls and Public Opinion—Some Puzzles and Paradoxes," *Trans-action*, Vol. 5, September, pp. 20–27.

Adler, Lee, and Irving Crespi, eds. (1966), *Attitude Research at Sea*, American Marketing Association.

Adler, Lee, Allen Greenberg, and D. B. Lucas (1965), "What Big Agency Men Think of Copy Testing Methods?" *Journal of Marketing Research*, Vol. 2, November, pp. 339–345.

Advertising Age (1967), "Wives over 45 Are More Adventurous Buyers, Study Finds," Vol. 38, October 30, p. 32.

Alderson, Wroe (1952), "Psychology for Marketing Economics," *Journal of Marketing*, October, pp. 119–135.

Alderson, Wroe, and Paul E. Green (1964), *Planning and Problem Solving in Marketing*, Richard D. Irwin.

Alderson, Wroe, and Robert E. Sessions (1957), *Basic Research Report on Consumer Behavior*, Alderson and Sessions Associates (April).

Alexander, Ralph S., James S. Cross, and Ross M. Cunningham (1961), *Industrial Marketing*, Richard D. Irwin.

Allport, Gordon W. (1935), "Attitudes," in C. Murchison, ed., *A Handbook of Social Psychology*, Clark University Press, pp. 798–844.

Anastasi, Anne (1958), *Differential Psychology*, 3rd ed., Macmillan Co.

Anastasi, Anne (1964), *Fields of Applied Psychology*, McGraw-Hill Book Company.

Anderson, H. H., and G. L. Anderson, eds. (1951), *An Introduction to Projective Techniques*, Prentice-Hall.

Anderson, L. R., and M. Fishbein (1965), "Prediction of Attitude from the Number, Strength, and Evaluative Aspect of Beliefs about Attitude Objects: A Comparison of Summation and Congruity Theories," *Journal of Personality and Social Psychology*, Vol. 2, September, pp. 437–443.

Anderson, T. W., and L. A. Goodman (1957), "Statistical Inference about Markov Chains," *The Annals of Mathematical Statistics*, Vol. 28, pp. 89–110.

Arndt, Johan (1966), "Word of Mouth Advertising: The Role of Product-Related Conversations in the Diffusion of a New Food Product," unpublished doctoral dissertation, Graduate School of Business, Harvard University.

Arndt, Johan (1967a), *Word of Mouth Advertising*, Advertising Research Foundation.

Arndt, Johan (1967b), "Role of Product-Related Conversations in the Diffusion of a New Product," *Journal of Marketing Research*, Vol. 4, August, pp. 291–295.

421

Arndt, Johan (1967c), "Word of Mouth Advertising and Informal Communication," in Donald F. Cox, ed., *Risk Taking and Information Handling in Consumer Behavior*, Graduate School of Business, Harvard University, pp. 189–239.

Arndt, Johan ed. (1968), *Insights Into Consumer Behavior*, Allyn & Bacon.

Atkin, K. L. (1962), "Advertising and Store Patronage," *Journal of Advertising Research*, Vol. 2, December, pp. 18–23.

Atkinson, John W., ed. (1958), *Motives in Fantasy, Action, and Society*, D. Van Nostrand Company.

Atkinson, John W. (1964), *An Introduction to Motivation*, D. Van Nostrand Company.

Baker, Stephen (1959), *Advertising Layout and Art Direction*, McGraw-Hill Book Company.

Barton, Samuel G. (1946), "The Movement of Branded Goods to the Consumer," in A. B. Blankenship, ed., *How to Conduct Consumer and Opinion Research*, Harper, pp. 58–70.

Bass, Frank M., et al., eds. (1961), *Mathematical Models and Methods in Marketing*, Richard D. Irwin.

Bass, Frank M. (1969), "A New Product Growth Model for Consumer Durables" *Management Science, Theory Series*, Vol. 15, January, pp. 215–227.

Bauer, Raymond A. (1960), "Consumer Behavior as Risk Taking," in R. S. Hancock, ed., *Dynamic Marketing for a Changing World*, Proceedings of the 43rd Conference of the American Marketing Association, pp. 389–400.

Bauer, Raymond A. (1961), "Risk Handling in Drug Adoption: The Role of Company Preference," *Public Opinion Quarterly*, Vol. 25, Winter, pp. 546–559.

Bauer, Raymond A. (1962), "A Functional Approach to Marketing Research," in William S. Decker, ed., *Emerging Concepts in Marketing*, Proceedings of the Winter Conference of the American Marketing Association, pp. 295–301.

Bauer, Raymond A. (1963a), "The Initiative of the Audience," *Journal of Advertising Research*, Vol. 3, June, pp. 2–7.

Bauer, Raymond A. (1963b), "The Role of the Audience in the Communications Process: Summary," in Stephen A. Greyser, ed., *Toward Scientific Marketing*, Proceedings of the Winter Conference of the American Marketing Association, pp. 73–82.

Bauer, Raymond A. (1965a), "A Revised Model of Source Effect," paper presented at the Annual Meeting of the American Psychological Association, Chicago.

Bauer, Raymond A. (1965b), "Food Costs and Values, Part I: Survey of Public Reaction," *Food Study for Grocery Manufacturers of America*, Arthur D. Little, Inc.

Bauer, Raymond A. (1967), *Social Indicators*, The M.I.T. Press.

Bauer, Raymond A., and Robert D. Buzzell (1964), "Mating Behavioral Science and Simulation," *Harvard Business Review*, Vol. 42, September-October, pp. 116–124.

Bauer, Raymond A., and Donald F. Cox (1963), "Rational Vs. Emotional Communications: A New Approach," in L. Arons and M. May, eds., *Televisoin and Human Behavior,* Appleton-Century-Crofts.

Bauer, Raymond A., and Stephen A. Greyser (1967), "The Dialogue That Never Happens," *Harvard Business Review,* Vol. 45, November-December, pp. 2–12.

Bauer, Raymond A., and Laurence H. Wortzel (1966), "Doctor's Choice: The Physician and His Sources of Information about Drugs," *Journal of Marketing Research,* Vol. 3, February, pp. 40–46.

Bayton, James A. (1958), "Motivation, Cognition, Learning—Basic Factors in Consumer Behavior," *Journal of Marketing,* Vol. 22, January, pp. 282–289.

Beal, G. M., and E. M. Rogers (1957), "Informational Sources in the Adoption Process of New Fabrics," *Journal of Home Economics,* Vol. 49, pp. 630–634.

Becker, S. L. (1963), "Research on Emotional and Logical Proofs," *Southern Speech Journal,* Vol. 28, pp. 198–207.

Berkowitz L., and D. R. Cottingham (1960), "The Interest Value and Relevance of Fear Arousing Communications," *Journal of Abnormal and Social Psychology,* Vol. 60, January, pp. 37–43.

Berlyne, D. E. (1960), *Conflict, Arousal, and Curiosity,* McGraw-Hill Book Company.

Berlyne, D. E. (1963), "Motivational Problems Raised by Exploratory and Epistemic Behavior," Sigmund Koch, ed., *Psychology: The Study of a Science,* McGraw-Hill Book Company, Vol. 5, pp. 284–364.

Berlyne, D. E. (1964), "Novelty," *New Society,* Vol. 3, May 28, pp. 23–24.

Berlyne, D. E. (1965), *Structure and Direction in Thinking,* John Wiley and Sons.

Berlyne, D. E. (1966), "Curiosity and Exploration," *Science,* Vol. 153, No. 3731, pp. 25–33.

Berlyne, D. E., and Sylvia Peckham (1966), "The Semantic Differential and Other Measures of Reaction to Visual Complexity," *Canadian Journal of Psychology,* Vol. 20, No. 2, pp. 125–135.

Berry, P. C. (1961), "Effect of Colored Illumination upon Perceived Temperature," *Journal of Applied Psychology,* Vol. 45, August, pp. 248–250.

Bogart, Leo (1964), *A Study of the Opportunity for Exposure to National Newspaper Advertising,* Bureau of Advertising.

Bogart, Leo, and B. Stuart Tolley (1964), "The Impact of Blank Space: An Experiment in Advertising Readership," *Journal of Advertising Research,* Vol. 4, June, pp. 21–27.

Borch, Karl (1968), "The Allais Paradox: A Comment," *Behavioral Science,* Vol. 13, November, pp. 488–489.

Bourne, Francis S. (1963), "Different Kinds of Decisions and Reference-Group Influence," in Perry Bliss, ed., *Marketing and the Behavioral Sciences,* Allyn and Bacon, pp. 247–255.

Brehm, Jack W., and Arthur R. Cohen (1962), *Explorations in Cognitive Dissonance,* John Wiley and Sons.

Britt, Steuart H., ed. (1966), *Consumer Behavior and the Behavioral Sciences,* John Wiley and Sons.

Brooks, John (1964), "Annals of Business: The Edsel" in Hiram C. Barksdale, ed., *Marketing in Progress,* Holt, Rinehart and Winston, pp. 419–440.

Brooks, Robert C., Jr. (1963), "Relating the Selling Effort to Patterns of Purchase Behavior," *Business Topics,* Vol. 11, Winter, pp. 73–79.

Brown, Arthur A., Frank T. Hulswit, and John D. Kettelle (1956), "A Study of Sales Operations," *Operations Research,* Vol. 4, June, pp. 296–308.

Brown, George H. (1952a), "Brand Loyalty—Fact or Fiction?" *Advertising Age,* Vol. 23, June 9, pp. 53–55; June 30, pp. 45–57.

Brown, George H. (1952b), "Coffee Buyers Loyal to Brands, Yet Two Thirds Buy Four or More Brands in a Year," *Advertising Age,* Vol. 23, July 14, pp. 54–56.

Brown, George H. (1952c), "99% of Flour Buyers Definitely Favor One Brand," *Advertising Age,* Vol. 23, July 28, pp. 54–56.

Brown, George H. (1952d) "75% of Chicago Families Buy Shampoo: Brand Loyalty Difficult to Assess," *Advertising Age,* Vol. 23, August 11, pp. 56–58.

Brown, George H. (1952e), "Study Shows Brand Loyalty Among Buyers of Soaps and Sudsers," *Advertising Age,* Vol. 23, October 6, pp. 82, 85–86.

Brown, George H. (1952f), "Study Finds Changing Purchase Patterns Are a Major Factor in the Concentrated Orange Juice Market," *Advertising Age,* Vol. 23, p. 77.

Brown, George H. (1953), "Brand Loyalty—Fact or Fiction?" *Advertising Age,* Vol. 24, January 26, pp. 75–76.

Brown, Judson Seise (1961), *The Motivation of Behavior,* McGraw-Hill Book Company.

Brown, Roger W. (1958), *Words and Things,* The Free Press.

Brown, Roger W. (1965), *Social Psychology,* The Free Press.

Bruner, Jerome S. (1957), "Discussion," *Contemporary Approaches to Cognition,* Harvard University Press, pp. 151–156.

Bruner, Jerome S., and L. Postman (1949), "On the Perception of Incongruity: A Paradigm," *Journal of Personality,* Vol. 18, December, pp. 206–223.

Bruner, Jerome S., L. Postman, and J. Rodrigues (1951), "Expectation and the Perception of Color," *American Journal of Psychology,* Vol. 64, April, pp. 216–227.

Bucklin, Louis P. (1963), "Retail Strategy and the Classification of Consumer Goods," *Journal of Marketing,* Vol. 27, January, pp. 50–55.

Bullock, H. A. (1961), "Consumer Motivation in Black and White" Part I, *Harvard Business Review,* Vol. 39 May-June, pp. 89–104; Part II, *Harvard Business Review,* Vol. 39, July-August, pp. 110–124.

Burt, Cyril (1950), "Factorial Analysis of Qualitative Data," *British Journal of Psychology* (*Statistical Section*), Vol. 3, November, pp. 166–185.

Burt, Cyril, W. F. Cooper, and J. L. Martin (1955), "A Psychological Study of Typography," *British Journal of Statistical Psychology*, Vol. 8, May, pp. 29–58.

Bush, G., and P. London (1960), "On the Disappearance of Knickers: Hypothesis for the Functional Analysis of The Psychology of Clothing," *Journal of Social Psychology*, Vol., 51, May, pp. 359–366.

Bush, Robert R., and Frederick Mosteller (1955), *Stochastic Models for Learning*, John Wiley and Sons.

Buzzell, Robert D. (1964), *Mathematical Models and Marketing Management*, Graduate School of Business Administration, Harvard University.

Buzzell, Robert D., and Robert E. M. Nourse (1967), *Product Innovation in Food Processing*, Graduate School of Business Administration, Harvard University.

Callazo, Clark, J. (1966), "Effects of Income upon Shopping Attitudes and Frustrations," *Journal of Retailing*, Spring, pp. 1–7.

Campbell, Brian M. (1969), 'The Existence and Determinants of Evoked Set in Brand Choice Behavior," unpublished doctoral dissertation, Columbia University.

Campbell, Donald T. (1947), "The Generality of Social Attitudes," unpublished doctoral dissertation, University of California, Berkeley.

Campbell, Donald T. (1950), "The Indirect Assessment of Social Attitudes," *Psychological Bulletin*, Vo. 47, January, pp. 15–38.

Campbell, Donald T. (1963), "Social Attitudes and Other Acquired Behavioral Dispositions" in Sigmund Koch, ed., *Psychology: A Study of a Science*, Vol. 6, McGraw-Hill Book Company, pp. 94–172.

Campbell, Donald T., and D. W. Fiske (1959), "Convergent and Discriminant Validation by the Multitrait-Multimethod Matrix," *Psychological Bulletin*, Vol. 56, March, pp. 81–105.

Campbell, N. R. (1920), *Physics, the Elements*, Cambridge University Press, republished as *Foundations of Science*, Dover, 1957.

Carlson, Earl R. (1956), "Attitude Change through Modification of Attitude Structure," *Journal of Abnormal and Social Psychology*, Vol. 52, March, pp. 256–261.

Carman, James M. (1965a), *Brand Switching and Linear Learning Models: Some Empirical Results*, Working Paper No. 20, Research Program in Marketing, Graduate School of Business, University of California, Berkeley.

Carman, James M. (1965b), *The Application of Social Class in Market Segmentation*, Institute of Business and Economic Research, University of California, Berkeley.

Carman, James M. (1968), *Correlates of Brand Loyalty: Some Positive Results*, Working Paper No. 26, Research Program in Marketing, Institute of Business and Economic Research, University of California, Berkeley.

Carroll, John B. (1964), "Words, Meanings and Concepts," in Janet A. Emig, James T. Fleming, and Helen M. Popp, eds., *Language and Learning*, Harcourt, Brace and World, pp. 73–101.

Cassady, Ralph, Jr., and Wylie L. Jones (1951), *The Nature of Competition in Gasoline Distribution at the Retail Level,* University of California Press.

Cattell, Raymond B. (1963), "The Structuring of Change by P-Technique and Incremental R-Technique," in Chester W. Harris, ed., *Problems in Measuring Change,* University of Wisconsin Press, pp. 167–198.

Chein, I. (1948), "Behavior Theory and the Behavior of Attitudes: Some Critical Comments" *Psychological Review,* Vol. 55, May, pp. 175–188.

Churchill, H. L. (1942), "How to Measure Brand Loyalty," *Advertising and Selling,* Vol. 35, pp. 24ff.

Cofer, C. N., and M. H. Appley (1964), *Motivation: Theory and Research,* John Wiley and Sons.

Cohen, Arthur R. (1964), *Attitude Change and Social Influence,* Basic Books.

Coleman, James S. (1964), *Introduction to Mathematical Sociology,* The Free Press.

Coleman, James, E. Katz, and H. Menzel (1959), "Social Processes in Physicians Adoption of a New Drug," *Journal of Chronic Diseases,* Vol. 9, January, pp. 1–19.

Coleman, Richard P. (1960), "The Significance of Social Stratification in Selling," in Martin L. Bell, ed., *Marketing: A Maturing Discipline,* Proceedings of the Winter Conference of the American Marketing Association, pp. 171–184.

Coombs, Clyde H. (1952), "A Theory of Psychological Scaling," *Bulletin of Engineering Research,* No. 34.

Coombs, Clyde H. (1964), *A Theory of Data,* John Wiley and Sons.

Coombs, Clyde H., and R. C. Kao (1955), "Nonmetric Factor Analysis," *Engineering Research Bulletin,* No. 38.

Cordozo, Richard N. (1965), "An Experimental Study of Customer Effort, Expectation, and Satisfaction," *Journal of Marketing Research,* Vol. 2, August, pp. 244–249.

Coulson, John S. (1966), "Buying Decisions within the Family and the Consumer-Brand Relationship," in Joseph W. Newman, ed., *On Knowing the Consumer,* John Wiley and Sons, pp. 59–66.

Cox, Donald F. (1962), "The Measurement of Information Value: A Study in Consumer Decision-Making," in William S. Decker, ed., *Emerging Concepts in Marketing,* Proceedings of the Winter Conference of the American Marketing Association, pp. 413–421.

Cox, Donald F. (1963), "The Audience as Communicators," in Stephen A. Greyser, ed., *Toward Scientific Marketing,* Proceedings of the Winter Conference of the American Marketing Association, pp. 58–72.

Cox, Donald F., ed. (1967), *Risk Taking and Information Handling in Consumer Behavior,* Graduate School of Business Administration, Harvard University.

Cox, Donald F., and Robert E. Good (1967), "How to Build a Marketing Information System," *Harvard Business Review,* Vol. 45, May-June, pp. 145–154.

Crane, Edgar (1965), *Marketing Communications,* John Wiley and Sons.

Cromwell, H. (1950), "The Relative Effects of Audience Attitude in the First versus the Second Argumentative Speech of a Series," *Speech Monographs,* Vol. 17, pp. 105–122.

Cronbach, Lee J., and P. E. Meehl (1955), "Construct Validity in Psychological Tests," *Psychological Bulletin,* Vol. 52, July, pp. 281–302.

Cunningham, Ross M. (1955), "Measurement of Brand Loyalty," *The Marketing Revolution,* Proceedings of the American Marketing Association, pp. 39-45.

Cunningham, Ross M. (1956a), "Brand Loyalty—What, Where, How Much?" *Harvard Business Review,* Vol. 34, January-February, pp. 116–128.

Cunningham, Ross M. (1959), "Brand Loyalty and Store Loyalty Interrelationships," in W. K. Dolva, ed., *Marketing Keys to Profit in the 1960's,* Proceedings of the American Marketing Association, pp. 201–214.

Cunningham, Scott M. (1966), "Perceived Risk as a Factor in the Diffusion of New Product Information," in Raymond M. Haas, ed., *Science, Technology, and Marketing,* Fall Conference Proceedings of the American Marketing Association, pp. 698–722.

Cunningham, Scott M. (1967a), "Perceived Risk as a Factor in Informal Consumer Communications," in Donald F. Cox, ed., *Risk Taking and Information Handling in Consumer Behavior,* Graduate School of Business, Harvard University, pp. 265–288.

Cunningham, Scott M. (1967b), "The Major Dimensions of Perceived Risk," in Donald F. Cox, ed., *Risk Taking and Information Handling in Consumer Behavior,* Graduate School of Business, Harvard University, pp. 82–108.

Cyert, R. M., J. G. March, and C. G. Moore (1962), "A Model of Retail Ordering and Pricing by a Department Store," in A. Kuehn, R. Frank, and W. Massy, eds., *Quantitative Methods in Marketing Analysis,* Richard D. Irwin, pp. 502–522.

Davis, R. C., and H. J. Smith (1933), "Determinants of Feeling Tone in Type Faces," *Journal of Applied Psychology,* Vol. 17, December, pp. 742–764.

Day, George S. (1967), "Buyer Attitudes and Brand Choice Behavior," unpublished doctoral dissertation, Columbia University.

Deese, James (1965), *The Structure of Associations in Language and Thought,* The Johns Hopkins Press.

DeFleur, M. L., and F. R. Westie (1963), "Attitude as a Scientific Concept," *Social Forces,* Vol. 42, pp. 17–31.

DeGrazia, Sebastian (1962), *Of Time, Work, and Leisure,* Twentieth Century Fund.

Diebold, Richard A., Jr. (1965), "A Survey of Psycholinguistic Research, 1954–1964," *Psycholinguistics,* pp. 209–276.

Dirksen, Charles J., Arthur Kroeger, and Lawrence C. Lockley (1963), *Readings in Marketing,* Richard D. Irwin.

DiVesta, F. J., and J. C. Merwin (1960), "The Effects of Need-Oriented Communications on Attitude Change," *Journal of Abnormal and Social Psychology,* Vol. 60, January, pp. 80–85.

Dolich, Ira J. (1967), "A Study of Congruence Relationships between Self Structures and Brands of Products," unpublished doctoral dissertation, University of Texas.

Dollard, John, and Neal E. Miller (1950), *Personality and Psychotherapy*, McGraw-Hill Book Company.

Doob, L. W. (1947), "The Behavior of Attitudes," *Psychological Review*, Vol. 54, May, pp. 135–156.

Dorcus, R. M. (1932), "Habitual Word Associations to Colors as a Possible Factor in Advertising," *Journal of Applied Psychology*, Vol. 16, June, pp. 277–287.

Draper, Jean E., and Larry H. Nolin (1964), "A Markov Chain Analysis of Brand Preferences," *Journal of Advertising Research*, Vol. 4, September, pp. 33–38.

Dulany, Don E. (1968), "Awareness, Rules and Propositional Control: A Confrontation with S-R Behavior Theory," in T. R. Dixon and D. L. Horton, eds., *Verbal Behavior and General Behavior Theory*, Prentice-Hall, pp. 340–387.

Dunn, S. Watson (1961), *Advertising: Its Role in Modern Marketing*, Holt, Rinehart and Winston.

Dutka, Solomon, and L. Frankel (1962), *Markov Chain Analysis: A New Tool of Marketers*, Audits and Surveys Company.

Eckart, C., and G. Young (1936), "The Approximation of One Matrix by Another of Lower Rank," *Psychometrika*, Vol. 1, September, pp. 211–218.

Egeth, Howard (1967), "Selective Attention," *Psychological Bulletin*, Vol. 67, January, pp. 41–57.

Ehrenberg, A. S. C. (1959), "The Pattern of Consumer Purchases," *Applied Statistics*, Vol. 8, March, pp. 26–41.

Ehrenberg, A. S. C. (1964), "Estimating the Proportion of Loyal Buyers," *Journal of Marketing Research*, Vol. 1, February, pp. 56–59.

Ehrenberg, A. S. C. (1965), "An Appraisal of Markov Brand-Switching Models," *Journal of Marketing Research*, Vol. 2, November, pp. 347–362.

Ehrenberg, A. S. C. (1966), "Intention-to-buy and Claimed Brand Usage," *Operations Research Quarterly*, Vol. 17, pp. 27–46.

Ehrlich, Danuta, Isaiah Guttman, Peter Shönbach, and Judson Mills (1957), "Post-decision Exposure to Relevant Information," *Journal of Abnormal and Social Psychology*, Vol. 54, January, pp. 98–102.

Eldersveld, S. J. (1956), "Experimental Propaganda Techniques and Voting Behavior," *American Political Science Review*, Vol. 50, pp. 154–165.

Ellis, Brian (1966), *Basic Concepts of Measurements*, Cambridge University Press.

Engel, James F. (1965), "Further Pursuit of the Dissonant Consumer: A Comment," *Journal of Marketing*, Vol. 29, April, pp. 33–34.

English, Horace B., and Ava Champney English (1958), *Psychological and Psychoanalytical Terms*, Longmans, Green.

Evans, Franklin B. (1959), "Psychological and Objective Factors in the Prediction of Brand Choice: Ford versus Chevrolet," *Journal of Business*, Vol. 32, October, pp. 340–369.

Farley, John U. (1964), "Brand Loyalty and the Economics of Information," *Journal of Business,* Vol. 37, October, pp. 9–14.

Farley, John U., and Alfred A. Kuehn (1965), "Stochastic Models of Brand Switching," in George Schwartz, ed., *Science in Marketing,* John Wiley and Sons.

Feldman, Shel (1966), *Cognitive Consistency,* Academic Press.

Feldman, Sidney P. (1966), "Some Dyadic Relationships Associated with Consumer Choice," in R. A. Haas, ed., *Science, Technology and Marketing,* Fall Conference Proceedings of the American Marketing Association, pp. 758–775.

Ferber, Robert (1962), "Research on Household Behavior," *American Economic Review,* Vol. 52, pp. 19–63.

Ferber, Robert (1966), "Anticipations Statistics and Consumer Behavior," *The American Statistician,* Vol. 20, October, pp. 20–24.

Ferber, Robert, and H. Wales, eds. (1958), *Motivation and Market Behavior,* Richard D. Irwin.

Ferster, C. B., and B. F. Skinner (1957), *Schedules of Reinforcement,* Appleton-Century-Crofts.

Festinger, Leon (1964), "Behavioral Support for Opinion Change," *Public Opinion Quarterly,* Vol. 28, pp. 404–417.

Fishbein, Martin (1963), "An Investigation of the Relationships between Beliefs about an Object and the Attitude toward that Object," *Human Relations,* Vol. 16, August, pp. 233–239.

Fishbein, Martin, ed., (1967), *Readings in Attitude Theory and Measurement,* John Wiley and Sons.

Foote, Nelson A., ed. (1961), *Household Decision Making,* New York University Press.

Fourt, L. A. (1960), "Applying Markov Chain Analysis to NCP Brand-Switching Data," unpublished memorandum, Market Research Corporation of America.

Frank, Ronald E. (1962), "Brand Choice as a Probability Process," *Journal of Business,* Vol 35, January, pp. 43–56.

Frank, Ronald E. (1967a), "Is Brand Loyalty a Useful Basis for Market Segmentation?" *Journal of Advertising Research,* Vol. 7, June, pp. 27–33.

Frank, Ronald E. (1967b), "Correlates of Buying Behavior for Grocery Products," *Journal of Marketing,* Vol. 31, October, pp. 48–53.

Frank, Ronald E., Paul E. Green, and H. F. Sieber, Jr. (1967), "Household Correlates of Purchase Price for Grocery Products," *Journal of Marketing Research,* Vol. 4, February, pp. 54–58.

Frank, Ronald E., Alfred A. Kuehn, and William F. Massy (1962), *Quantitative Techniques in Marketing Analysis,* Richard D. Irwin.

Frank, Ronald E., and William F. Massy (1963), "Innovation and Brand Choice: The Folgers Invasion," in Stephen Greyser, ed., *Toward Scientific Marketing,* Proceedings of the Winter Conference of the American Marketing Association, pp. 96–107.

Frank, Ronald E., W. F. Massy, and Donald G. Morrison (1964), "The Determinants

Hovland, Carl I. (1959), "Reconciling Con...g Results Derived from Experimental and Survey Studies of Attitude Change, ...rican Psychologist, Vol. 14, January, pp. 8–17.

Hovland, Carl I., I. L. Janis, and H. H. Kelly (1...Communication and Persuasion, Yale University Press.

Hovland, Carl I., A. A. Lumsdaine, and F. D. Sheffi...Mass Communications, Princeton University Pre...

Hovland, Carl I., and W. Mandell (1952), "An Experi...Comparison of Con...sion-Drawing by the Communicator and by the Aud...Journal of Abnormal and Social Psychology, Vol. 47, July, pp. 581–588.

Hovland, Carl I., and M. J. Rosenberg, eds. (1960), Attitude...nization and Change, Yale University Press.

Hovland Carl I., and W. Weiss (1951), "The Influence of Sourc...edibility on Communication Effectiveness," Public Opinion Quarterly, 15, pp. 635–650.

Howard, John A. (1963), Marketing Management: Analysis and Plan...g, rev. ed., Richard D. Irwin.

Howard, John A. (1965), Marketing Theory, Allyn and Bacon.

Howard, John A. (1966), Testimony before the Stagger's Committee of the U.S. House of Representatives, August.

Howard, John A. (1968), "Are Systems Systematic?" in D. N. Slate and Robert Ferber, eds., Systems: Research and Applications for Marketing, Bureau of Economic and Business Research, University of Illinois, pp. 3–8.

Howard, John A., and Charles G. Moore, Jr. (1963), A Descriptive Model of the Purchasing Function, unpublished monograph, University of Pittsburgh.

Howard, John A., and William M. Morgenroth (1968), "Information Processing Model of Executive Decision," Management Science, Vol. 14, March, pp. 416–428.

Howard, John A., and Jagdish N. Sheth (1968a), "A Theory of Buyer Behavior," Rivesta Internazionale de Scienze Economiche e Commerciali, Vol. 15, pp. 589–618.

Howard, John A., and Jagdish N. Sheth (1968b), "Summary of the Theory of Buyer Behavior," in J. B. Kernan and M. S. Sommers, eds., Perspectives in Marketing Theory, Appleton-Century-Crofts, pp. 154–173.

Howard, Ronald A. (1963), "On Methods: Stochastic Process Models of Consumer Behavior," Journal of Advertising Research, Vol. 3, September, pp. 35–42.

Hull, Clark L. (1943), Principles of Behavior, D. Appleton-Century Company.

Hull, Clark L. (1952), A Behavior System, Yale University Press.

Janis, I. L. (1954), "Personality Correlates of Susceptibility to Persuasion," Journal of Personality, Vol. 22, June, pp. 504–518.

Janis, I. L. (1955), "Anxiety Indices Related to Susceptibility to Persuasion," Journal of Abnormal and Social Psychology, Vol. 51, November, pp. 663–667.

Janis, I. L. (1958), *Psychological Stress,* John Wiley and Sons.

Janis, I. L. (1959), "Motivational Factors in the Resolution of Decisional Conflicts," in M. R. Jones, ed., *Nebraska Symposium on Motivation,* Vol. 8, University of Nebraska Press.

Janis, I. L. (1962), "The Psychological Effects of Warnings," in G. W. Baker and D. W. Chapman, eds., *Man and Society in Disaster,* Basic Books.

Janis, I. L. (1967), "Effects of Fear Arousal on Attitude Change: Recent Developments in Theory and Experimental Research," in L. Berkowitz, ed., *Advances in Experimental Social Psychology,* Vol. 3, Academic Press, pp. 166–224.

Janis, I. L., and Rosalind L. Feierabend (1957), "Effects of Alternative Ways of Ordering Pro and Con Arguments in Persuasive Communications," in C. I. Hovland, ed., *Order of Presentation in Persuasion,* Yale University Press, pp. 115–128.

Janis, I. L., and S. Feshbach (1953), "Effects of Fear-Arousing Communications," *Journal of Abnormal and Social Psychology,* Vol. 48, January pp. 78–92.

Janis, I. L., and P. B. Field (1959), "Sex Differences and Personality Factors Related to Persuasibility," in C. I. Hovland and I. L. Janis, eds., *Personality and Persuasibility,* Yale University Press, pp. 55–68.

Johnson, Robert P. (1968), *Study of Intentions vs. Behavior,* unpublished manuscript, Graduate School of Business, Columbia University.

Juster, F. T. (1964), *Anticipations and Purchases: An Analysis of Consumer Behavior,* Princeton University Press.

Juster, F. T. (1966), "Consumer Buying Intentions and Purchase Probability: An Experiment in Survey Design," *Journal of the American Statistical Association,* Vol. 61, No. 315, pp. 658–697.

Kash, Don E. (1968), "Research and Development at the University," *Science,* Vol. 160, pp. 1313–1318.

Kassarjian, Harold H. (1968), "Consumer Behavior: A Field Theoretical Approach" in R. L. King, ed., *Marketing and the New Science of Planning,* Proceedings of the American Marketing Association, pp. 285–289.

Kassarjian, Harold H. (1969), "The Negro and American Advertising" *Journal of Marketing Research,* Vol. 6, pp. 29–39.

Katona, George C. (1963), "The Relationship between Psychology and Economics," in Sigmund Koch, ed., *Psychology: A Study of a Science,* Vol. 6, pp. 639–676.

Katona, George C., and Eva Mueller (1954), "A Study of Purchase Decisions," in L. H. Clark, ed., *Consumer Behavior: The Dynamics of Consumer Reactions,* Vol. 1, New York University Press, pp. 30–87.

Katz, Daniel (1960), "The Functional Approach to the Study of Attitudes," *Public Opinion Quarterly,* Vol. 24, pp. 163–204.

Katz, Daniel (1967), "The Practice and Potential of Survey Methods in Psychological Research," Charles Y. Glock, ed., *Survey Research in Social Sciences,* Russell Sage Foundation.

Katz, Daniel, and E. Stotland (1959), "A Preliminary Statement to a Theory of Attitude Structure and Change," in Sigmund Koch, ed., *Psychology: A Study of a Science*, Vol. 3, pp. 423–475.

Katz, Elihu (1957), "The Two-Step Flow of Communication: An Up-to-Date Report on an Hypothesis," *Public Opinion Quarterly*, Vol. 21, Spring, pp. 70–82.

Katz, Elihu (1968), "On Reopening the Question of Selectivity in Exposure to Mass Communication," in R. P. Abelson et al., eds., *Theories of Cognitive Consistency*, Rand McNally.

Katz, Elihu, and P. F. Lazarsfeld (1955), *Personal Influence*, The Free Press of Glencoe.

Kelman, Herbert C. (1958), "Compliance, Identification and Internalization: Three Processes of Opinion Change," *Journal of Conflict Resolution*, Vol. 2, pp. 51–60.

Kelman, Herbert C. (1961), "Processes of Opinion Change," *Public Opinion Quarterly*, Vol. 25, pp. 57–78.

Kelman, Herbert C., and Alice H. Eagly (1965), "Attitude Toward the Communicator, Perception of Communication Content and Attitude Change," *Journal of Personality and Social Psychology*, Vol. 1, January, pp. 63–78.

Kelman, Herbert C., and C. I. Hovland (1953), " 'Reinstatement' of the Communicator in Delayed Measurement of Opinion Change," *Journal of Abnormal and Social Psychology*, Vol. 48, July, pp. 327–335.

Kemeny, John G., and J. Laurie Snell (1957), "Markov Processes in Learning Theory," *Psychometrika*, Vol. 22, September, pp. 221–230.

Kenkel, William F. (1961), "Husband-Wife Interaction in Decision Making and Decision Choices," *The Journal of Social Psychology*, Vol. 54, August, pp. 255–262.

Kenkel, William F., and Dean K. Hoffman (1956), "Real and Conceived Roles in Family Decision Making," *Marriage and the Family*, Vol. 17, November, pp. 311–316.

Kerby, Joe Kent (1966), "The Role of Semantic Generalization in the Formation of Attitudes toward Various Products Bearing a Common Brand Name," unpublished doctoral dissertation, Columbia University.

King, Charles W., and John O. Summers (1967), "Dynamics of Interpersonal Communication: The Interaction Dyad," in Donald F. Cox, ed., *Risk Taking and Information Handling in Consumer Behavior*, Graduate School of Business, Harvard University, pp. 240–264.

Klapper, J. T. (1960), *The Effects of Mass Communication*, The Free Press.

Kleppner, Otto (1966), *Advertising Procedure*, 5th ed., Prentice-Hall.

Kluckhohn, Clyde (1954), "Culture and Behavior," Gardner Lindzey, ed., *Handbook of Social Psychology*, Vol. 2, pp. 921–976.

Knepprath, E., and T. Clevenger (1965), "Reasoned Discourse and Motive Appeals in Selected Political Speeches," *Quarterly Journal of Speech*, Vol. 51, pp. 52–56.

Koch, Sigmund (1954), "Clark L. Hull," in A. T. Poffenberger, ed., *Modern Learning Theory*, Appleton-Century-Crofts, pp. 1–176.

Kogan, Nathan, and Michael A. Wallach (1964), *Risk Taking: A Study in Cognition and Personality*, Holt, Rinehart and Winston.

Kollat, David T., and Ronald T. Willett (1967), "Customer Impulse Purchasing Behavior," *Journal of Marketing Research*, Vol. 4, February, pp. 21–31.

Koponen, Arthur (1960), "Personality Characteristics of Purchasers," *Journal of Advertising Research*, Vol. 1, September, pp. 6–12.

Korzybski, A. (1941), *Science and Sanity: An Introduction to Non-Aristotelian Systems and General Semantics*, International Non-Aristotelian Library Publishing Company.

Kover, Arthur J. (1967), "Models of Man as Defined by Marketing Research," *Journal of Marketing Research*, Vol. 4, May, pp. 129–132.

Krugman, Herbert E. (1964), "Some Applications of Pupil Measurement," *Journal of Marketing Research*, Vol. 1, November, pp. 15–19.

Krugman, Herbert E. (1967), "Processes Underlying Exposure to Advertising," Mimeographed, Seventy-fifth Annual Convention, American Psychological Association.

Kruskal, J. B. (1964), "Multidimensional Scaling by Optimizing Goodness of Fit to a Nonmetric Hypothesis," *Psychometrika*, Vol. 29, December, pp. 1–27.

Kuehn, Alfred A. (1958), "An Analysis of the Dynamics of Consumer Behavior and Its Implications for Marketing Management," unpublished doctoral dissertation Graduate School of Industrial Administration, Carnegie Institute of Technology.

Kuehn, Alfred A. (1962), "Consumer Brand Choice as a Learning Process," *Journal of Advertising Research*, Vol. 2, December, pp. 10–17.

Kuehn, Alfred A. (1963), "Demonstration of a Relationship between Psychological Factors and Brand Choice," *Journal of Business*, Vol. 36, April, pp. 237–241.

Kuehn, Alfred A., and Albert C. Rohloff (1965), "New Dimensions in Analysis of Brand-Switching," in Frederick F. Webster, ed., *New Directions in Marketing*, American Marketing Association, pp. 297–308.

Laird, Donald A. (1950), "Customs Are Hard to Change," *Personnel Journal*, pp. 402–405.

Lancaster, Kelvin (1966a), "Change and Innovation in the Technology of Consumption," in Harold F. Williamson and Gertrude Tait, eds., *Papers and Proceedings of the Seventy-Eighth Annual Meeting of the American Economic Association*, pp. 14–23.

Lancaster, Kelvin (1966b), "A New Approach to Consumer Theory," *Journal of Political Economy*, Vol. 74, April, pp. 132–157.

Lansing, John B., and Leslie Kish (1957), "Family Life Cycle as an Independent Variable," *American Sociological Review*, Vol. 22, pp. 512–519.

Lanzetta, John T. (1967), "Uncertainty as a Motivating Variable," Mimeo, Conference on Experimental Social Psychology, Vienna, Austria.

Lasswell, H. D. (1948), "The Structure and Function of Communication in Society," in L. Bryson, ed., *Communication of Ideas*, Harper.

Lasswell, H. D., and A. Kaplan (1950), *Power and Society*, Yale University Press.

Lavidge, Robert C., and Gary A. Steiner (1961), "A Model for Predictive Measurements of Advertising Effectiveness," *Journal of Marketing*, Vol. 25, October, pp. 59–62.

Lawrence, Douglas H. (1963), "The Nature of a Stimulus: Some Relationships between Learning and Perception," in Sigmund Koch, ed., *Psychology: A Study of a Science*, Vol. 5, McGraw-Hill Book Company, pp. 179–212.

Lazarsfeld, Paul F. (1954), *Mathematical Thinking in the Social Sciences*, The Free Press.

Lazarsfeld, Paul F. (1959), "Latent Structure Analysis," in Sigmund Koch, ed., *Psychology: A Study of a Science*, McGraw-Hill Book Company, Vol. 3, pp. 476–543.

Lazarsfeld, Paul F., and Patricia L. Kendall (1948), *Radio Listening in America*, Prentice-Hall.

Leavitt, Harold J. (1954), "A Note on Some Experimental Findings about the Meaning of Price," *Journal of Business*, Vol. 27, July, pp. 205–210.

Lee, Dorothy (1957), "The Cultural and Emotional Values of Food," *Merrill-Palmer Quarterly*, Vol. 3, Winter, pp. 84–88.

LeGrand, Bruce, and Jon G. Udell (1964), "Consumer Behavior in the Market Place," *Journal of Retailing*, Vol. 40, Fall, pp. 32–40.

Leventhal, H. (1965), "Fear Communications in the Acceptance of Preventive Health Practices," Department of Psychology, Yale University, January (mimeographed).

Leventhal, H., and P. Niles (1964), "A Field Experiment on Fear-Arousal with Data on the Validity of Questionnaire Measures," *Journal of Personality*, Vol. 32, pp. 459–479.

Leventhal, H., and P. Niles (1965), "Persistence of Influence for Varying Durations of Exposure to Threat Stimuli," *Psychological Reports*, Vol. 16, pp. 223–233.

Leventhal, H., R. Singer, and S. Jones (1965), "Effects of Fear and Specificity of Recommendation upon Attitudes and Behavior," *Journal of Personality and Social Psychology*, Vol. 2, July, pp. 20–29.

Leventhal, H., and Jean C. Watts (1966), "Sources of Resistance to Fear-Arousing Communications on Smoking and Lung Cancer," *Journal of Personality*, Vol. 34, June, pp. 155–175.

Lewin, K. (1951), *Field Theory in Social Science*, Harper and Brothers.

Lewin, K. (1958), "Group Decision and Social Change," in E. E. Maccoby et al., eds., *Readings in Social Psychology*, Henry Holt and Company, 3rd ed., pp. 197–211.

Lewin, K., Tamarra Dembo, Leon Festinger, and Pauline Snedden Sears (1944), "Level of Aspiration," in J. McV. Hunt, ed., *Personality and the Behavior Disorders*, Vol. I, Ronald Press, pp. 333–378.

Likert, R. (1932), "A Technique for the Measurement of Attitudes," *Archives of Psychology*, Vol 22, No. 140, pp. 44–53.

Lingoes, J. C., and L. Guttman (1967), "Nonmetric Factor Analysis: A Rank Reducing Alternative to Linear Factor Analysis," *Multivariate Behavioral Research*, Vol. 2, October, pp. 485–506.

Lipstein, Benjamin (1959), "The Dynamics of Brand Loyalty and Brand Switching," Proceedings of Advertising Research Foundation, pp. 101–108.

Lipstein, Benjamin (1965), "A Mathematical Model of Consumer Behavior," *Journal of Marketing Research*, Vol. 2, August, pp. 259–265.

Little, John D. C. (1964), "Mathematical Marketing Models," talk given before the Philadelphia Chapter of the Operations Research Society of America, October 22.

Logan, Frank A., Daniel L. Olmsted, Burton S. Rosner, Richard D. Schwartz, and Carl M. Stevens (1955), *Behavior Theory and Social Science*, Yale University Press.

Lord, Frederick M. (1956), "The Measurement of Growth," *Educational and Psychological Measurement*, Vol. 16, pp. 421–437.

Lo Sciuto, Leonard A., Larry H. Strassmann, and William D. Wells (1967), "Advertising Weight and the Reward Value of the Brand," *Journal of Advertising Research*, Vol. 7, June, pp. 34–38.

Lotshaw, Elmer P. (1969), "Industrial Marketing and the JMR," *Journal of Marketing Research*, Vol. 6, February, p. 109.

Lucas, Darrell B. (1937), "The Impression Values of Fixed Advertising Locations in the *Saturday Evening Post*," *Journal of Applied Psychology*, Vol. 21, pp. 613–631.

Lucas, Darrell B. (1940), "A Rigid Technique for Measuring the Impression Values of Specific Magazine Advertisements," *Journal of Applied Psychology*, Vol. 24, pp. 778–790.

Lucas, Darrell B., and S. A. Britt (1950), *Advertising Psychology and Research*, McGraw-Hill Book Company.

Lucas, Darrell B., and S. A. Britt (1963), *Measuring Advertising Effectiveness*, McGraw-Hill Book Company.

Luce, R. Duncan (1959), *Individual Choice Behavior*, John Wiley and Sons.

Lynes, Russell (1949), *The Tastemakers*, Harper and Brothers, pp. 315–320.

MacCorquodale, Kenneth, and Paul E. Meehl (1948), "On a Distinction between Hypothetical Constructs and Intervening Variables," *Psychological Review*, Vol. 55, pp. 95–107.

MacLeod, R. B. (1947), "The Phenomenological Approach to Social Psychology," *Psychological Review*, Vol. 54, pp. 193–210.

McClelland, D. C., ed. (1955), *Studies in Motivation*, Appleton-Century-Crofts.

McClelland, D. C. (1961), *The Achieving Society*, D. Van Nostrand Company.

McClelland, D. C., J. W. Atkinson, R. A. Clark, and E. L. Lowell (1953), *The Achievement Motive*, Appleton-Century-Crofts.

McConnell, J. Douglas (1968), "The Development of Brand Loyalty: An Experimental Study," *Journal of Marketing Research*, Vol. 5, February, pp. 13–20.

McGuire, William J. (1961), "The Effectiveness of Supportive and Refutational Defenses in Immunizing and Restoring Beliefs against Persuasion," *Sociometry*, Vol. 24, pp. 84–97.

McGuire, William J. (1963), *Effectiveness of Fear Appeals in Advertising*, Advertising Research Foundation (August).

McGuire, William J. (1964), "Inducing Resistance to Persuasion: Some Contemporary Approaches," in L. Berkowitz, ed., *Advances in Experimental Social Psychology*, Vol. 1, Academic Press, pp. 191–229.

McGuire, William J. (1966a), "Attitudes and Opinions," *Annual Review of Psychology*, Vol. 17, pp. 475–514.

McGuire, William J. (1966b), Research Proposal to National Science Foundation, Mimeographed, University of California.

McGuire, William J. (1967), "Some Impending Reorientations in Social Psychology: Some Thoughts Provoked by Kenneth Ring," *Journal of Experimental Social Psychology*, Vol. 3, pp. 124–139.

McGuire, William J. (1968a), "Personality and Susceptibility to Social Influence," in E. F. Boyatta and W. W. Lambert, eds., *Handbook of Personality Theory and Research*, Rand McNally, in press.

McGuire, William J. (1968b), "Nature of Attitudes and Attitude Change," in G. Lindzey and E. Aronson, eds., *Handbook of Social Psychology*, rev. ed., Addison-Wesley Publishing Company, in press.

McGuire, Wi'liam J. (1968c), "Résumé and Response from the Consistency Theory Viewpoint," in R. P. Abelson et al., *Theories of Cognitive Consistency: A Sourcebook*, Rand McNally, pp. 275–302.

McGuire, William J. (1968d), "Selective Exposure: A Summing Up," in R. P. Abelson et al., eds., *Theories of Cognitive Consistency: A Sourcebook*, Rand McNally, pp. 797–800.

McGuire, William J. (1968e), "Theory of the Structure of Human Thought," in R. P. Abelson et al., eds., *Theories of Cognitive Consistency: A Sourcebook*, Rand McNally, pp. 140–162.

McGuire, William J., and D. Papageorgis (1961), "The Relative Efficacy of Various Types of Prior Belief-Defense in Producing Immunity against Persuasion," *Journal of Abnormal and Social Psychology*, Vol. 62, March, pp. 327–337.

Maccoby, E. E., T. M. Newcomb, and E. L. Hartley, eds. (1958), *Readings in Social Psychology*, 3rd ed., Holt, Rinehart and Winston.

Maffei, Richard B. (1960), "Brand Preferences and Simple Markov Processes," *Operations Research*, Vol. 8, March-April, pp. 210–218.

Maffei, Richard B. (1961), "Brand Preferences and Market Dynamics," *Journal of Industrial Economics*, Vol. 9, April, pp. 119–131.

Maier, N. R. F., and R. A. Maier (1957), "An Experimental Test of the Effects of 'Developmental' versus 'Free' Discussions on the Quality of Group Decisions," *Journal of Applied Psychology*, Vol. 41, October, pp. 320–323.

Mandell, Maurice I. (1968), *Advertising*, Prentice-Hall.

March, James G., and Herbert A. Simon (1958), *Organizations*, John Wiley and Sons.

Marcus, A. S., and R. A. Bauer (1964), "Yes: These are Generalized Opinion Leaders," *Public Opinion Quarterly*, Vol. 28, Winter, pp. 628–632.

Margenau, R. (1950), *The Nature of Physical Reality*, McGraw-Hill Book Company.

Martineau, P. (1957), *Motivation in Advertising*, McGraw-Hill Book Company.

Massy, William F., and Donald S. Morrison (1968), "Comments on Ehrenberg's Appraisal of Brand-Switching Models," *Journal of Marketing Research*, Vol. 5, pp. 225–229.

Merton, Robert K. (1957), *Social Theory and Social Structure*, The Free Press.

Mertes, John E. (1964), "A Retail Structure Theory for Site Analysis," *Journal of Retailing*, Vol. 40, Summer, pp. 19–30.

Messick, Samuel J. (1956), "Some Recent Theoretical Developments in Multidimensional Scaling," *Educational and Psychological Measurement*, Vol. 16, pp. 82–100.

Messick, Samuel, and R. P. Abelson (1956), "The Additive Constant Problem in Multidimensional Scaling," *Psychometrika*, Vol. 21, March, pp. 1–15.

Miller, George A. (1956), "The Magical Number Seven, Plus or Minus Two: Some Limits on Our Capacity for Processing Information," *Psychological Review*, Vol. 63, pp. 81–97.

Miller, George A., Eugene Galanter, and Karl Pribram, (1960), *Plans and the Structure of Behavior*, Holt, Rinehart and Winston.

Miller, Neal E. (1959), "Liberalization of Basic S-R Concepts: Extensions to Conflict, Behavior, Motivation, and Social Learning," in Sigmund Koch, ed., *Psychology: A Study of a Science*, McGraw-Hill Book Company, Vol. 2, pp. 196–292.

Mitchell, Walter G. (1967), "Systematic Synthesis of Advertising Research Verbatims," *Journal of Advertising Research*, Vol. 7, September, pp. 37–40.

Modigliani, Franco, and Kalman J. Cohen (1961), *The Role of Anticipations and Plans in Economic Behavior and Their Place in Economic Analysis and Forecasting*, University of Illinois Press.

Moffitt, J. W., and R. Stagner (1956), "Perceptual Rigidity and Closure as Functions of Anxiety," *Journal of Abnormal Social Psychology*, Vol. 52, May, pp. 354–357.

Montgomery, D. B. (1967), "Stochastic Modeling of the Consumer," *Industrial Management Review*, Vol. 8, pp. 31–42.

Morrison, Donald G. (1965), "Stochastic Models for Time Series with Applications in Marketing," *Technical Report No. 8, Program in Operations Research*, Stanford University.

Morrison, Donald G. (1966), "Interpurchase Time and Brand Loyalty," *Journal of Marketing Research*, Vol. 3, August, pp. 289–292.

Morrison, Donald G. (1967), "On the Consistency of Preference in Allais' Paradox," *Behavioral Science,* Vol. 12, September, pp. 373–383.

Moscovici, Serge (1963), "Attitudes and Opinions," *Annual Review of Psychology,* Vol. 14, pp. 231–260.

Mueller, Eva (1958), "The Desire for Innovations in Household Goods," in L. H. Clark, ed., *Consumer Behavior,* Vol. 3, Survey Research Center, University of Michigan.

Murphy, M. P., and R. D. Buzzell (1963), "The Conceptual Basis of the Schwerin Advertising Effectiveness Model," paper presented to Advertising Research Foundation, Operations Research Discussion Group, November 7, 1963.

Murray, D. C., and H. L. Deabler (1957), "Colors and Mood-Tones," *Journal of Applied Psychology,* Vol. 41, October, pp. 279–283.

Myers, John G. (1966), "Patterns of Interpersonal Influence in the Adoption of New Products," in Raymond M. Haas, ed., *Science Technology and Marketing,* Proceedings of the Fall Conference of the American Marketing Association, pp. 750–757.

Myers, John G. (1967), "Determinants of Private Brand Attitude," *Journal of Marketing Research,* Vol. 4, February, pp. 73–81.

Myers, John G. (1968), *Consumer Image and Attitude,* Institute of Business and Economic Research, University of California, Berkeley.

Newell, Allen, J. C. Shaw, and Herbert A. Simon (1958), "Elements of a Theory of Human Problem Solving," *Psychological Review,* Vol. 65, pp. 151–166.

Nicosia, F. M. (1964), "Opinion Leadership and the Flow of Communication: Some Problems and Prospects," in L. George Smith, ed., *Reflections on Progress in Marketing,* Educators Conference of the American Marketing Association, pp. 340–358.

Nicosia, F. M. (1965), "Panel Designs and Analysis in Marketing," in P. D. Bennett, ed., *Economic Growth, Competition and World Markets,* Proceedings of the American Marketing Association, pp. 222–243.

Nicosia, F. M. (1966), *Consumer Decision Processes,* Prentice-Hall.

Niles, P. (1964), "The Relationship of Susceptibility and Anxiety to Acceptance of Fear-Arousing Communications," unpublished doctoral dissertation, Yale University.

Nuttall, C. G. F. (1962), "TV Commercial Audiences in the United Kingdom," *Journal of Advertising Research,* Vol. 2, September, pp. 19–28.

Ogilvy, David (1963), *Confessions of an Advertising Man,* Atheneum Publishers.

Oppenheimer, Robert (1956), "Analogy in Science," *American Psychologist,* Vol. 11, March, pp. 127–135.

Osgood, Charles E. (1949), "The Similarity Paradox in Human Learning: A Resolution," *Psychological Review,* Vol. 56, May, pp. 132–143.

Osgood, Charles E. (1957a), "A Behavioristic Analysis of Perception and Language as Cognitive Phenomena," *Contemporary Approaches to Cognition,* Harvard University Press, pp. 75–118.

Osgood, Charles E. (1957b), "Motivational Dynamics of Language Behavior," in Marshall R. Jones, ed., *Nebraska Symposium on Motivation,* University of Nebraska Press, pp. 348–424.

Osgood, Charles E. (1959), "The Representation Model and Relevant Research Methods," in Ithiel de Sola Pool, ed., *Trends in Content Analysis,* University of Illinois Press, pp. 33–88.

Osgood, Charles E. (1962), "Studies in the Generality of Affective Meaning Systems," *American Psychologist,* Vol. 17, January, pp. 10–28.

Osgood, Charles E. (1963a), "On Understanding and Creating Sentences," *American Psychologist,* Vol. 18, December, pp. 735–751.

Osgood, Charles E. (1963b), "Psycholinguistics," in Sigmund Koch, ed., *Psychology: A Study of a Science,* Vol. 6, pp. 244–316.

Osgood, Charles E. (1964), "Semantic Differential Technique in the Comparative Study of Cultures," *American Anthropologist,* Vol. 66, No. 3, Part 2, pp. 171–200.

Osgood, Charles E., George J. Suci, and Percy H. Tannenbaum (1957), *The Measurement of Meaning,* University of Illinois Press.

Palda, Kristian S. (1966), "The Hypothesis of a Hierarchy of Effects: A Partial Evaluation," *Journal of Marketing Research,* Vol. 3, February, pp. 13–24.

Paterson, D. G., and M. A. Tinker (1940), *How to Make Type Readable,* Harper and Brothers.

Patterson, Don D., and Arthur J. McAnally (1947), "The Family Panel: A Technique for Diagnosing Sales Ills," *Sales Management,* Vol. 59, October, pp. 134–136.

Payne, Buryl (1966), "A Descriptive Theory of Information." *Behavioral Science,* Vol. 11, July, pp. 295–305.

Peak, Helen (1955), "Attitude and Motivation," in M. R. Jones, ed., *Nebraska Symposium on Motivation,* University of Nebraska Press, pp. 149–188.

Pellemans, Paul A. (1969), "Investigations on the Relationships Existing Between the Attitude toward the Brand and the Intention to Buy the Same Brand," unpublished doctoral dissertation, Graduate School of Business, Columbia University.

Perry, Michael (1968), "Computer Simulation of Consumer Brand Choice," unpublished doctoral dissertation, Graduate School of Business, Columbia University.

Pettigrew, Thomas F. (1958), "The Measurement and Correlates of Category Width as a Cognitive Variable," *Journal of Personality,* Vol. 26, December, pp. 532–544.

Poffenberger, A. T. (1928), *Psychology in Advertising,* Shaw.

Poffenberger, A. T., and Bernice E. Barrows (1924), "The Feeling Value of Lines," *Journal of Applied Psychology,* Vol. 8, June, pp. 187–205.

Poffenberger, A. T., and R. B. Franklin, (1923), "A Study of the Appropriateness of Type Faces," *Journal of Applied Psychology*, Vol. 7, December, pp. 312–329.

Polli, Rolando, and Victor J. Cook (1967), "A Test of the Product Life Cycle as a Model of Sales Behavior," *Marketing Science Institute Working Paper*, P-43-3.

Postman, L., and Brown, D. R. (1952), "The Perceptual Consequences of Success and Failure," *Journal of Abnormal and Social Psychology*, Vol. 47, April, pp. 213–221.

Printers' Ink (1958a), "What New Products mean to Companies: Growth, a Longer Life, Bigger Profits," June 13, pp. 21–28, and October 31, pp. 21–27.

Printers' Ink (1958b), "Family Buying Decisions: Who Makes Them, Who Influences Them?" September 19, pp. 21–29.

Quandt, R. E., and W. J. Baumol (1966), "The Demand for Abstract Transport Modes: Theory and Measurement," *Journal of Regional Science*, Vol. 6, pp. 13–26.

Rao, C. R. (1958), "Some Statistical Methods for Comparison of Growth Curves," *Biometrika*, Vol. 14, pp. 1–17.

Rarick, Galen Ronald (1963), "Effects of Two Components of Communicator Prestige," unpublished doctoral dissertation, Stanford University.

Reeves, Rosser (1961), *Reality in Advertising*, Alfred A. Knopf.

Reissman, Leonard (1959), *Class in American Society*, The Free Press.

Reitman, Walter (1965), *Cognition and Thought: An Information Processing Approach*, John Wiley and Sons.

Reitman, Walter (1966), "Information Processing Models, Computer Simulation and the Psychology of Thinking," *Information Processing Working Paper #7* (*1P-7*), Department of Psychology, University of Michigan, Revised, November.

Reynolds, William H. (1965), "More Sense about Market Segmentation," *Harvard Business Review*, Vol. 43, September-October, pp. 107–114.

Rhine, R. J. (1958), "A Concept-Formation Approach to Attitude Acquisition," *Psychological Review*, Vol. 65, pp. 362–370.

Rhine, R. J., and B. A. Silun (1958), "Acquisition and Change of a Concept Attitude as a Function of Consistency of Reinforcement," *Journal of Experimental Psychology*, Vol. 55, June, pp. 524–529.

Rich, Stuart U., and Subhash C. Jain (1968), "Social Class and Life Cycle as Predictors of Shopping Behavior," *Journal of Marketing Research*, Vol. 5, January, pp. 41–49.

Riesman, David (1950), *The Lonely Crowd*, Doubleday and Company.

Robertson, Thomas S. (1968), "Purchase Sequence Responses: Innovators vs. Non-Innovators," *Journal of Advertising Research*, Vol. 8, March, pp. 47–54.

Robertson, Thomas S., and John R. Rossiter, "Fashion Diffusion. The Interplay of Innovator and Opinion Leader Roles" undated, unpublished manuscript.

Robinson, I. P. (1948), "The Effects of Differential Degrees of Similarity of Stimulus-Response Relations on Transfer of Verbal Learning," *American Psychologist,* Vol. 3, p. 250.

Robinson, Patrick J., and David J. Luck (1964), *Promotional Decision Making: Practice and Theory,* McGraw-Hill Book Company, pp. 216–220.

Rogers, E. M. (1962), *Diffusion of Innovations,* The Free Press.

Rohloff, A. C. (1963), "New Ways to Analyze Brand-to-Brand Competition" in Stephen Greyser, ed., *Toward Scientific Marketing,* Proceedings of the Winter Conference of the American Marketing Association, pp. 224–232.

Rosenberg, Milton J. (1956), "Cognitive Structure and Attitudinal Affect," *Journal of Abnormal and Social Psychology,* Vol. 53, November, pp. 367–372.

Rosenberg, Milton J. (1960), "An Analysis of Affective-Cognitive Consistency," in C. I. Hovland and M. J. Rosenberg, eds., *Attitude Organization and Change,* Yale University Press, pp. 15–64.

Rosenberg, Milton J., and R. P. Abelson (1960), "An Analysis of Cognitive Balancing," in C. I. Hovland and M. J. Rosenberg, eds., *Attitude Organization and Change,* Yale University Press, pp. 112–163.

Rosenblatt, M. (1960), "An Aggregation Problem for Markov Chains," in Robert E. Machob, ed., *Information and Decision Processes,* McGraw-Hill Book Company, pp. 87–92.

Rothman, J. (1964), "Formulation of an Index of Propensity to Buy," *Journal of Marketing Research,* Vol. 1, May, pp. 21–25.

Rotzoll, Kim B. (1967), "The Effect of Social Stratification on Market Behavior," *Journal of Advertising Research,* Vol. 7, March, pp. 22–27.

Royce, J. R. (1963), "Factors as Theoretical Constructs," *American Psychologist,* Vol. 18, August, pp. 522–527.

Rudolph, H. J. (1947), *Attention and Interest Factors in Advertising,* Funk and Wagnalls (in association with Printers' Ink Publishing Company).

Ryan, T. A., and C. B. Schwartz (1956), "Speed of Perception as a Function of Mode of Representation," *American Journal of Psychology,* Vol. 69, March, pp. 60–69.

Rychlak, Joseph F. (1968), *A Philosophy of Science for Personality Theory,* Houghton Mifflin Company.

Sarnoff, I., and D. Katz (1954), "The Motivational Bases of Attitude Change," *Journal of Abnormal and Social Psychology,* Vol. 49, January, pp. 115–124.

Schiller, G. (1935), "An Experimental Study of the Appropriateness of Color and Type in Advertising," *Journal of Applied Psychology,* Vol. 19, December, pp. 652–664.

Schwartz, Alvin (1966), "The Influence of Media Characteristics on Coupon Redemption," *Journal of Marketing,* Vol. 30, January, pp. 41–46.

Schwerin, H. C. (1955), "Television and Radio Commercials," in *Annual Marketing*

Research Conference, Business Papers No. 31, Bureau of Business Research, University of Michigan.

Sethi, S. Prakash (1968), "An Investigation into the Mediating Effects of Socio-Psychological Variables between Advertising Stimulus and Brand Loyalty," unpublished doctoral dissertation, Columbia University.

Sharp, H., and P. Mott (1956), "Consumer Decisions in the Metropolitan Family," *Journal of Marketing,* Vol. 21, October, pp. 149–156.

Shepard, Roger N. (1962), "The Analysis of Proximities: Multidimensional Scaling With an Unknown Distance Function, I and II" *Psychometrika,* Vol. 27, June, pp. 125–140; Vol. 27, September, 219–246.

Shepard, Roger N. (1963), "An Analysis of Proximities as a Technique for the Study of Information Processing in Man," *Human Factors,* Vol. 5, pp. 33–48.

Shepard, Roger N. (1964). "On Subjectively Optimum Selection among Multiattribute Alternatives," in Magnard W. Shelly and Stern L. Bryan, eds., *Human Judgments and Optimality,* John Wiley and Sons, pp. 257–281.

Sherif, Caroline W., Muzafer Sherif, and Roger E. Nebergall (1965), *Attitude and Attitude Change,* W. B. Saunders Company.

Sherif, Muzafer (1968), "Self-Concept," in David L. Sills, ed., *International Encyclopedia of the Social Sciences,* Vol. 14, pp. 150–159.

Sherif, Muzafer, and C. I. Hovland (1961), *Social Judgment,* Yale University Press.

Sherif, Muzafer, and Bertram L. Koslin (1960), "The 'Institutional' vs. 'Behavioral' Controversy in Social Science with Special Reference to Political Science," Institute of Group Relations, University of Oklahoma.

Sheth, Jagdish N. (1966), "A Behavioral and Quantitative Investigation of Brand Loyalty," unpublished doctoral dissertation, University of Pittsburgh.

Sheth, Jagdish N. (1967), "A Review of Buyer Behavior," *Management Science,* Vol. 13, August, B-718–B756.

Sheth, Jagdish N. (1968a), "How Adults Learn Brand Preference," *Journal of Advertising Research,* September, pp. 25–38.

Sheth, Jagdish N. (1968b), "A Factor Analytic Model of Brand Loyalty," *Journal of Marketing Research,* Vol. 5, November, pp. 395–404.

Sheth, Jagdish N. (1968c), "Cognitive Dissonance, Brand Preference and Product Familiarity," in Johan Arndt, ed., *Insights into Consumer Behavior,* Allyn and Bacon, pp. 41–54.

Sheth, Jagdish N. (1968d), "Perceived Risk and Diffusion of Innovations," in Johan Arndt, ed. *Insights into Consumer Behavior,* Allyn and Bacon, pp. 173–188.

Sheth, Jagdish N. (1968e), "Applications of Multivariate Methods in Marketing," in Robert L. King, ed., *Marketing and the New Science of Planning,* Proceedings of the American Marketing Association, pp. 259–265.

Sheth, Jagdish N. (1968f), "Influence of Brand Preference on Post-Decision Dissonance," *Journal of Indian Academy of Applied Psychology,* No. 3, pp. 73–77.

Sheth, Jagdish N. (1968g), "Multivariate Analysis of Marketing Data," Working Paper No. 14, Graduate School of Business, Columbia University.

Sheth, Jagdish N. (1969a), "Projective Attitudes toward Instant Coffee in Late Sixties," Working Paper No. 18, Graduate School of Business, Columbia University.

Sheth, Jagdish N. (1969b), How Advertising Works, IAA-ARF Joint Publication on Multiple Measures of Advertising, in press.

Sheth, Jagdish N. (1969c), "Using Factor Analysis to Estimate Parameters," Journal of the American Statistical Association, in press.

Sheth, Jagdish N. (1969d), "Heavy Users and Early Adoption of Innovations," Working Paper No. 17, Graduate School of Business, Columbia University.

Sheth, Jagdish N. (1969e), "Factor Analysis of Classifactory Data," Working Paper No. 21, Graduate School of Business, Columbia University.

Sheth, Jagdish N. (1969f), "Recency Effect and the Linear Learning Model," Working Paper No. 22, Graduate School of Business, Columbia University.

Sheth, Jagdish N. (1969g), "Attitude-Behavior Discrepancy in Buying Electrical Motors," Working Paper No. 23, Graduate School of Business, Columbia University.

Sheth, Jagdish N. (1969h), "Measurement of Multidimensional Brand Loyalty of a Consumer" Working Paper No. 24, Graduate School of Business, Columbia University.

Sheth, Jagdish N. (1969i), "Importance of Word-of-Mouth in the Diffusion of Low-Risk and Highly-Advantageous Innovations," Working Paper No. 16, Graduate School of Business, Columbia University.

Sheth, Jagdish, N., and L. Winston Ring (1968), "Correlates of General Attitudes," unpublished working paper, graduate School of Business, Columbia University.

Sheth, Jagdish N., and M. Venkatesan (1968), "Risk-Reduction Processes in Repetitive Consumer Behavior," Journal of Marketing Research, Vol. 5, No. 3, pp. 307–310.

Shuchman, Abe, and Michael Perry (1969), "Self-Confidence and Persuasibility in Marketing: A Reappraisal," Journal of Marketing Research, Vol. 6, May, pp. 146–155.

Siegel, Sidney (1956), Nonparametric Statistics for the Behavioral Sciences, McGraw-Hill Book Company.

Simon, Herbert A. (1954), "Some Strategic Considerations in the Construction of Social Sciences Models," in P. F. Lazarsfeld, ed., Mathematical Thinking in the Social Sciences, The Free Press.

Simon, Herbert A. (1960), Administrative Behavior, The Macmillan Company.

Simon, Herbert A. (1963), "Economics and Psychology," in Sigmund Koch, ed., Psychology: A Study of a Science, Vol. 6, McGraw-Hill Book Company, pp. 685–723.

Simon, Herbert A. (1968), "The Future of Information Processing Technology," Management Science, Vol. 14, May, pp. 619–624.

Simon, Lonard S., and Melvin R. Marks (1965), "Consumer Behavior during the New York Newspaper Strike," *Journal of Advertising Research,* Vol. 5, March, pp. 9–17.

Singer, R. P. (1965), "The Effects of Fear-Arousing Communication on Attitude Change and Behavior," unpublished doctoral dissertation, University of Connecticut.

Skinner, B. F. (1953), *Science and Human Behavior,* The Macmillan Company.

Skinner, B. F. (1956), "A Case History in Scientific Method," *American Psychologist,* Vol. 11, May, pp. 221–233.

Smith, G. H. (1954), *Motivation Research in Advertising and Marketing,* McGraw-Hill Book Company.

Smith, M. Brewster (1949), "Personal Values as Determinants of a Political Attitude," *Journal of Psychology,* Vol. 28, pp. 477–486.

Smith, M. Brewster, Jerome S. Bruner, and Robert W. White (1956), *Opinion and Personality,* John Wiley and Sons.

Smith, Steward A. (1965), "Factors Influencing the Relationship Between Buying Plans and Ad Readership," *Journal of Marketing Research,* Vol. 2, February, pp. 40–44.

Spence, Kenneth Wartenbee (1960), *Behavior Theory and Learning: Selected Papers,* Prentice-Hall.

Staats, A. W., and C. K. Staats (1958), "Attitudes Established by Classical Conditioning," *Journal of Abnormal and Social Psychology,* Vol. 57, pp. 37–40.

Stanley, Thomas Blaine (1954), *The Technique of Advertising Production,* 2nd ed., Prentice-Hall.

Starch, D. (1956), "How Do Size and Color of Advertisements Affect Readership," *Starch Tested Copy,* No. 74.

Starch, D. (1957), "Readership and Size of Advertisement," *Starch Tested Copy,* No. 82.

Starch, D. (1961a), "Do Inside Positions Differ in Readership?" *Starch Tested Copy,* No. 95.

Starch, D. (1961b), *Measuring Product Sales Made by Advertising,* Daniel Starch and Staff.

Starch, D. (1961c), "Readership of Drawings and Photographs," *Starch Tested Copy,* No. 91.

Starch, D., and Staff (1961), "Is Preferred Position Worth It?" *Starch Tested Copy,* No. 94.

Stefflre, V. J. (1965), "Simulation of Peoples Behavior toward New Objects and Events," *American Behavioral Scientist,* Vol. 8, pp. 12–15.

Steiner, Gary A. (1966), "The People Look at Commercials: A Study of Audience Behavior," *Journal of Business,* Vol. 39, April, pp. 272–304.

Stevens, Stanley S. (1939), "On the Problem of Scales for the Measurement of Psychological Magnitudes," *F. Unif. Sci.,* Vol. 9, pp. 94–99.

Stevens, S. S. (1946), "On the Theory of Scales of Measurement," *Science,* Vol. 103, pp. 677–680.

Stevens, Stanley S. (1951), *Handbook of Experimental Psychology,* John Wiley and Sons.

Stigler, George J. (1952), *The Theory of Price,* rev. ed., The Macmillan Company.

Strauss, George (1962), "Tactics of Lateral Relationship: The Purchasing Agent," *Administrative Science Quarterly,* September, pp. 161–186.

Strauss, George (1964), "Work-Flow Functions, Interfunctionary Rivalry and Professionalism: A Case Study of Purchasing Agents," Institute of Industrial Relations, University of California, Berkeley.

Styan, G. P. H., and Harry Smith, Jr. (1964), "Markov Chains Applied to Marketing," *Journal of Marketing Research,* Vol. 1, February, pp. 50–55.

Suppes, Patrick (1966), *Information Processing and Choice Behavior,* Technical Report No. 91, Institute for Mathematical Studies in the Social Sciences, Stanford University.

Swed, F. S., and C. Eisenhart (1943), "Tables for Testing Randomness of Grouping in a Sequence of Alternatives," *Annals of Mathematical Statistics,* Vol. 14, pp. 66–87.

Tanaka, Yasumasa, Tadasu Oyama, and Charles E. Osgood (1963), "A Cross-Culture and Cross-Concept Study of the Generality of Semantic Spaces," *Journal of Verbal Learning and Verbal Behavior,* Vol. 2, December, pp. 392–405.

Tax, Sol (1958), "Changing Consumption in Indian Guatemala," in Lincoln Clark, ed., *Consumer Behavior: Research on Consumer Reactions,* Harper and Brothers, pp. 227–238.

Thurstone, L. L. (1928), "Attitude Can Be Measured," *Journal of Sociology,* Vol. 33, pp. 529–554.

Tinker, M. A. (1958), "Recent Studies of Eye Movements in Reading," *Psychological Bulletin,* Vol. 55, pp. 215–231.

Tinker, M. A. (1963), *Legibility of Print,* Iowa State University Press.

Torgerson, Warren S. (1958), *Theory and Methods of Scaling,* John Wiley and Sons.

Tucker, Ledyard R. (1958), "Determination of Parameters of a Functional Relation by Factor Analysis," *Psychometrika,* Vol. 23, March, pp. 19–23.

Tucker, Ledyard R. (1959), "Determination of Generalized Learning Curves by Factor Analysis," Educational Testing Service.

Tucker, Ledyard R. (1966), "Learning Theory and Multivariate Experiment: Illustration by Determination of Generalized Learning Curves," in R. B. Cattell, ed., *Handbook of Multivariate Experimental Psychology,* Rand McNally, pp. 476–501.

Tucker, Ledyard R., and S. Messick (1960), "Individual Differences in Multidimensional Scaling," *E.T.S. Memo Rm 60-15,* Educational Testing Service.

Tucker, Ledyard R., and S. Messick (1963), "An Individual Difference Model for Multi-dimensional Scaling," *Psychometrika*, Vol. 28, pp. 333–367.

Tucker, W. T., and John J. Painter (1961), "Personality and Product Use," *Journal of Applied Psychology*, Vol. 45, October, pp. 325–329.

Tull, D. S., R. A. Boring, and M. H. Gonsior (1964), "A Note on the Relationship of Price and Imputed Quality," *Journal of Business*, Vol. 37, April, pp. 186–191.

Twedt, Dik W. (1952), "A Multiple Factor Analysis of Advertising Readership" *Journal of Applied Psychology*, Vol. 36, June, pp. 207–215.

Twedt, Dik Warren (1964), "How Important to Marketing Strategy Is the 'Heavy User'?" *Journal of Marketing*, Vol. 28, January, pp. 71–72.

Venkatesan, M. and J. N. Sheth (1968), "An Experimental Study in Risk Reduction," in Robert L. King, ed., *Marketing and the New Science of Planning*, Proceedings of the American Marketing Association, pp. 213–214.

Wales, Hugh G., Dwight Gentry, and Max Wales (1958), *Advertising Copy Layout and Typography*, The Ronald Press Company.

Wallace, Anthony F. C. (1961), "On Being Just Complicated Enough," *Anthropology*, Vol. 47, pp. 458–464.

Watson, J. B. (1925), *Behaviorism*, Norton.

Weinberg, Robert S. (1960), *An Analytical Approach to Advertising Expenditure Strategy*, Association of National Advertisers.

Weiss, W. (1960), "Emotional Arousal and Attitude Change," *Psychological Reports*, Vol. 6, April, pp. 267–280.

Weitzman, R. A. (1963), "A Factor Analytic Method for Investigating Differences between Groups of Individual Learning Curves," *Psychometrika*, Vol. 28, pp. 69–80.

Wells, William D. (1961), "Measuring Readiness to Buy," *Harvard Business Review*, Vol. 39, July-August, pp. 81–87.

Wells, William D. (1966), "General Personality Tests and Consumer Behavior," in Joseph W. Newman, ed., *On Knowing the Consumer*, John Wiley and Sons, pp. 187–190.

Westfall, Ralph (1962), "Psychological Factors in Predicting Product Choice," *Journal of Marketing*, Vol. 26, April, pp. 34–40.

Westfall, Ralph, Harper Boyd, and Donald T. Campbell, (1957), "The Use of Structured Techniques in Motivation Research," *Journal of Marketing*, Vol. 22, October, pp. 134–139.

Wexner, Lois B. (1954), "The Degree to Which Colors (Hues) Are Associated with Mood-Tones," *Journal of Applied Psychology*, Vol. 38, December, pp. 432–435.

Wilding, John, and Raymond A. Bauer (1968), "Consumer Goals and Reactions to a Communication Source," *Journal of Marketing Research*, Vol. 5, February, pp. 73–77.

Wilkening, E. A. (1958), "Joint Decision-Making in Farm Families as a Function of Status and Role," *American Sociological Review,* Vol. 23, pp. 187–192.

Wind, Yoram (1966), "Industrial Buying Behavior: Source Loyalty in the Purchase of Industrial Components," unpublished doctoral dissertation, Graduate School of Business, Stanford University.

Winick, C. (1959), "Art Work versus Photography: An Experimental Study," *Journal of Applied Psychology,* Vol. 43, pp. 180–182.

Wolgast, E. H. (1958), "Do Husbands or Wives Make the Purchasing Decisions?" *Journal of Marketing,* Vol. 23, October, pp. 151–158.

Womer, Stanley (1944), "Some Applications of the Continuous Consumer Panel," *Journal of Marketing,* Vol. 9, October, pp. 132–136.

Woodlock, J. W. (1964), "A Clue to Purchase Patterns—Markov's Mathemagic," *Sales Management,* Vol. 93, September, pp. 71–72.

Wylie, Ruth C. (1961), *The Self Concept,* University of Nebraska Press.

Young, G., and A. S. Householder (1938), "Matrix Approximation and Latent Roots," *American Mathematical Monthly,* Vol. 45, pp. 165–171.

Young, Michael (1952), "Distribution of Income within the Family," *The British Journal of Sociology,* Vol. 3, pp. 305–321.

Zajonc, Robert B. (1954), "Structure of the Cognitive Field," unpublished doctoral dissertation, University of Michigan.

Zajonc, Robert B. (1965), "The Attitudinal Effects of Mere Exposure," *Technical Report No. 34,* Institute for Social Research, University of Michigan.

Index